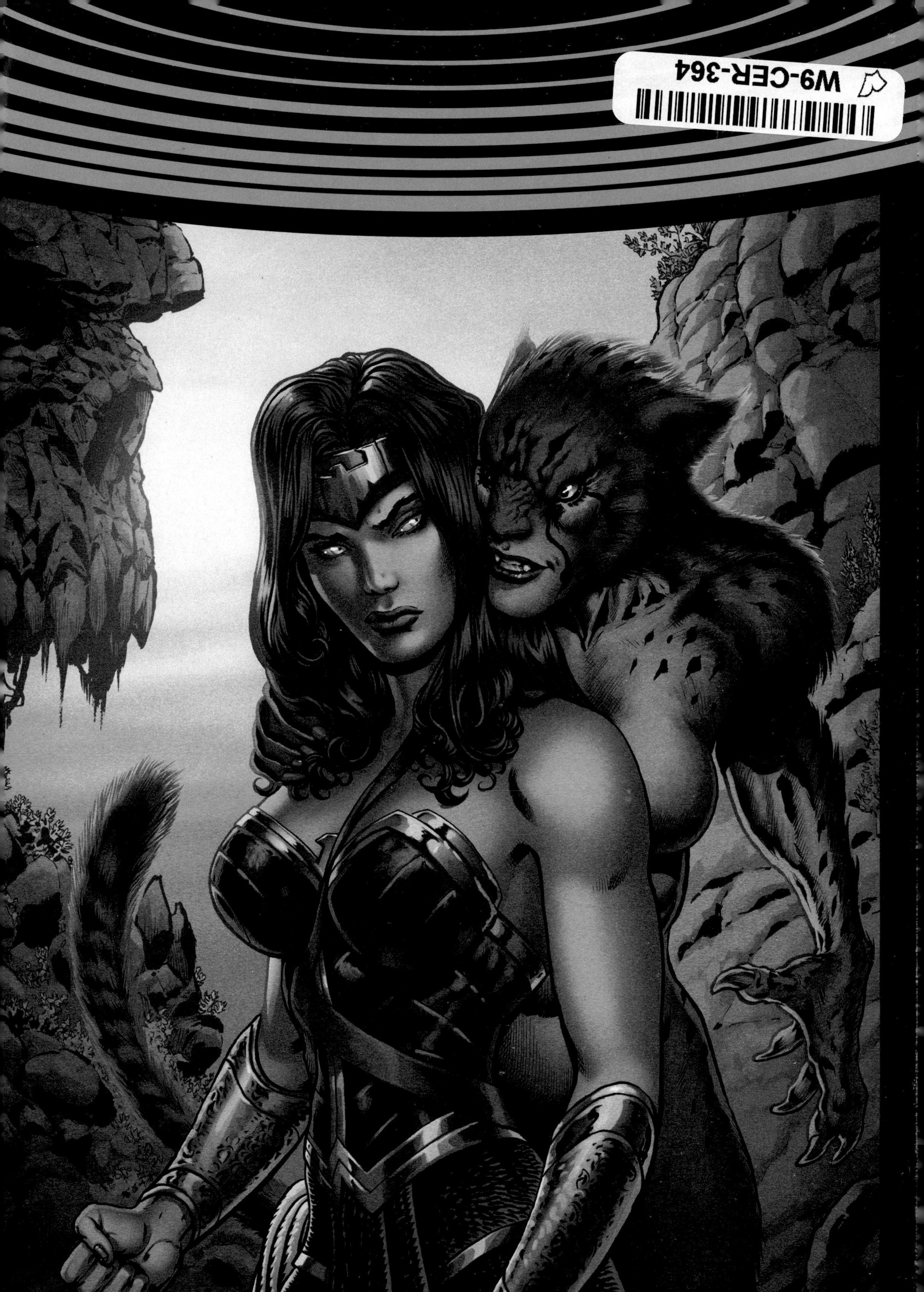

WONDER WOMAN

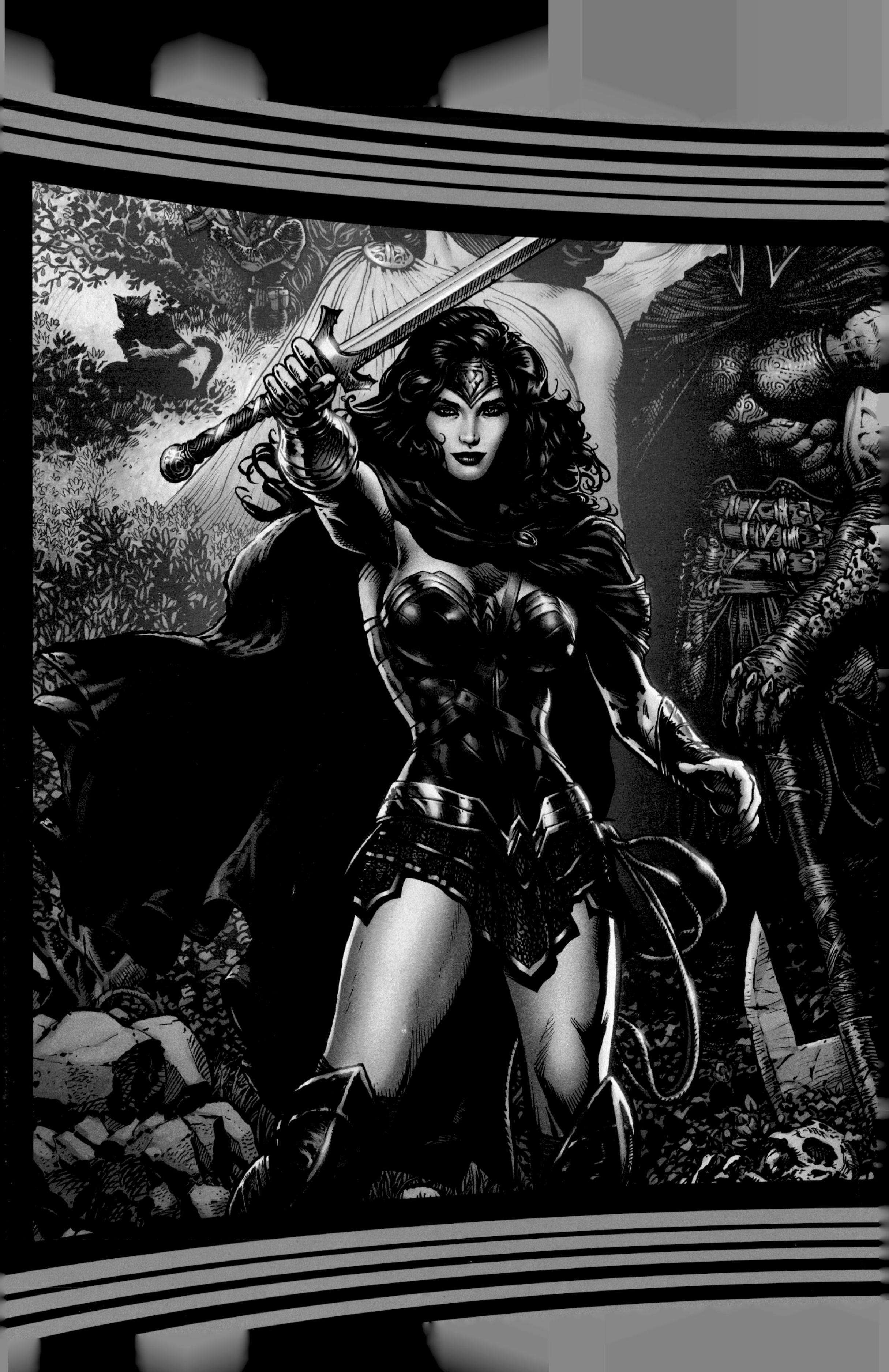

WONDER WOMAN

VOL.1 THE LIES

GREG RUCKA
writer

LIAM SHARP
artist

MATTHEW CLARK
penciller (pages 7-26)

SEAN PARSONS
inker (pages 7-26)

LAURA MARTIN
JEREMY COLWELL
colorists

JODI WYNNE
letterer

LIAM SHARP & LAURA MARTIN
collection and original series cover artists

Special thanks to Paulo Siqueira

WONDER WOMAN created by WILLIAM MOULTON MARSTON

CHRIS CONROY MARK DOYLE Editors – Original Series ✳ **DAVE WIELGOSZ** Assistant Editor – Original Series ✳ **JEB WOODARD** Group Editor – Collected Editions
ROBIN WILDMAN Editor – Collected Edition ✳ **STEVE COOK** Design Director – Books ✳ **LOUIS PRANDI** Publication Design

BOB HARRAS Senior VP – Editor-in-Chief, DC Comics

DIANE NELSON President ✳ **DAN DiDIO** Publisher ✳ **JIM LEE** Publisher ✳ **GEOFF JOHNS** President & Chief Creative Officer
AMIT DESAI Executive VP – Business & Marketing Strategy, Direct to Consumer & Global Franchise Management
SAM ADES Senior VP – Direct to Consumer ✳ **BOBBIE CHASE** VP – Talent Development ✳ **MARK CHIARELLO** Senior VP – Art, Design & Collected Editions
JOHN CUNNINGHAM Senior VP – Sales & Trade Marketing ✳ **ANNE DePIES** Senior VP – Business Strategy, Finance & Administration
DON FALLETTI VP – Manufacturing Operations ✳ **LAWRENCE GANEM** VP – Editorial Administration & Talent Relations ✳ **ALISON GILL** Senior VP – Manufacturing & Operations
HANK KANALZ Senior VP – Editorial Strategy & Administration ✳ **JAY KOGAN** VP – Legal Affairs ✳ **THOMAS LOFTUS** VP – Business Affairs ✳ **JACK MAHAN** VP – Business Affairs
NICK J. NAPOLITANO VP – Manufacturing Administration ✳ **EDDIE SCANNELL** VP – Consumer Marketing ✳ **COURTNEY SIMMONS** Senior VP – Publicity & Communications
JIM (SKI) SOKOLOWSKI VP – Comic Book Specialty Sales & Trade Marketing ✳ **NANCY SPEARS** VP – Mass, Book, Digital Sales & Trade Marketing

WONDER WOMAN VOLUME 1: THE LIES

DC Comics, 2900 West Alameda Ave., Burbank, CA 91505
Printed by LSC Communications, Salem, VA, USA. 1/20/17. First Printing.
ISBN: 978-1-4012-6778-0
Barnes & Noble exclusive edition ISBN: 978-1-4012-7635-5

Library of Congress Cataloging-in-Publication Data is available.

PEFC Certified

Printed on paper from
sustainably managed
forests, controlled
sources

PEFC/29-31-337   www.pefc.org

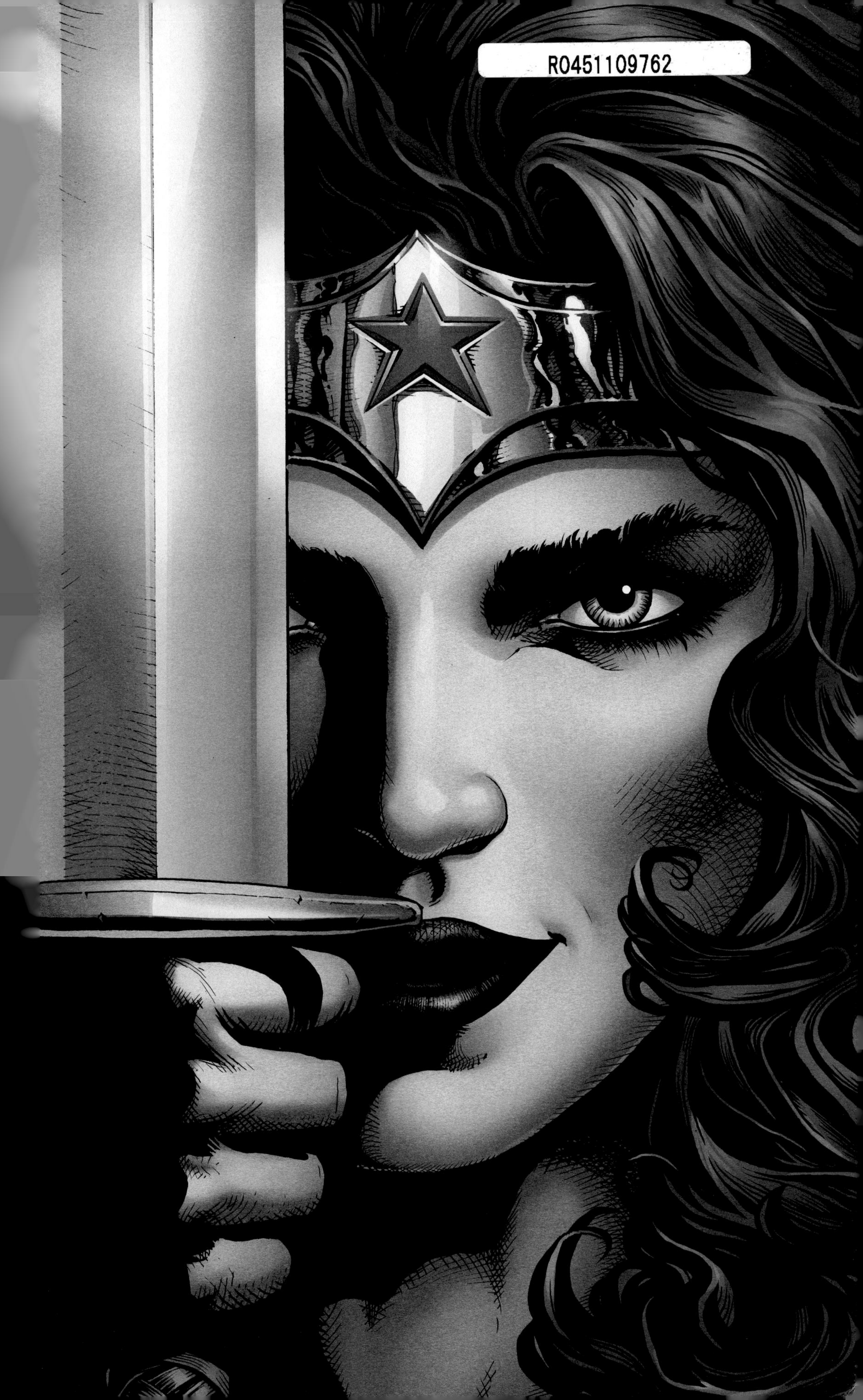

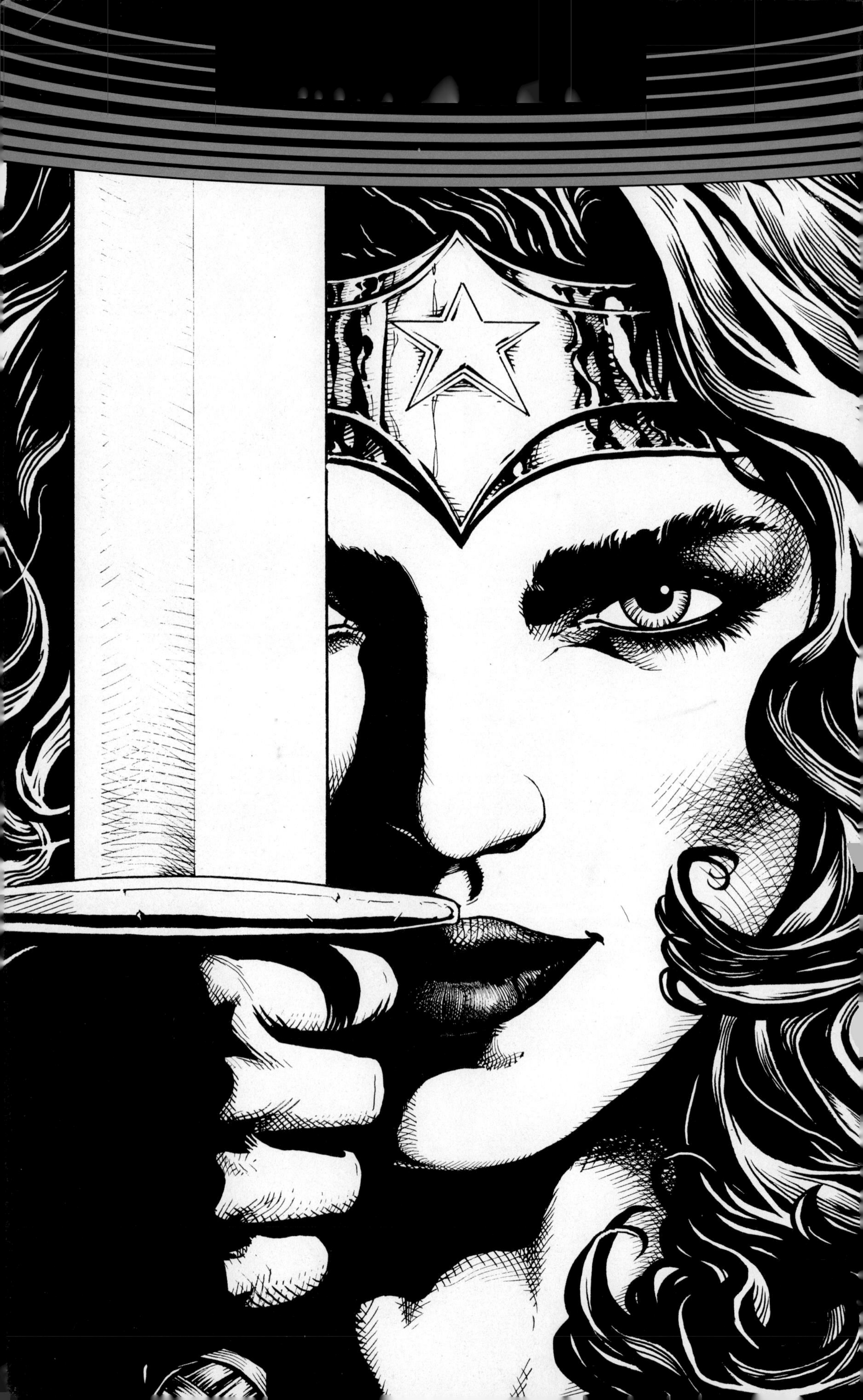

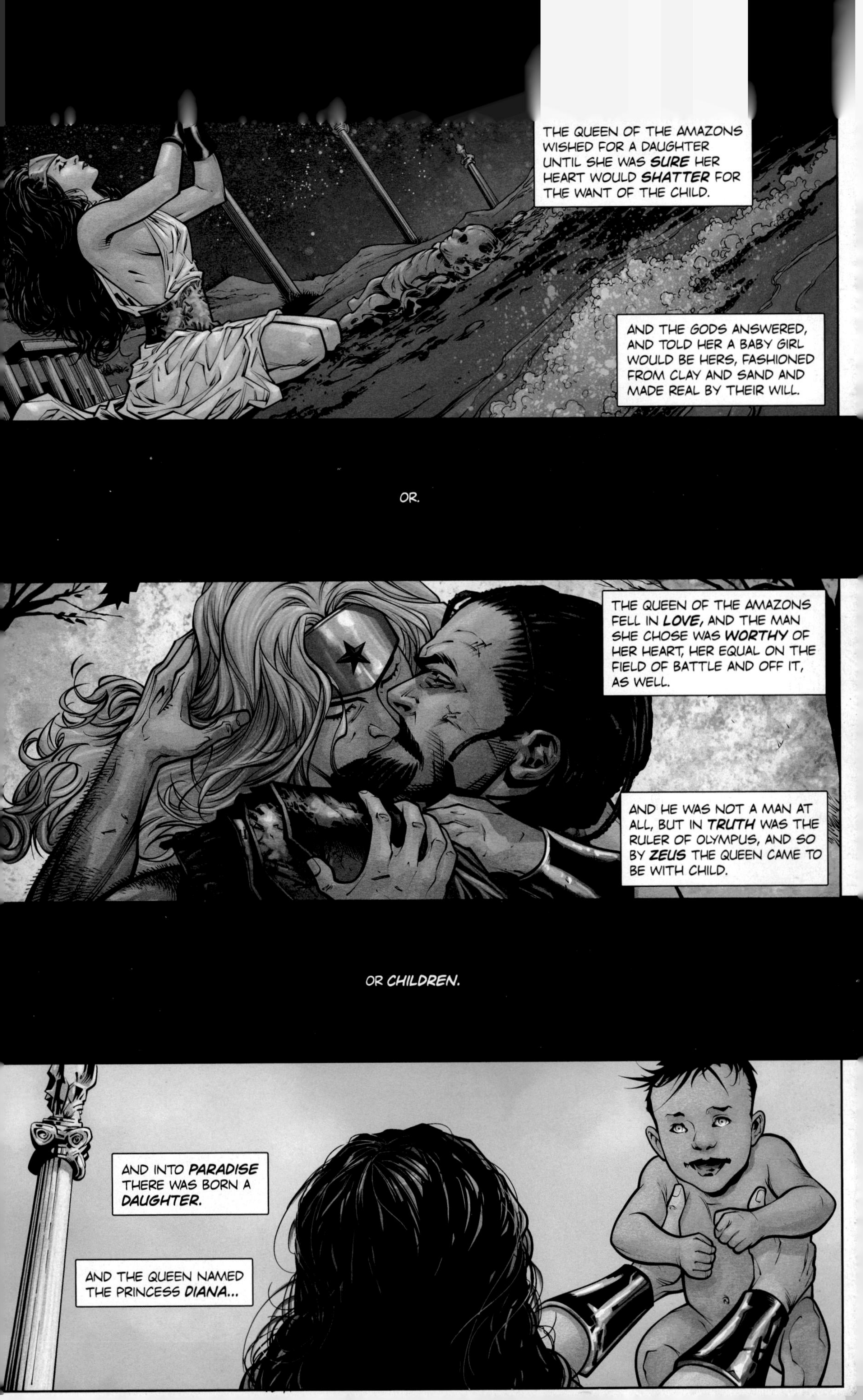
THE QUEEN OF THE AMAZONS WISHED FOR A DAUGHTER UNTIL SHE WAS SURE HER HEART WOULD SHATTER FOR THE WANT OF THE CHILD.
AND THE GODS ANSWERED, AND TOLD HER A BABY GIRL WOULD BE HERS, FASHIONED FROM CLAY AND SAND AND MADE REAL BY THEIR WILL.
OR.
THE QUEEN OF THE AMAZONS FELL IN LOVE, AND THE MAN SHE CHOSE WAS WORTHY OF HER HEART, HER EQUAL ON THE FIELD OF BATTLE AND OFF IT, AS WELL.
AND HE WAS NOT A MAN AT ALL, BUT IN TRUTH WAS THE RULER OF OLYMPUS, AND SO BY ZEUS THE QUEEN CAME TO BE WITH CHILD.
OR CHILDREN.
AND INTO PARADISE THERE WAS BORN A DAUGHTER.
AND THE QUEEN NAMED THE PRINCESS DIANA...

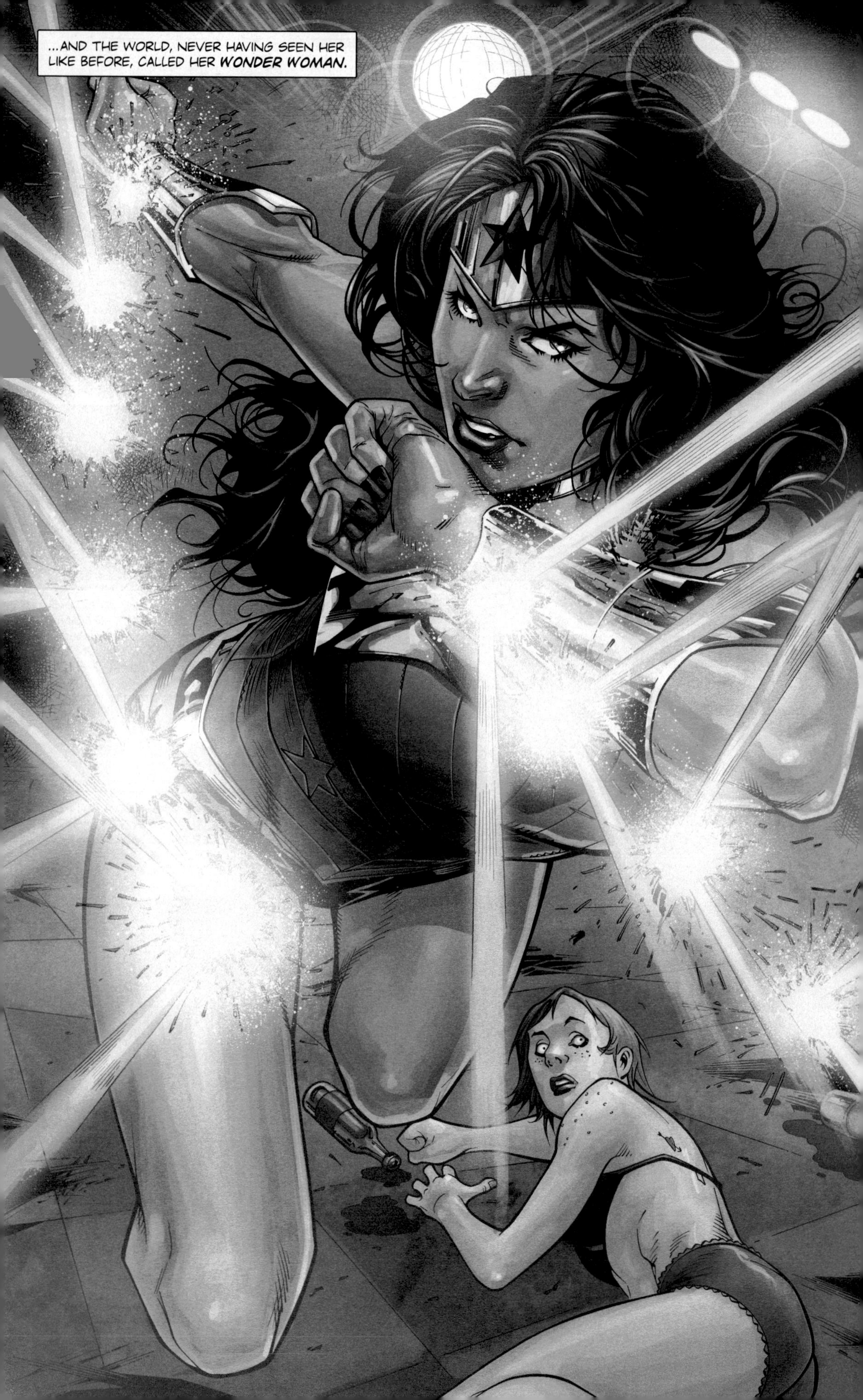
...AND THE WORLD, NEVER HAVING SEEN HER LIKE BEFORE, CALLED HER WONDER WOMAN.

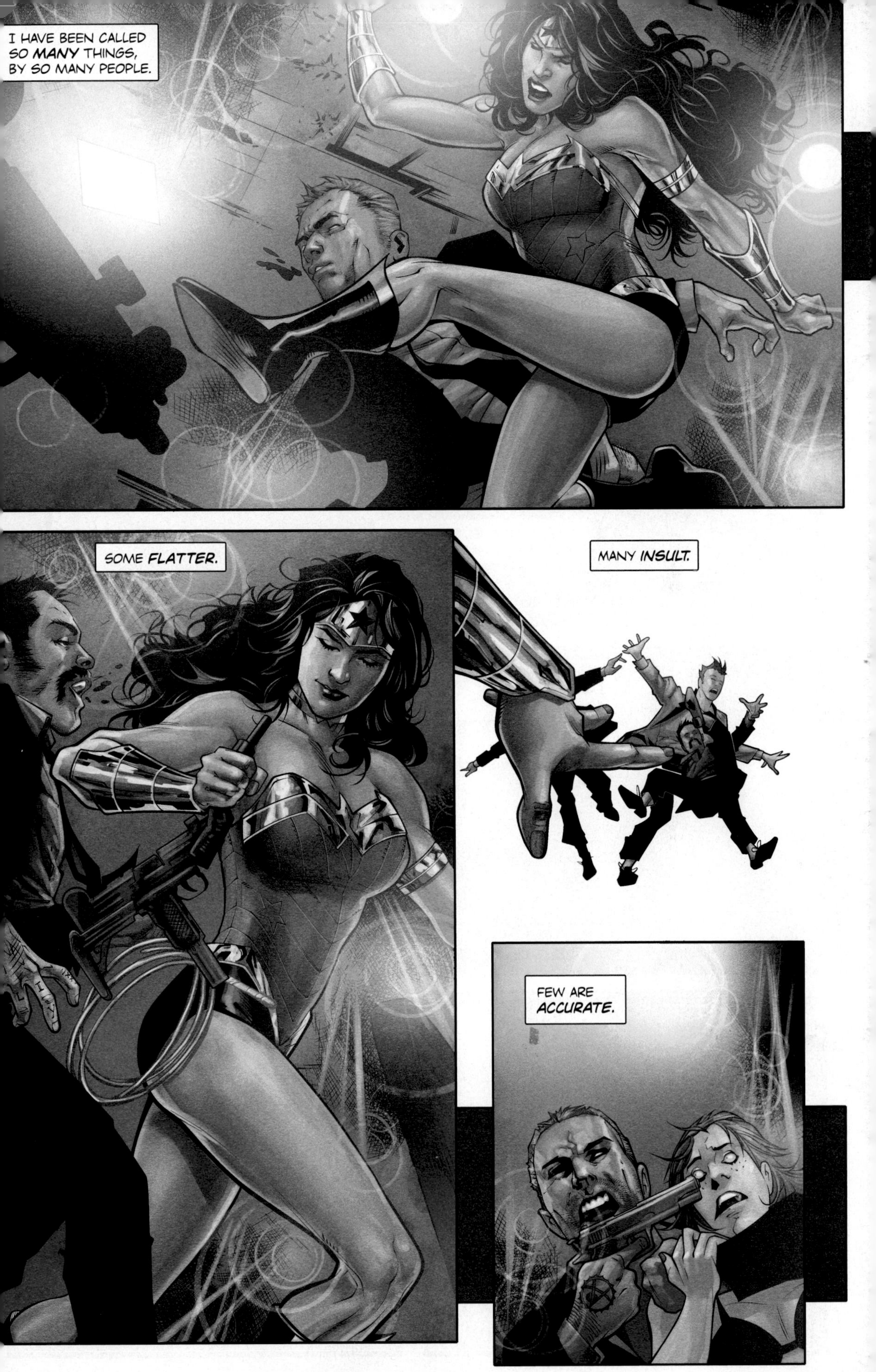
I HAVE BEEN CALLED SO MANY THINGS, BY SO MANY PEOPLE.
SOME FLATTER.
MANY INSULT.
FEW ARE ACCURATE.

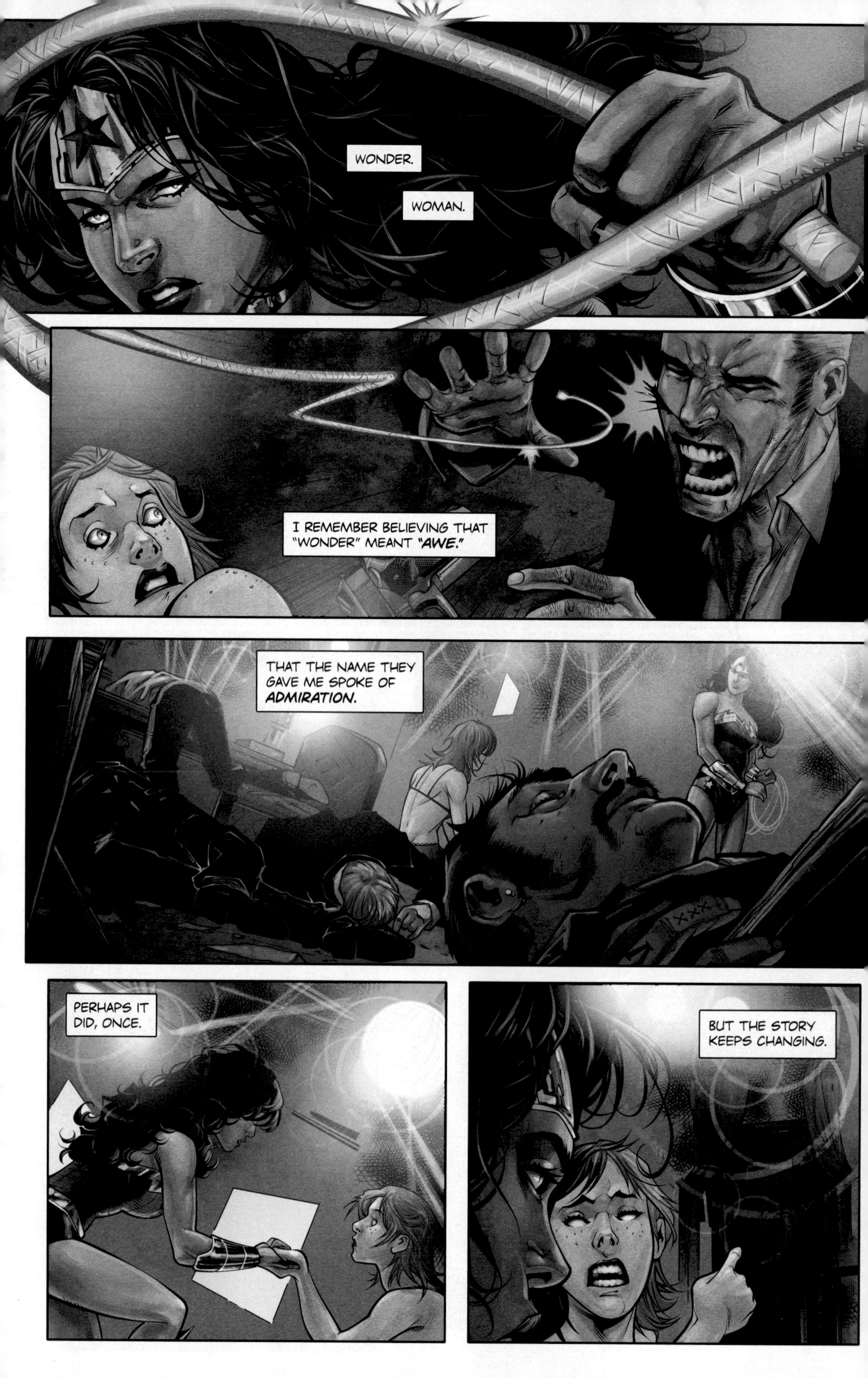
WONDER.
WOMAN.
I REMEMBER BELIEVING THAT "WONDER" MEANT "AWE."
THAT THE NAME THEY GAVE ME SPOKE OF ADMIRATION.
PERHAPS IT DID, ONCE.
BUT THE STORY KEEPS CHANGING.

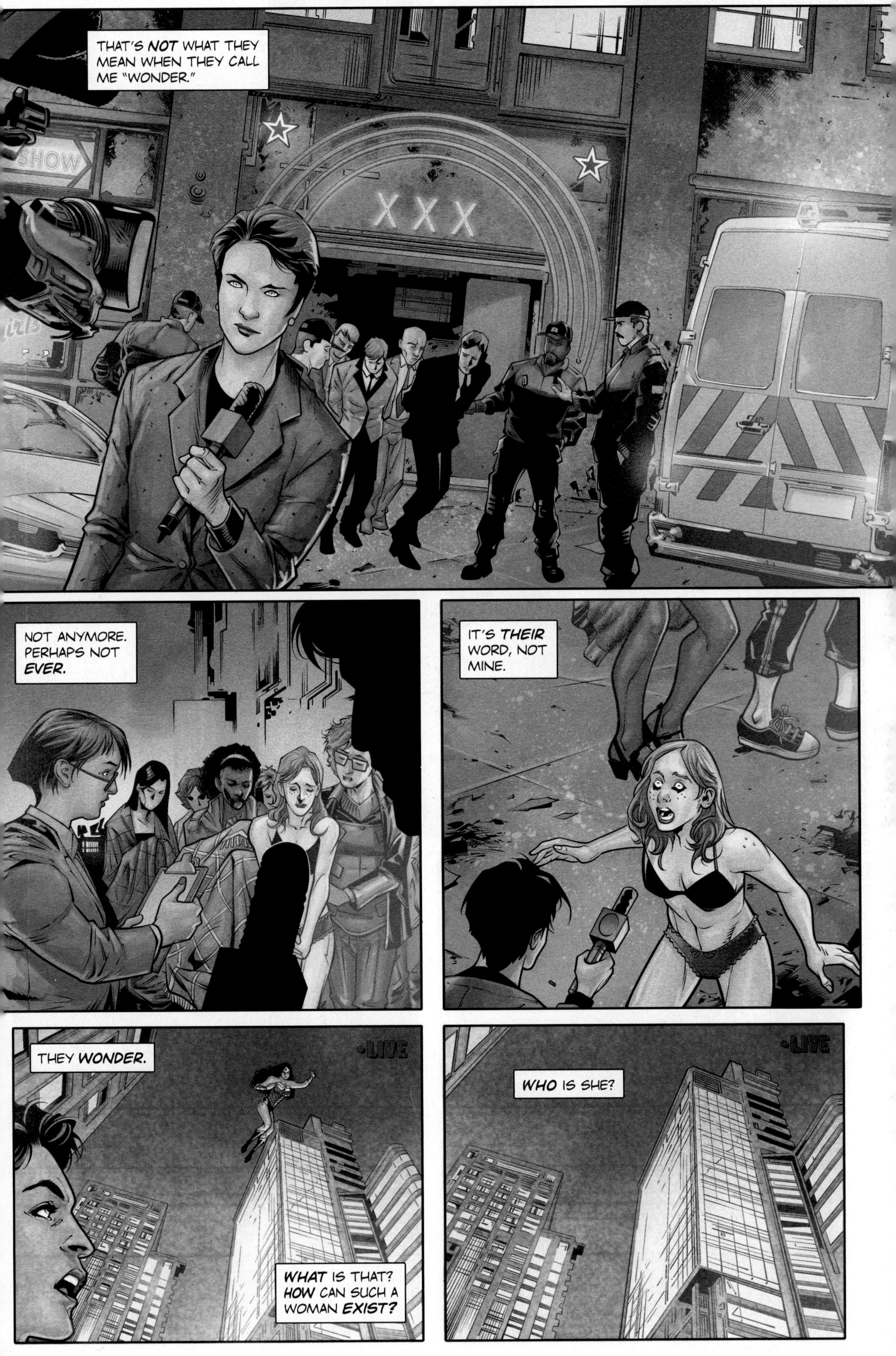
THAT'S NOT WHAT THEY MEAN WHEN THEY CALL ME "WONDER."
SHOW
XXX
NOT ANYMORE. PERHAPS NOT EVER.
IT'S THEIR WORD, NOT MINE.
THEY WONDER.
LIVE
WHAT IS THAT? HOW CAN SUCH A WOMAN EXIST?
LIVE
WHO IS SHE?

THE TRUTH IS, I NO LONGER **KNOW**.

THE TRUTH...

...MATTERS....

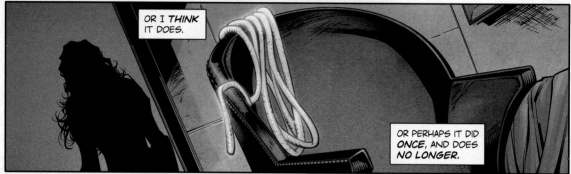

OR I **THINK** IT DOES.

OR PERHAPS IT DID **ONCE**, AND DOES **NO LONGER**.

OR PERHAPS IT **NEVER** DID.

BUT THAT SEEMS... **WRONG**.

IT **SHOULD** MATTER. IT SHOULD MATTER A **GREAT DEAL**.

OR PERHAPS IT SHOULDN'T. THE STORY KEEPS **CHANGING**.

THIS IS THE **HELM** OF THE **GOD OF WAR**. WORN BY **ARES**, WON BY **ME**.

I **THINK** I AM THE GOD OF WAR.

YET I THINK THAT **CANNOT** BE TRUE.

WAR...

...THE **FIRST** CASUALTY OF WAR...

...IS **TRUTH**.

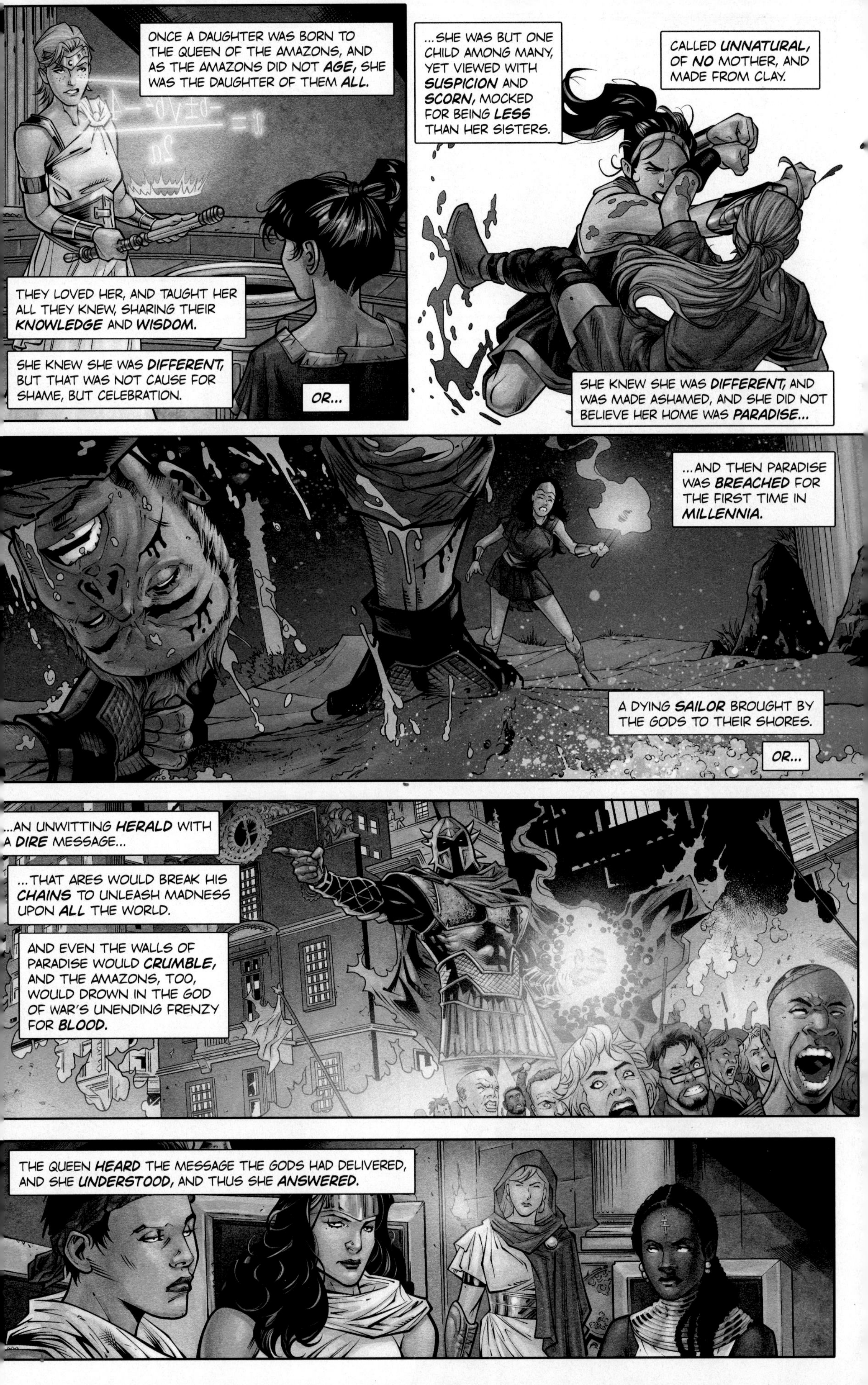
ONCE A DAUGHTER WAS BORN TO THE QUEEN OF THE AMAZONS, AND AS THE AMAZONS DID NOT AGE, SHE WAS THE DAUGHTER OF THEM ALL.
THEY LOVED HER, AND TAUGHT HER ALL THEY KNEW, SHARING THEIR KNOWLEDGE AND WISDOM.
SHE KNEW SHE WAS DIFFERENT, BUT THAT WAS NOT CAUSE FOR SHAME, BUT CELEBRATION.
OR...
...SHE WAS BUT ONE CHILD AMONG MANY, YET VIEWED WITH SUSPICION AND SCORN, MOCKED FOR BEING LESS THAN HER SISTERS.
CALLED UNNATURAL, OF NO MOTHER, AND MADE FROM CLAY.
SHE KNEW SHE WAS DIFFERENT, AND WAS MADE ASHAMED, AND SHE DID NOT BELIEVE HER HOME WAS PARADISE...
...AND THEN PARADISE WAS BREACHED FOR THE FIRST TIME IN MILLENNIA.
A DYING SAILOR BROUGHT BY THE GODS TO THEIR SHORES.
OR...
...AN UNWITTING HERALD WITH A DIRE MESSAGE...
...THAT ARES WOULD BREAK HIS CHAINS TO UNLEASH MADNESS UPON ALL THE WORLD.
AND EVEN THE WALLS OF PARADISE WOULD CRUMBLE, AND THE AMAZONS, TOO, WOULD DROWN IN THE GOD OF WAR'S UNENDING FRENZY FOR BLOOD.
THE QUEEN HEARD THE MESSAGE THE GODS HAD DELIVERED, AND SHE UNDERSTOOD, AND THUS SHE ANSWERED.

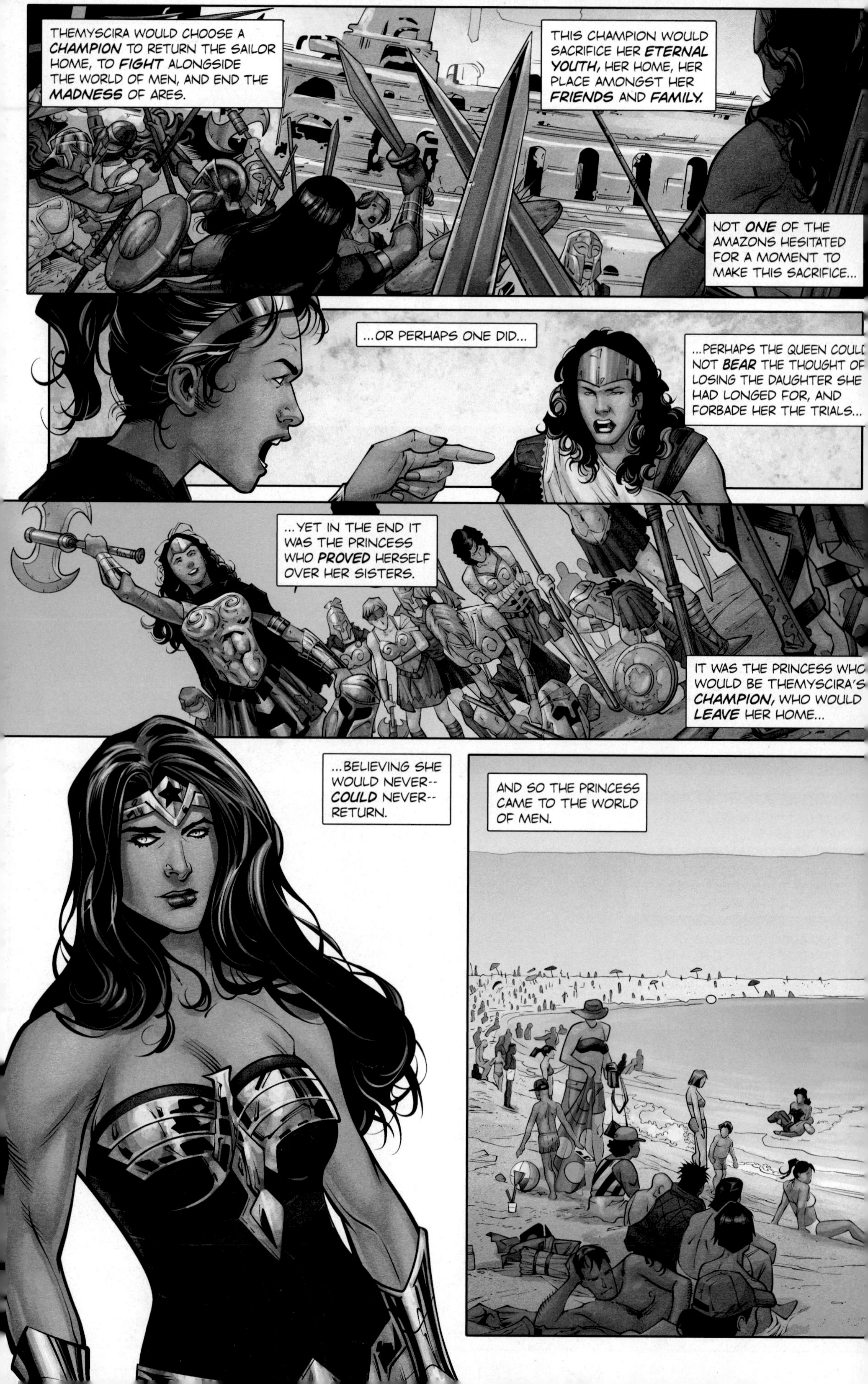
THEMYSCIRA WOULD CHOOSE A CHAMPION TO RETURN THE SAILOR HOME, TO FIGHT ALONGSIDE THE WORLD OF MEN, AND END THE MADNESS OF ARES.
THIS CHAMPION WOULD SACRIFICE HER ETERNAL YOUTH, HER HOME, HER PLACE AMONGST HER FRIENDS AND FAMILY.
NOT ONE OF THE AMAZONS HESITATED FOR A MOMENT TO MAKE THIS SACRIFICE...
...OR PERHAPS ONE DID...
...PERHAPS THE QUEEN COULD NOT BEAR THE THOUGHT OF LOSING THE DAUGHTER SHE HAD LONGED FOR, AND FORBADE HER THE TRIALS...
...YET IN THE END IT WAS THE PRINCESS WHO PROVED HERSELF OVER HER SISTERS.
IT WAS THE PRINCESS WHO WOULD BE THEMYSCIRA'S CHAMPION, WHO WOULD LEAVE HER HOME...
...BELIEVING SHE WOULD NEVER-- COULD NEVER-- RETURN.
AND SO THE PRINCESS CAME TO THE WORLD OF MEN.

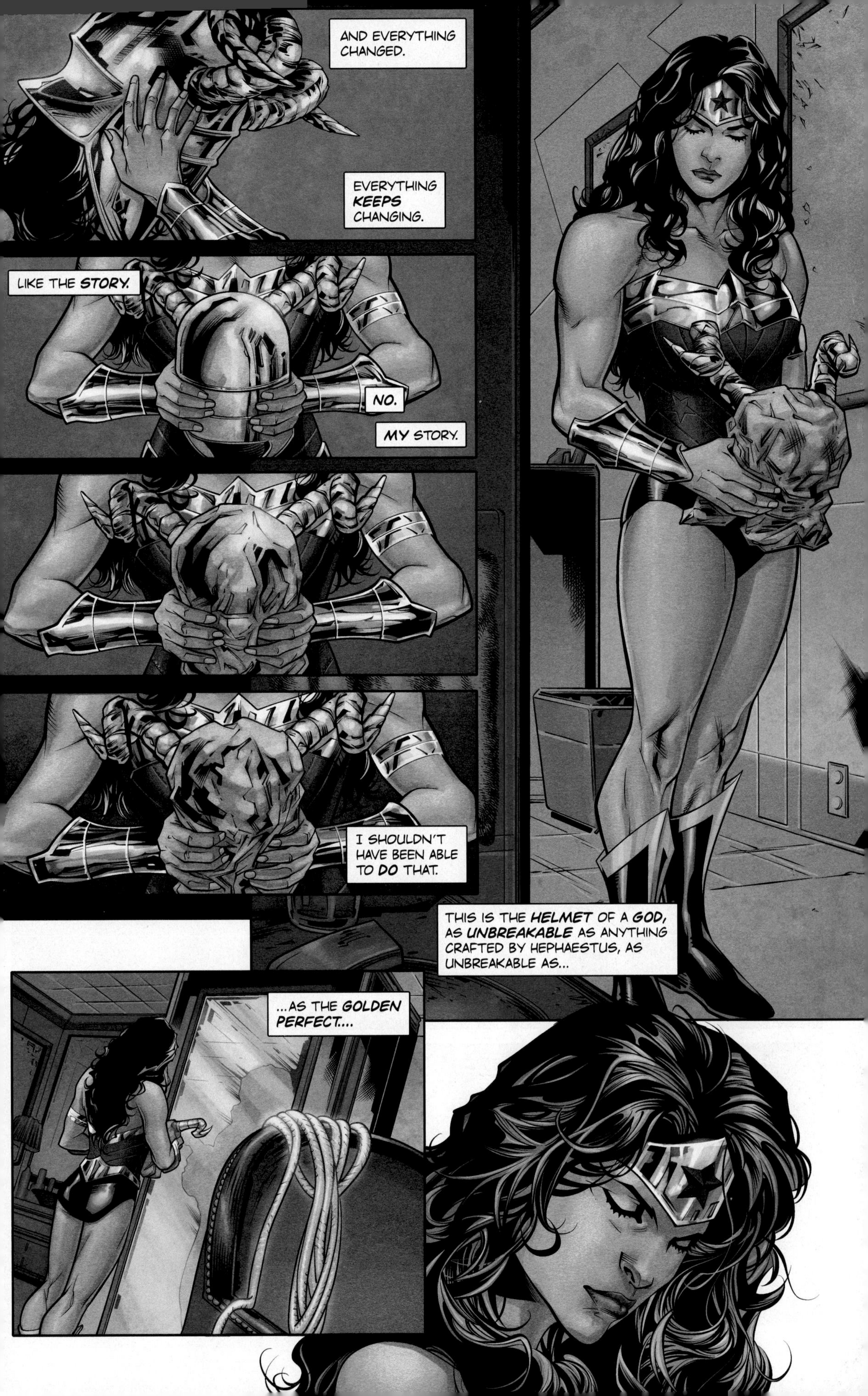
AND EVERYTHING CHANGED.
EVERYTHING **KEEPS** CHANGING.
LIKE THE **STORY.**
NO.
MY STORY.
I SHOULDN'T HAVE BEEN ABLE TO **DO** THAT.
THIS IS THE **HELMET** OF A **GOD,** AS **UNBREAKABLE** AS ANYTHING CRAFTED BY HEPHAESTUS, AS UNBREAKABLE AS...
...AS THE **GOLDEN PERFECT....**

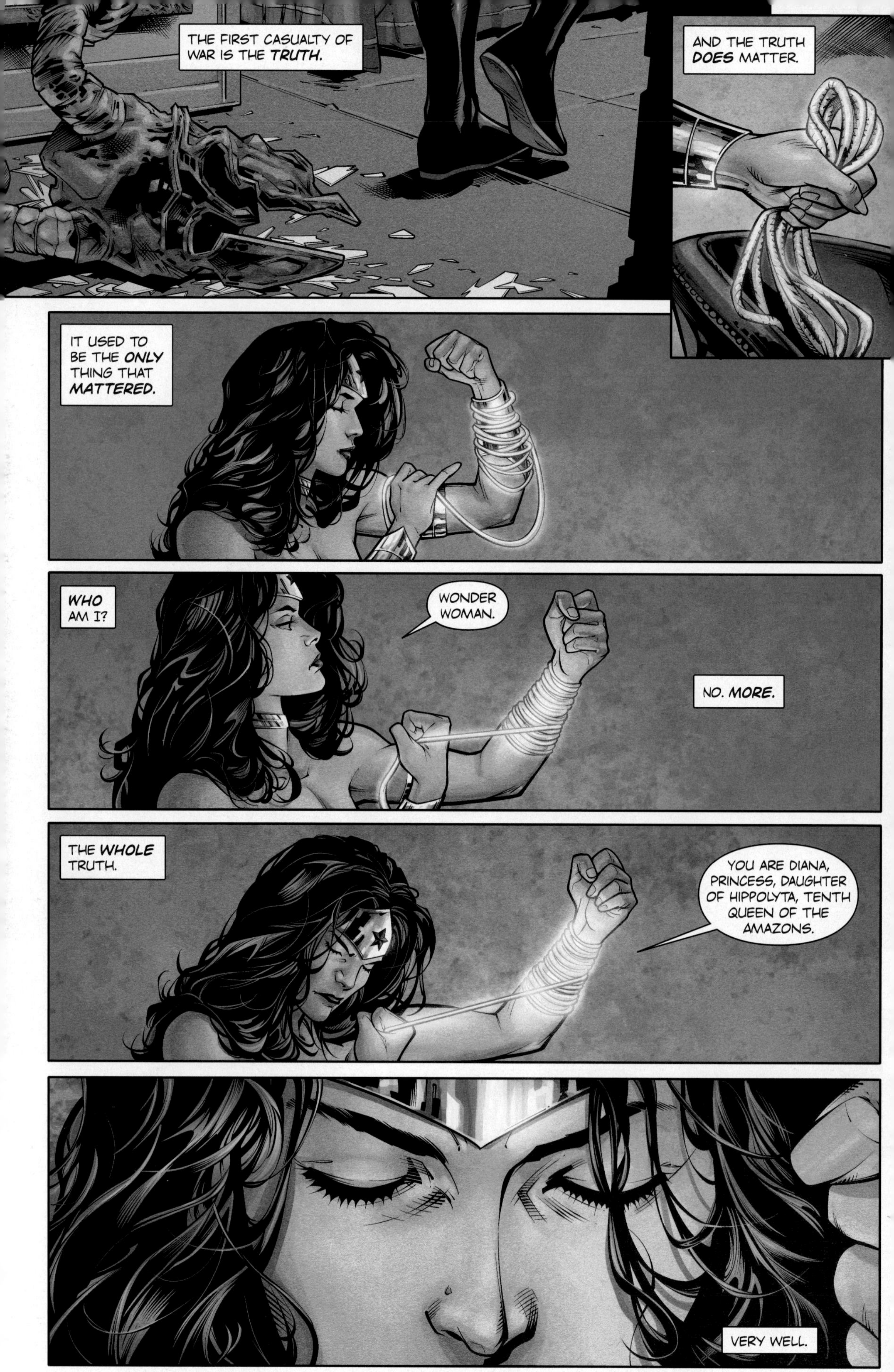
THE FIRST CASUALTY OF WAR IS THE TRUTH.
AND THE TRUTH DOES MATTER.
IT USED TO BE THE ONLY THING THAT MATTERED.
WHO AM I?
WONDER WOMAN.
NO. MORE.
THE WHOLE TRUTH.
YOU ARE DIANA, PRINCESS, DAUGHTER OF HIPPOLYTA, TENTH QUEEN OF THE AMAZONS.
VERY WELL.

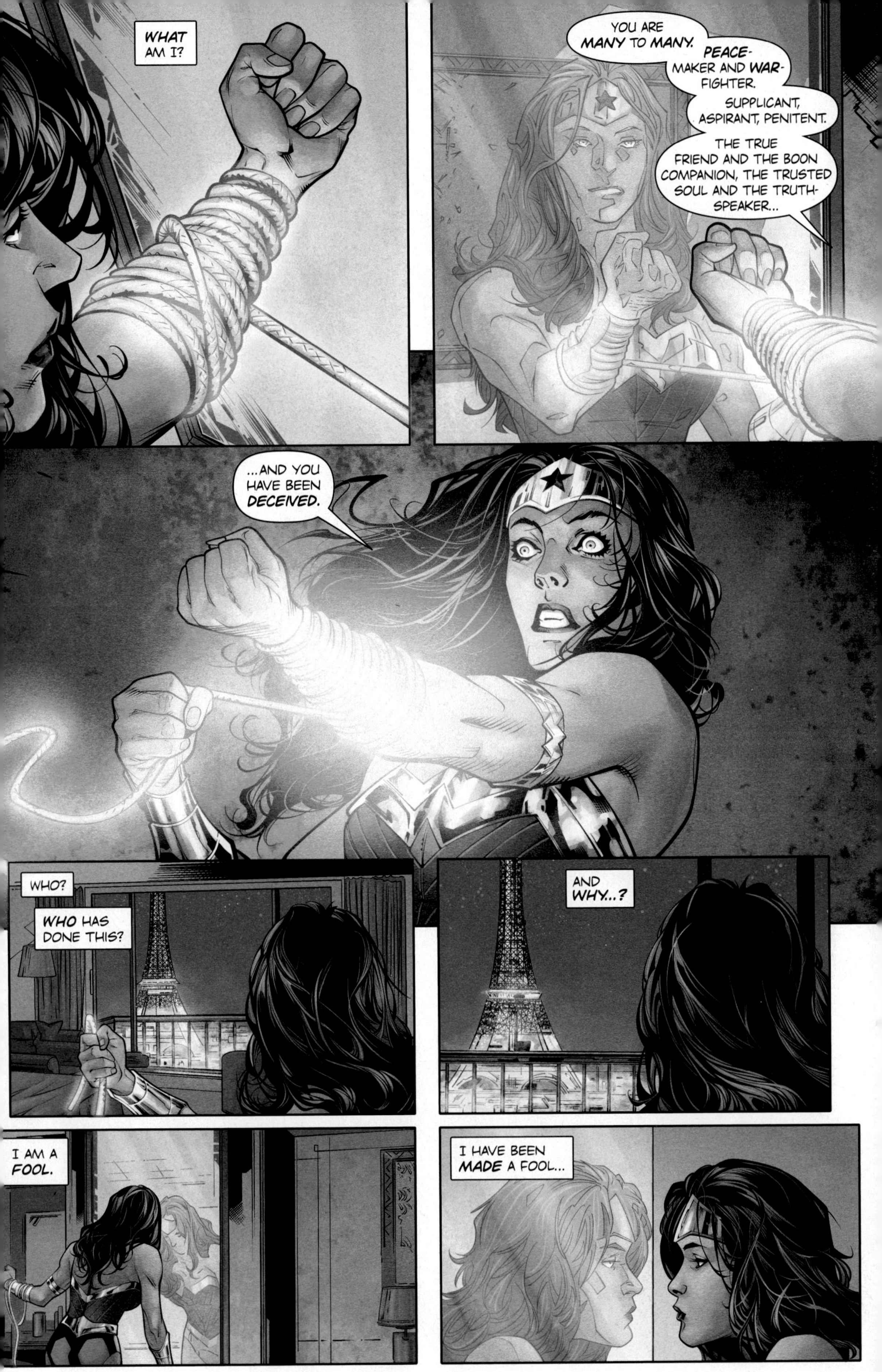
WHAT AM I?
YOU ARE MANY TO MANY. PEACE-MAKER AND WAR-FIGHTER.
SUPPLICANT, ASPIRANT, PENITENT.
THE TRUE FRIEND AND THE BOON COMPANION, THE TRUSTED SOUL AND THE TRUTH-SPEAKER...
...AND YOU HAVE BEEN DECEIVED.
WHO?
WHO HAS DONE THIS?
AND WHY...?
I AM A FOOL.
I HAVE BEEN MADE A FOOL...

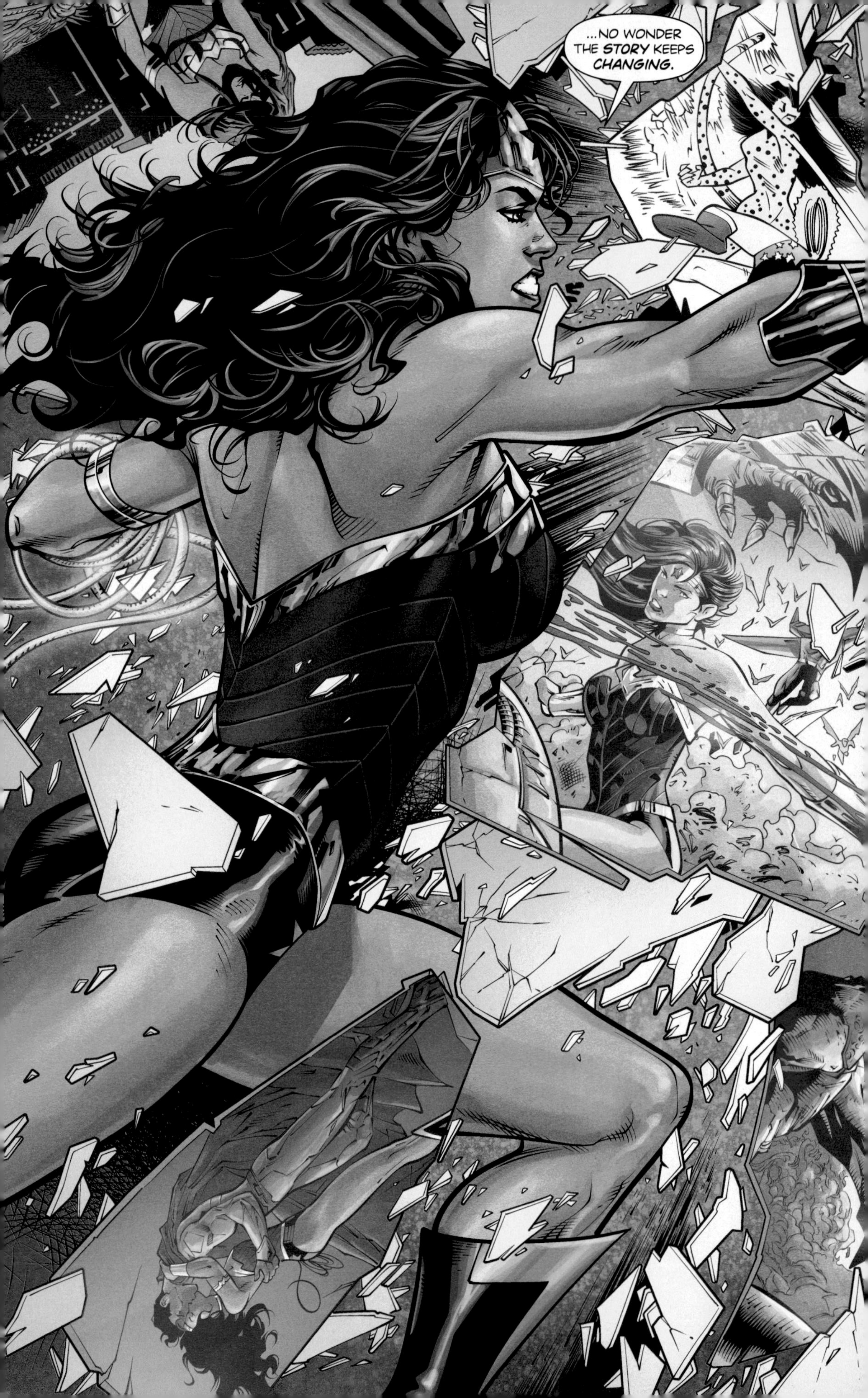
...NO WONDER THE STORY KEEPS CHANGING.

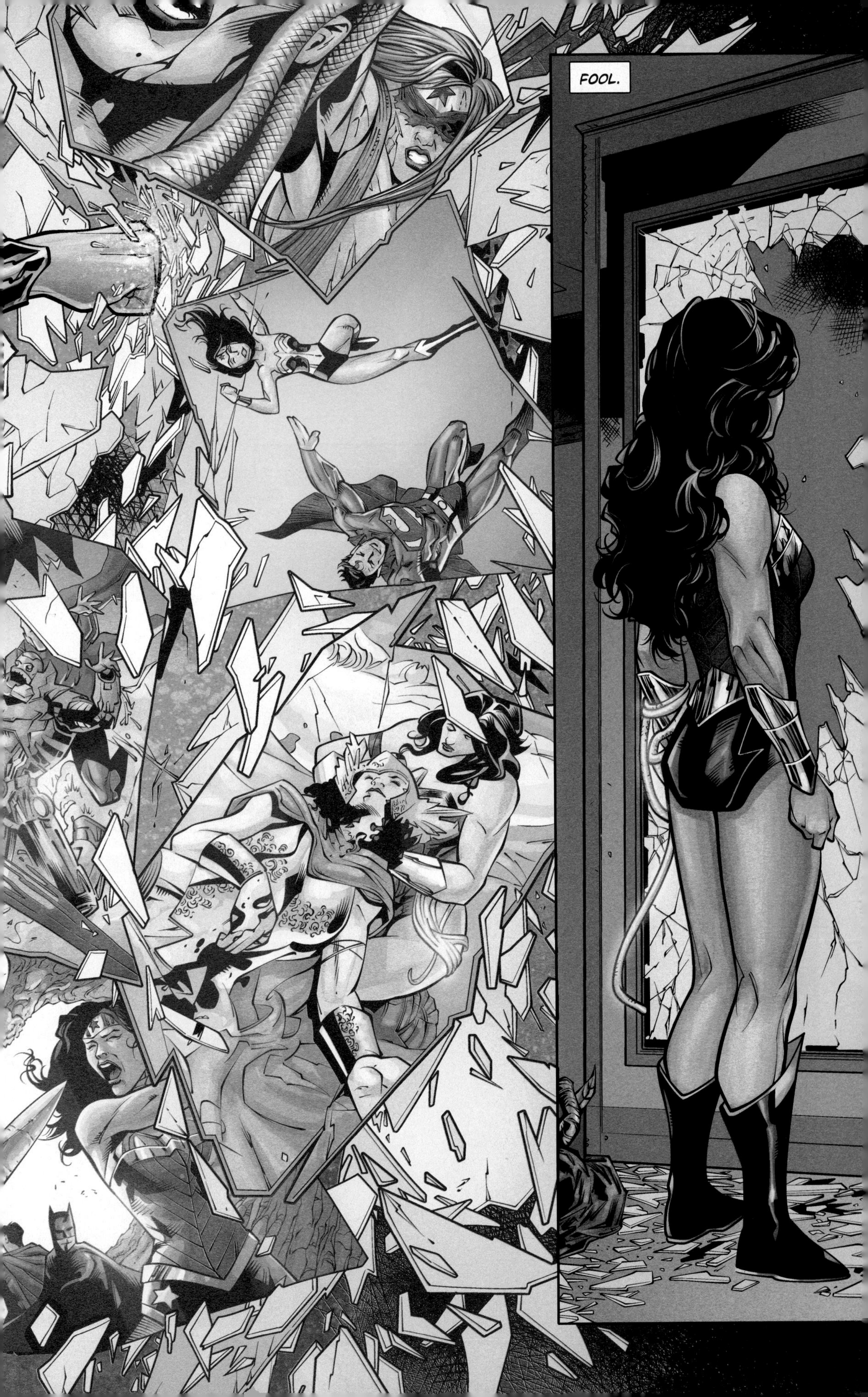
FOOL.

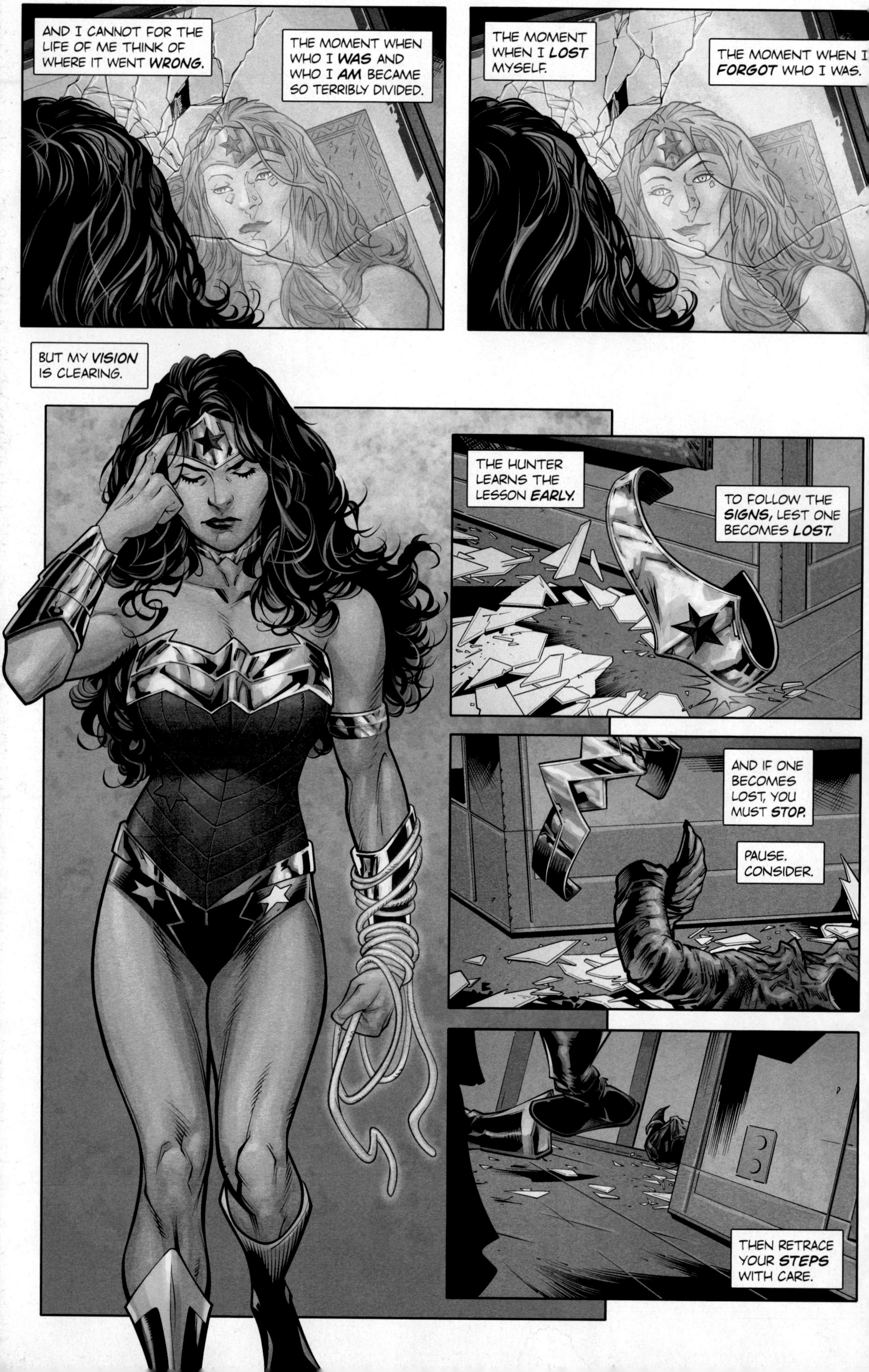
AND I CANNOT FOR THE LIFE OF ME THINK OF WHERE IT WENT WRONG.
THE MOMENT WHEN WHO I WAS AND WHO I AM BECAME SO TERRIBLY DIVIDED.
THE MOMENT WHEN I LOST MYSELF.
THE MOMENT WHEN I FORGOT WHO I WAS.
BUT MY VISION IS CLEARING.
THE HUNTER LEARNS THE LESSON EARLY.
TO FOLLOW THE SIGNS, LEST ONE BECOMES LOST.
AND IF ONE BECOMES LOST, YOU MUST STOP.
PAUSE. CONSIDER.
THEN RETRACE YOUR STEPS WITH CARE.

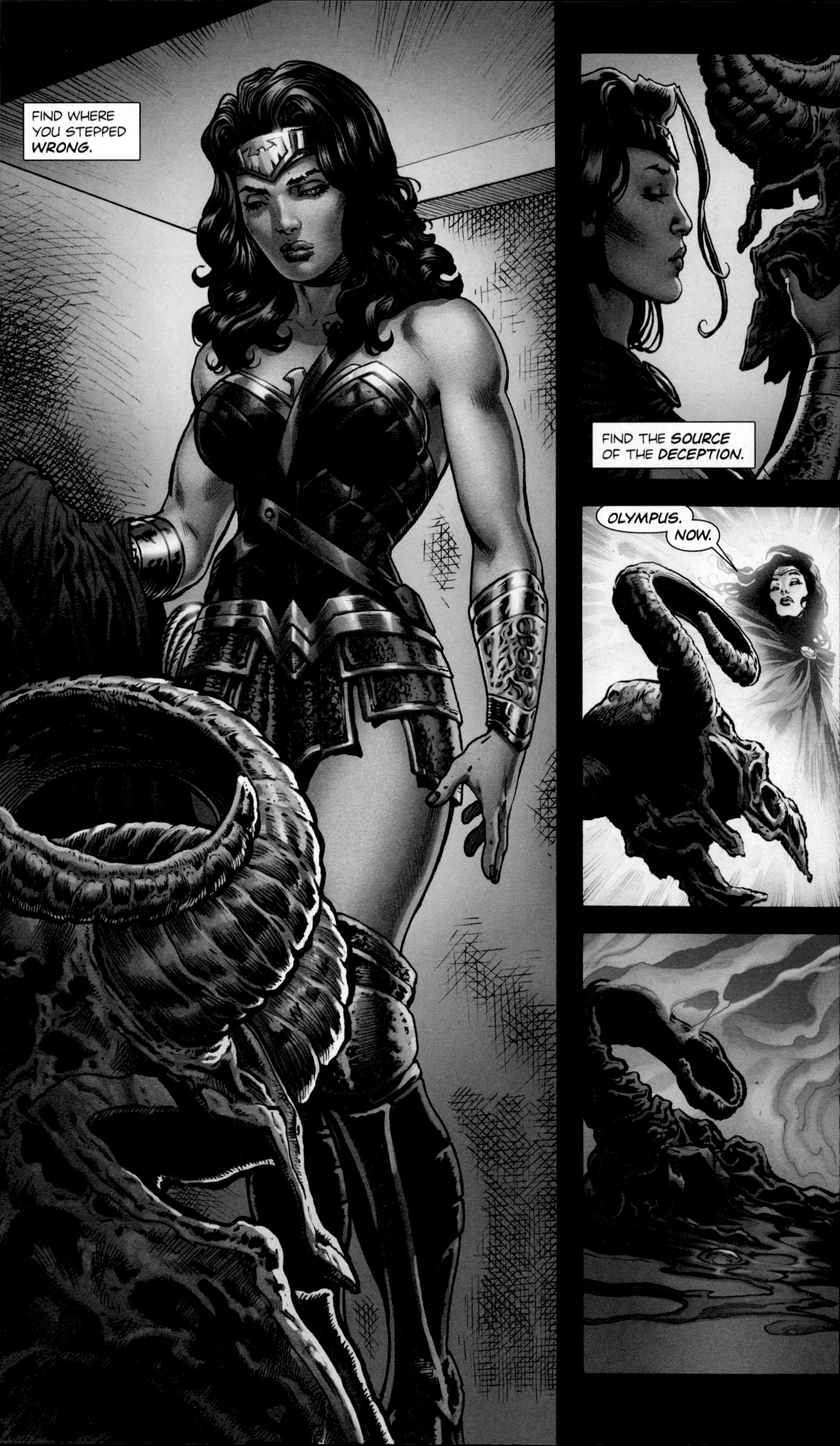
FIND WHERE YOU STEPPED WRONG.
FIND THE SOURCE OF THE DECEPTION.
OLYMPUS. NOW.

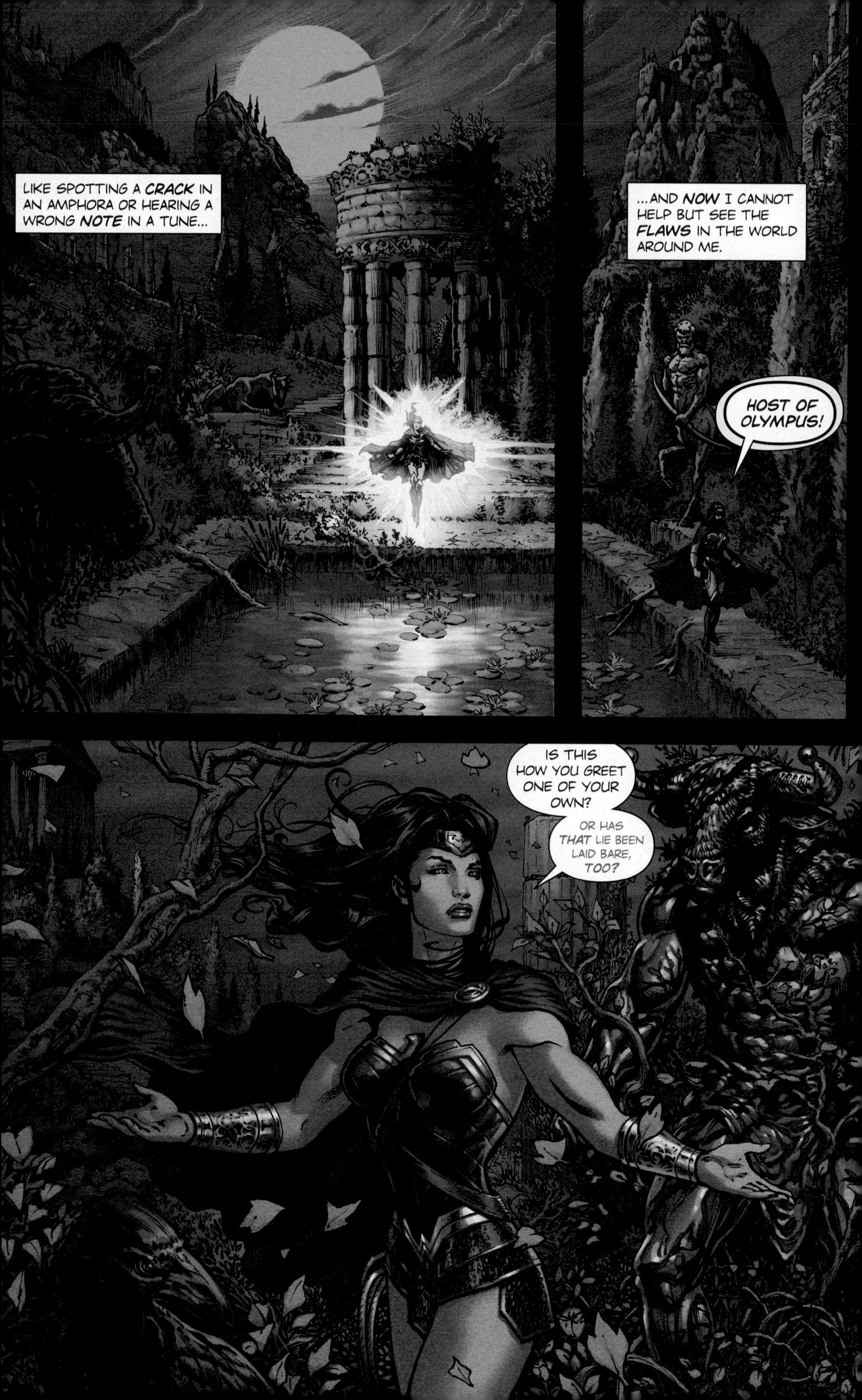
LIKE SPOTTING A CRACK IN AN AMPHORA OR HEARING A WRONG NOTE IN A TUNE...
...AND NOW I CANNOT HELP BUT SEE THE FLAWS IN THE WORLD AROUND ME.
HOST OF OLYMPUS!
IS THIS HOW YOU GREET ONE OF YOUR OWN?
OR HAS THAT LIE BEEN LAID BARE, TOO?

AUTOMATONS.

THE WORK OF HEPHAESTUS.

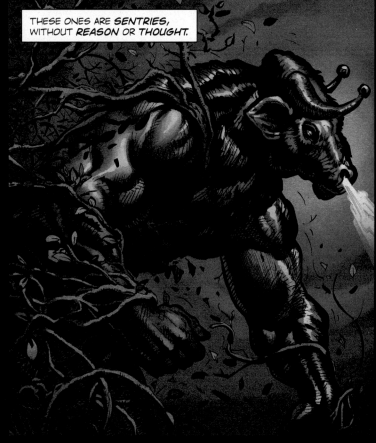

THESE ONES ARE **SENTRIES,** WITHOUT **REASON** OR **THOUGHT.**

THEY CAN DO **ONLY** AS THEY HAVE BEEN **INSTRUCTED,** NO MORE AND NO LESS.

NO REMORSE, NOR HESITATION. NO REGRET, NOR CONSCIENCE.

AND THEY WILL **NEVER** RELENT.

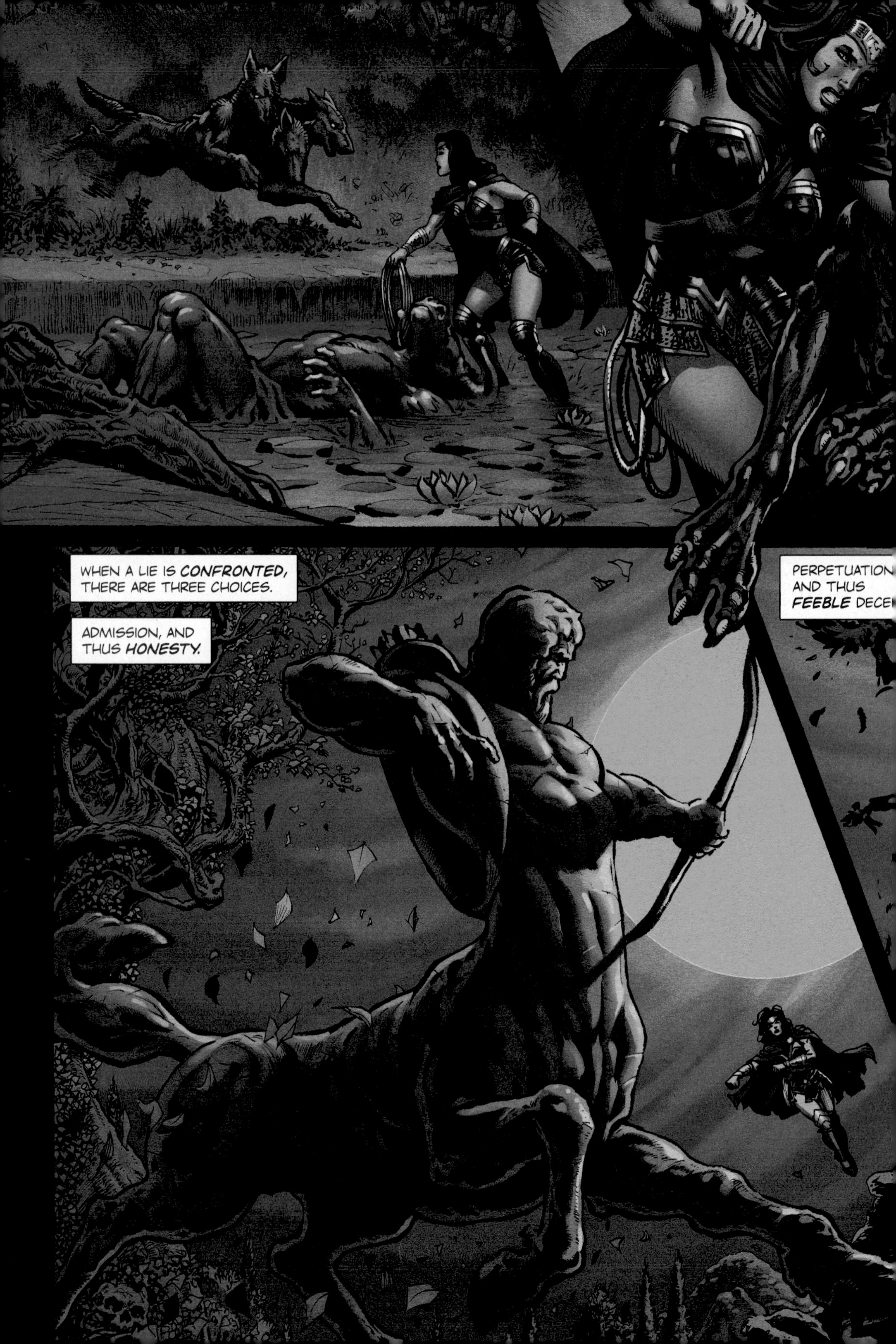

WHEN A LIE IS CONFRONTED, THERE ARE THREE CHOICES.
ADMISSION, AND THUS HONESTY.
PERPETUATION AND THUS FEEBLE DECE

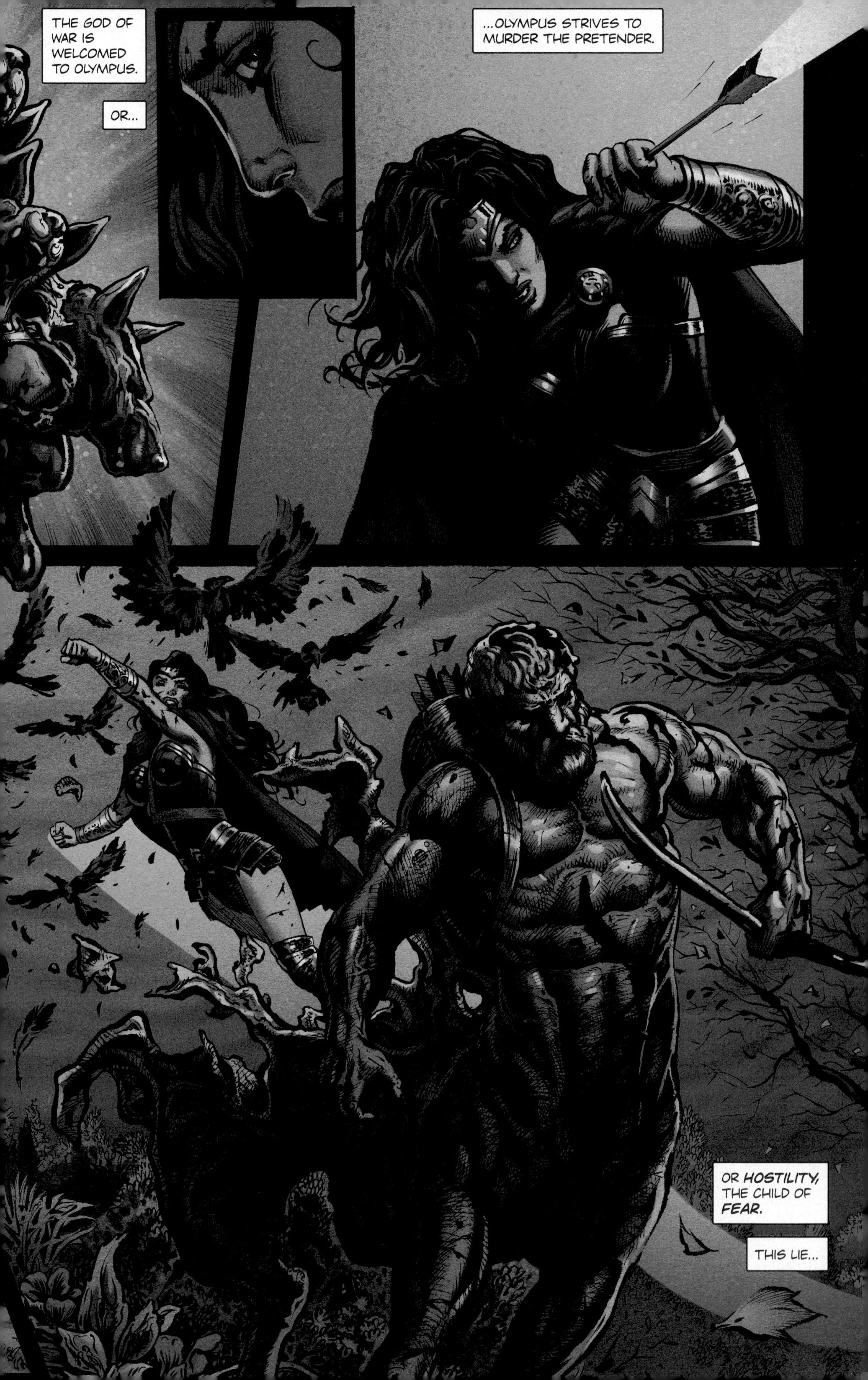
THE GOD OF WAR IS WELCOMED TO OLYMPUS.
OR...
...OLYMPUS STRIVES TO MURDER THE PRETENDER.
OR HOSTILITY, THE CHILD OF FEAR.
THIS LIE...

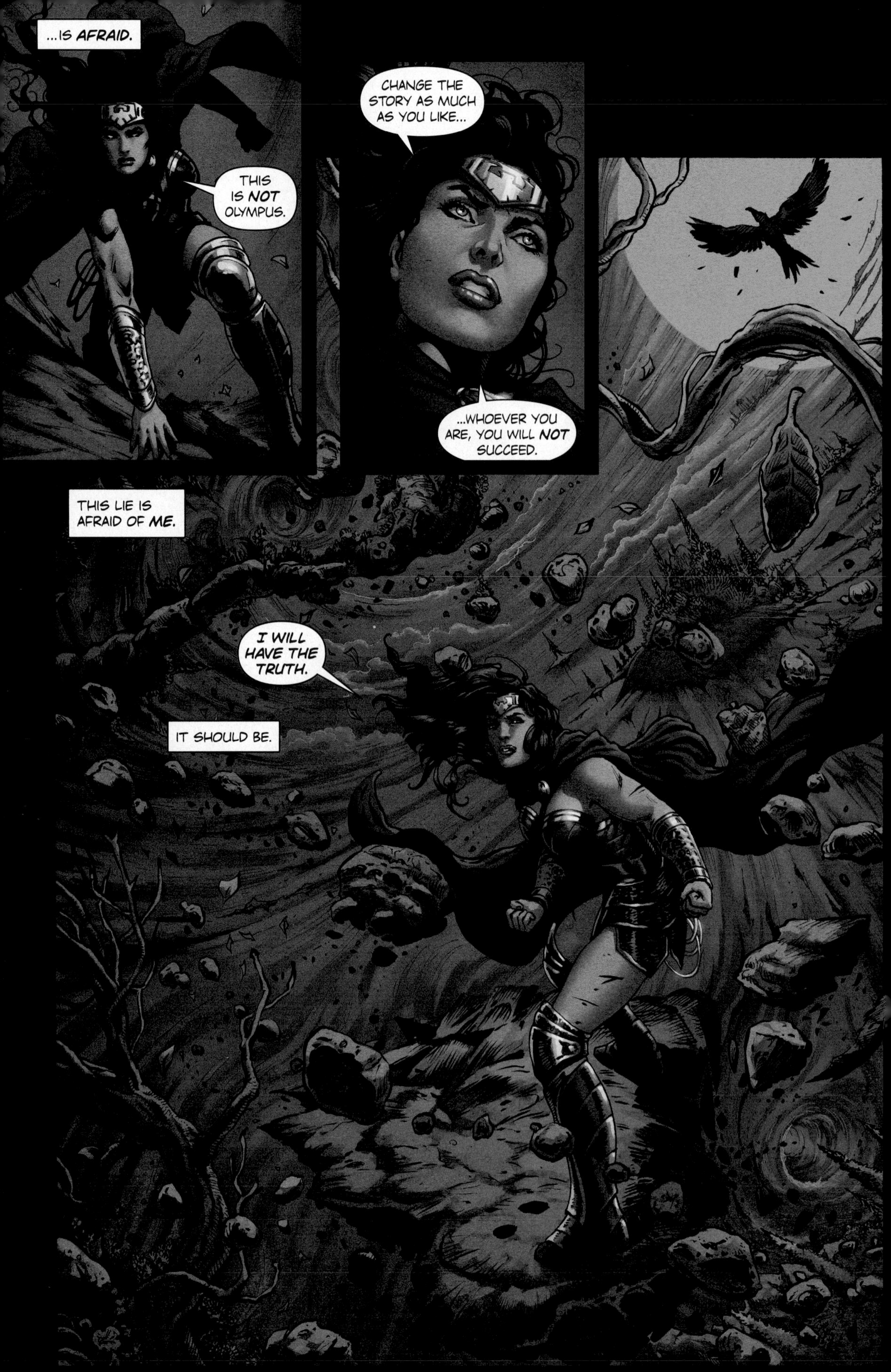

...IS AFRAID.
THIS IS NOT OLYMPUS.
CHANGE THE STORY AS MUCH AS YOU LIKE...
...WHOEVER YOU ARE, YOU WILL NOT SUCCEED.
THIS LIE IS AFRAID OF ME.
I WILL HAVE THE TRUTH.
IT SHOULD BE.

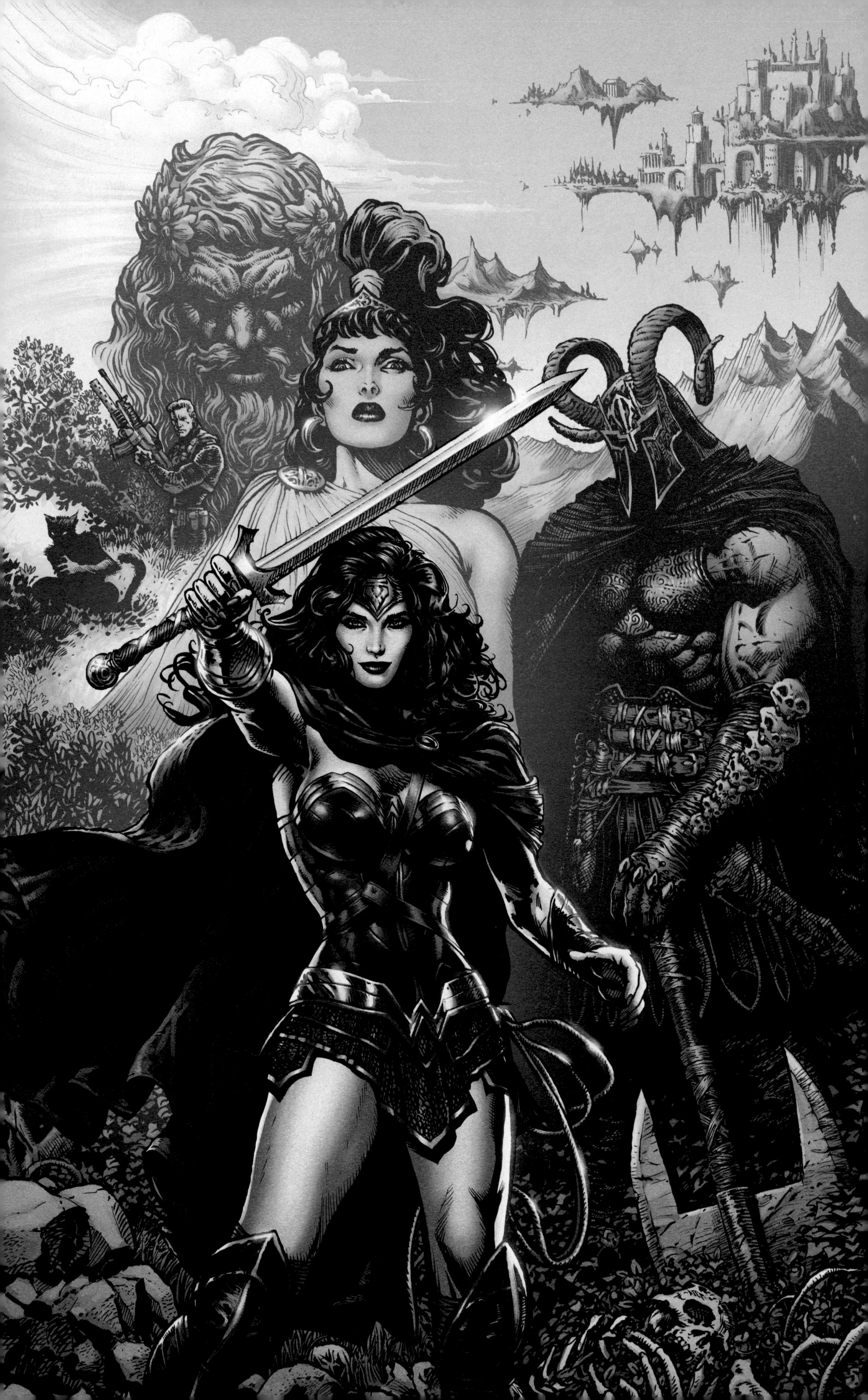

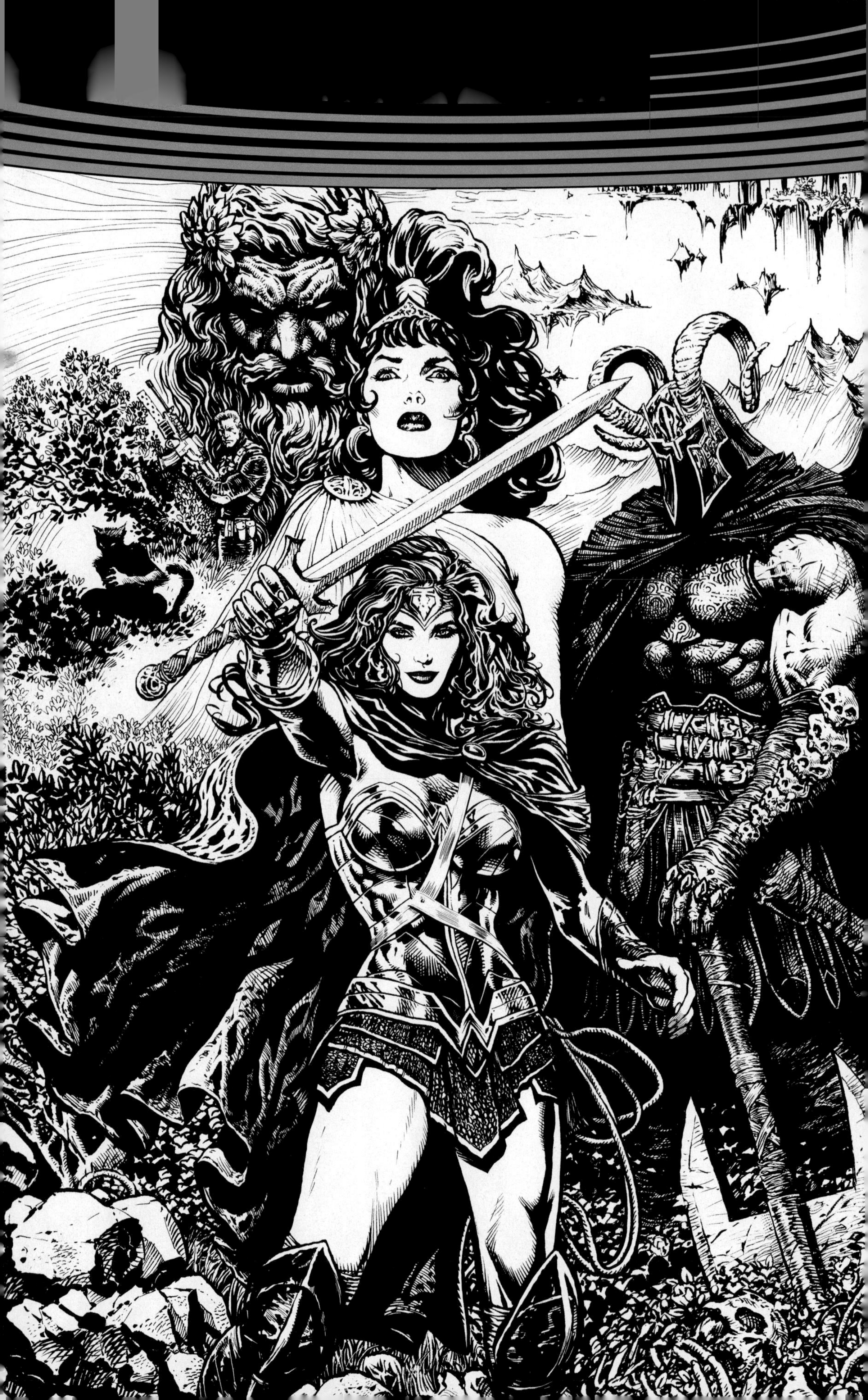

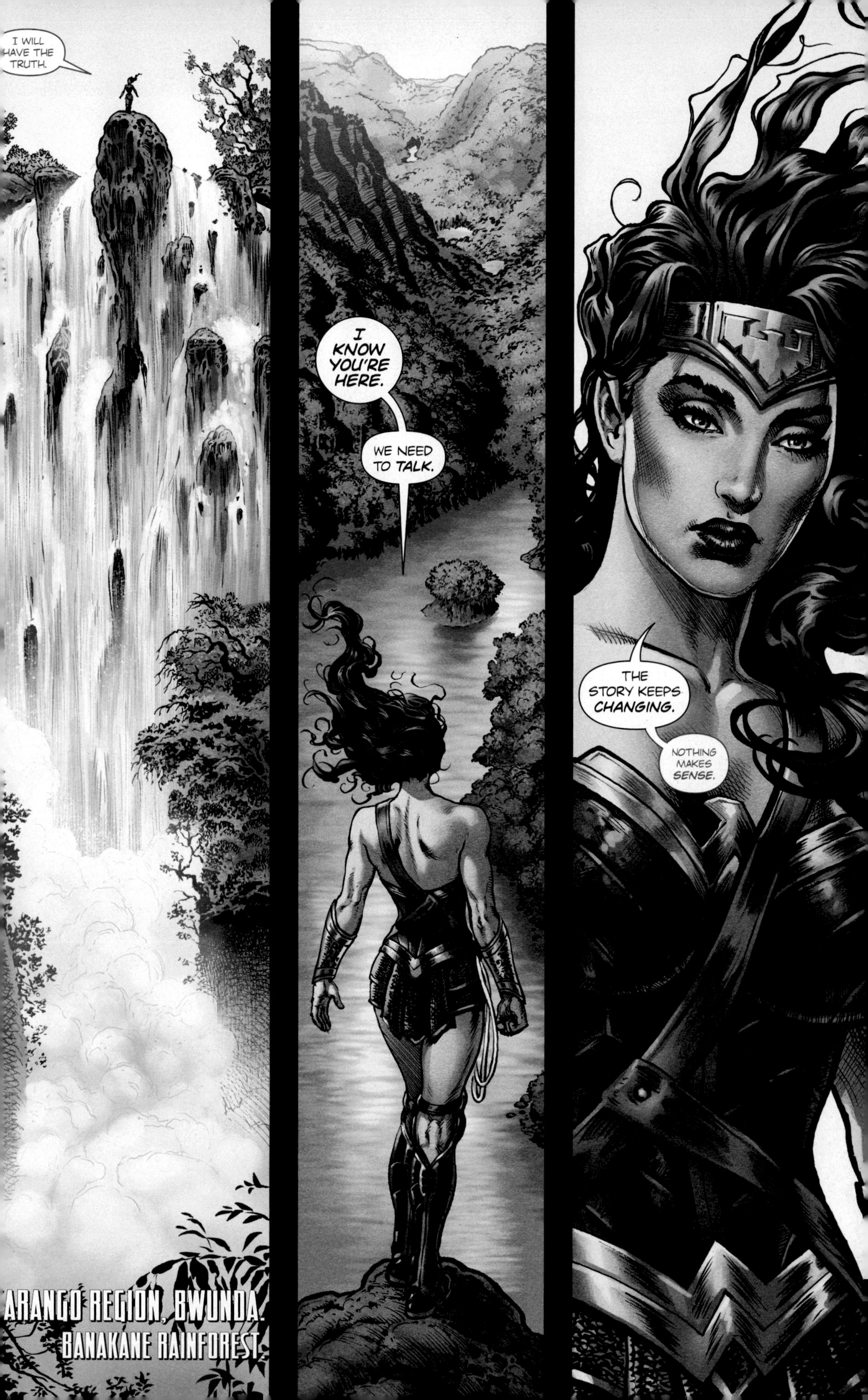
I WILL HAVE THE TRUTH.
I KNOW YOU'RE HERE.
WE NEED TO TALK.
THE STORY KEEPS CHANGING.
NOTHING MAKES SENSE.
ARANGO REGION, BWUNDA.
BANAKANE RAINFOREST.

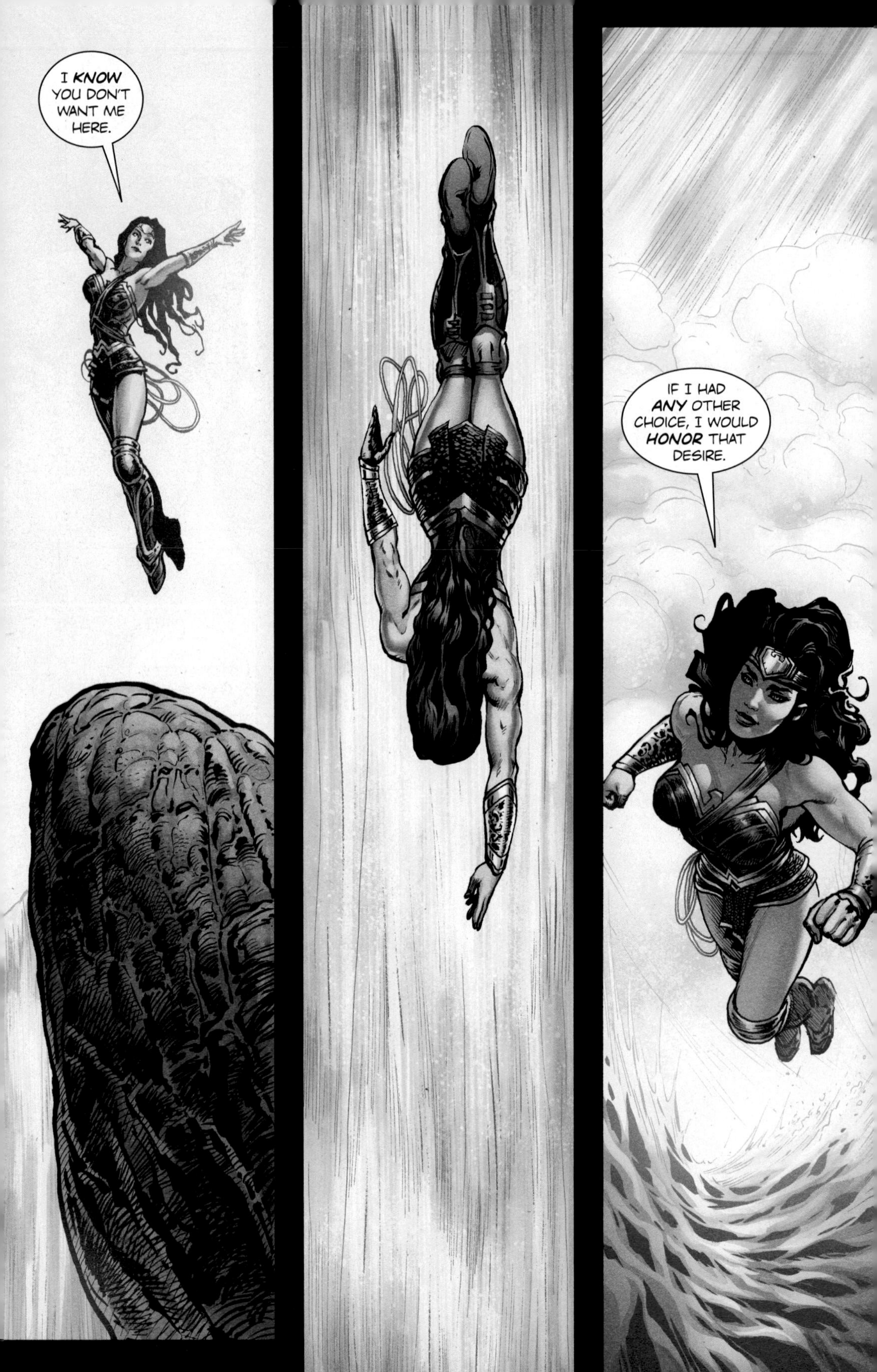
I KNOW YOU DON'T WANT ME HERE.
IF I HAD ANY OTHER CHOICE, I WOULD HONOR THAT DESIRE.

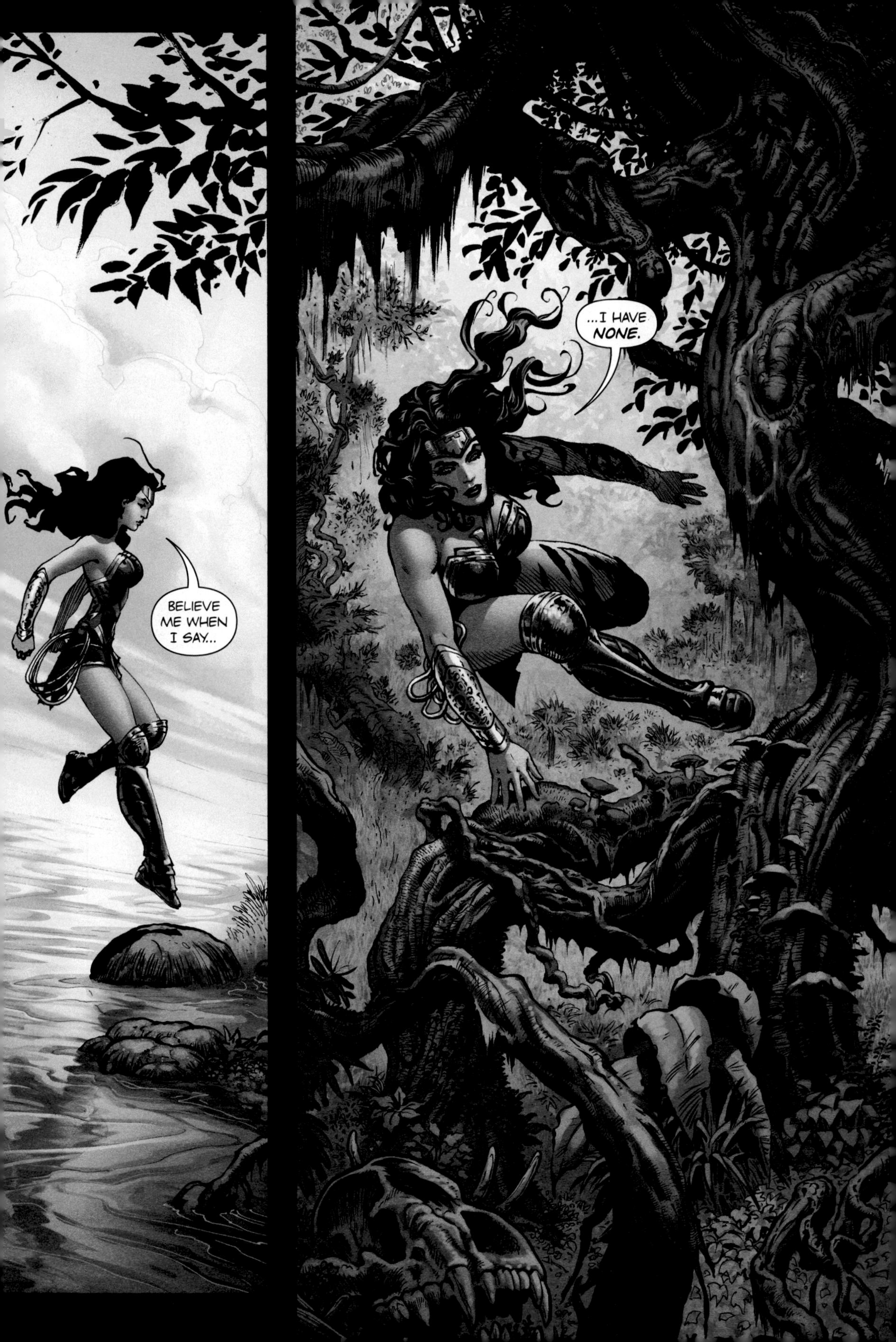
BELIEVE ME WHEN I SAY...
...I HAVE NONE.

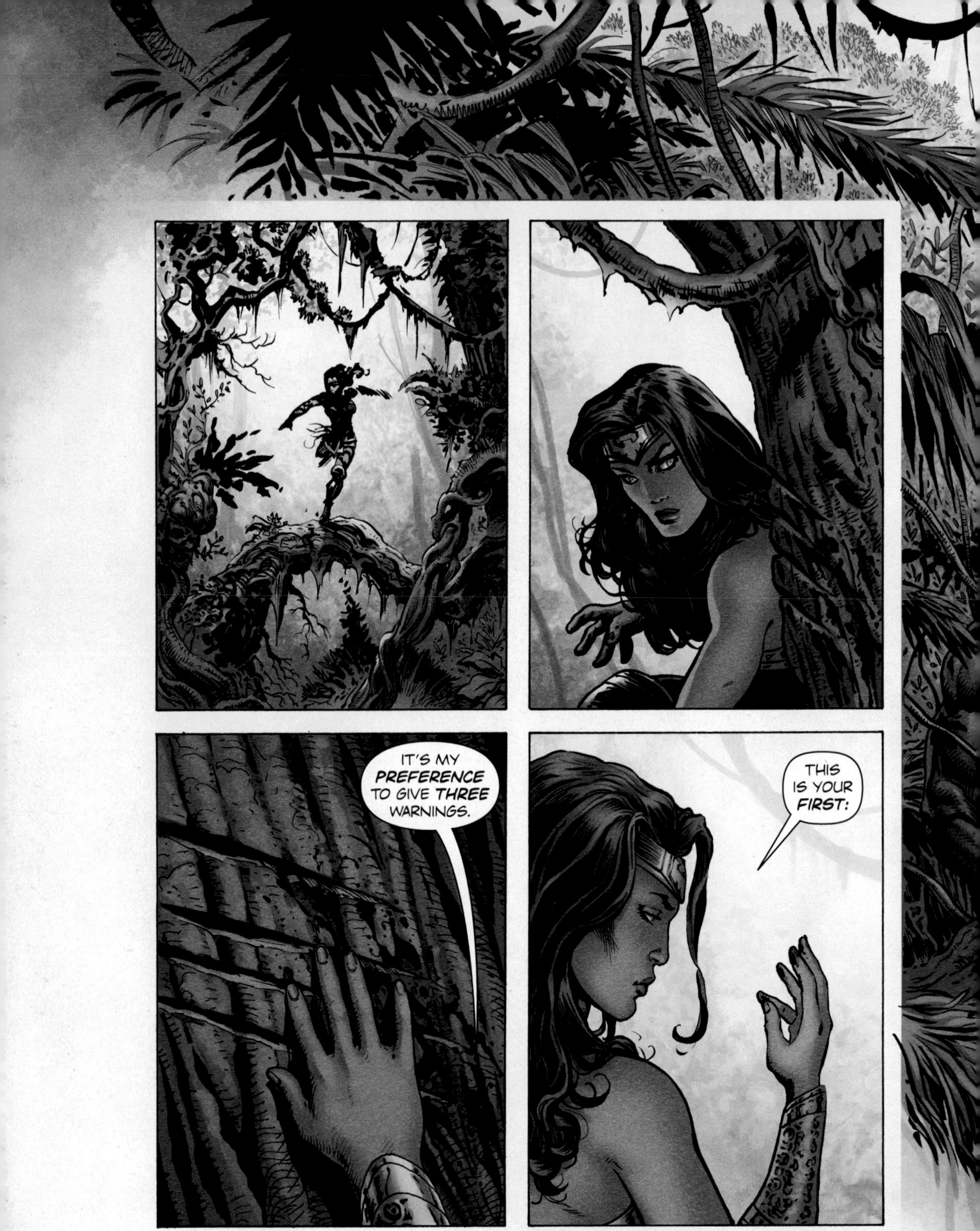
IT'S MY PREFERENCE TO GIVE THREE WARNINGS.
THIS IS YOUR FIRST:

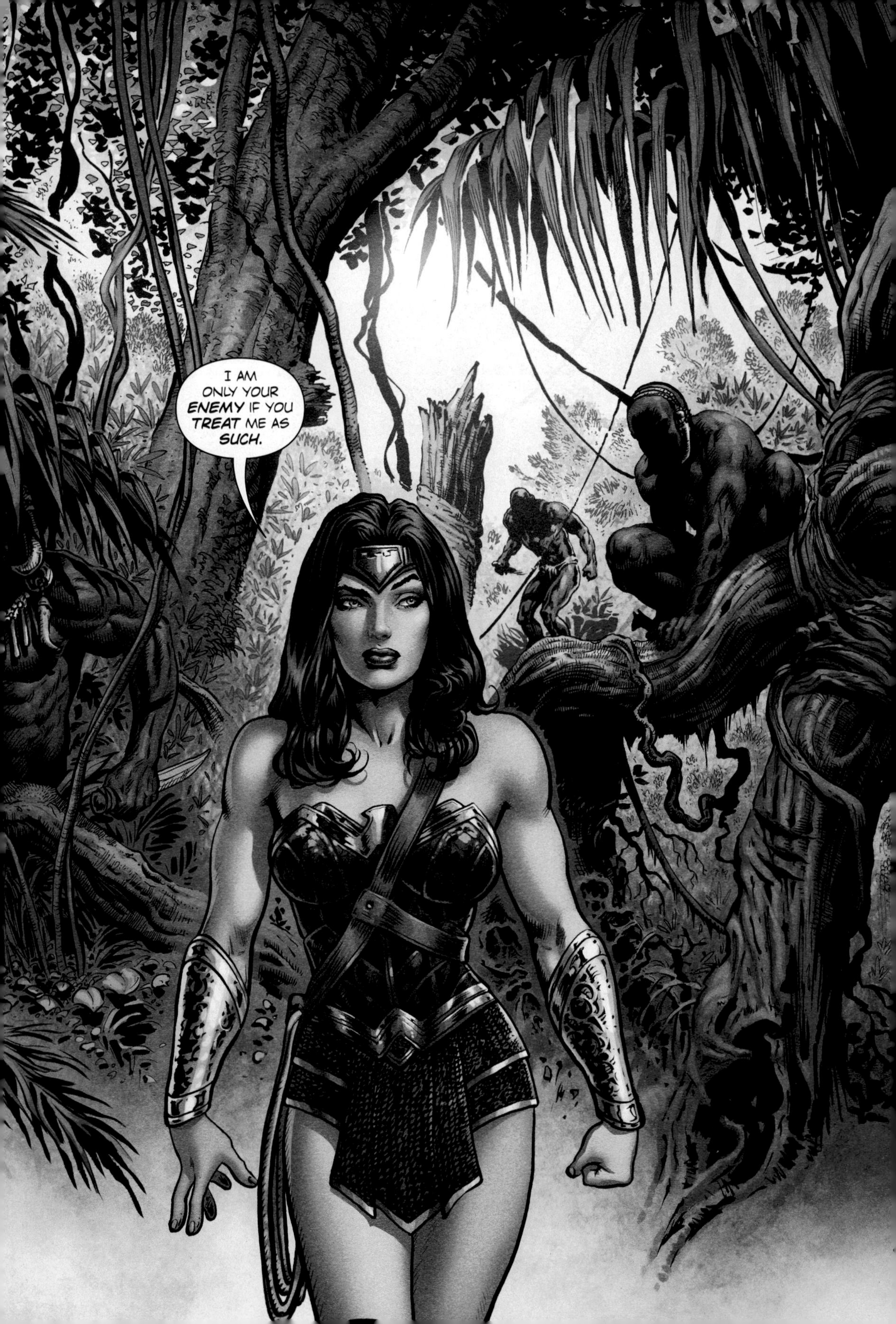
I AM ONLY YOUR ENEMY IF YOU TREAT ME AS SUCH.

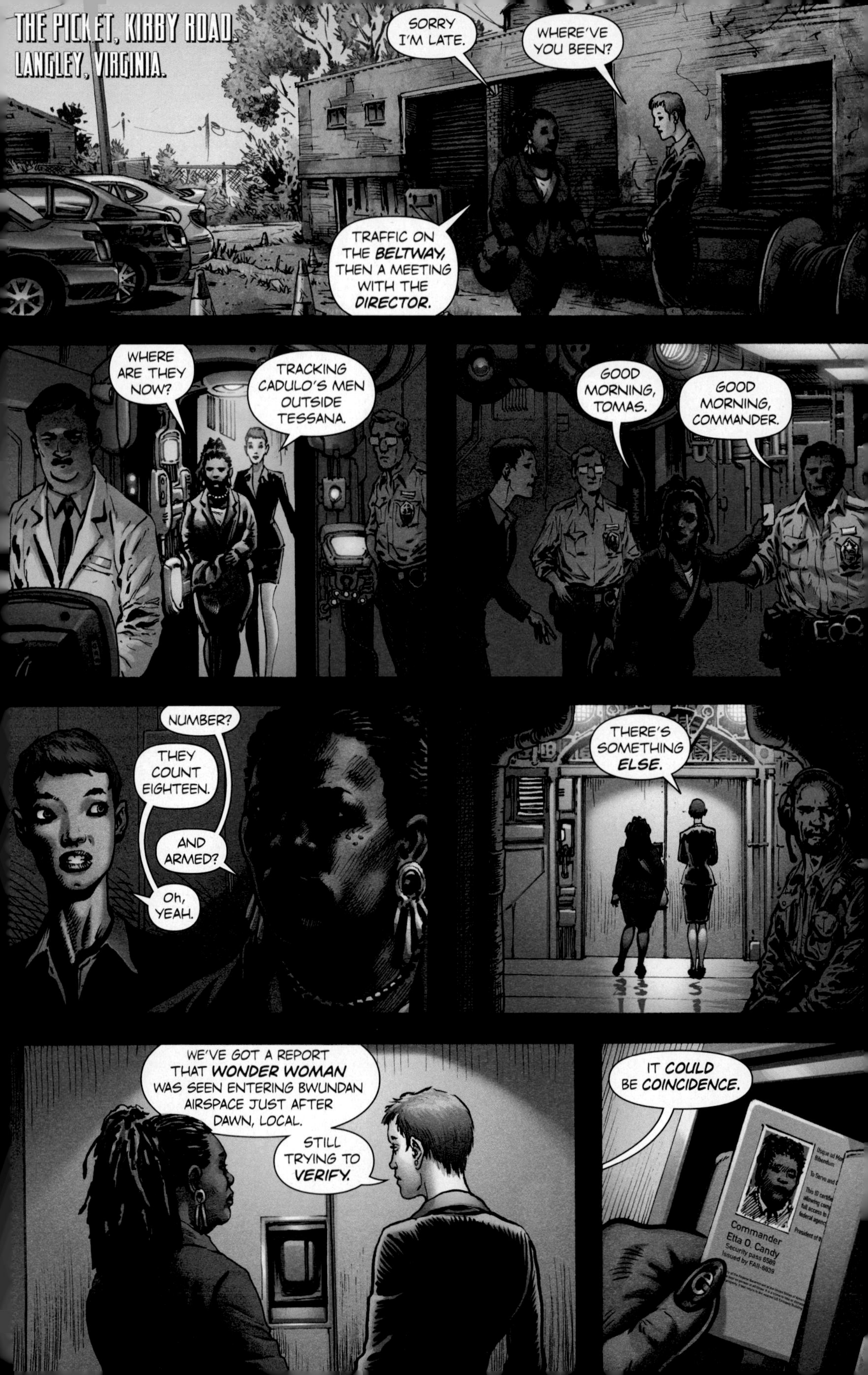
THE PICKET, KIRBY ROAD.
LANGLEY, VIRGINIA.
SORRY I'M LATE.
WHERE'VE YOU BEEN?
TRAFFIC ON THE **BELTWAY,** THEN A MEETING WITH THE **DIRECTOR.**
WHERE ARE THEY NOW?
TRACKING CADULO'S MEN OUTSIDE TESSANA.
GOOD MORNING, TOMAS.
GOOD MORNING, COMMANDER.
NUMBER?
THEY COUNT EIGHTEEN.
AND ARMED?
Oh, YEAH.
THERE'S SOMETHING **ELSE.**
WE'VE GOT A REPORT THAT **WONDER WOMAN** WAS SEEN ENTERING BWUNDAN AIRSPACE JUST AFTER DAWN, LOCAL.
STILL TRYING TO **VERIFY.**
IT **COULD** BE **COINCIDENCE.**
Commander
Etta O. Candy

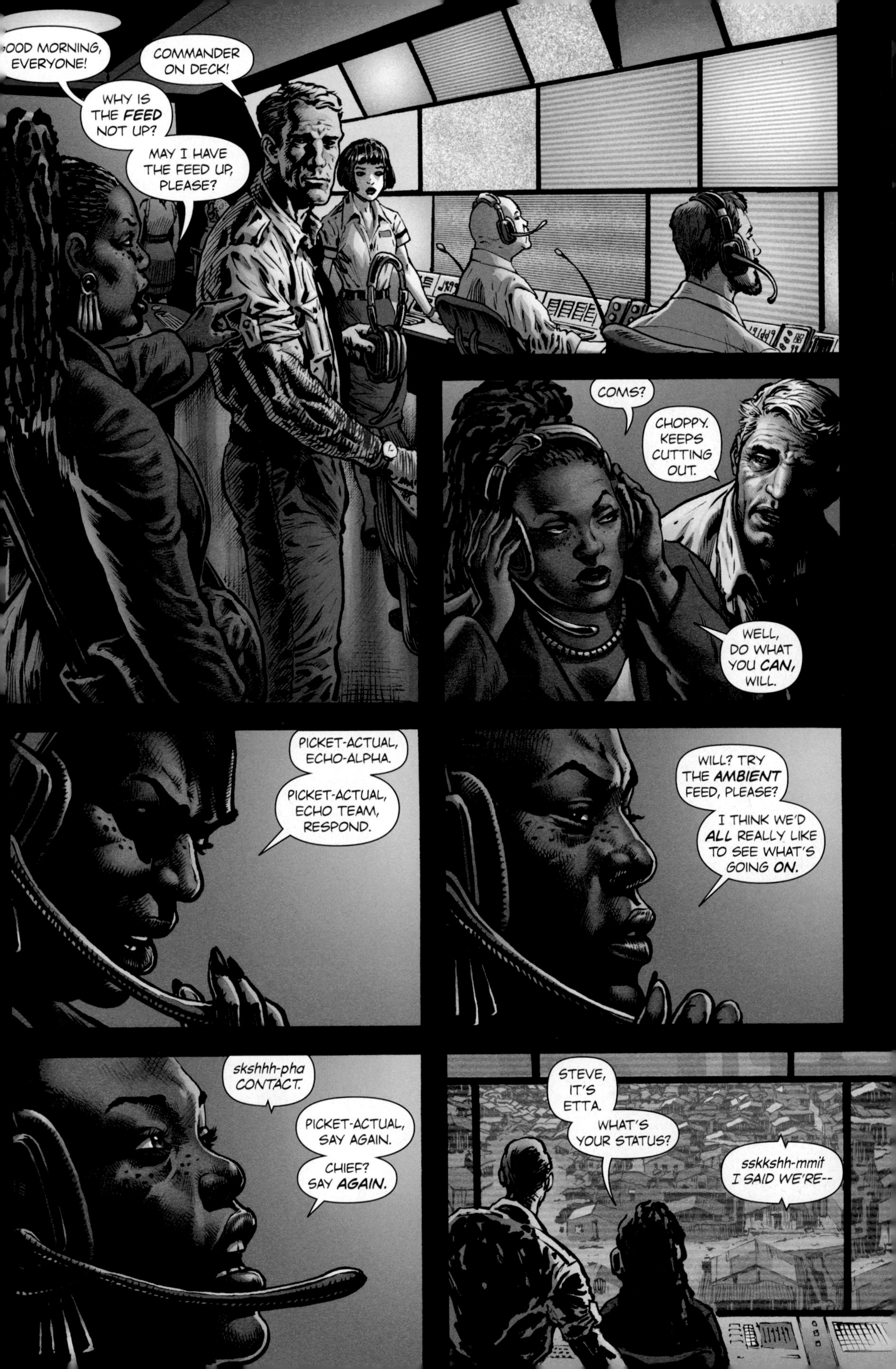
GOOD MORNING, EVERYONE!
COMMANDER ON DECK!
WHY IS THE **FEED** NOT UP?
MAY I HAVE THE FEED UP, PLEASE?
COMS?
CHOPPY. KEEPS CUTTING OUT.
WELL, DO WHAT YOU **CAN,** WILL.
PICKET-ACTUAL, ECHO-ALPHA.
PICKET-ACTUAL, ECHO TEAM, RESPOND.
WILL? TRY THE **AMBIENT** FEED, PLEASE?
I THINK WE'D **ALL** REALLY LIKE TO SEE WHAT'S GOING **ON.**
skshhh-pha CONTACT.
PICKET-ACTUAL, SAY AGAIN.
CHIEF? SAY **AGAIN.**
STEVE, IT'S ETTA.
WHAT'S YOUR STATUS?
sskkshh-mmit I SAID WE'RE--

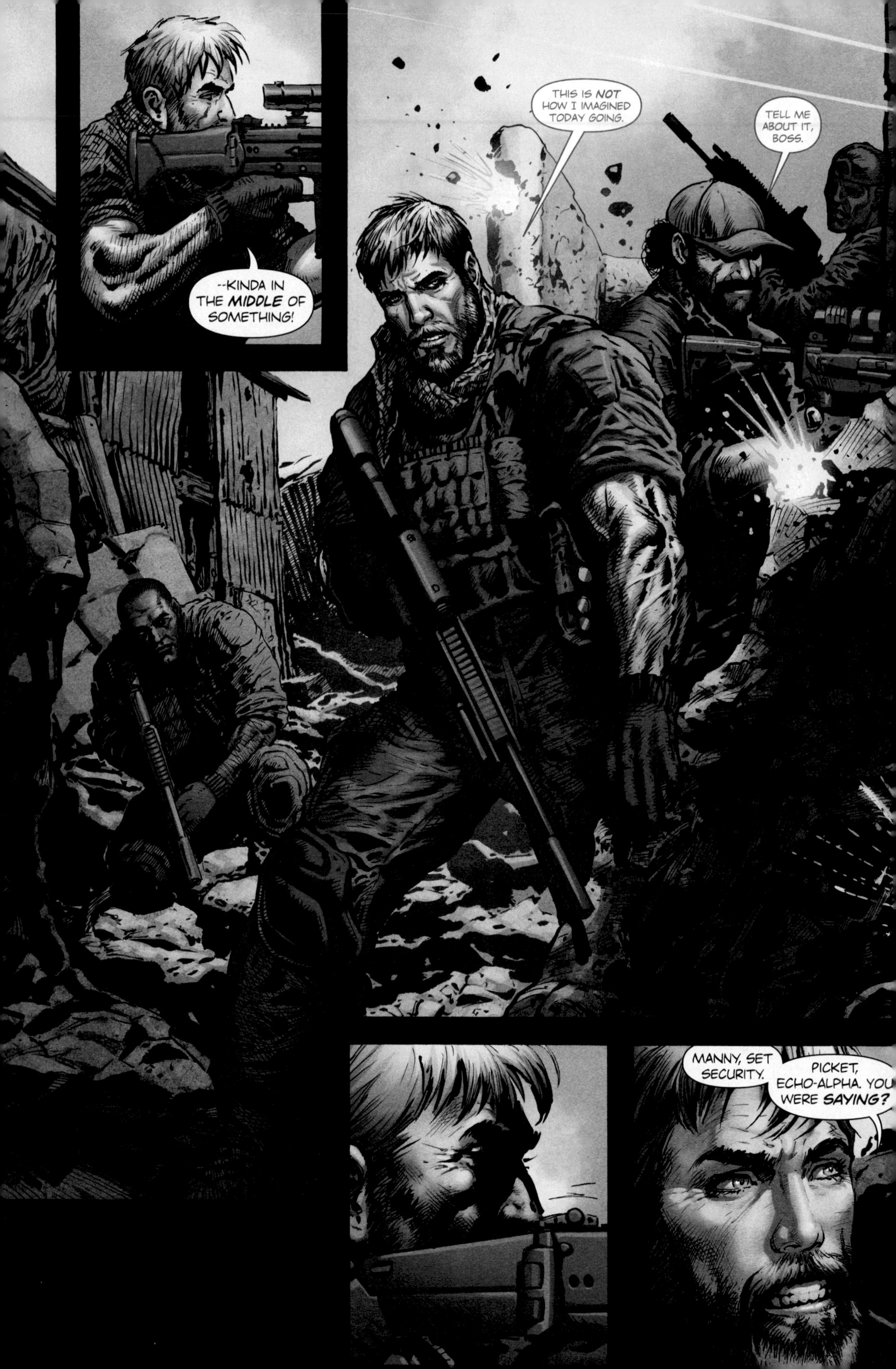
--KINDA IN THE MIDDLE OF SOMETHING!
THIS IS NOT HOW I IMAGINED TODAY GOING.
TELL ME ABOUT IT, BOSS.
MANNY, SET SECURITY.
PICKET, ECHO-ALPHA. YOU WERE SAYING?

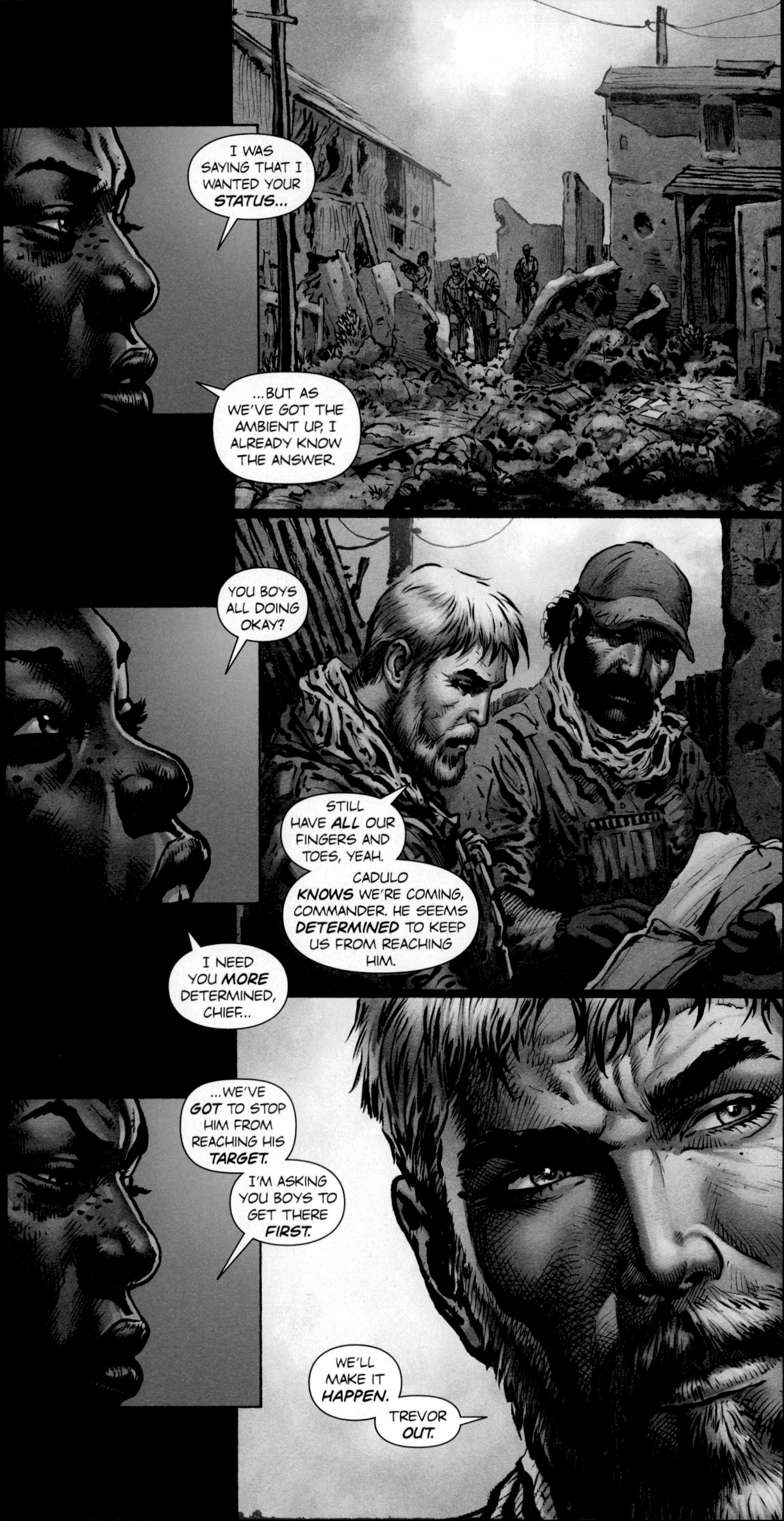
I WAS SAYING THAT I WANTED YOUR STATUS...
...BUT AS WE'VE GOT THE AMBIENT UP, I ALREADY KNOW THE ANSWER.
YOU BOYS ALL DOING OKAY?
STILL HAVE ALL OUR FINGERS AND TOES, YEAH.
CADULO KNOWS WE'RE COMING, COMMANDER. HE SEEMS DETERMINED TO KEEP US FROM REACHING HIM.
I NEED YOU MORE DETERMINED, CHIEF...
...WE'VE GOT TO STOP HIM FROM REACHING HIS TARGET.
I'M ASKING YOU BOYS TO GET THERE FIRST.
WE'LL MAKE IT HAPPEN.
TREVOR OUT.

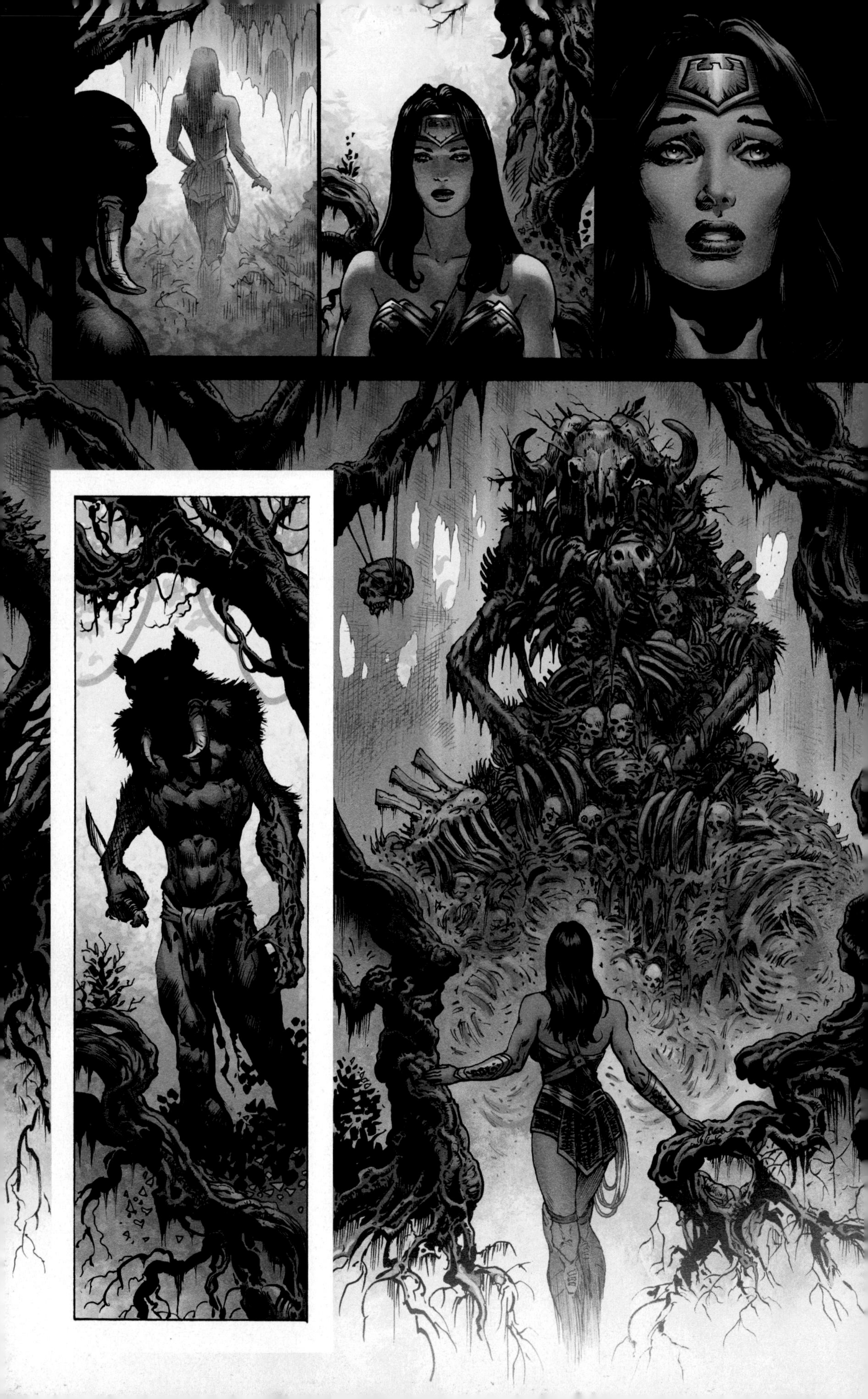

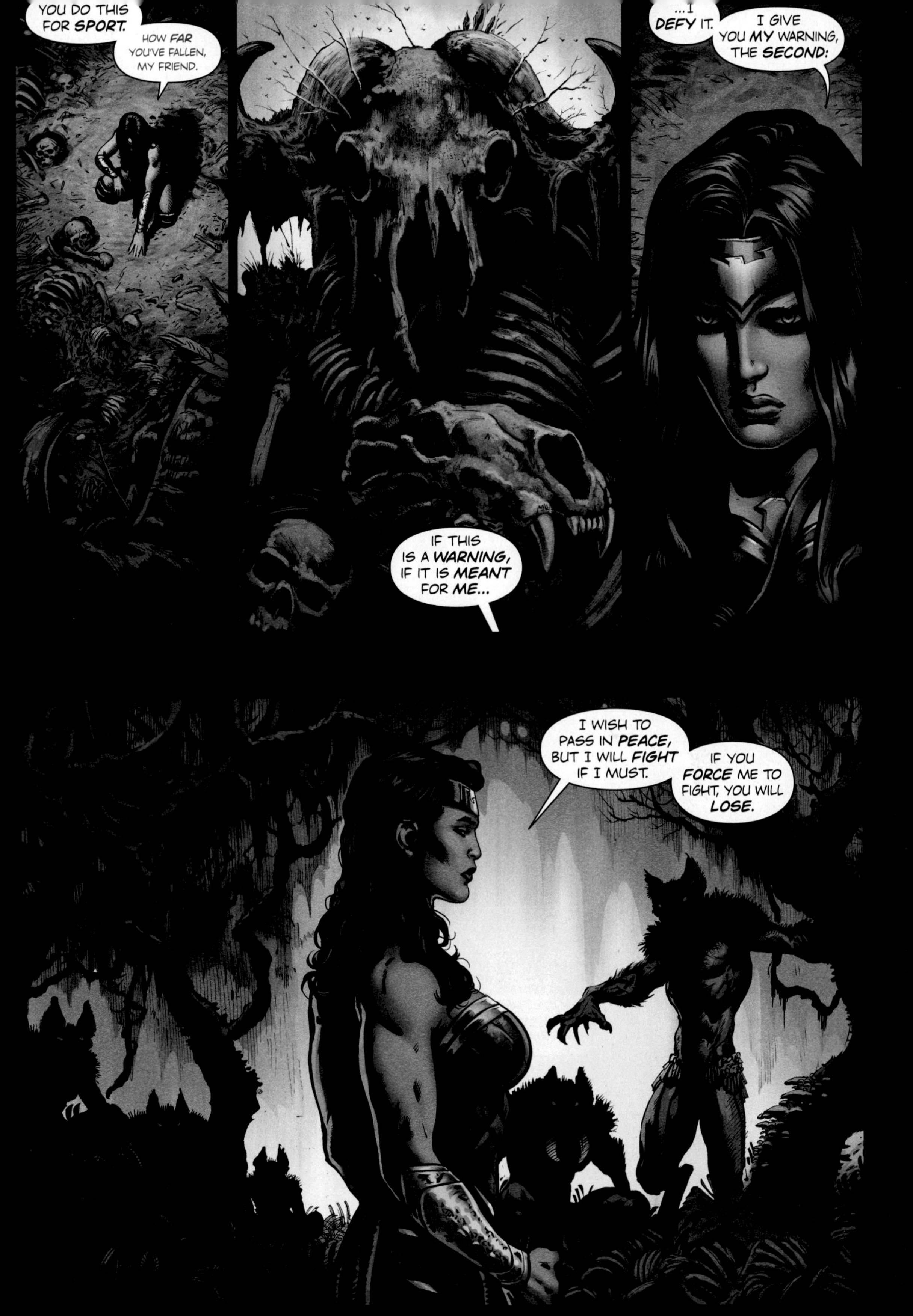
YOU DO THIS FOR SPORT.
HOW FAR YOU'VE FALLEN, MY FRIEND.
IF THIS IS A WARNING, IF IT IS MEANT FOR ME...
...I DEFY IT.
I GIVE YOU MY WARNING, THE SECOND:
I WISH TO PASS IN PEACE, BUT I WILL FIGHT IF I MUST.
IF YOU FORCE ME TO FIGHT, YOU WILL LOSE.

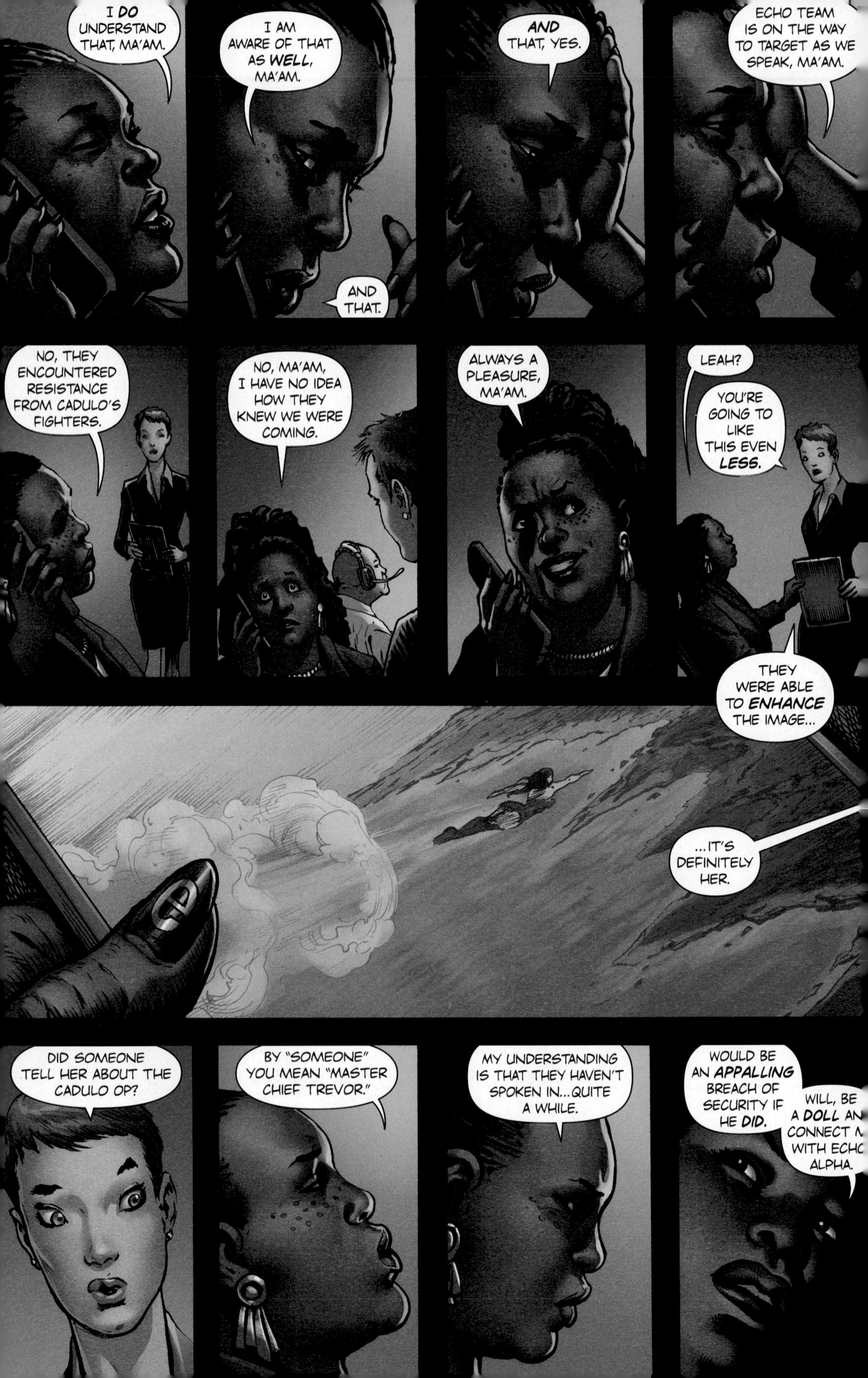

I DO UNDERSTAND THAT, MA'AM.
I AM AWARE OF THAT AS WELL, MA'AM.
AND THAT.
AND THAT, YES.
ECHO TEAM IS ON THE WAY TO TARGET AS WE SPEAK, MA'AM.
NO, THEY ENCOUNTERED RESISTANCE FROM CADULO'S FIGHTERS.
NO, MA'AM, I HAVE NO IDEA HOW THEY KNEW WE WERE COMING.
ALWAYS A PLEASURE, MA'AM.
LEAH?
YOU'RE GOING TO LIKE THIS EVEN LESS.
THEY WERE ABLE TO ENHANCE THE IMAGE...
...IT'S DEFINITELY HER.
DID SOMEONE TELL HER ABOUT THE CADULO OP?
BY "SOMEONE" YOU MEAN "MASTER CHIEF TREVOR."
MY UNDERSTANDING IS THAT THEY HAVEN'T SPOKEN IN...QUITE A WHILE.
WOULD BE AN APPALLING BREACH OF SECURITY IF HE DID.

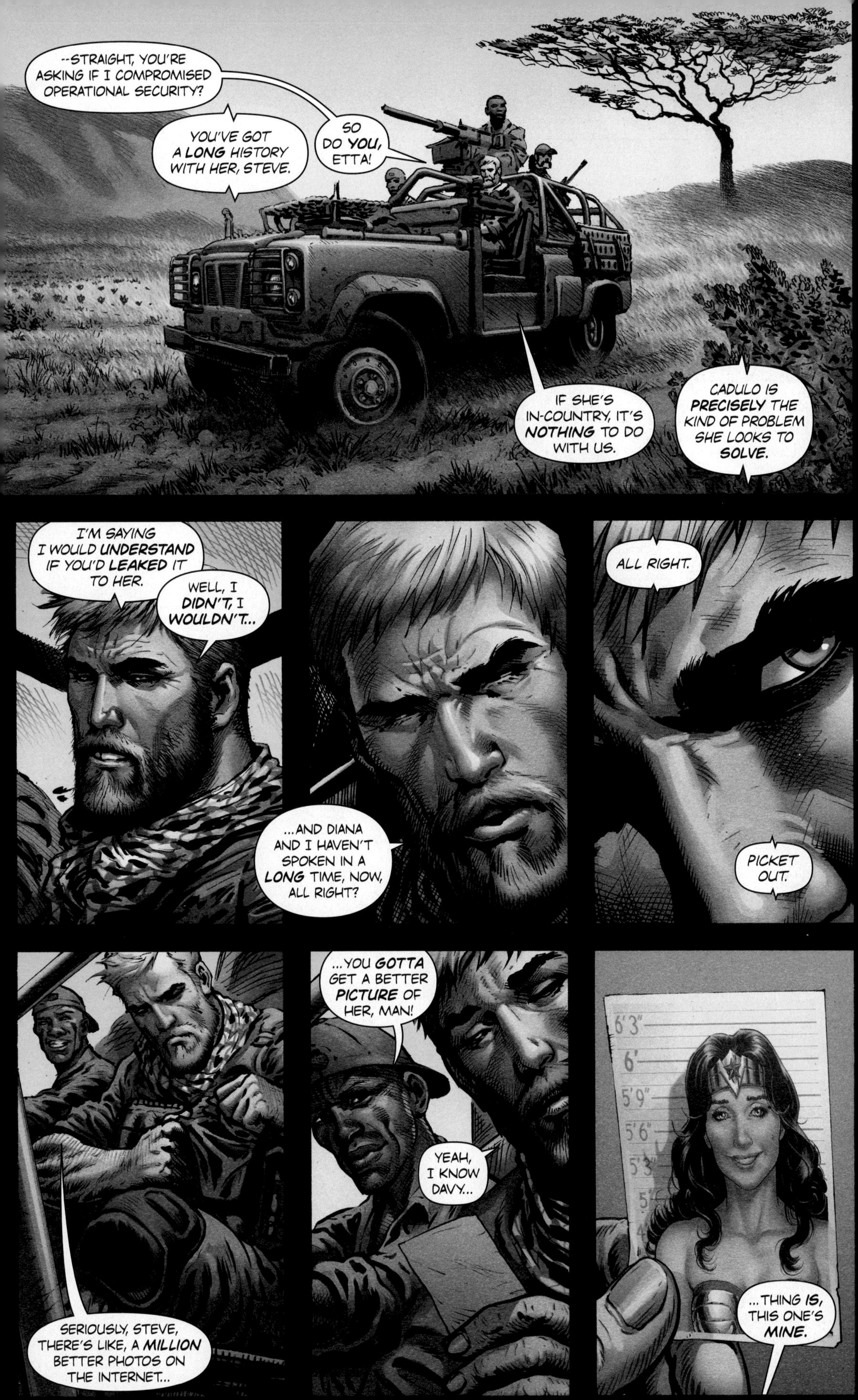
--STRAIGHT, YOU'RE ASKING IF I COMPROMISED OPERATIONAL SECURITY?
SO DO YOU, ETTA!
YOU'VE GOT A LONG HISTORY WITH HER, STEVE.
IF SHE'S IN-COUNTRY, IT'S NOTHING TO DO WITH US.
CADULO IS PRECISELY THE KIND OF PROBLEM SHE LOOKS TO SOLVE.
I'M SAYING I WOULD UNDERSTAND IF YOU'D LEAKED IT TO HER.
WELL, I DIDN'T, I WOULDN'T...
...AND DIANA AND I HAVEN'T SPOKEN IN A LONG TIME, NOW, ALL RIGHT?
ALL RIGHT.
PICKET OUT.
SERIOUSLY, STEVE, THERE'S LIKE, A MILLION BETTER PHOTOS ON THE INTERNET...
...YOU GOTTA GET A BETTER PICTURE OF HER, MAN!
YEAH, I KNOW DAVY...
6'3"
6'
5'9"
5'6"
...THING IS, THIS ONE'S MINE.

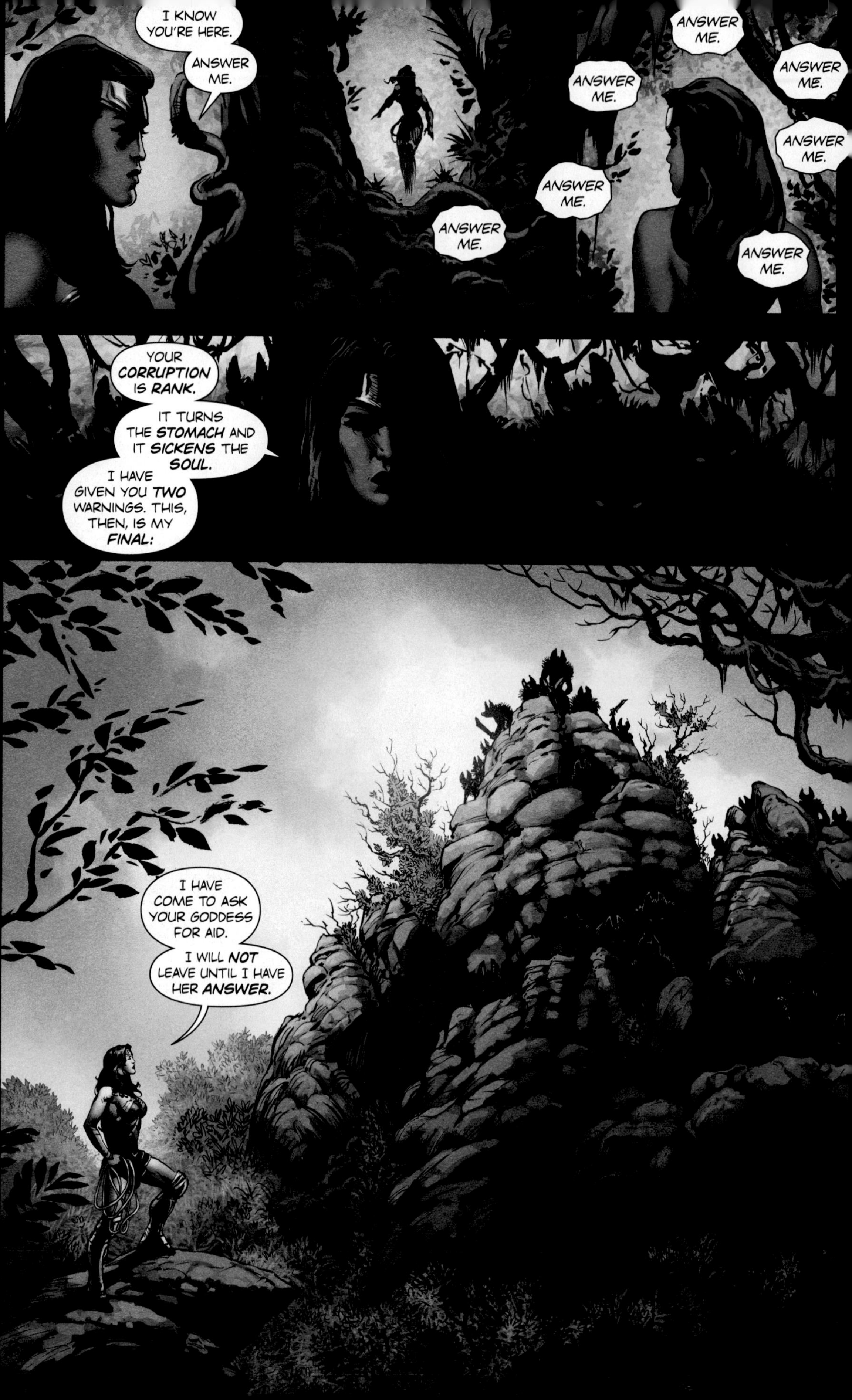
I KNOW YOU'RE HERE.
ANSWER ME.
ANSWER ME.
ANSWER ME.
ANSWER ME.
ANSWER ME.
ANSWER ME.
ANSWER ME.
ANSWER ME.
YOUR CORRUPTION IS RANK.
IT TURNS THE STOMACH AND IT SICKENS THE SOUL.
I HAVE GIVEN YOU TWO WARNINGS. THIS, THEN, IS MY FINAL:
I HAVE COME TO ASK YOUR GODDESS FOR AID.
I WILL NOT LEAVE UNTIL I HAVE HER ANSWER.

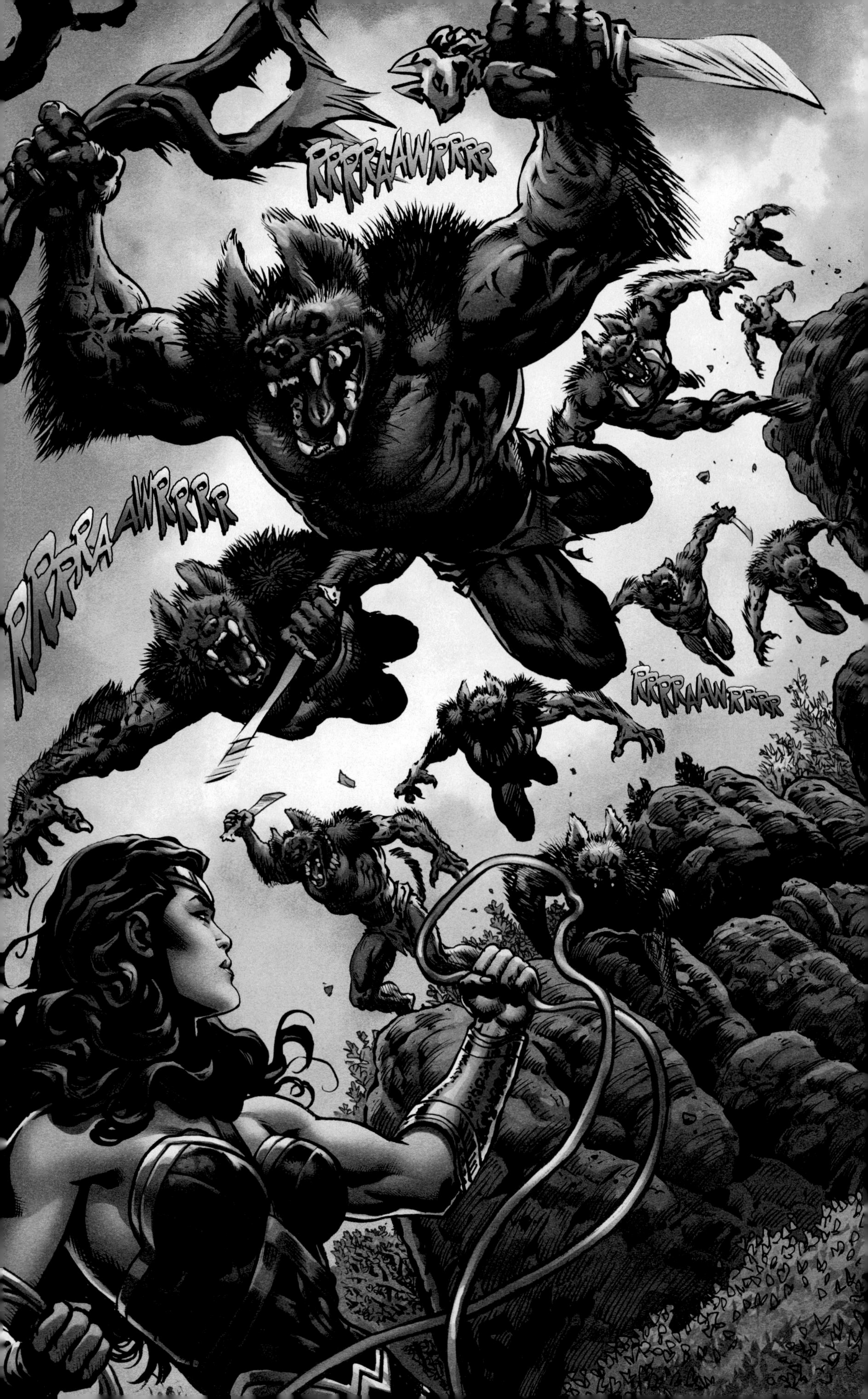
RRRRAAWRRRR
RRRRRAAWRRRR
RRRRAAWRRRR

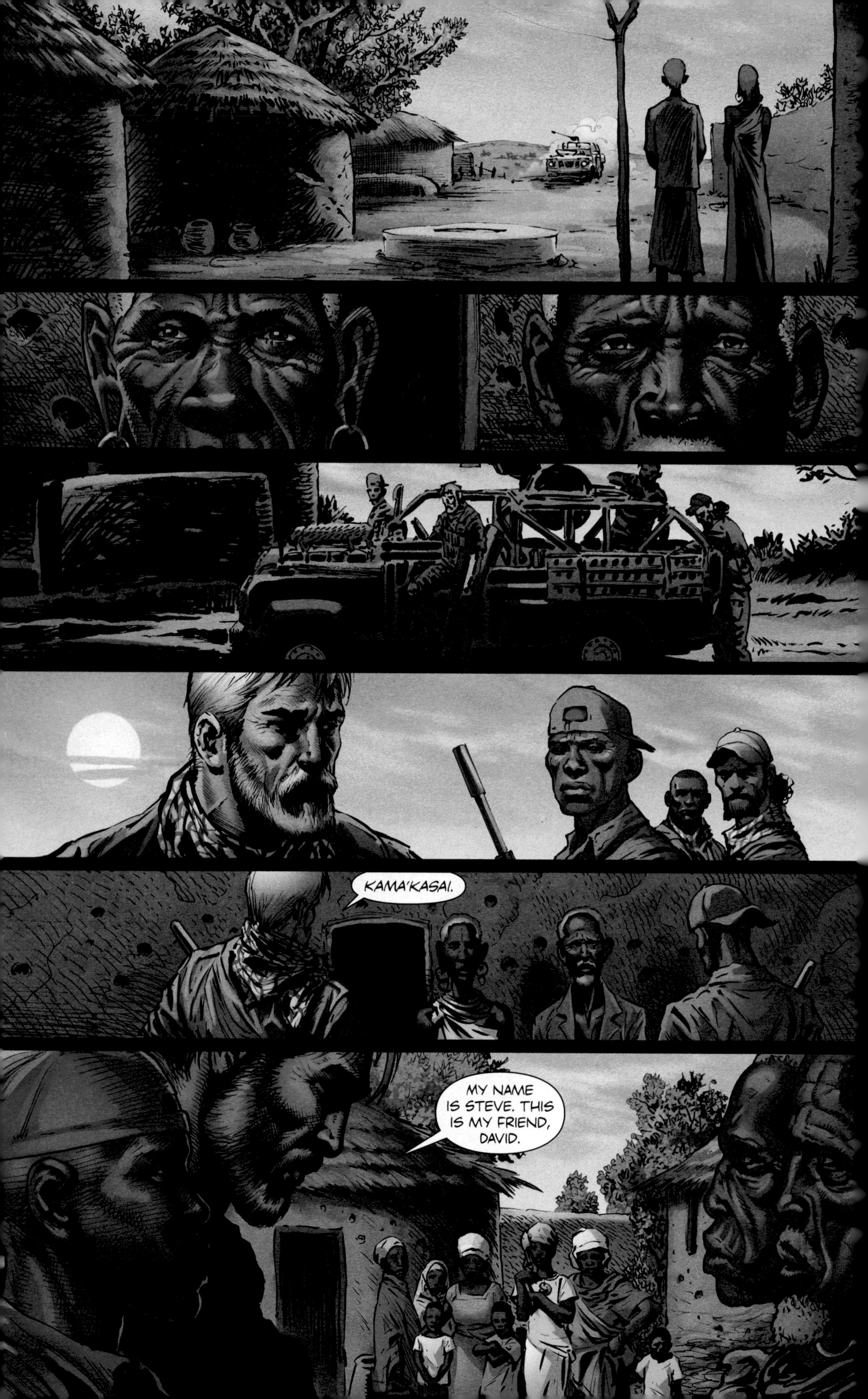
KAMA'KASAI.
MY NAME IS STEVE. THIS IS MY FRIEND, DAVID.

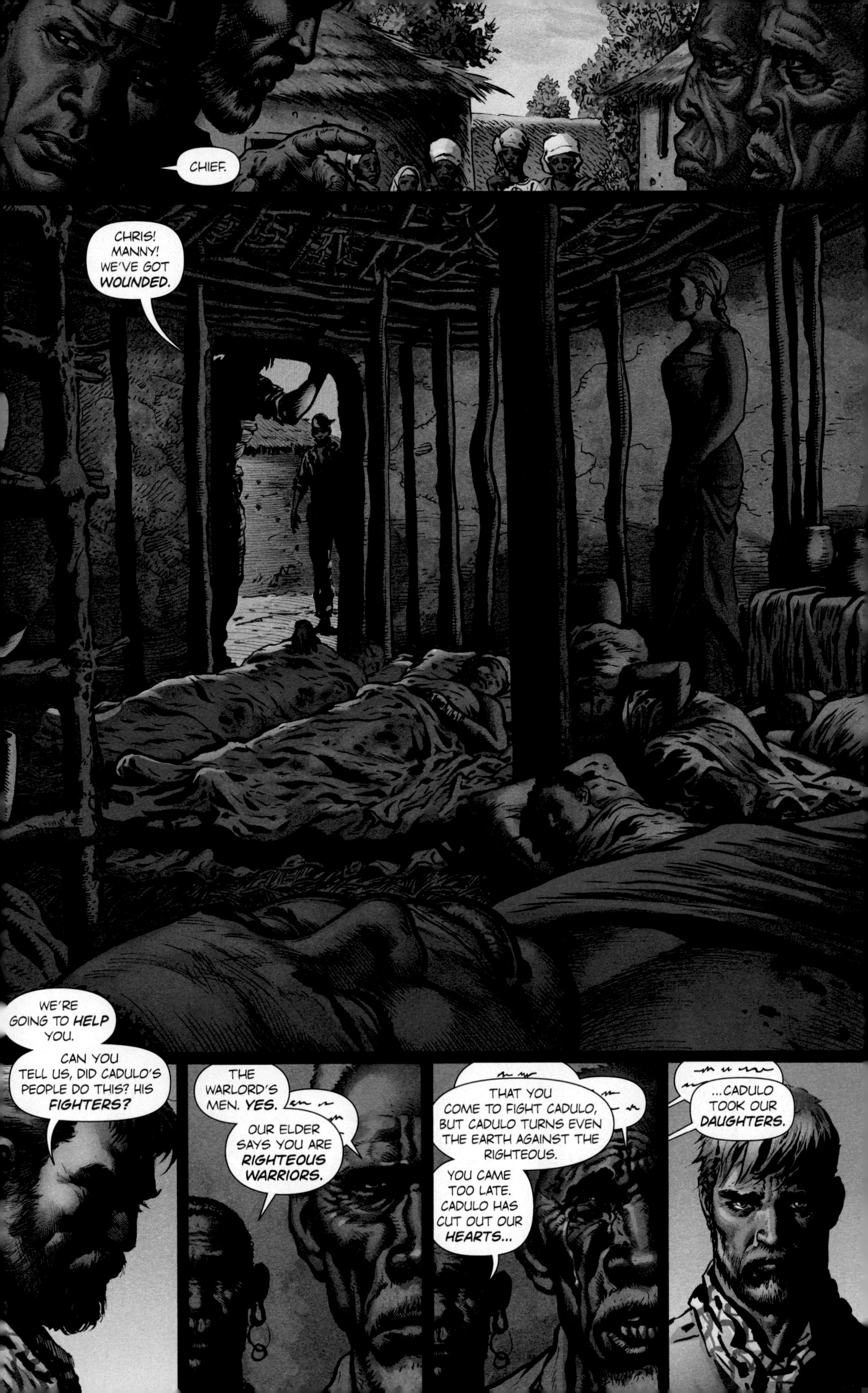
CHIEF.
CHRIS! MANNY! WE'VE GOT **WOUNDED.**
WE'RE GOING TO **HELP** YOU.
CAN YOU TELL US, DID CADULO'S PEOPLE DO THIS? HIS **FIGHTERS?**
THE WARLORD'S MEN. **YES.**
OUR ELDER SAYS YOU ARE **RIGHTEOUS WARRIORS.**
THAT YOU COME TO FIGHT CADULO, BUT CADULO TURNS EVEN THE EARTH AGAINST THE RIGHTEOUS.
YOU CAME TOO LATE. CADULO HAS CUT OUT OUR **HEARTS...**
...CADULO TOOK OUR **DAUGHTERS.**

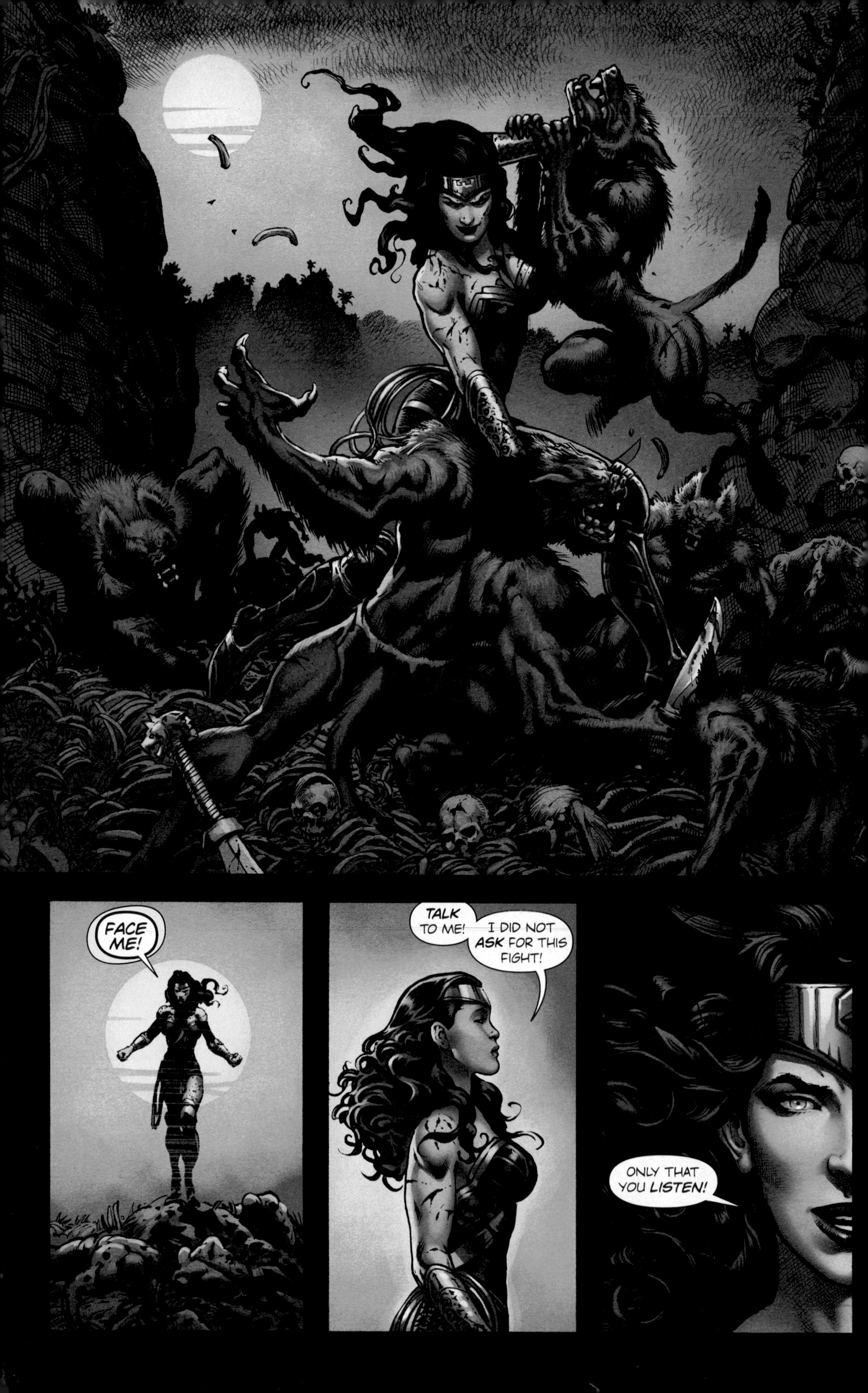
FACE ME!
TALK TO ME!
I DID NOT ASK FOR THIS FIGHT!
ONLY THAT YOU LISTEN!

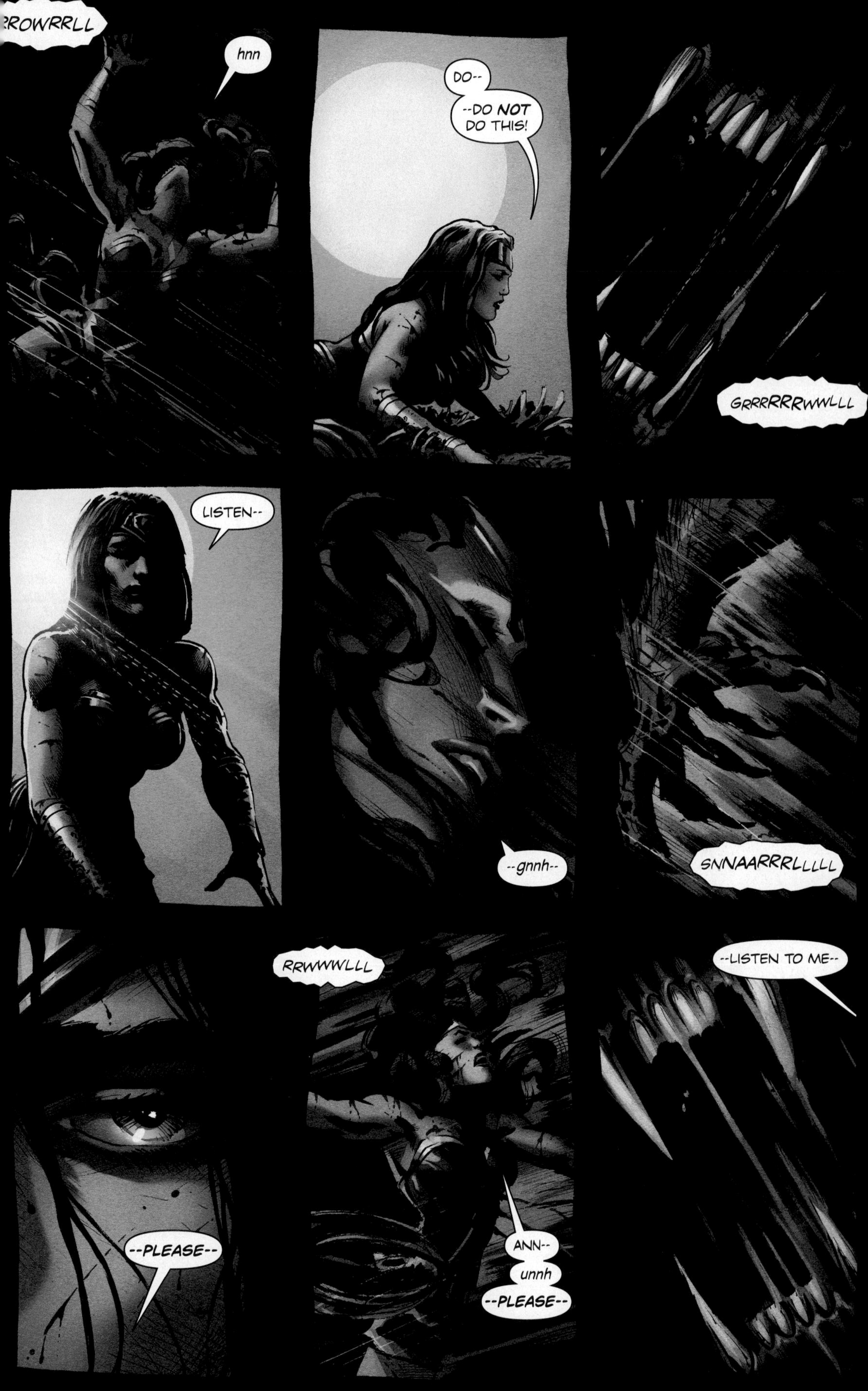
RROWRRLL
hnn
DO--
--DO **NOT** DO THIS!
GRRRRRRWWLLL
LISTEN--
--gnnh--
SNNAARRRLLLLL
RRWWWLLL
--LISTEN TO ME--
--PLEASE--
ANN--
unnh
--PLEASE--

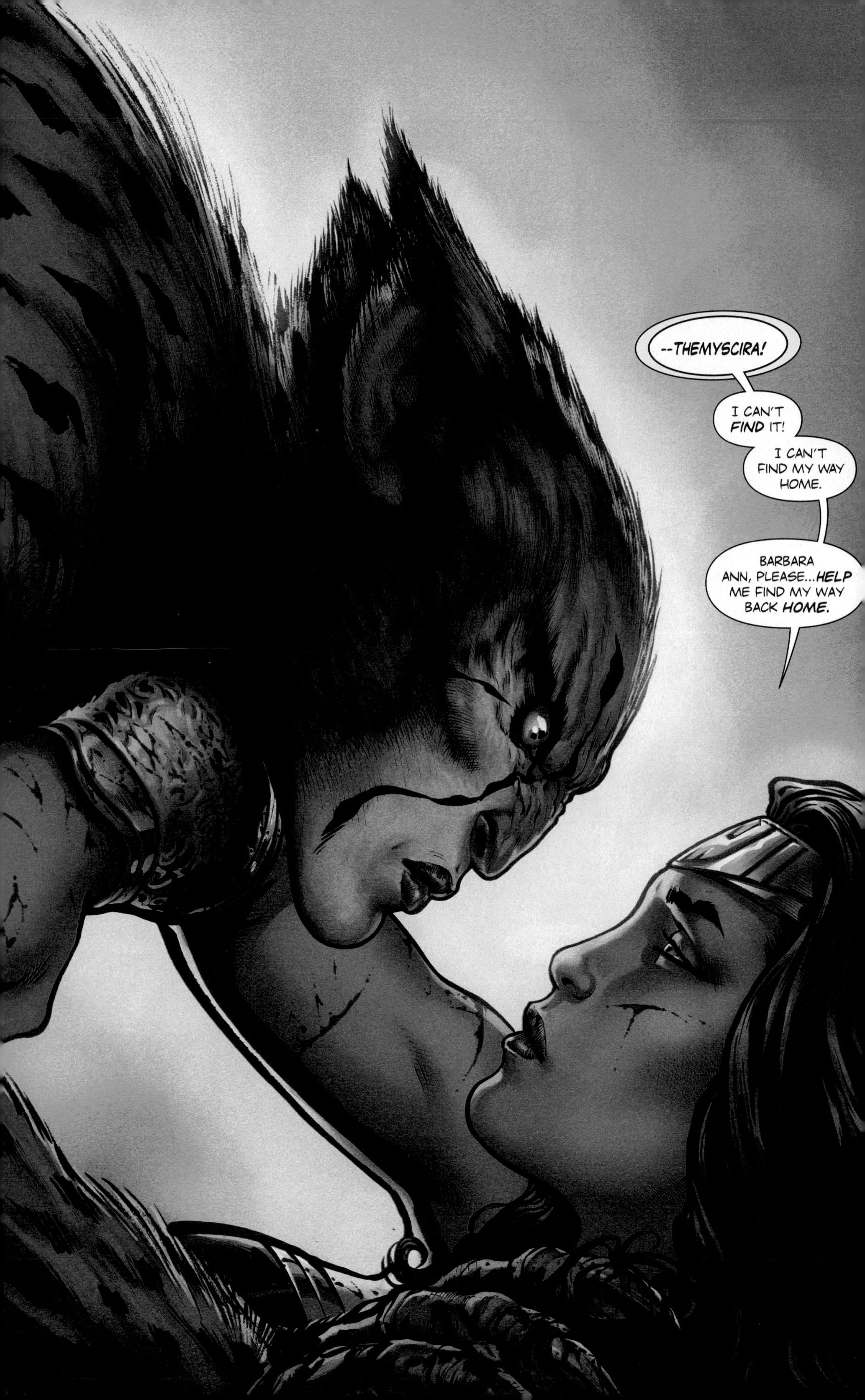
--THEMYSCIRA!
I CAN'T FIND IT!
I CAN'T FIND MY WAY HOME.
BARBARA ANN, PLEASE...HELP ME FIND MY WAY BACK HOME.

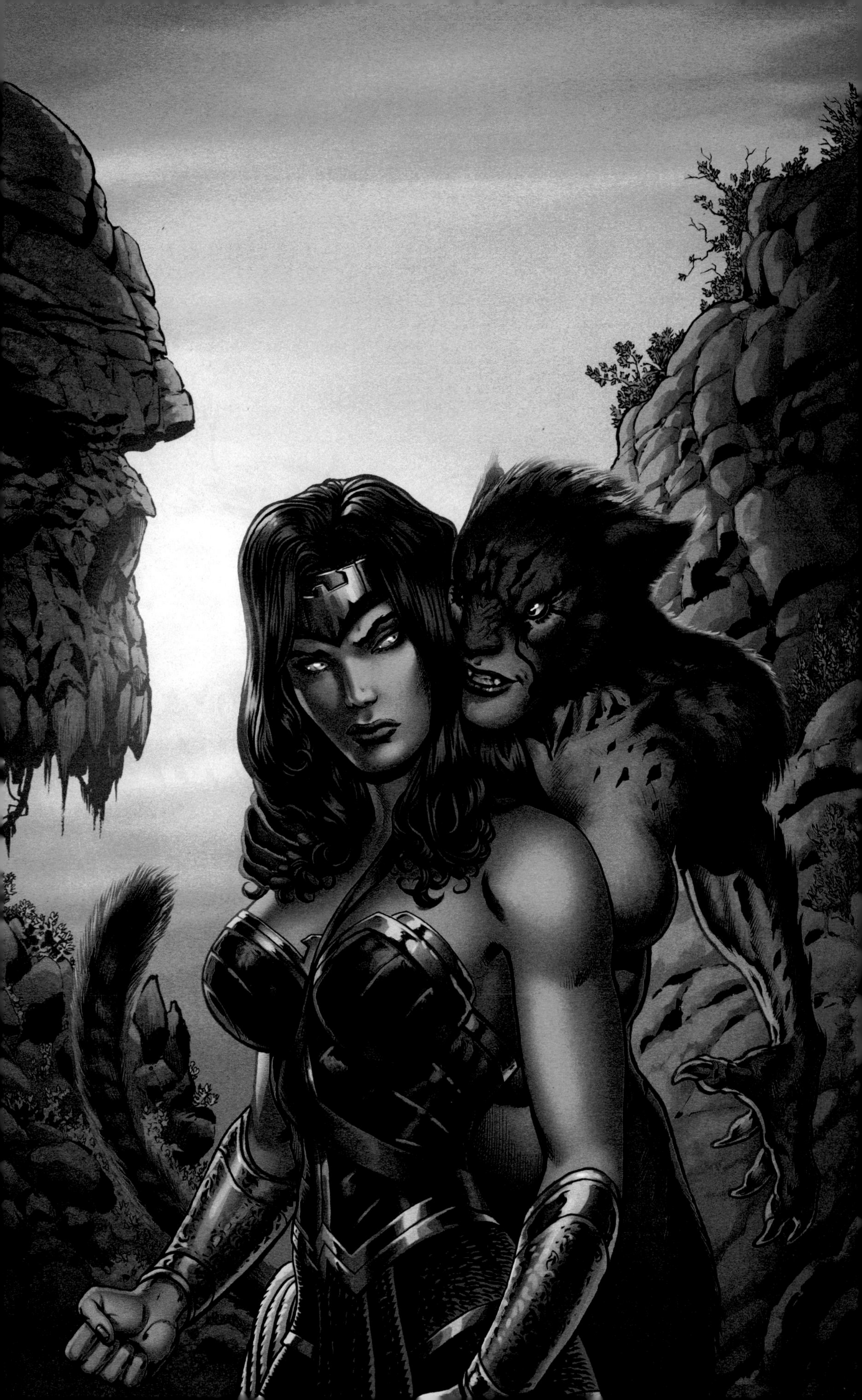

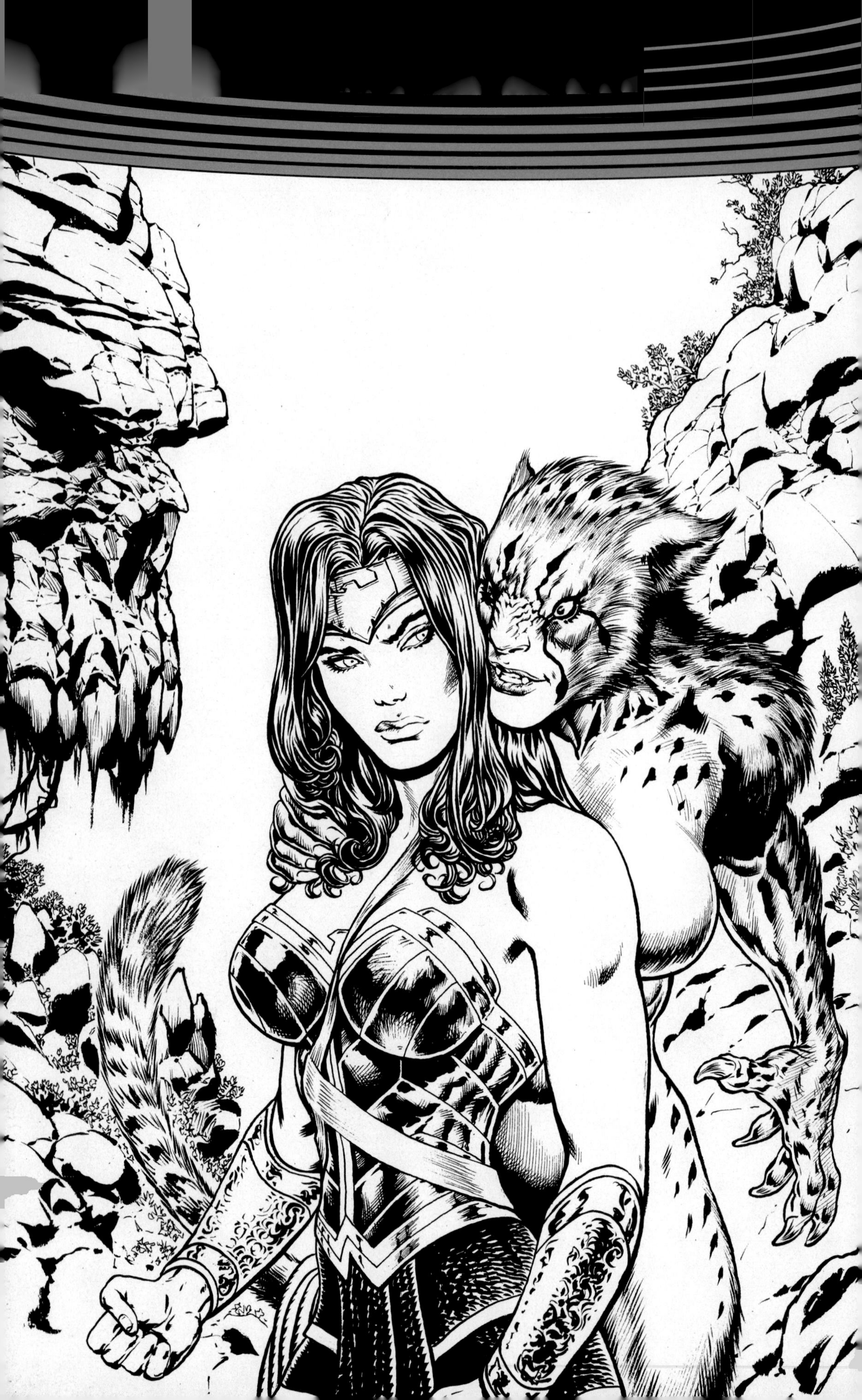

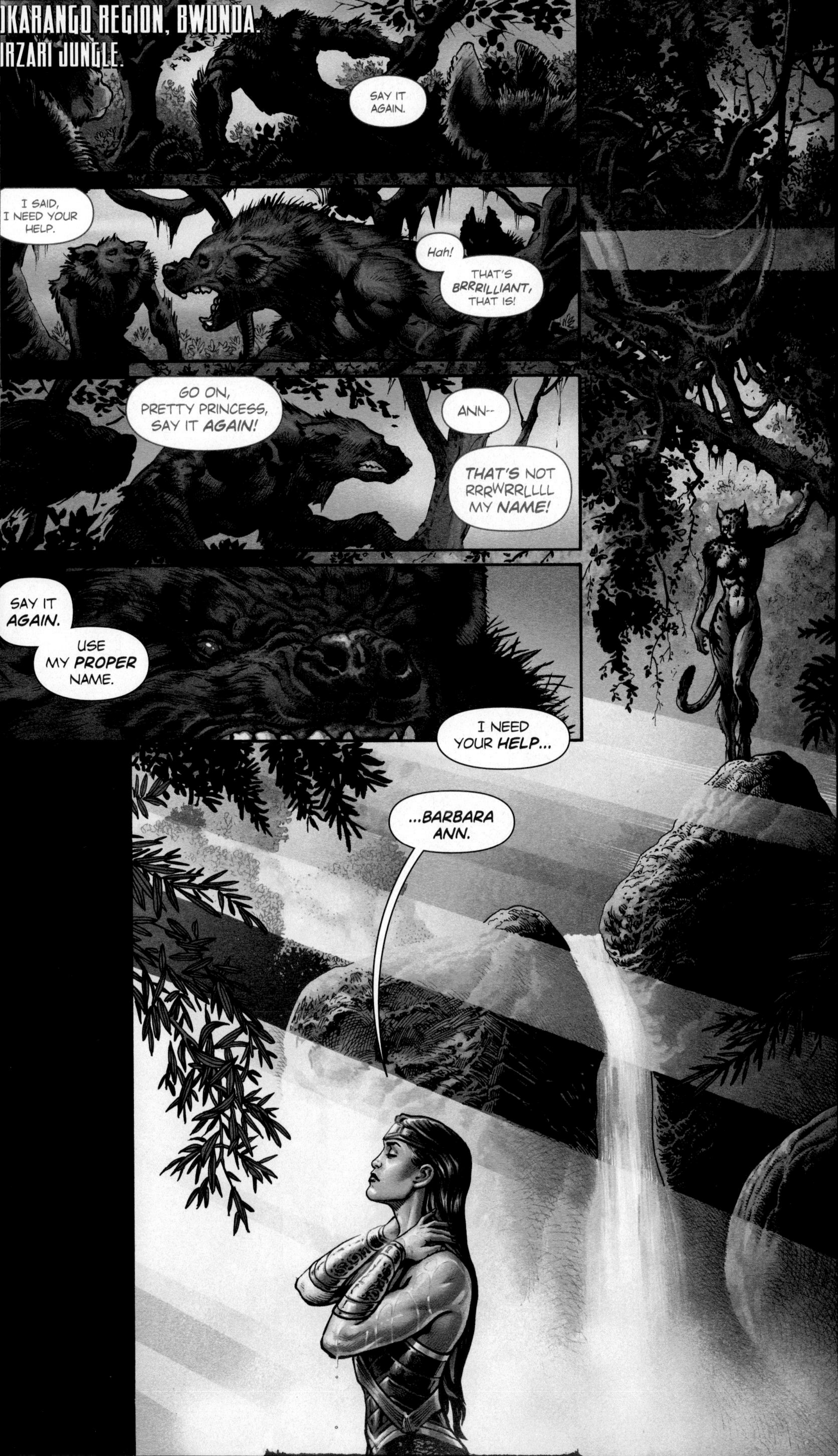

OKARANGO REGION, BWUNDA.
IRZARI JUNGLE.
SAY IT AGAIN.
I SAID, I NEED YOUR HELP.
Hah!
THAT'S BRRRILLIANT, THAT IS!
GO ON, PRETTY PRINCESS, SAY IT AGAIN!
ANN--
THAT'S NOT RRRWRRLLLL MY NAME!
SAY IT AGAIN.
USE MY PROPER NAME.
I NEED YOUR HELP...
...BARBARA ANN.

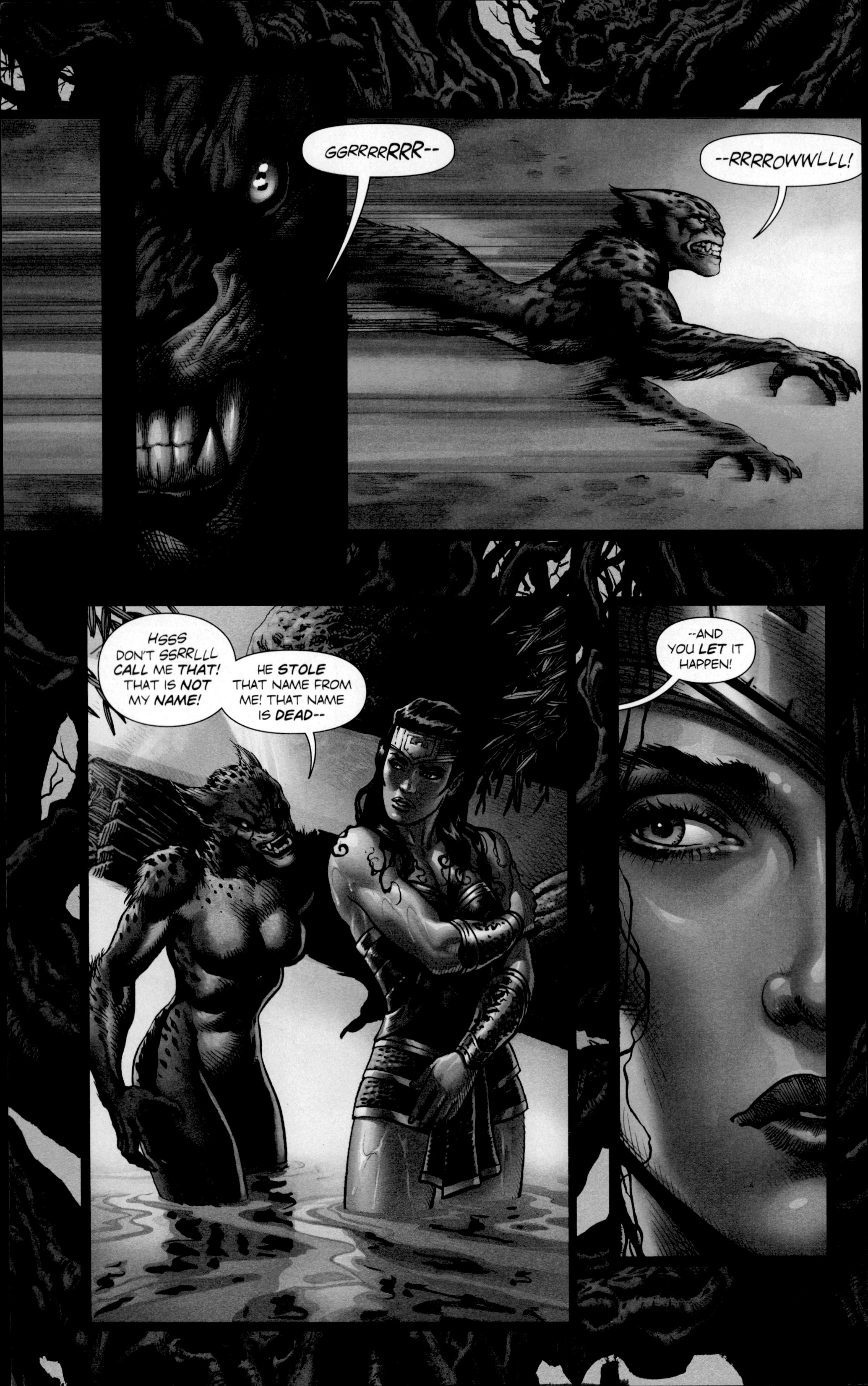
GGRRRRRRR--
--RRRROWWLLL!
HSSS DON'T SSRRLLL CALL ME THAT! THAT IS NOT MY NAME!
HE STOLE THAT NAME FROM ME! THAT NAME IS DEAD--
--AND YOU LET IT HAPPEN!

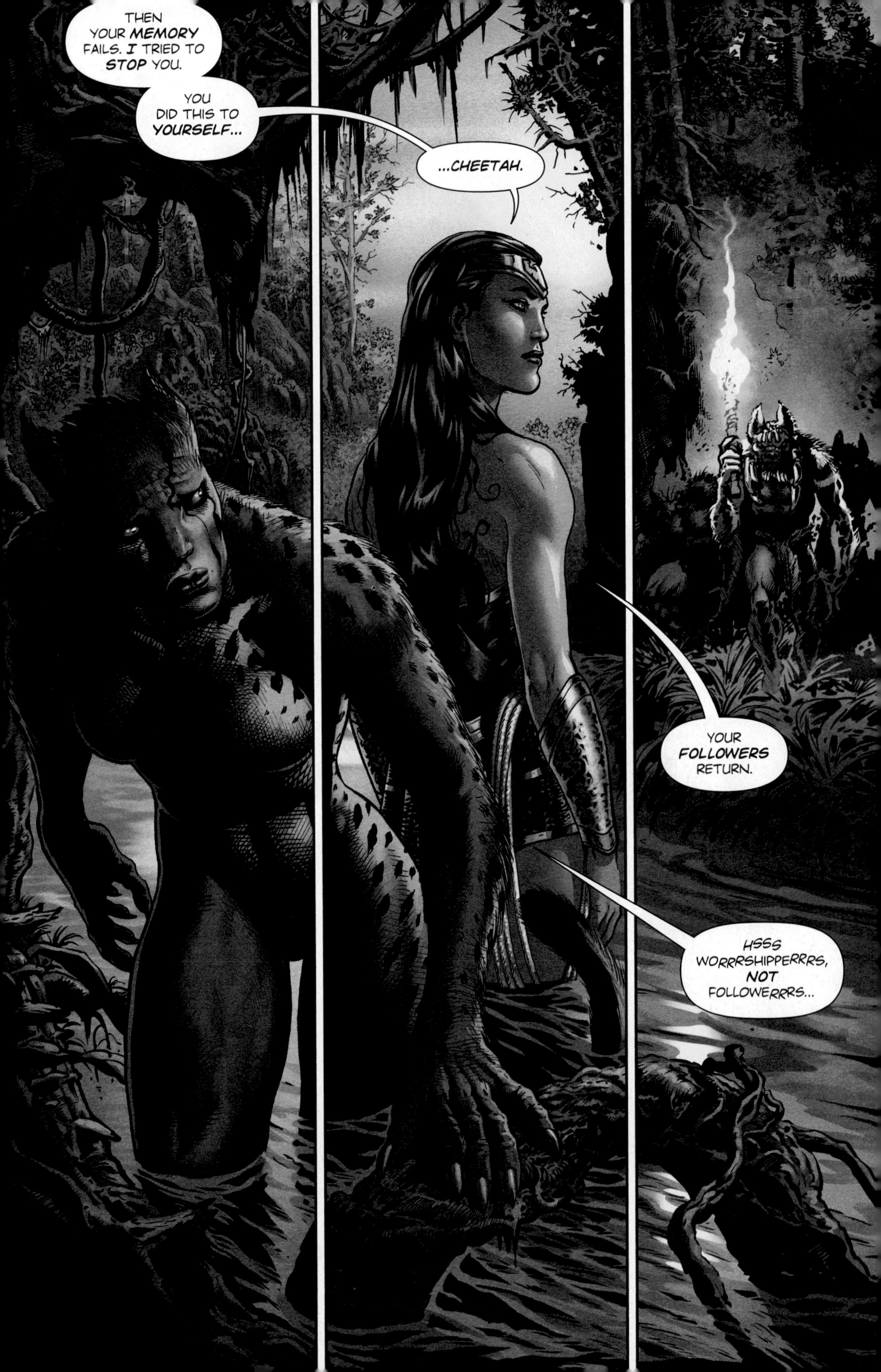

THEN YOUR MEMORY FAILS. I TRIED TO STOP YOU.
YOU DID THIS TO YOURSELF...
...CHEETAH.
YOUR FOLLOWERS RETURN.
HSSS WORRRSHIPPERRRS, NOT FOLLOWERRRS...

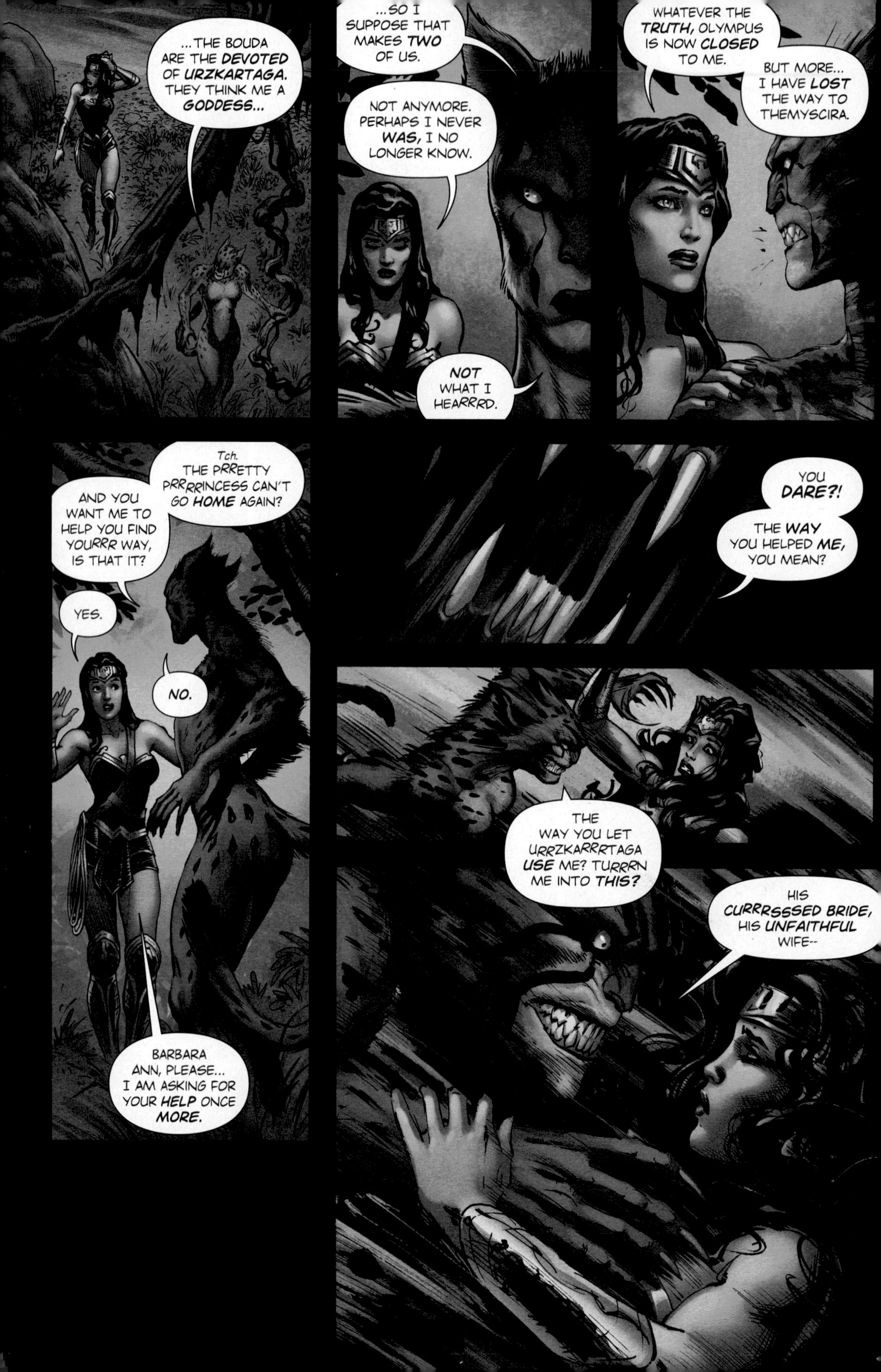
...THE BOUDA ARE THE DEVOTED OF URZKARTAGA. THEY THINK ME A GODDESS...
...SO I SUPPOSE THAT MAKES TWO OF US.
NOT ANYMORE. PERHAPS I NEVER WAS, I NO LONGER KNOW.
NOT WHAT I HEARRRD.
WHATEVER THE TRUTH, OLYMPUS IS NOW CLOSED TO ME.
BUT MORE... I HAVE LOST THE WAY TO THEMYSCIRA.
Tch. THE PRRETTY PRRRRINCESS CAN'T GO HOME AGAIN?
AND YOU WANT ME TO HELP YOU FIND YOURRR WAY, IS THAT IT?
YES.
NO.
BARBARA ANN, PLEASE... I AM ASKING FOR YOUR HELP ONCE MORE.
YOU DARE?!
THE WAY YOU HELPED ME, YOU MEAN?
THE WAY YOU LET URRZKARRRTAGA USE ME? TURRRN ME INTO THIS?
HIS CURRRSSSED BRIDE, HIS UNFAITHFUL WIFE--

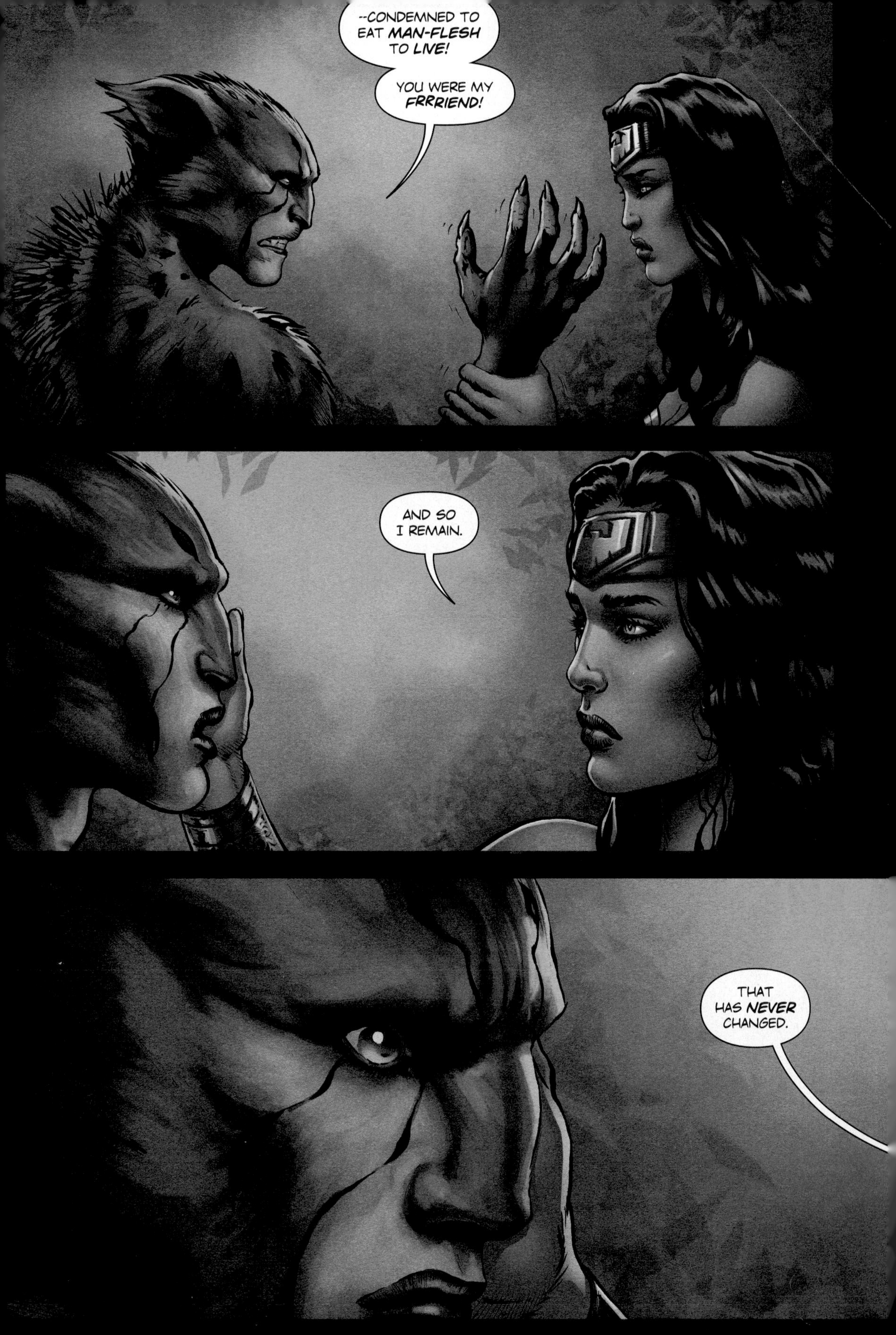
--CONDEMNED TO EAT **MAN-FLESH** TO **LIVE!**
YOU WERE MY **FRRRIEND!**
AND SO I REMAIN.
THAT HAS **NEVER** CHANGED.

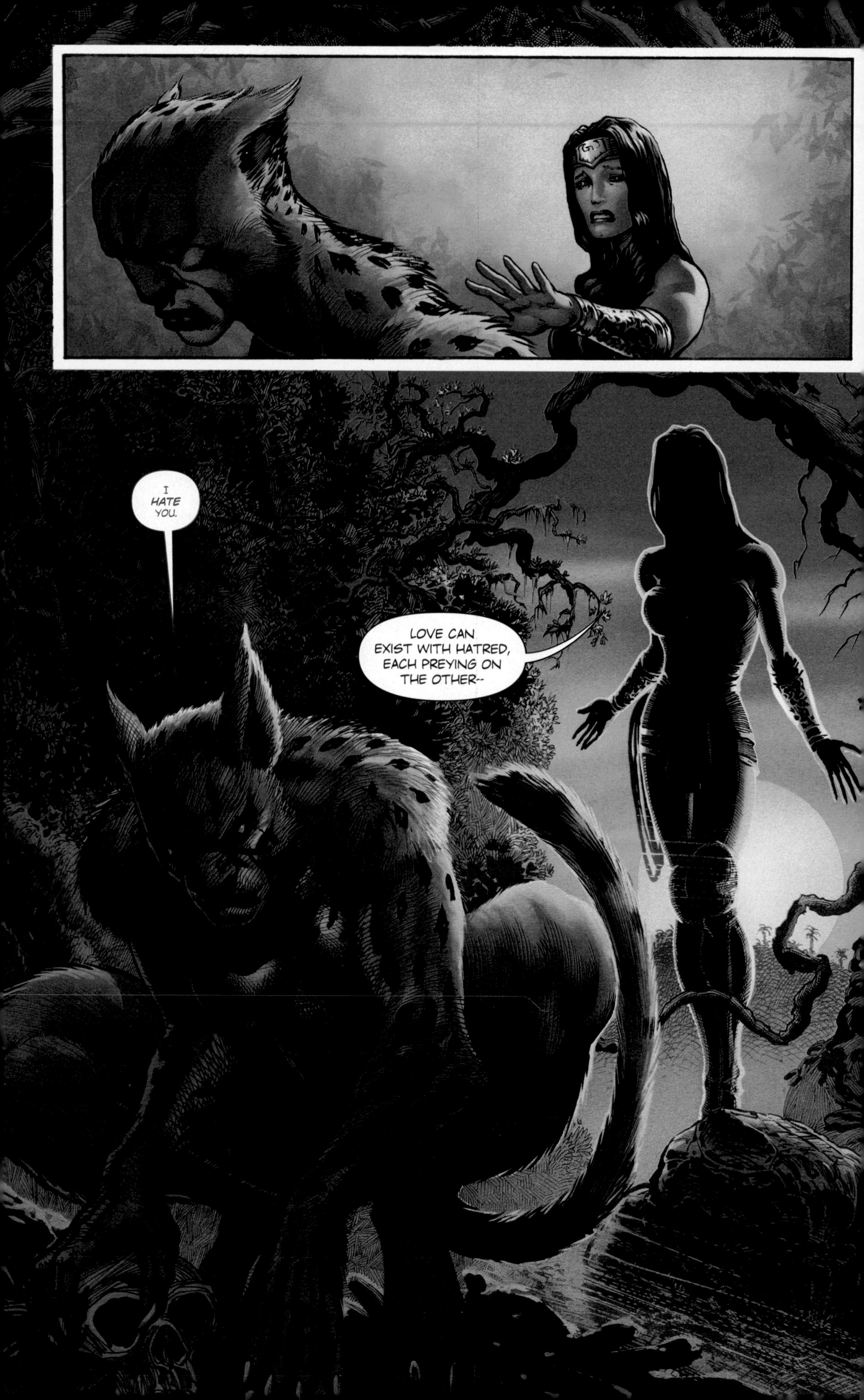
I HATE YOU.
LOVE CAN EXIST WITH HATRED, EACH PREYING ON THE OTHER--

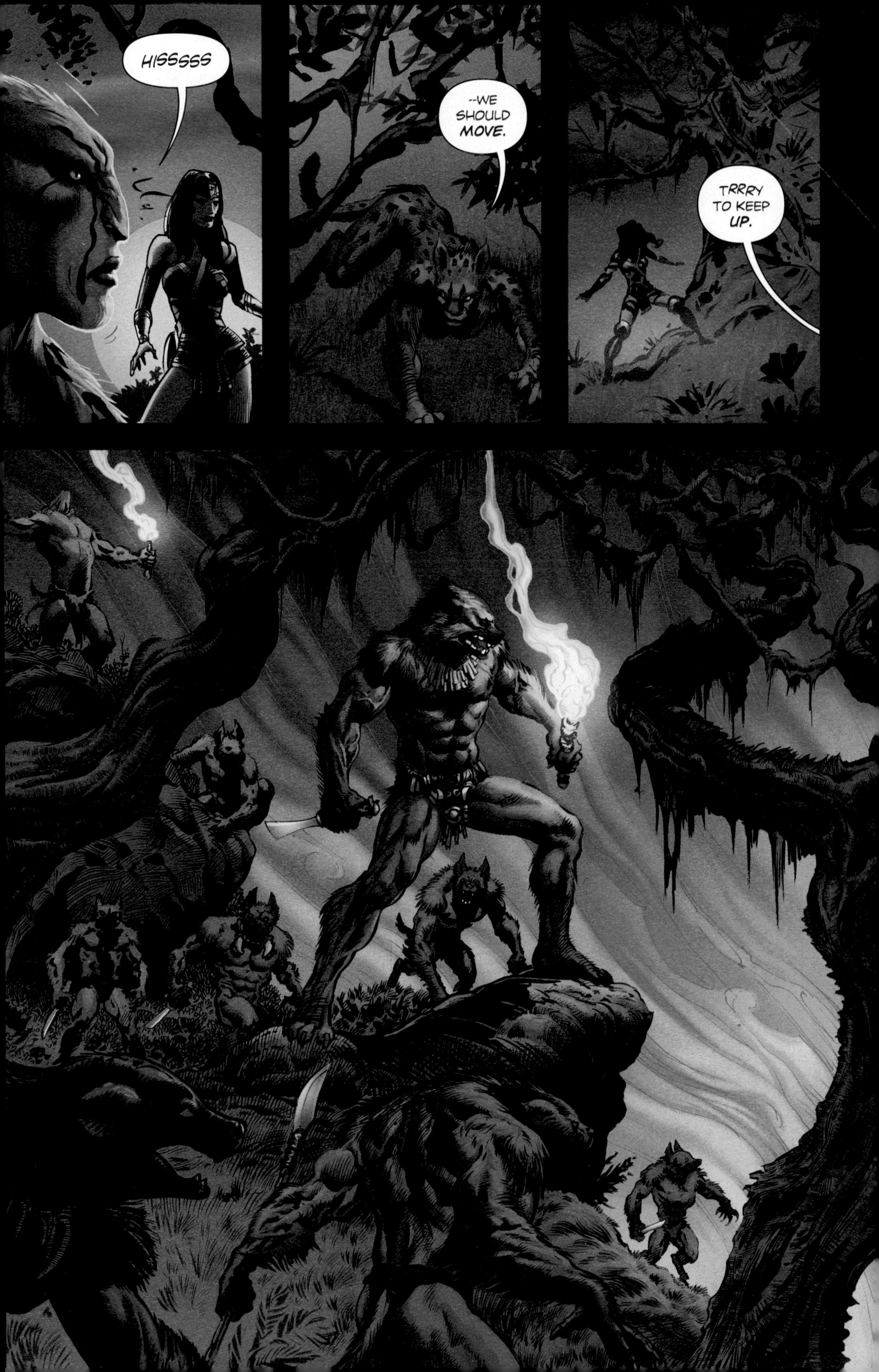
HISSSSS
--WE SHOULD MOVE.
TRRRY TO KEEP UP.

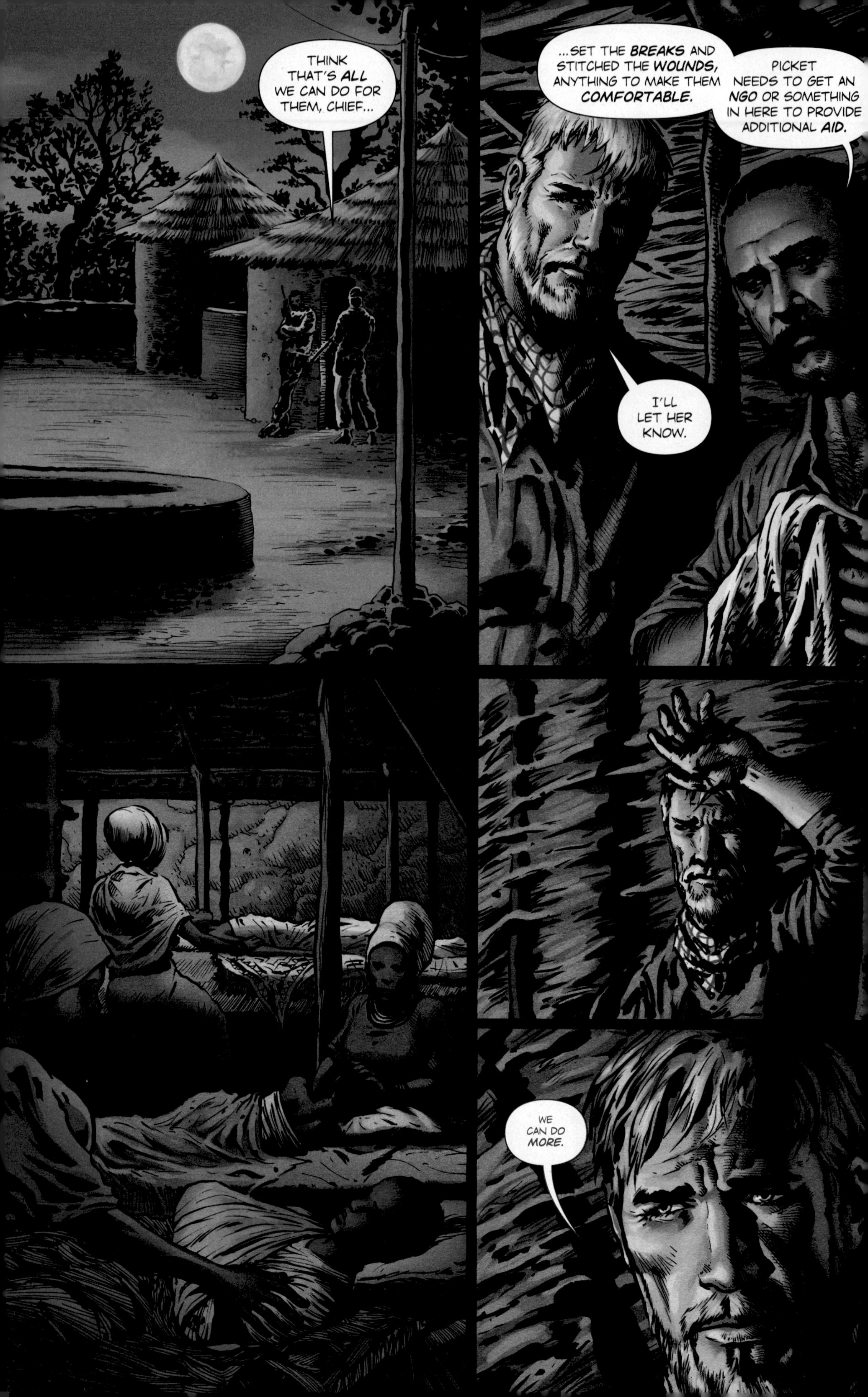
THINK THAT'S ALL WE CAN DO FOR THEM, CHIEF...
...SET THE BREAKS AND STITCHED THE WOUNDS, ANYTHING TO MAKE THEM COMFORTABLE.
PICKET NEEDS TO GET AN NGO OR SOMETHING IN HERE TO PROVIDE ADDITIONAL AID.
I'LL LET HER KNOW.
WE CAN DO MORE.

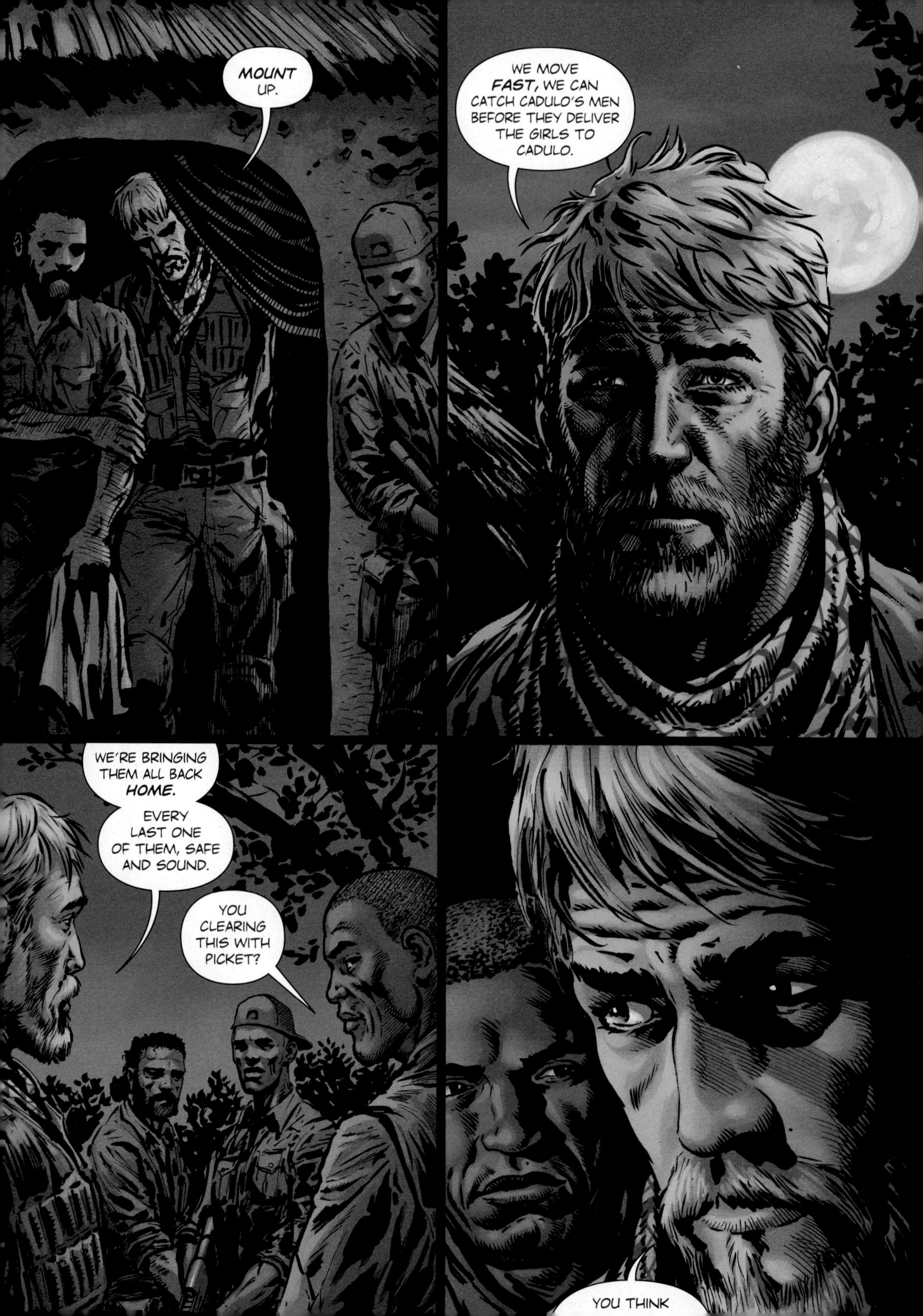
MOUNT UP.
WE MOVE FAST, WE CAN CATCH CADULO'S MEN BEFORE THEY DELIVER THE GIRLS TO CADULO.
WE'RE BRINGING THEM ALL BACK HOME.
EVERY LAST ONE OF THEM, SAFE AND SOUND.
YOU CLEARING THIS WITH PICKET?
YOU THINK

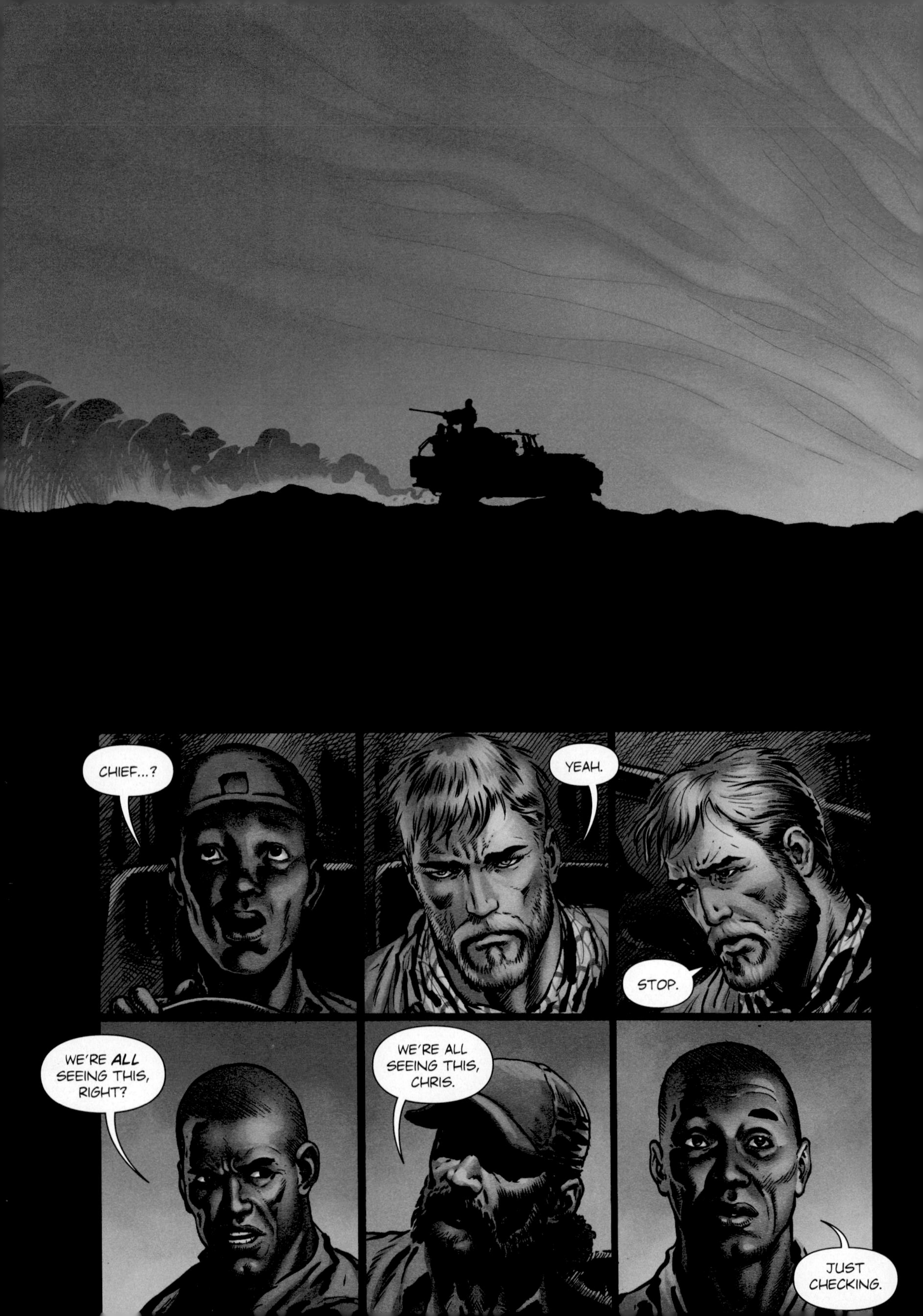
CHIEF...?
YEAH.
STOP.
WE'RE **ALL** SEEING THIS, RIGHT?
WE'RE ALL SEEING THIS, CHRIS.
JUST CHECKING.

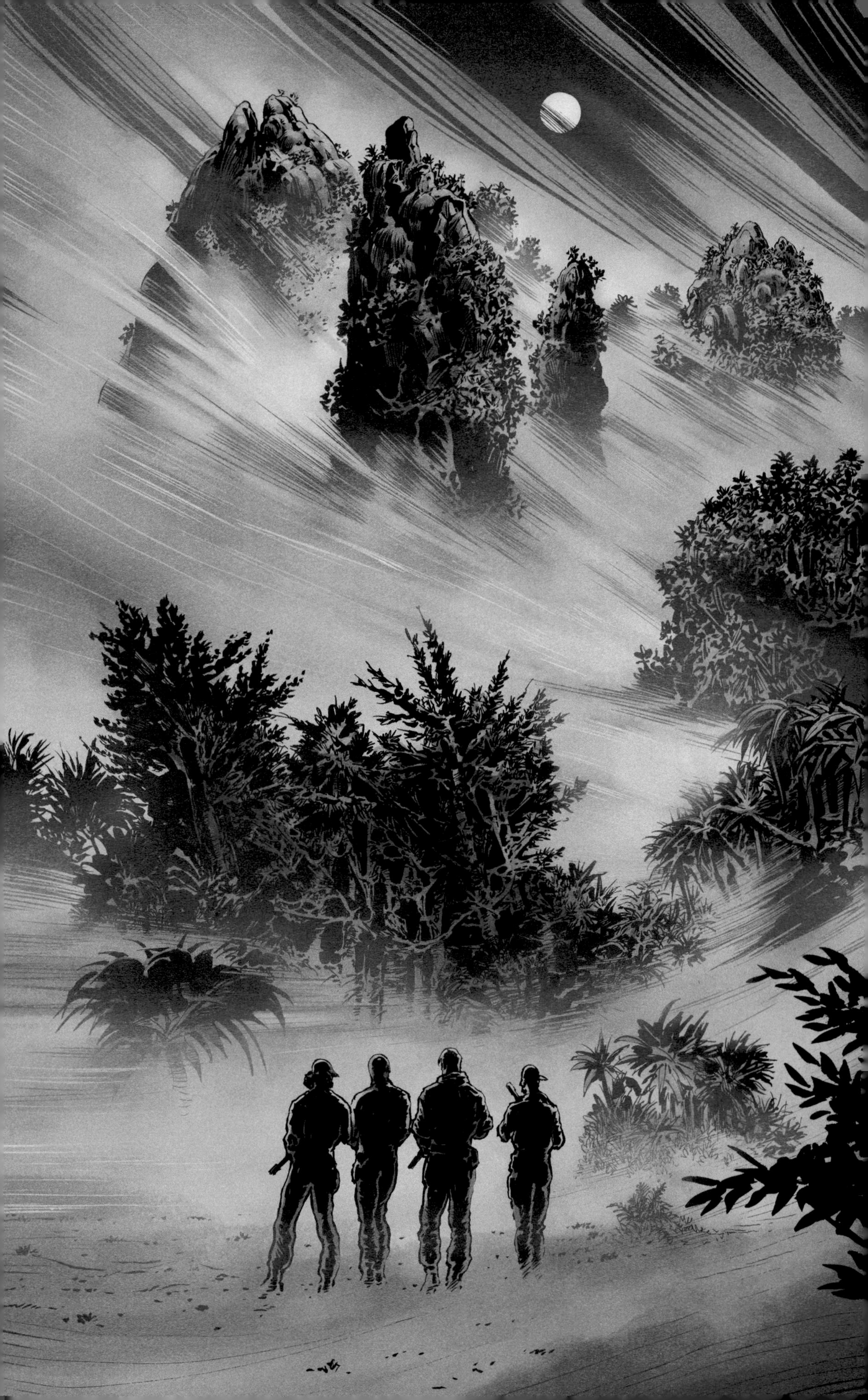

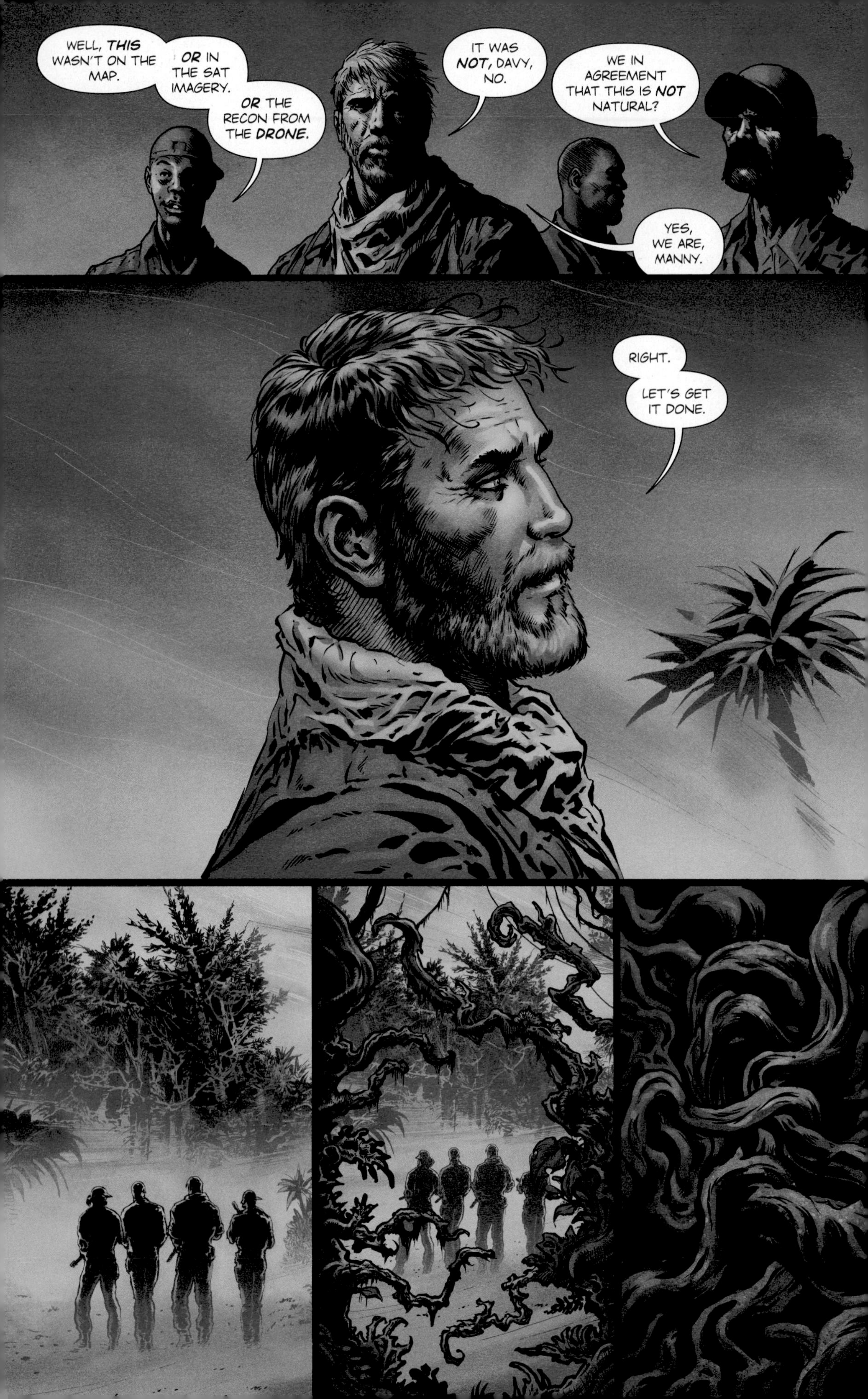
WELL, **THIS** WASN'T ON THE MAP.
OR IN THE SAT IMAGERY.
OR THE RECON FROM THE **DRONE.**
IT WAS **NOT,** DAVY, NO.
WE IN AGREEMENT THAT THIS IS **NOT** NATURAL?
YES, WE ARE, MANNY.
RIGHT.
LET'S GET IT DONE.

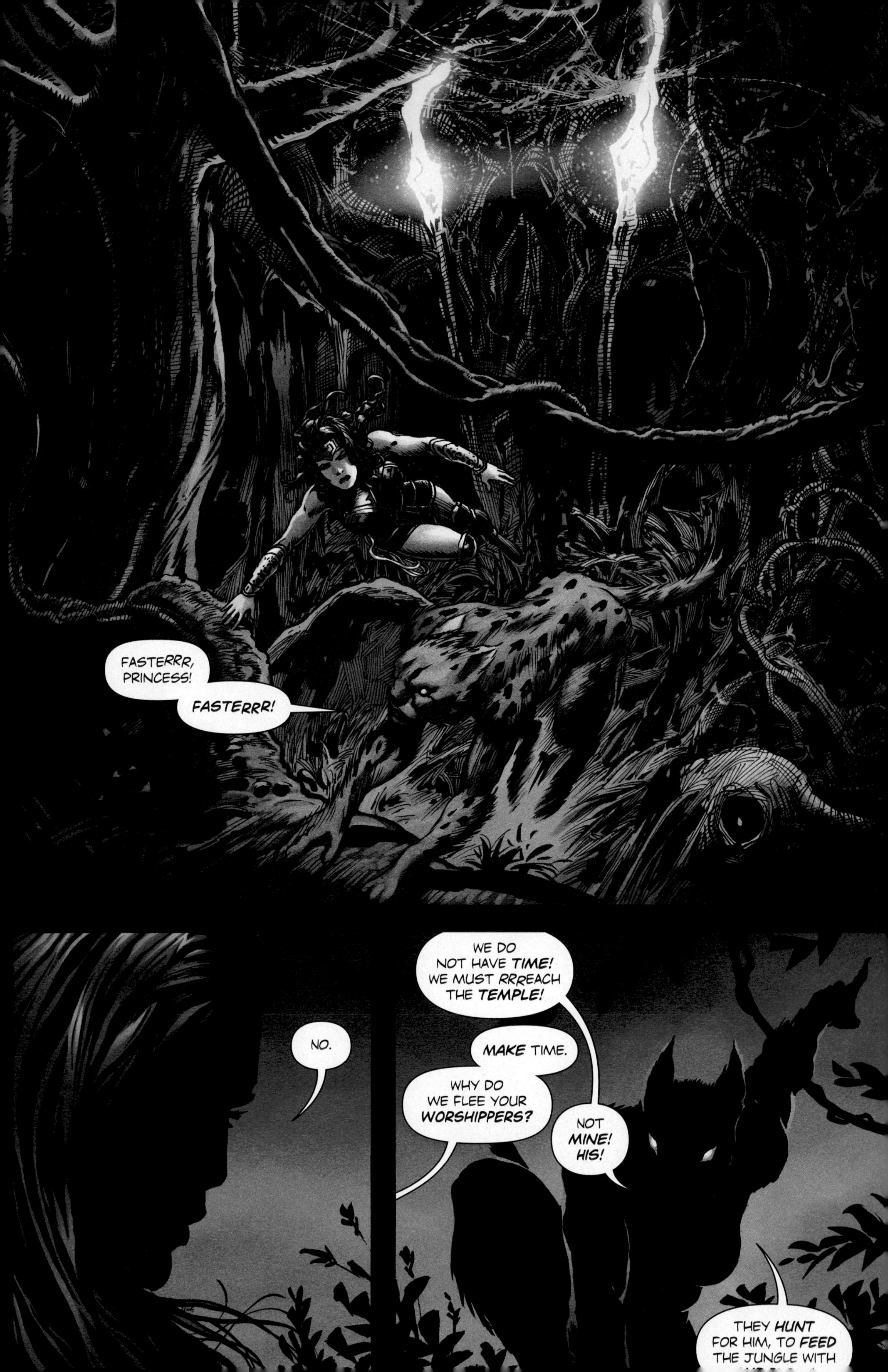
FASTERRR, PRINCESS!
FASTERRR!
NO.
WE DO NOT HAVE TIME! WE MUST RRREACH THE TEMPLE!
MAKE TIME.
WHY DO WE FLEE YOUR WORSHIPPERS?
NOT MINE! HIS!
THEY HUNT FOR HIM, TO FEED THE JUNGLE WITH

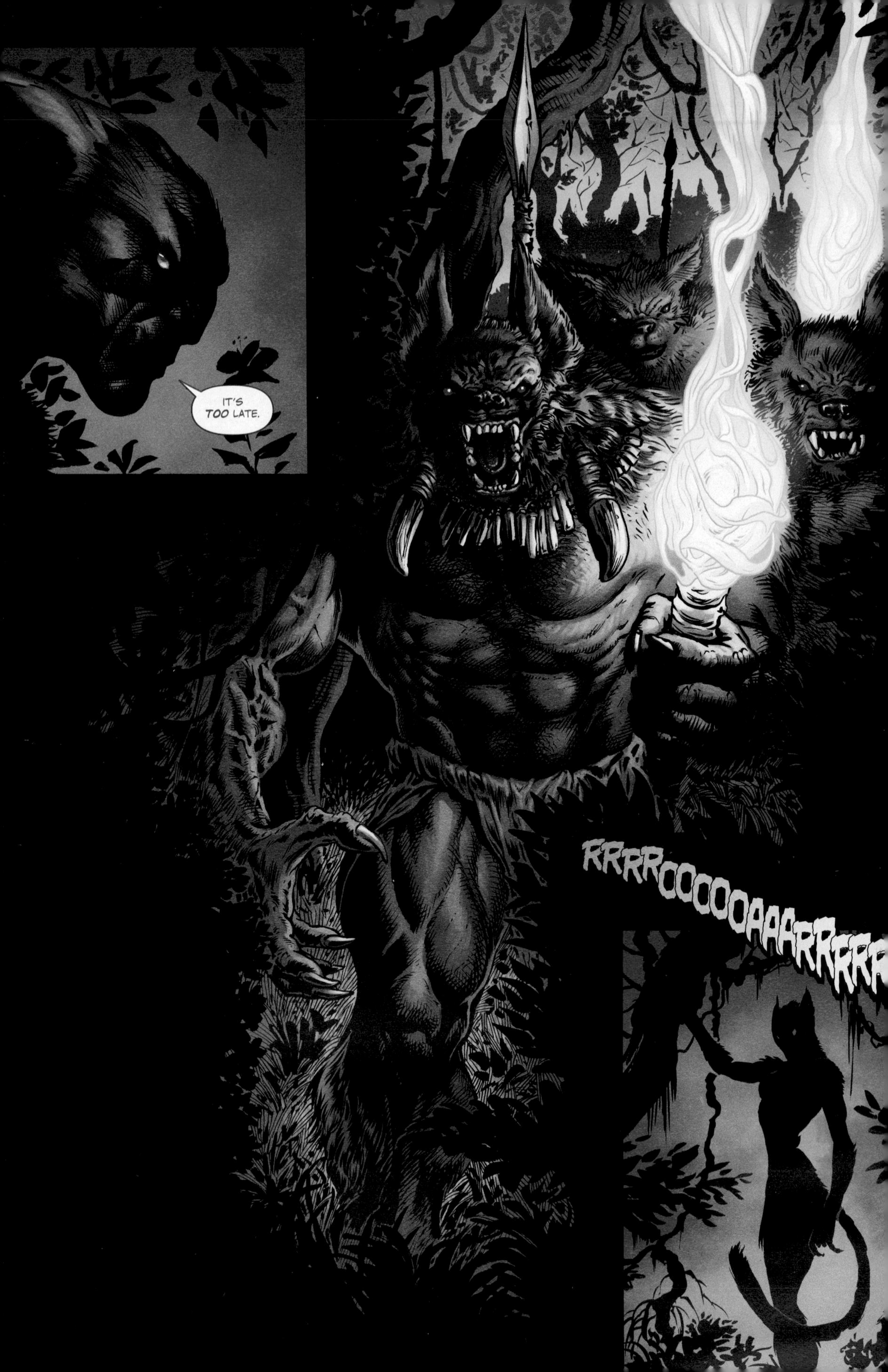
IT'S TOO LATE.
RRRROOOOOOAAARRRRR

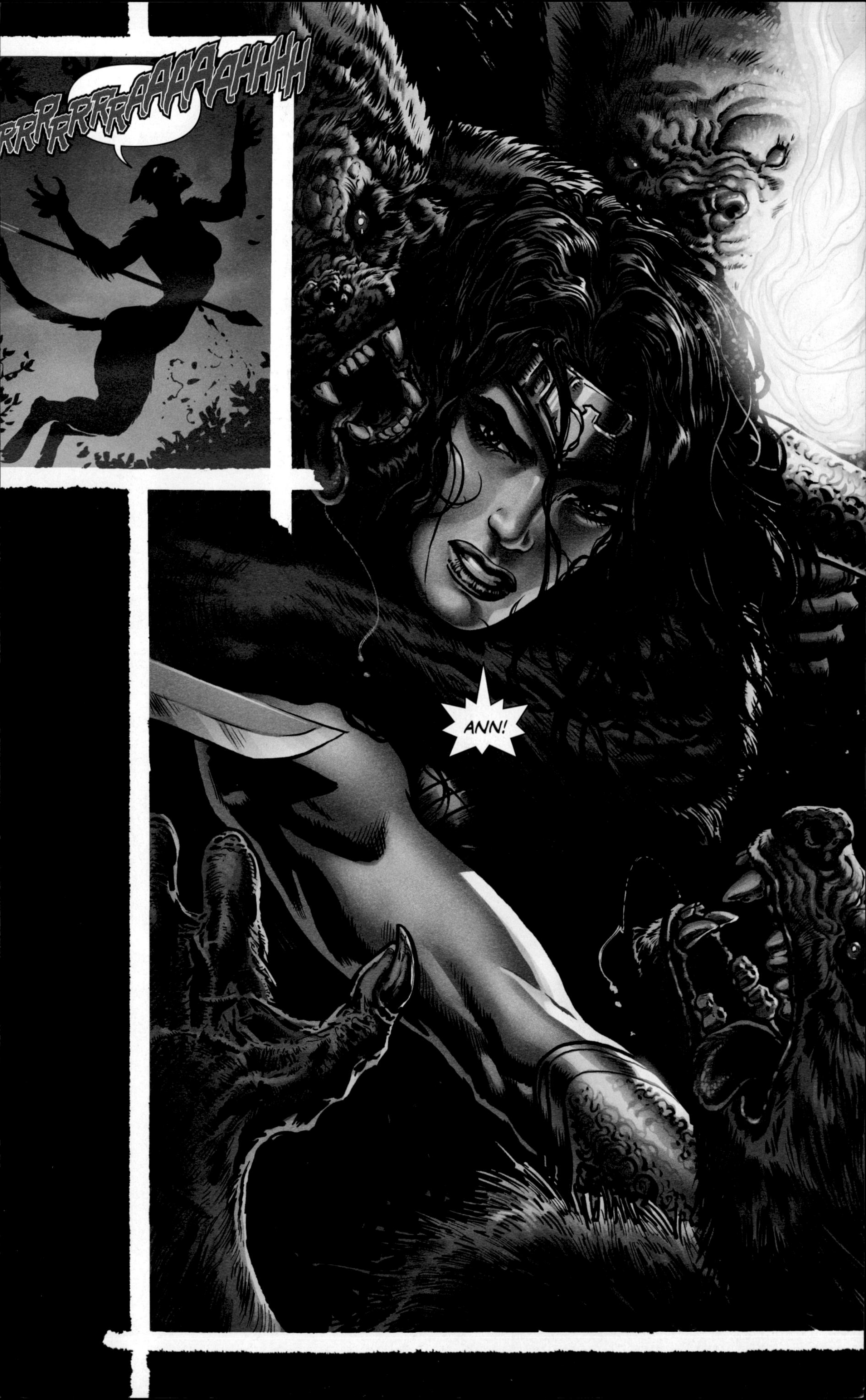
RRRRRRRRAAAAAHHHH
ANN!

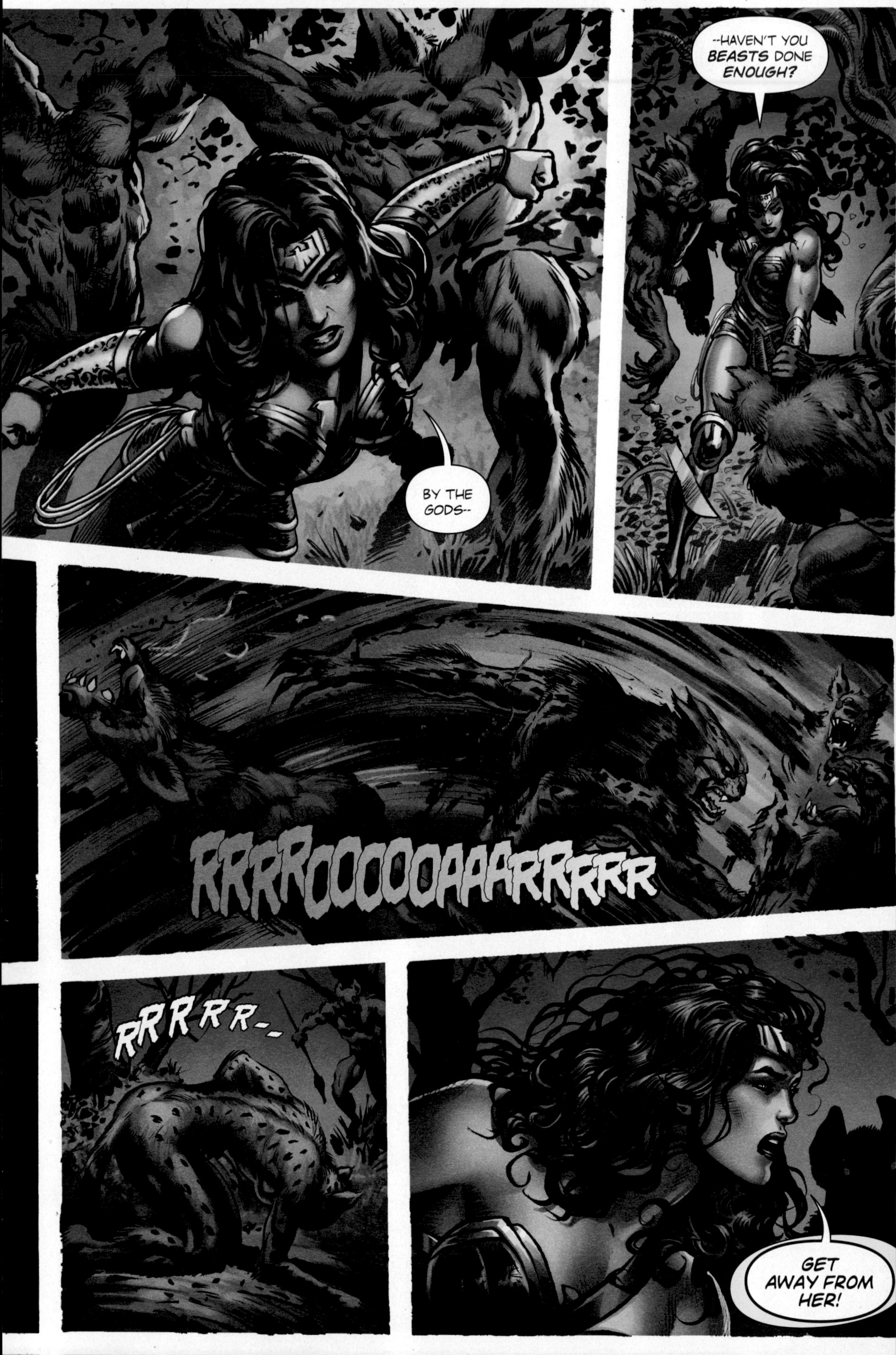
BY THE GODS--
--HAVEN'T YOU BEASTS DONE ENOUGH?
RRRROOOOOOAAARRRRR
RRRRR--
GET AWAY FROM HER!

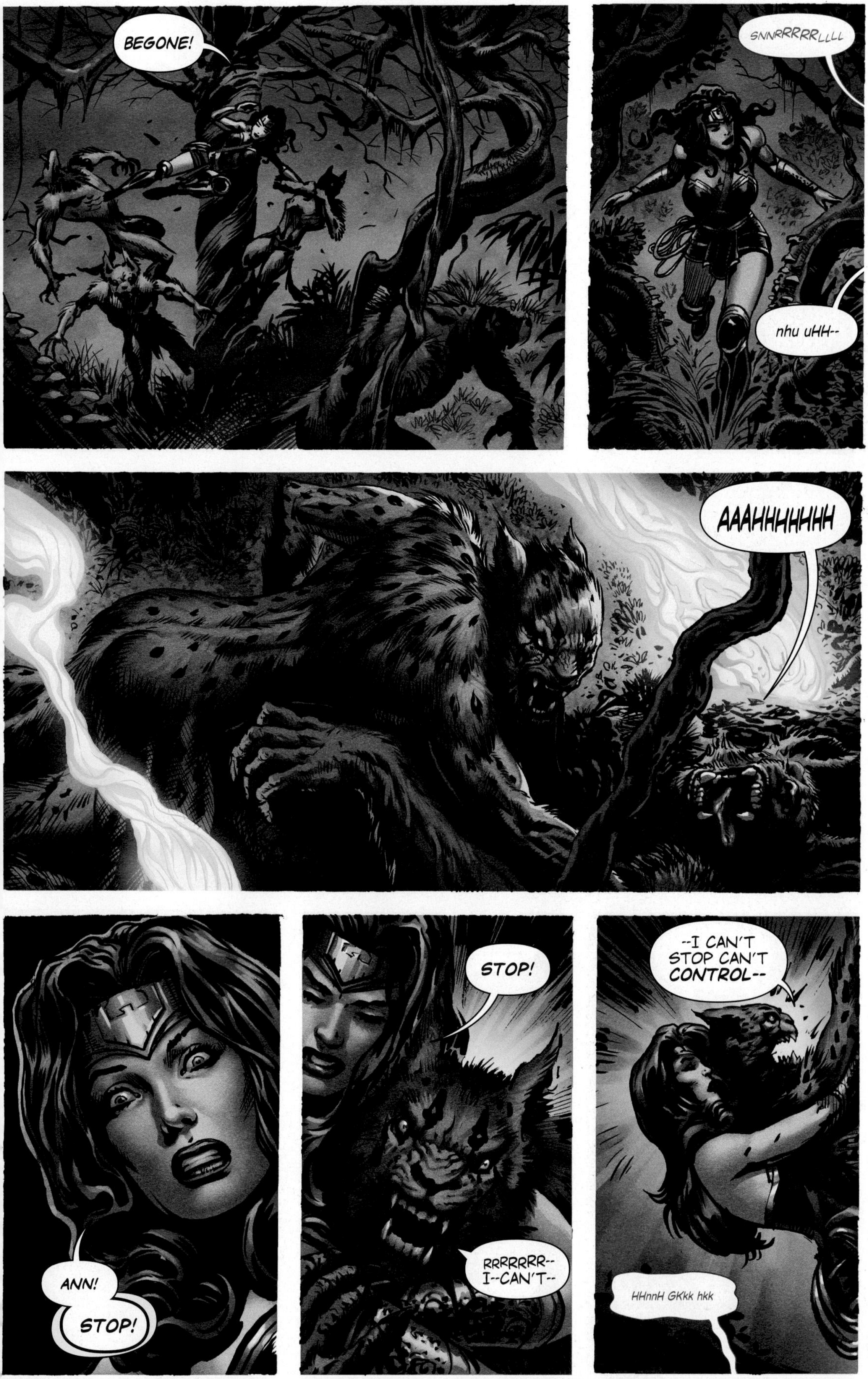
BEGONE!
SNNRRRRRLLLL
nhu uHH--
AAAHHHHHHH
ANN!
STOP!
STOP!
RRRRRRR--
I--CAN'T--
--I CAN'T
STOP CAN'T
CONTROL--
HHnnH GKkk hkk

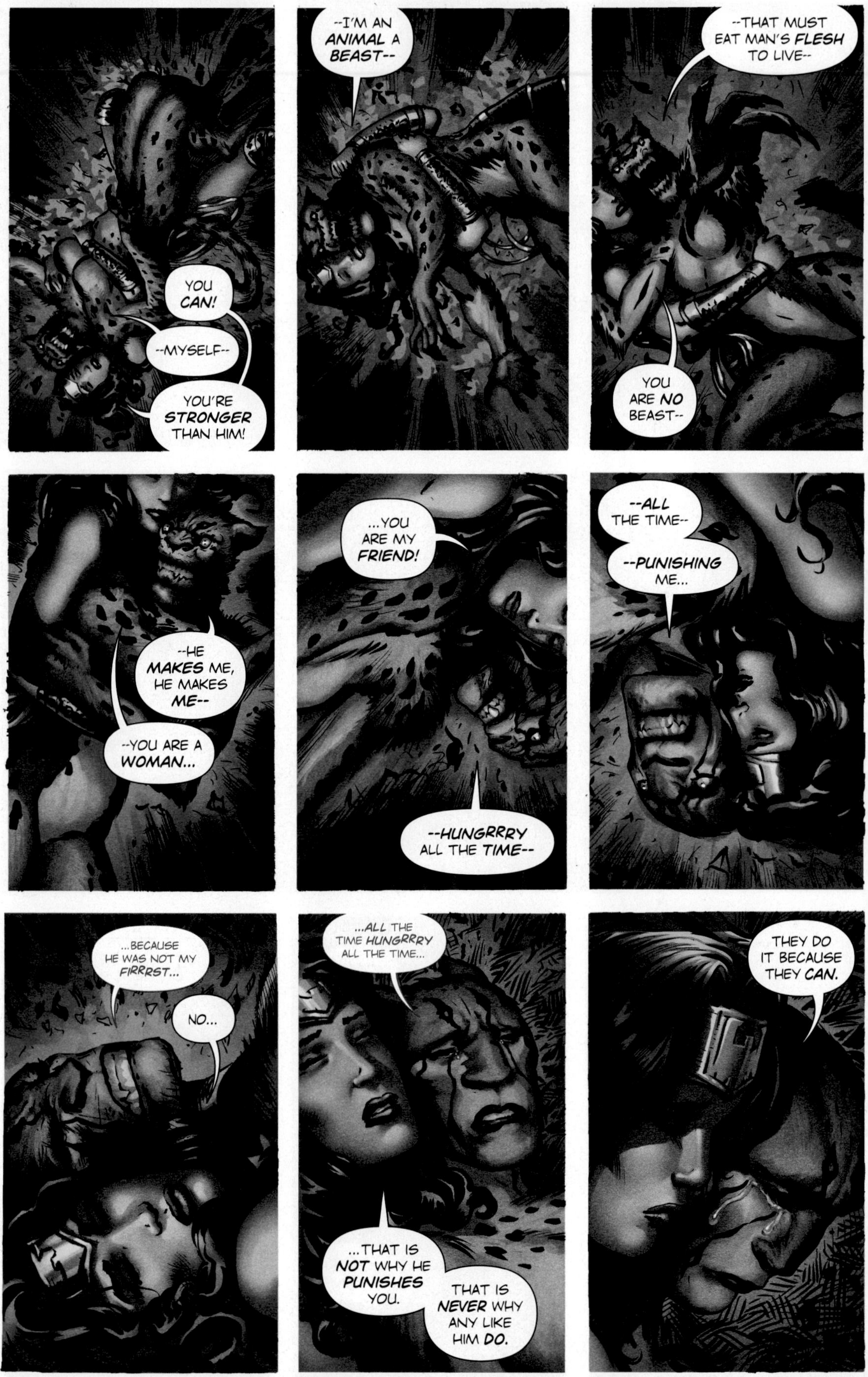
YOU CAN!
--MYSELF--
YOU'RE STRONGER THAN HIM!
--I'M AN ANIMAL A BEAST--
--THAT MUST EAT MAN'S FLESH TO LIVE--
YOU ARE NO BEAST--
--HE MAKES ME, HE MAKES ME--
--YOU ARE A WOMAN...
...YOU ARE MY FRIEND!
--HUNGRRRY ALL THE TIME--
--ALL THE TIME--
--PUNISHING ME...
...BECAUSE HE WAS NOT MY FIRRRST...
NO...
...ALL THE TIME HUNGRRRY ALL THE TIME...
...THAT IS NOT WHY HE PUNISHES YOU.
THAT IS NEVER WHY ANY LIKE HIM DO.
THEY DO IT BECAUSE THEY CAN.

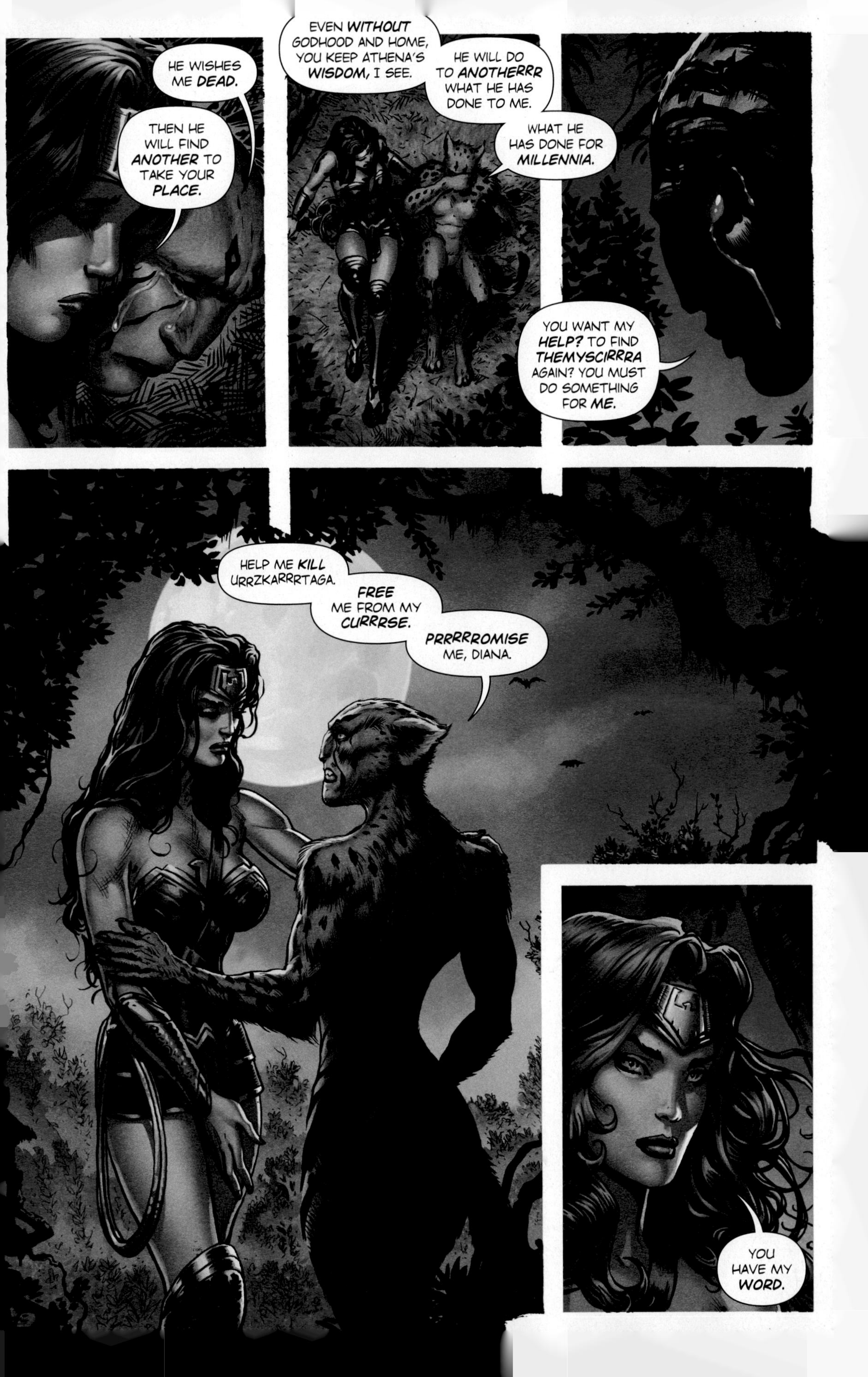
HE WISHES ME DEAD.
THEN HE WILL FIND ANOTHER TO TAKE YOUR PLACE.
EVEN WITHOUT GODHOOD AND HOME, YOU KEEP ATHENA'S WISDOM, I SEE.
HE WILL DO TO ANOTHERRR WHAT HE HAS DONE TO ME.
WHAT HE HAS DONE FOR MILLENNIA.
YOU WANT MY HELP? TO FIND THEMYSCIRRRA AGAIN? YOU MUST DO SOMETHING FOR ME.
HELP ME KILL URRZKARRRTAGA.
FREE ME FROM MY CURRRSE.
PRRRRROMISE ME, DIANA.
YOU HAVE MY WORD.

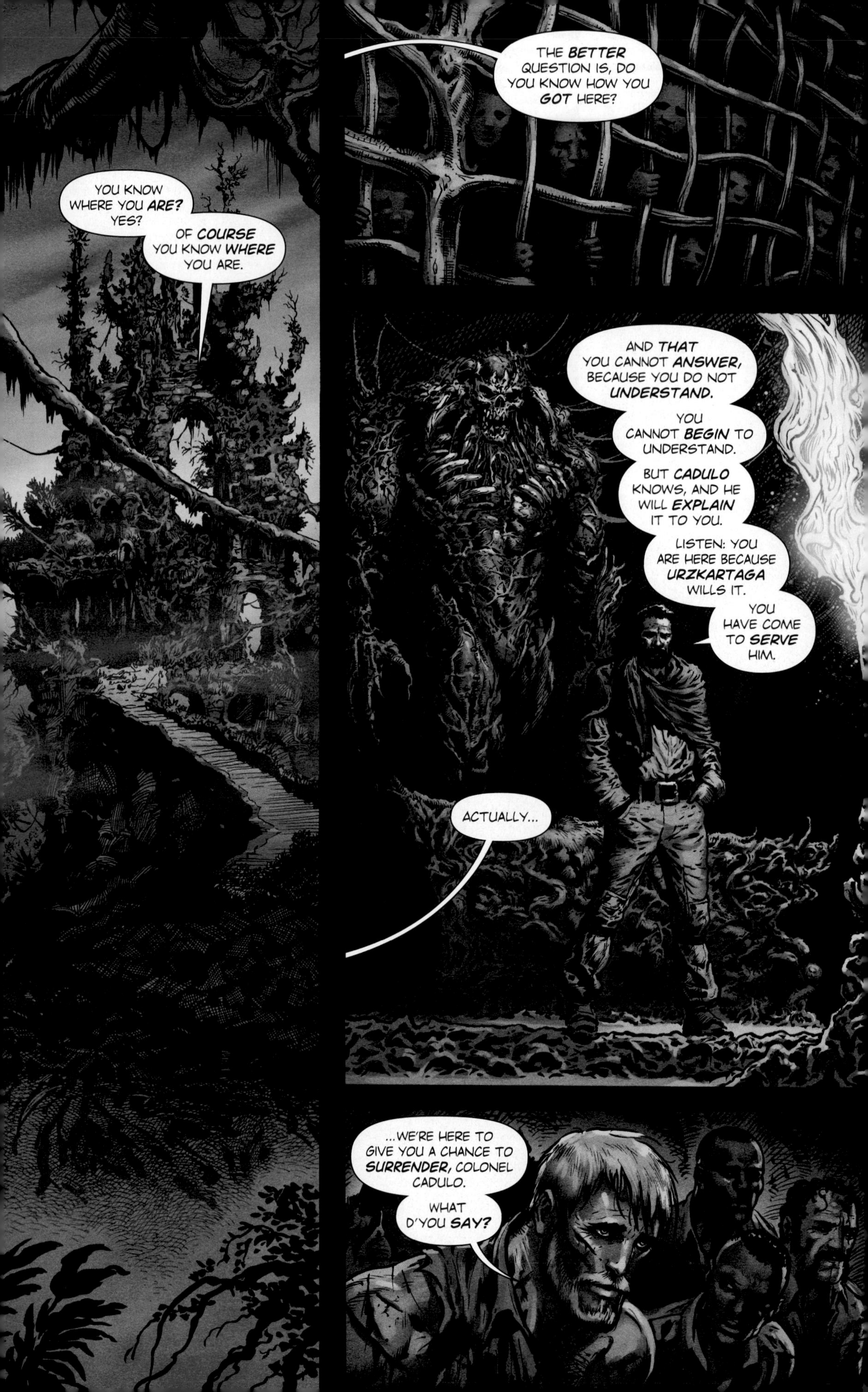

YOU KNOW WHERE YOU ARE? YES?
OF COURSE YOU KNOW WHERE YOU ARE.
THE BETTER QUESTION IS, DO YOU KNOW HOW YOU GOT HERE?
AND THAT YOU CANNOT ANSWER, BECAUSE YOU DO NOT UNDERSTAND.
YOU CANNOT BEGIN TO UNDERSTAND.
BUT CADULO KNOWS, AND HE WILL EXPLAIN IT TO YOU.
LISTEN: YOU ARE HERE BECAUSE URZKARTAGA WILLS IT.
YOU HAVE COME TO SERVE HIM.
ACTUALLY...
...WE'RE HERE TO GIVE YOU A CHANCE TO SURRENDER, COLONEL CADULO.
WHAT D'YOU SAY?

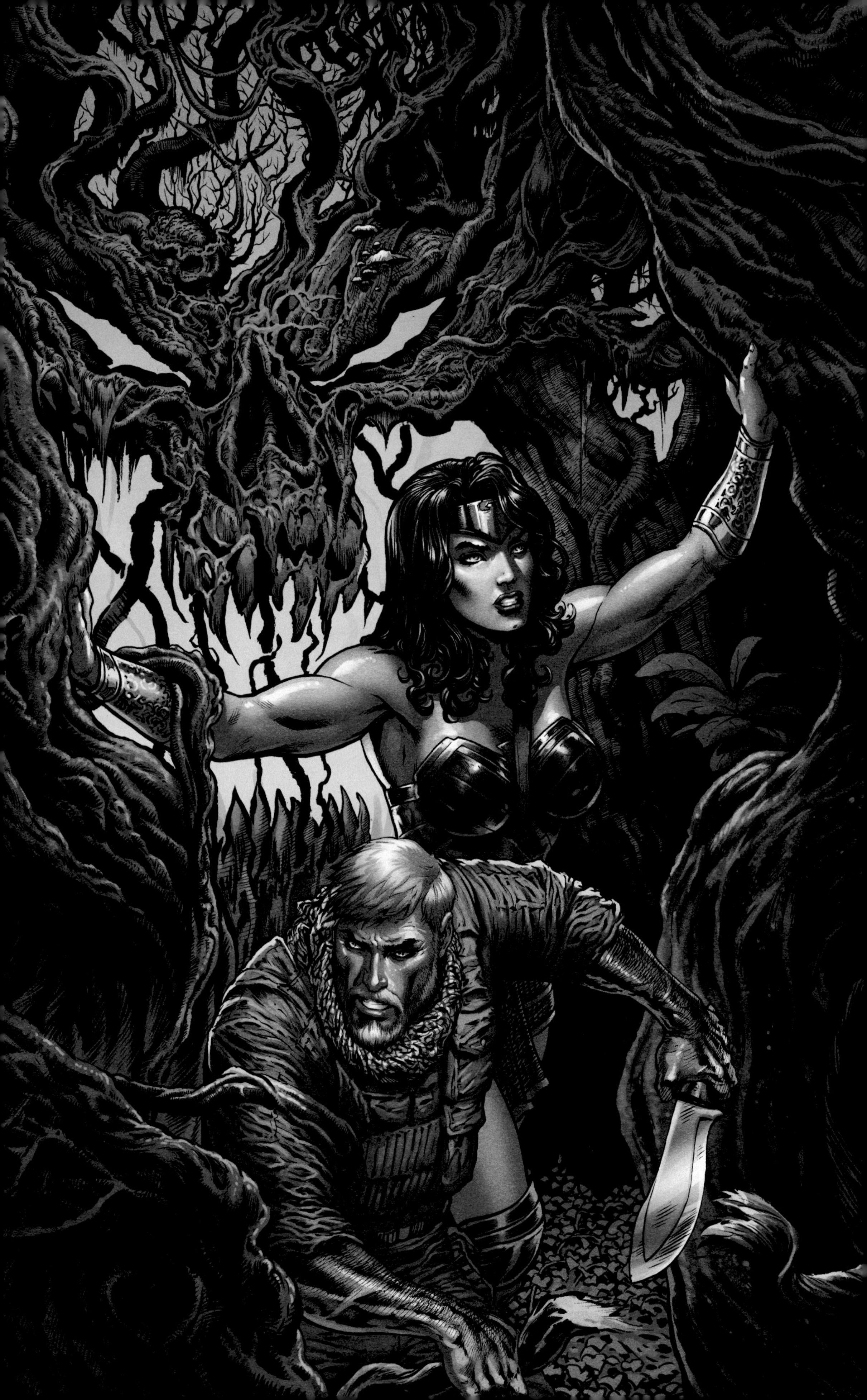

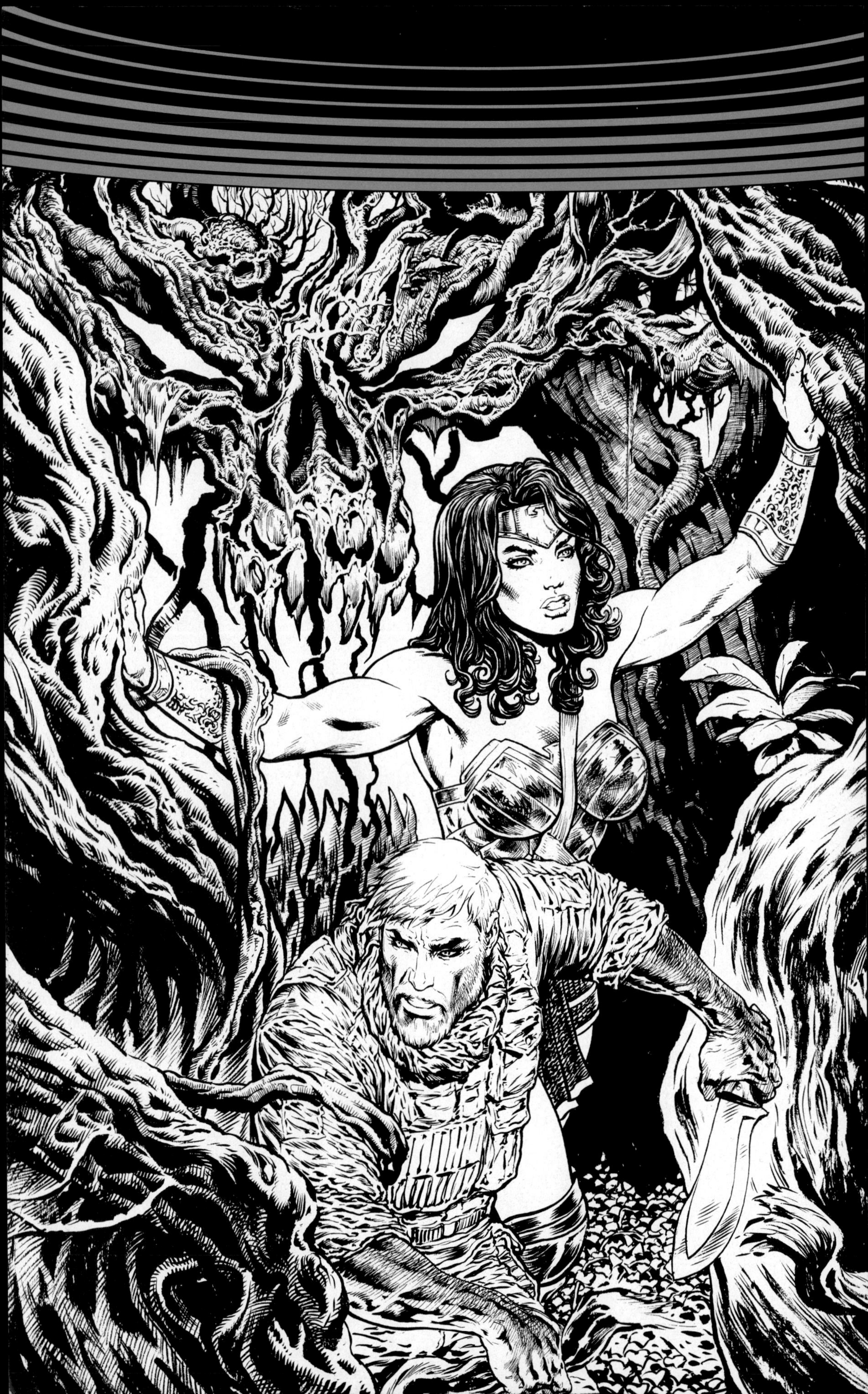

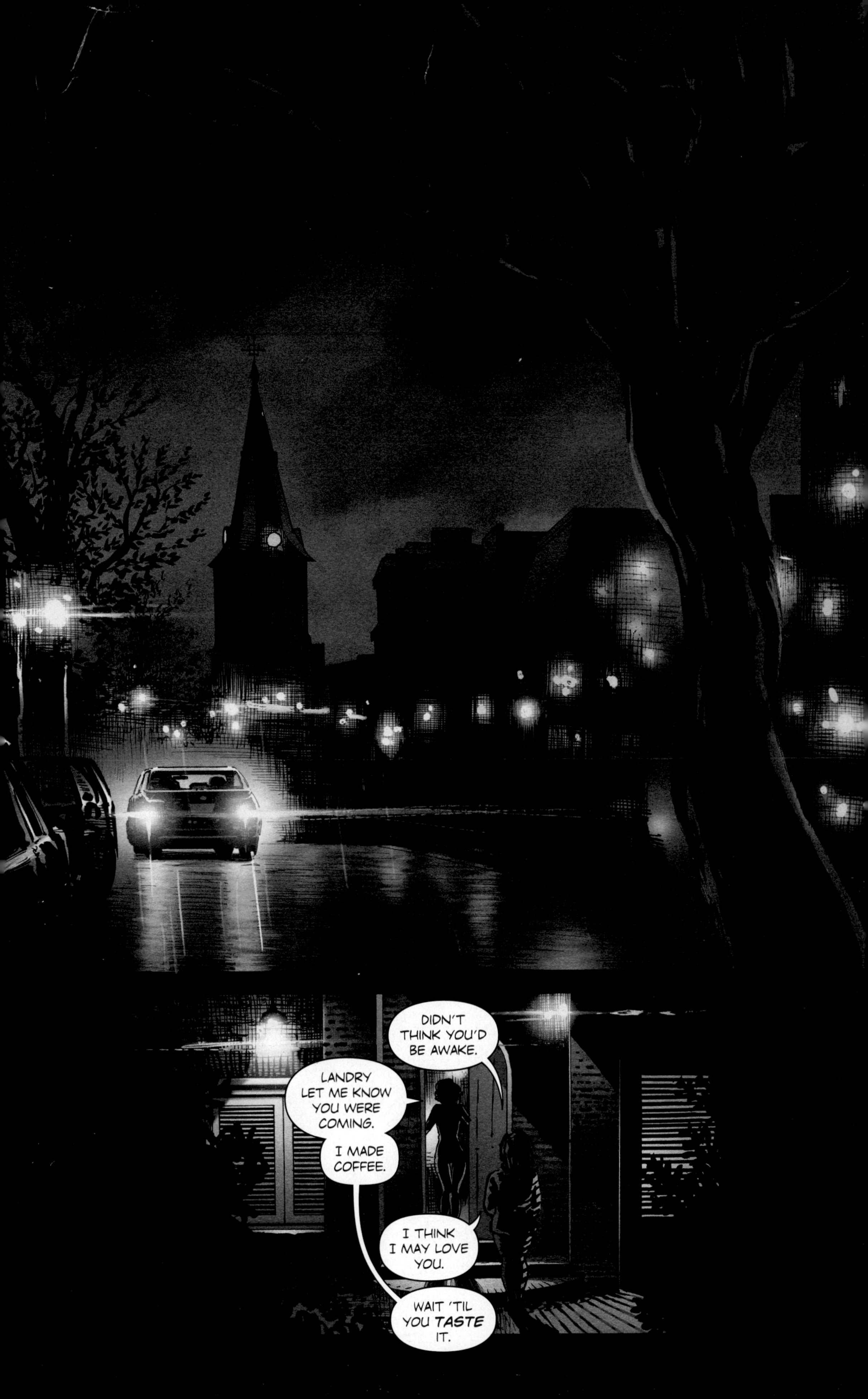
DIDN'T THINK YOU'D BE AWAKE.
LANDRY LET ME KNOW YOU WERE COMING.
I MADE COFFEE.
I THINK I MAY LOVE YOU.
WAIT 'TIL YOU *TASTE* IT.

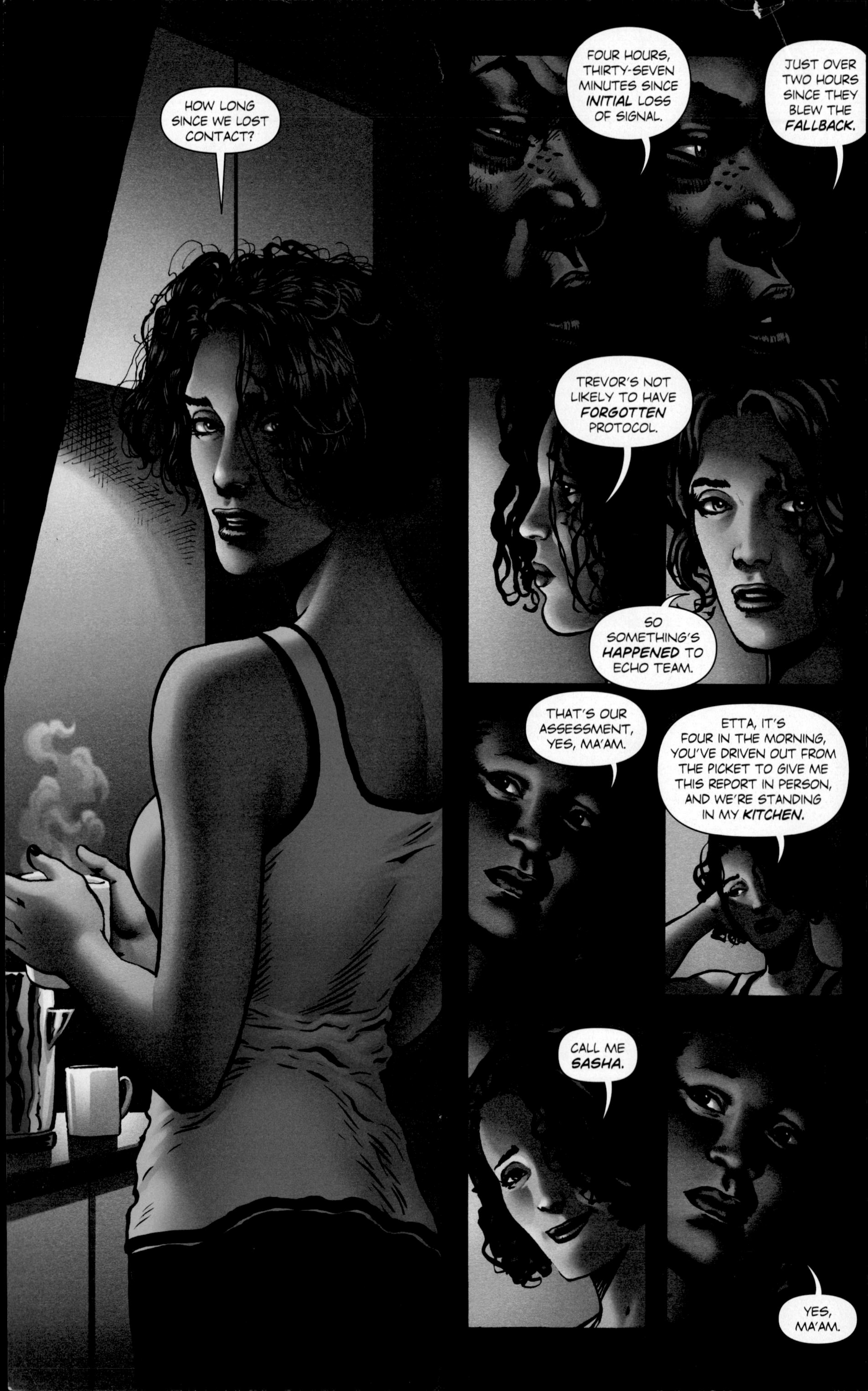

HOW LONG SINCE WE LOST CONTACT?
FOUR HOURS, THIRTY-SEVEN MINUTES SINCE INITIAL LOSS OF SIGNAL.
JUST OVER TWO HOURS SINCE THEY BLEW THE FALLBACK.
TREVOR'S NOT LIKELY TO HAVE FORGOTTEN PROTOCOL.
SO SOMETHING'S HAPPENED TO ECHO TEAM.
THAT'S OUR ASSESSMENT, YES, MA'AM.
ETTA, IT'S FOUR IN THE MORNING, YOU'VE DRIVEN OUT FROM THE PICKET TO GIVE ME THIS REPORT IN PERSON, AND WE'RE STANDING IN MY KITCHEN.
CALL ME SASHA.
YES, MA'AM.

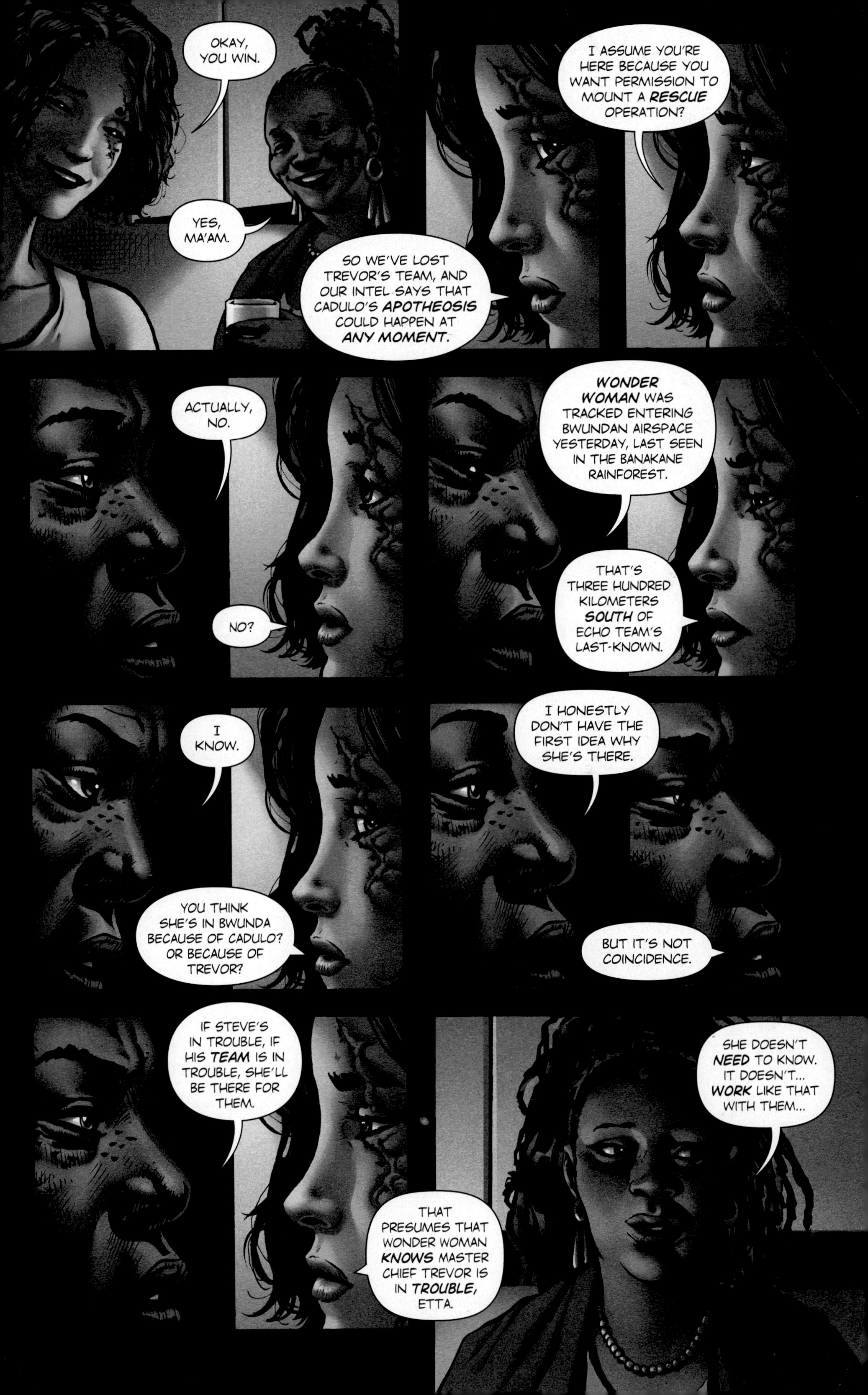
OKAY, YOU WIN.
YES, MA'AM.
SO WE'VE LOST TREVOR'S TEAM, AND OUR INTEL SAYS THAT CADULO'S APOTHEOSIS COULD HAPPEN AT ANY MOMENT.
I ASSUME YOU'RE HERE BECAUSE YOU WANT PERMISSION TO MOUNT A RESCUE OPERATION?
ACTUALLY, NO.
NO?
WONDER WOMAN WAS TRACKED ENTERING BWUNDAN AIRSPACE YESTERDAY, LAST SEEN IN THE BANAKANE RAINFOREST.
THAT'S THREE HUNDRED KILOMETERS SOUTH OF ECHO TEAM'S LAST-KNOWN.
I KNOW.
YOU THINK SHE'S IN BWUNDA BECAUSE OF CADULO? OR BECAUSE OF TREVOR?
I HONESTLY DON'T HAVE THE FIRST IDEA WHY SHE'S THERE.
BUT IT'S NOT COINCIDENCE.
IF STEVE'S IN TROUBLE, IF HIS TEAM IS IN TROUBLE, SHE'LL BE THERE FOR THEM.
THAT PRESUMES THAT WONDER WOMAN KNOWS MASTER CHIEF TREVOR IS IN TROUBLE, ETTA.
SHE DOESN'T NEED TO KNOW. IT DOESN'T... WORK LIKE THAT WITH THEM...

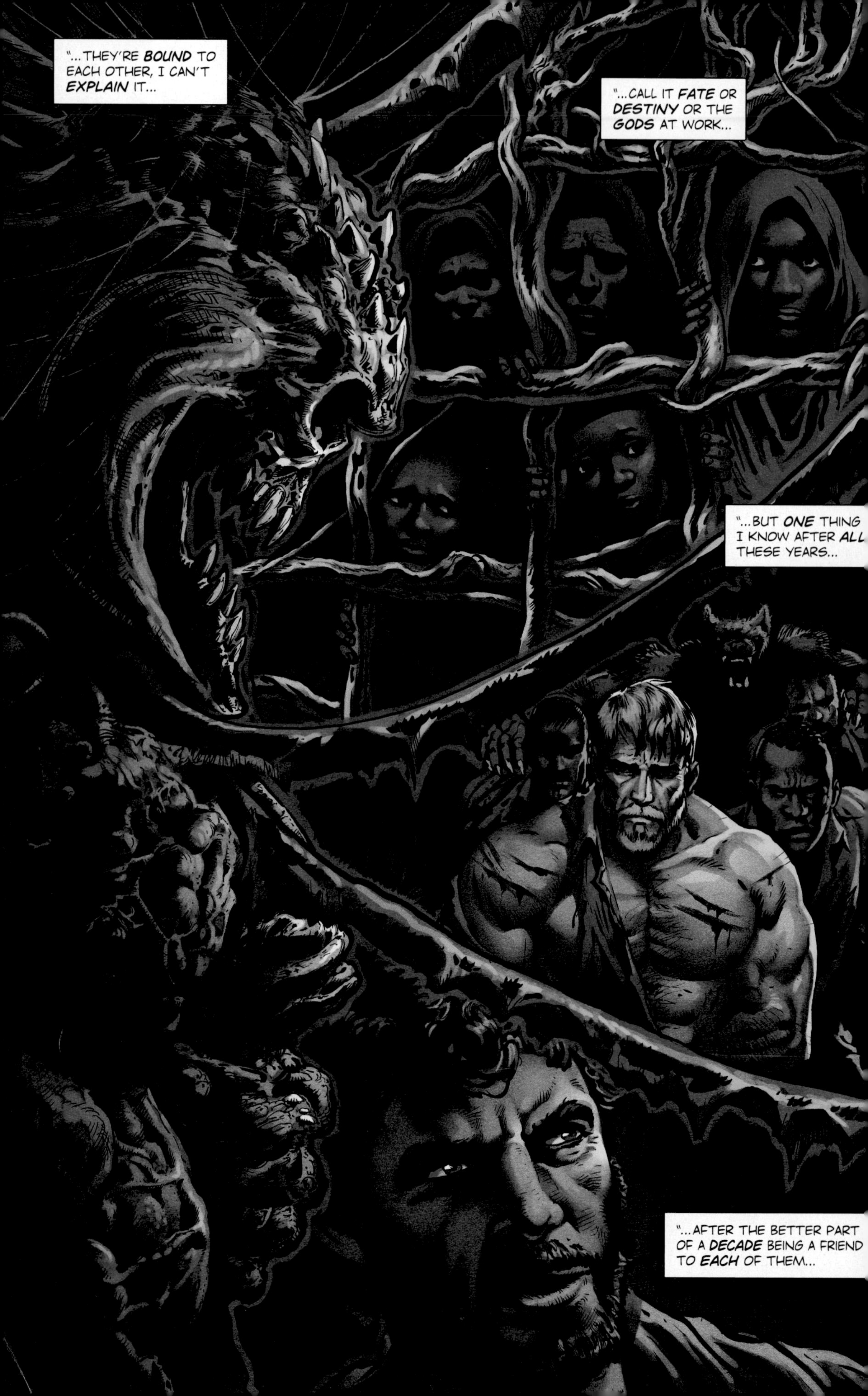
"...THEY'RE BOUND TO EACH OTHER, I CAN'T EXPLAIN IT...
"...CALL IT FATE OR DESTINY OR THE GODS AT WORK...
"...BUT ONE THING I KNOW AFTER ALL THESE YEARS...
"...AFTER THE BETTER PART OF A DECADE BEING A FRIEND TO EACH OF THEM...

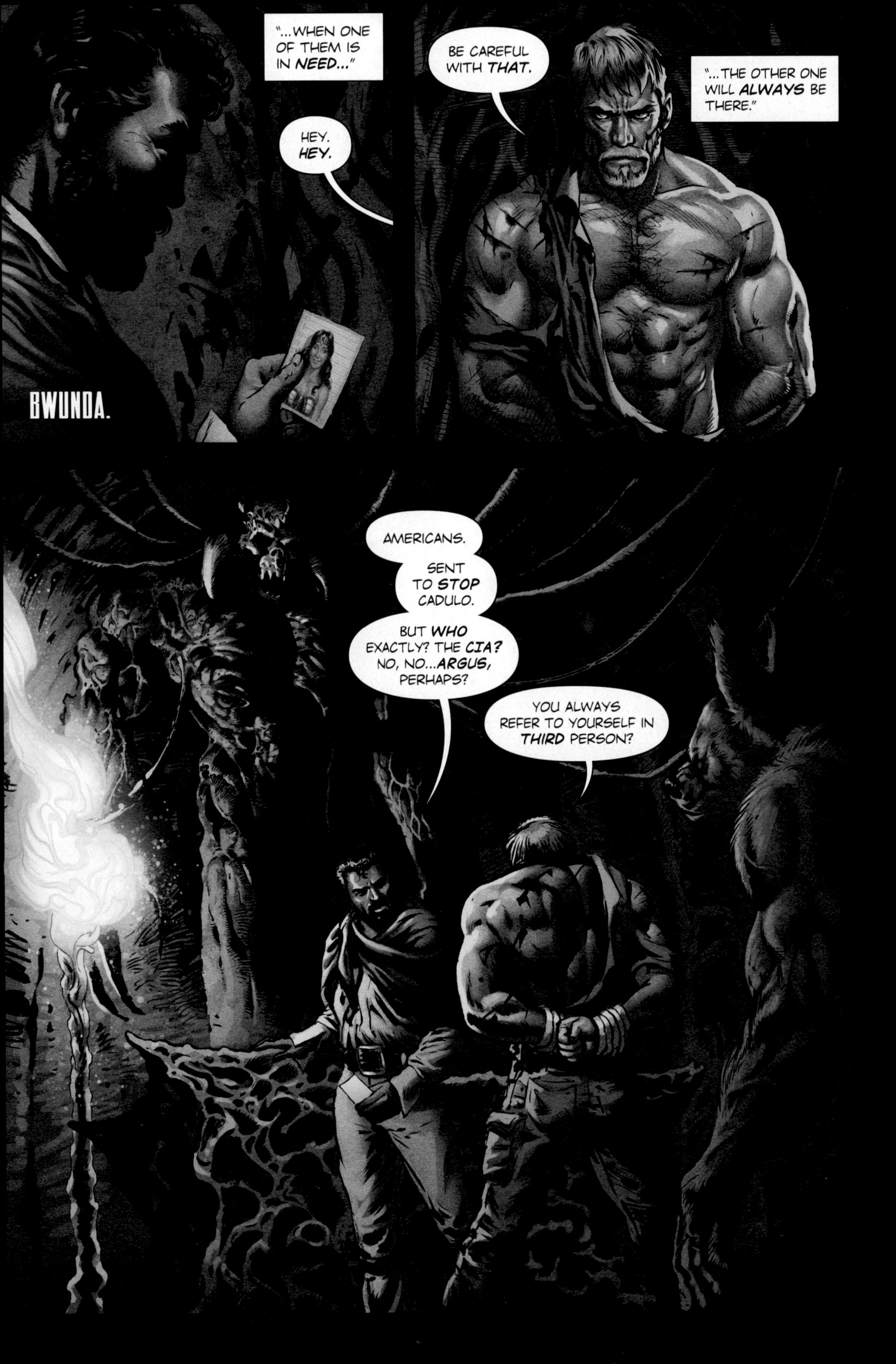
"...WHEN ONE OF THEM IS IN NEED..."
HEY. HEY.
BWUNDA.
BE CAREFUL WITH THAT.
"...THE OTHER ONE WILL ALWAYS BE THERE."
AMERICANS.
SENT TO STOP CADULO.
BUT WHO EXACTLY? THE CIA? NO, NO...ARGUS, PERHAPS?
YOU ALWAYS REFER TO YOURSELF IN THIRD PERSON?

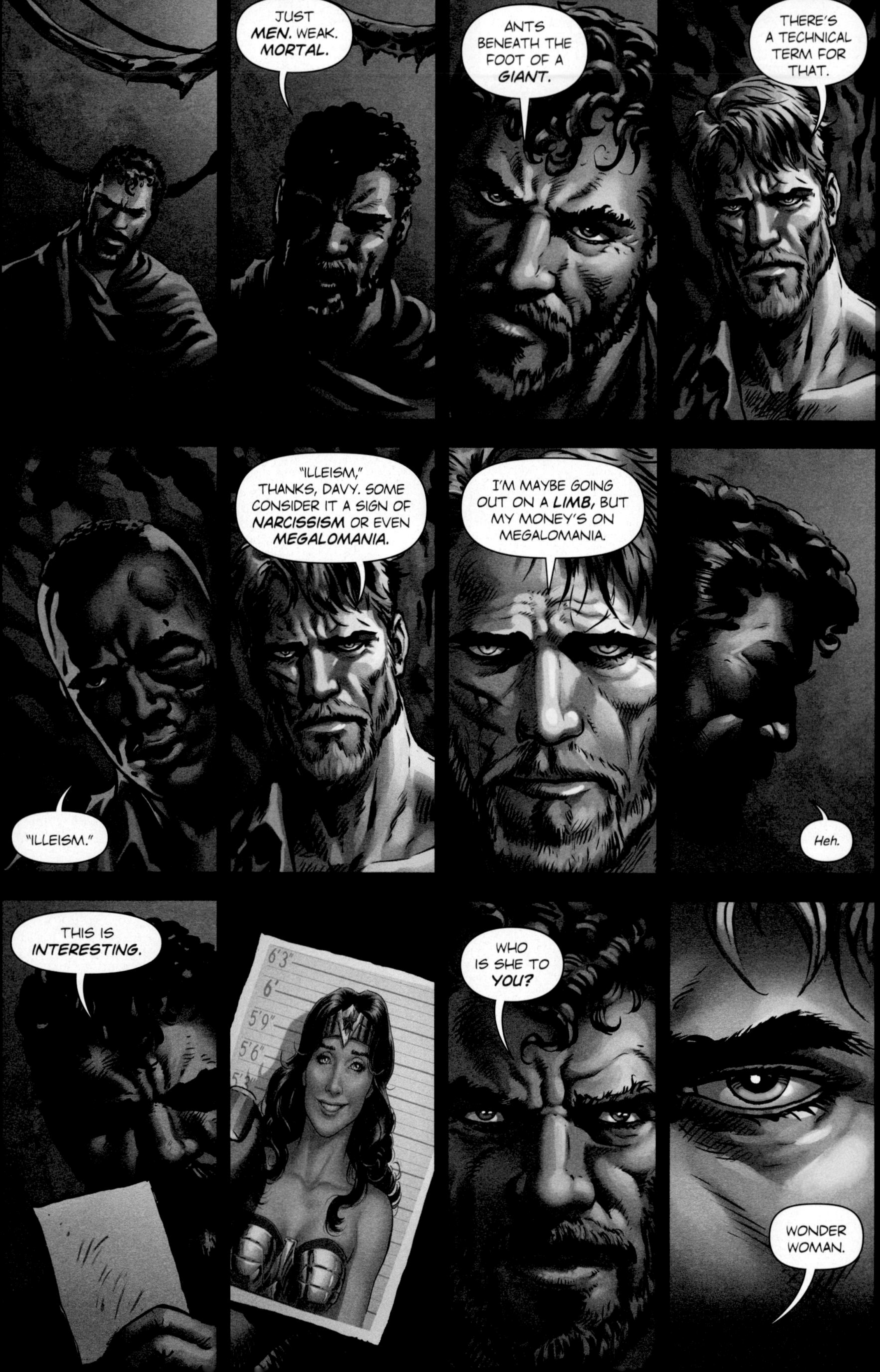
JUST MEN. WEAK. MORTAL.
ANTS BENEATH THE FOOT OF A GIANT.
THERE'S A TECHNICAL TERM FOR THAT.
"ILLEISM."
"ILLEISM," THANKS, DAVY. SOME CONSIDER IT A SIGN OF NARCISSISM OR EVEN MEGALOMANIA.
I'M MAYBE GOING OUT ON A LIMB, BUT MY MONEY'S ON MEGALOMANIA.
Heh.
THIS IS INTERESTING.
6'3"
6'
5'9"
5'6"
WHO IS SHE TO YOU?
WONDER WOMAN.

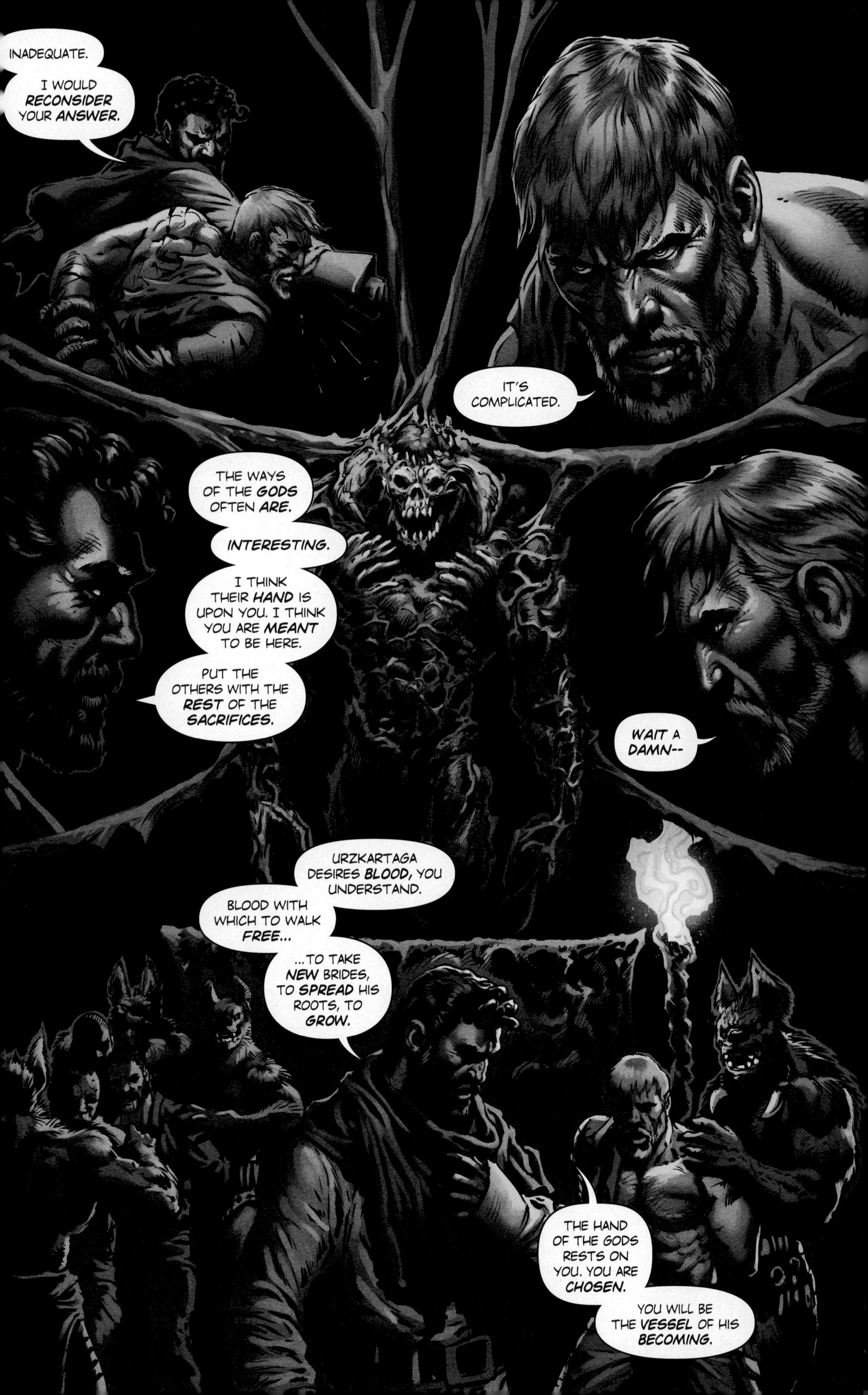
INADEQUATE.
I WOULD RECONSIDER YOUR ANSWER.
IT'S COMPLICATED.
THE WAYS OF THE GODS OFTEN ARE.
INTERESTING.
I THINK THEIR HAND IS UPON YOU. I THINK YOU ARE MEANT TO BE HERE.
PUT THE OTHERS WITH THE REST OF THE SACRIFICES.
WAIT A DAMN--
URZKARTAGA DESIRES BLOOD, YOU UNDERSTAND.
BLOOD WITH WHICH TO WALK FREE...
...TO TAKE NEW BRIDES, TO SPREAD HIS ROOTS, TO GROW.
THE HAND OF THE GODS RESTS ON YOU. YOU ARE CHOSEN.
YOU WILL BE THE VESSEL OF HIS BECOMING.

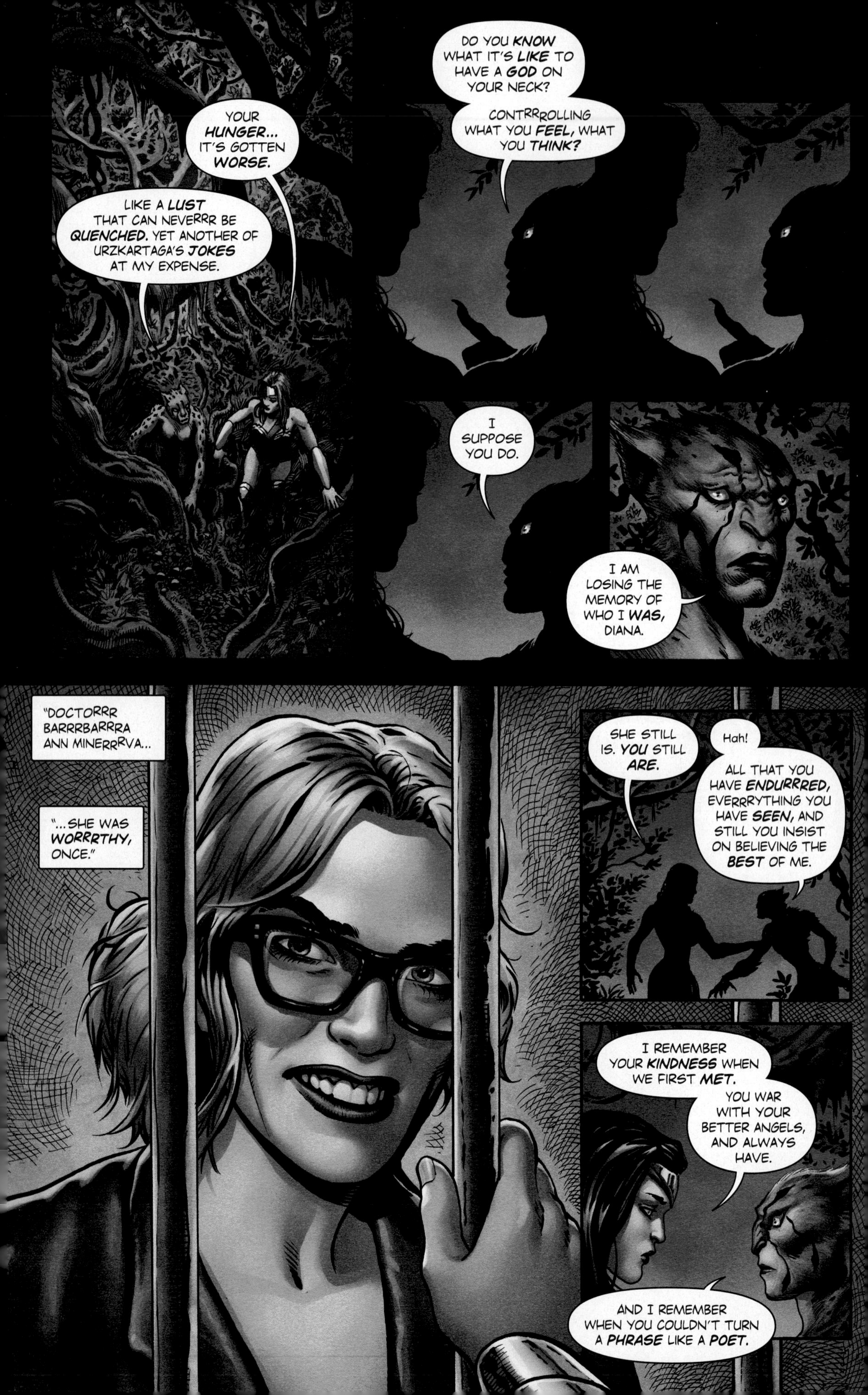

YOUR HUNGER... IT'S GOTTEN WORSE.
LIKE A LUST THAT CAN NEVERRR BE QUENCHED. YET ANOTHER OF URZKARTAGA'S JOKES AT MY EXPENSE.
DO YOU KNOW WHAT IT'S LIKE TO HAVE A GOD ON YOUR NECK?
CONTRRROLLING WHAT YOU FEEL, WHAT YOU THINK?
I SUPPOSE YOU DO.
I AM LOSING THE MEMORY OF WHO I WAS, DIANA.
"DOCTORRR BARRRBARRRA ANN MINERRRVA...
"...SHE WAS WORRRTHY, ONCE."
SHE STILL IS. YOU STILL ARE.
Hah!
ALL THAT YOU HAVE ENDURRRED, EVERRRYTHING YOU HAVE SEEN, AND STILL YOU INSIST ON BELIEVING THE BEST OF ME.
I REMEMBER YOUR KINDNESS WHEN WE FIRST MET.
YOU WAR WITH YOUR BETTER ANGELS, AND ALWAYS HAVE.
AND I REMEMBER WHEN YOU COULDN'T TURN A PHRASE LIKE A POET.

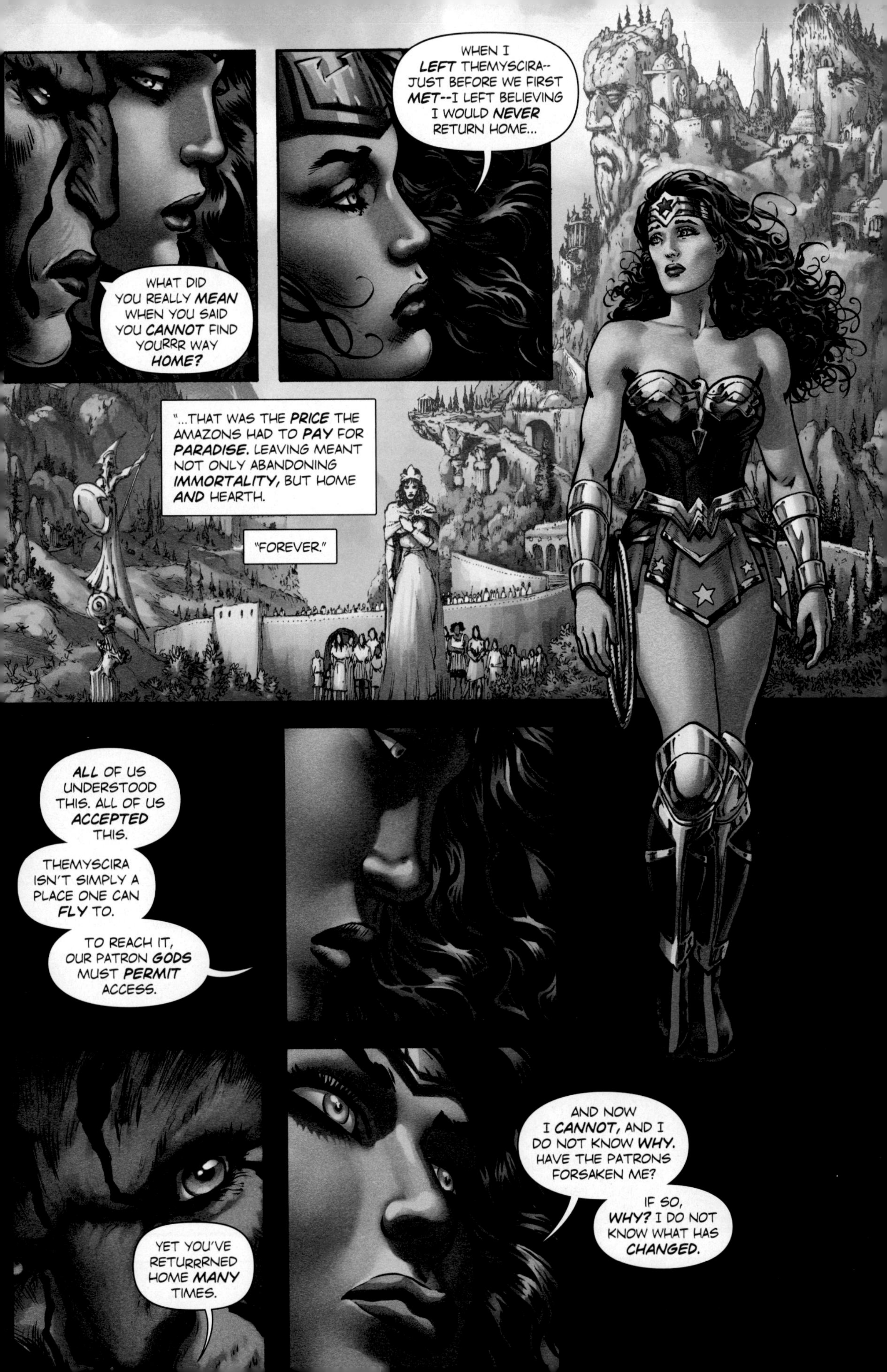
WHAT DID YOU REALLY MEAN WHEN YOU SAID YOU CANNOT FIND YOURRR WAY HOME?
WHEN I LEFT THEMYSCIRA--JUST BEFORE WE FIRST MET--I LEFT BELIEVING I WOULD NEVER RETURN HOME...
"...THAT WAS THE PRICE THE AMAZONS HAD TO PAY FOR PARADISE. LEAVING MEANT NOT ONLY ABANDONING IMMORTALITY, BUT HOME AND HEARTH.
"FOREVER."
ALL OF US UNDERSTOOD THIS. ALL OF US ACCEPTED THIS.
THEMYSCIRA ISN'T SIMPLY A PLACE ONE CAN FLY TO.
TO REACH IT, OUR PATRON GODS MUST PERMIT ACCESS.
YET YOU'VE RETURRRNED HOME MANY TIMES.
AND NOW I CANNOT, AND I DO NOT KNOW WHY. HAVE THE PATRONS FORSAKEN ME?
IF SO, WHY? I DO NOT KNOW WHAT HAS CHANGED.

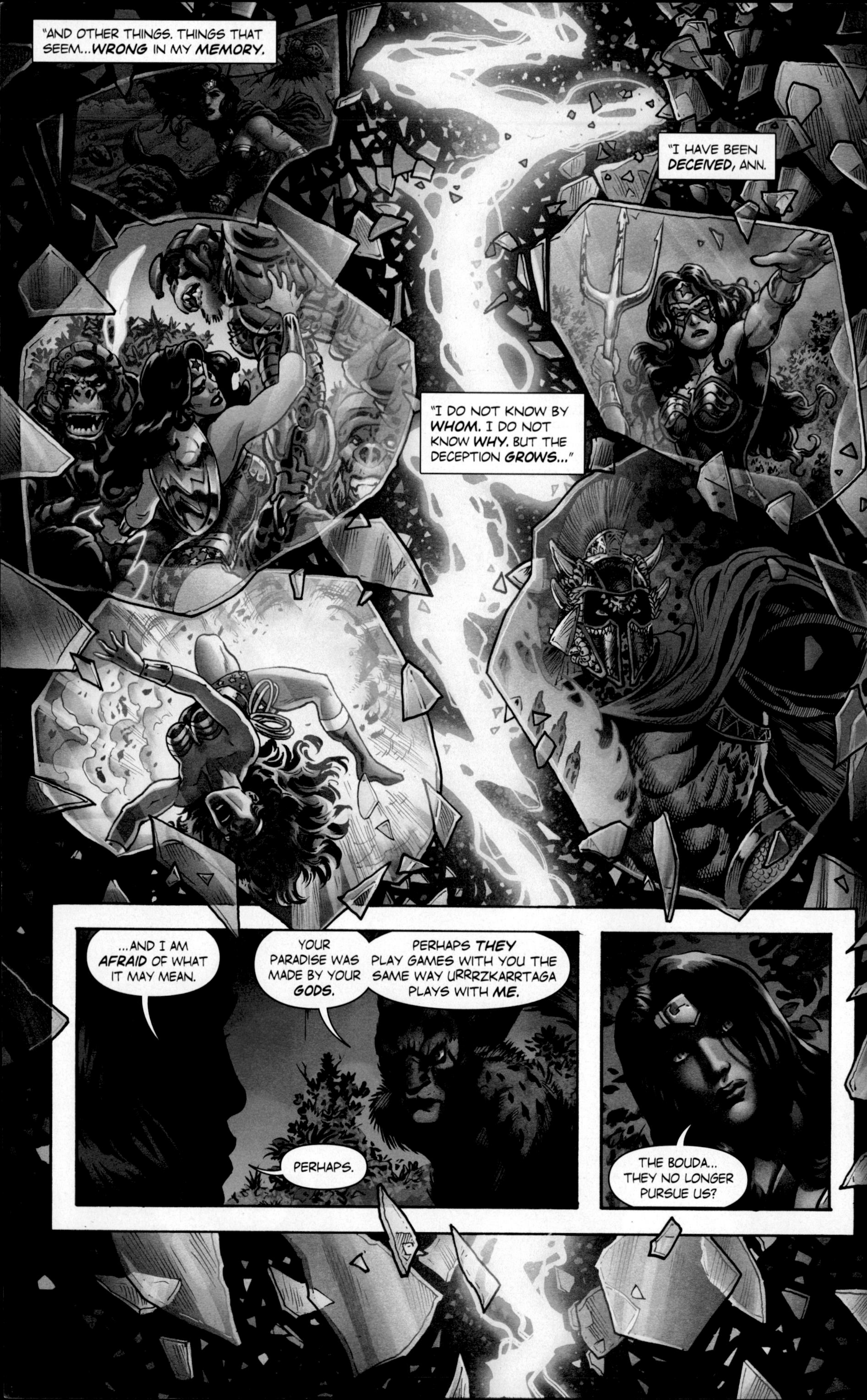
"AND OTHER THINGS. THINGS THAT SEEM...WRONG IN MY MEMORY.
"I HAVE BEEN DECEIVED, ANN.
"I DO NOT KNOW BY WHOM. I DO NOT KNOW WHY. BUT THE DECEPTION GROWS..."
...AND I AM AFRAID OF WHAT IT MAY MEAN.
YOUR PARADISE WAS MADE BY YOUR GODS.
PERHAPS THEY PLAY GAMES WITH YOU THE SAME WAY URRRZKARRTAGA PLAYS WITH ME.
PERHAPS.
THE BOUDA... THEY NO LONGER PURSUE US?

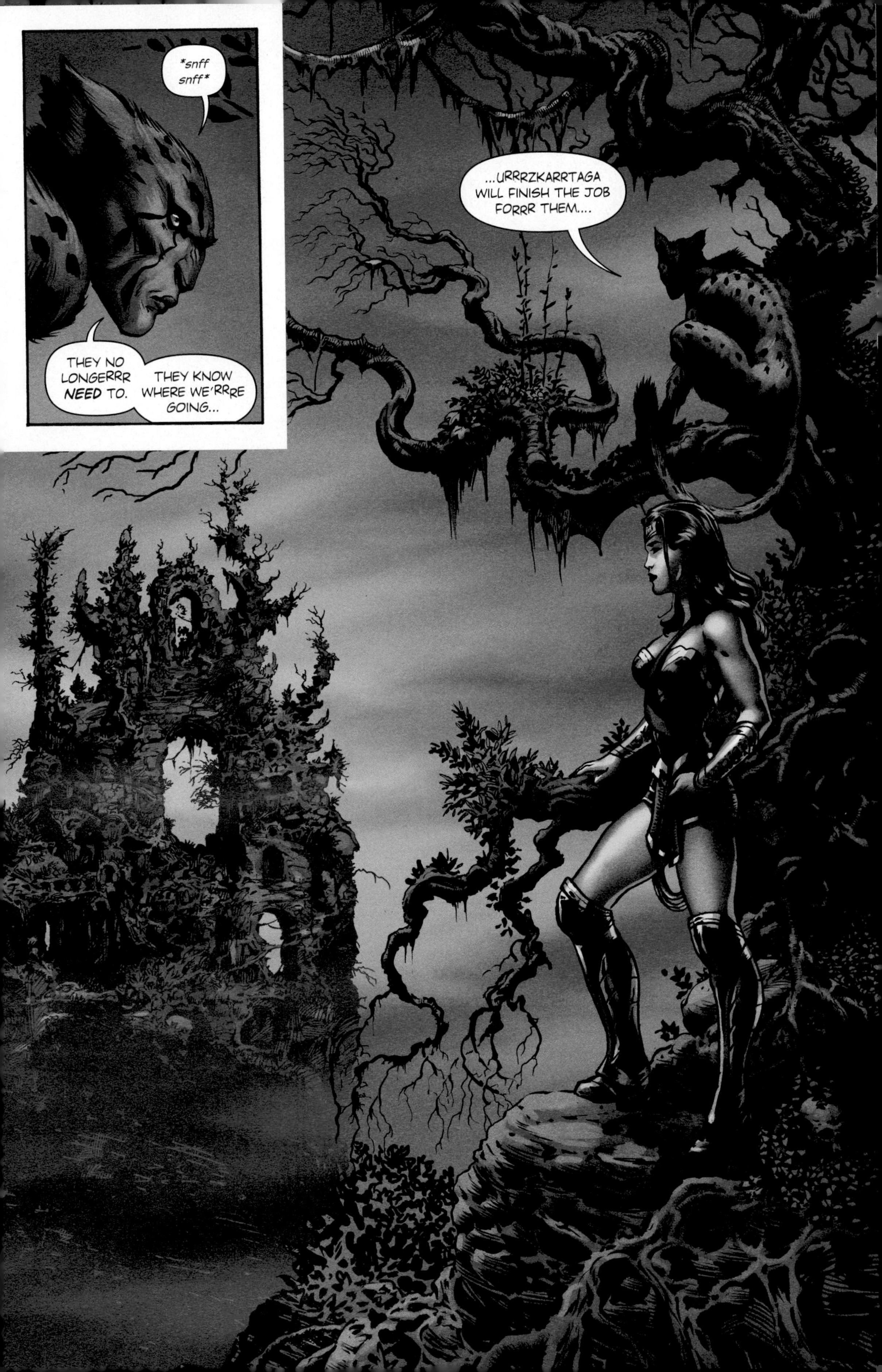
*snff
snff*
THEY NO LONGERRR NEED TO.
THEY KNOW WHERE WE'RRRE GOING...
...URRRZKARRTAGA WILL FINISH THE JOB FORRR THEM....

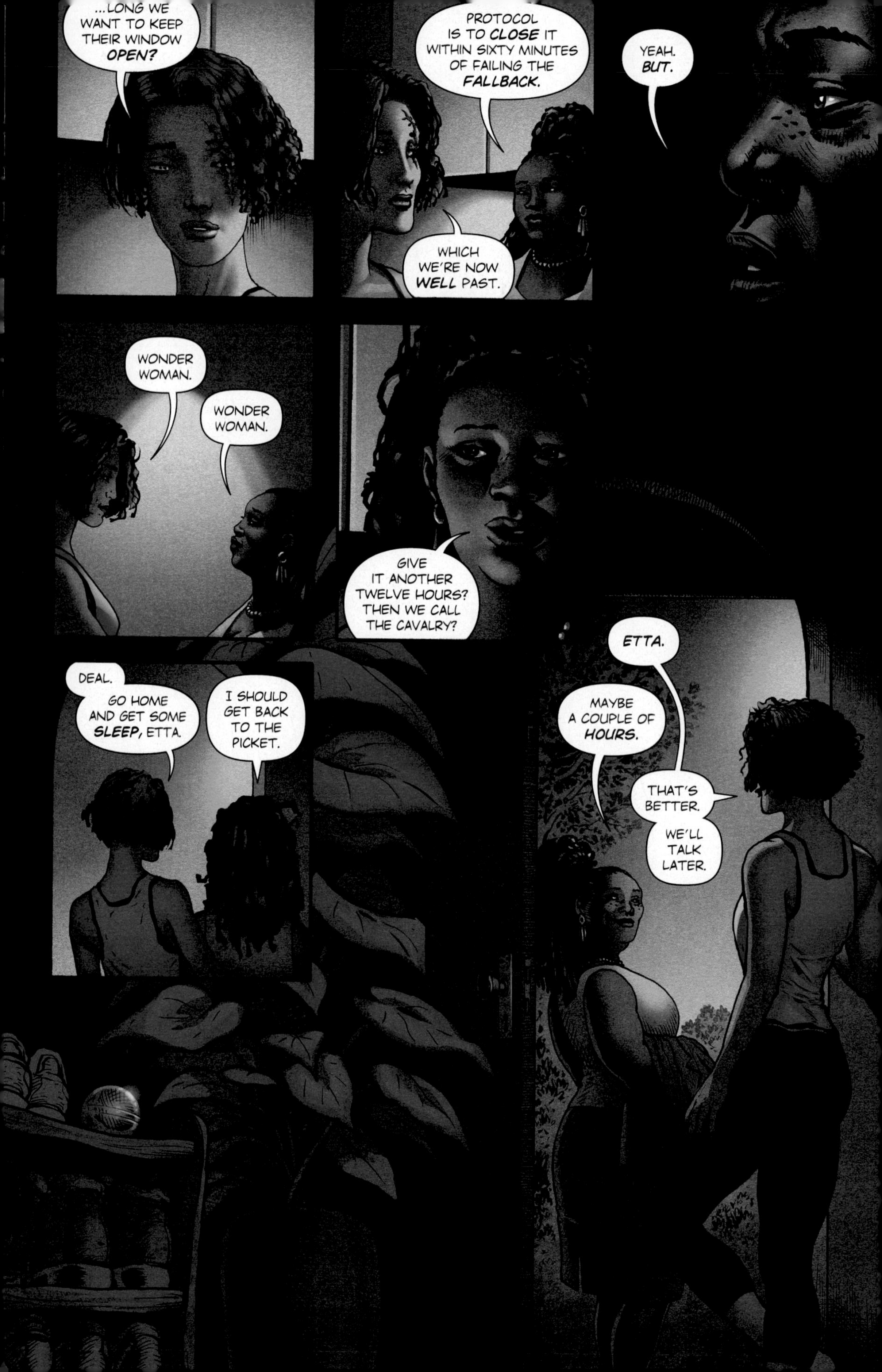
...LONG WE WANT TO KEEP THEIR WINDOW OPEN?
PROTOCOL IS TO CLOSE IT WITHIN SIXTY MINUTES OF FAILING THE FALLBACK.
WHICH WE'RE NOW WELL PAST.
YEAH. BUT.
WONDER WOMAN.
WONDER WOMAN.
GIVE IT ANOTHER TWELVE HOURS? THEN WE CALL THE CAVALRY?
DEAL.
GO HOME AND GET SOME SLEEP, ETTA.
I SHOULD GET BACK TO THE PICKET.
ETTA.
MAYBE A COUPLE OF HOURS.
THAT'S BETTER.
WE'LL TALK LATER.

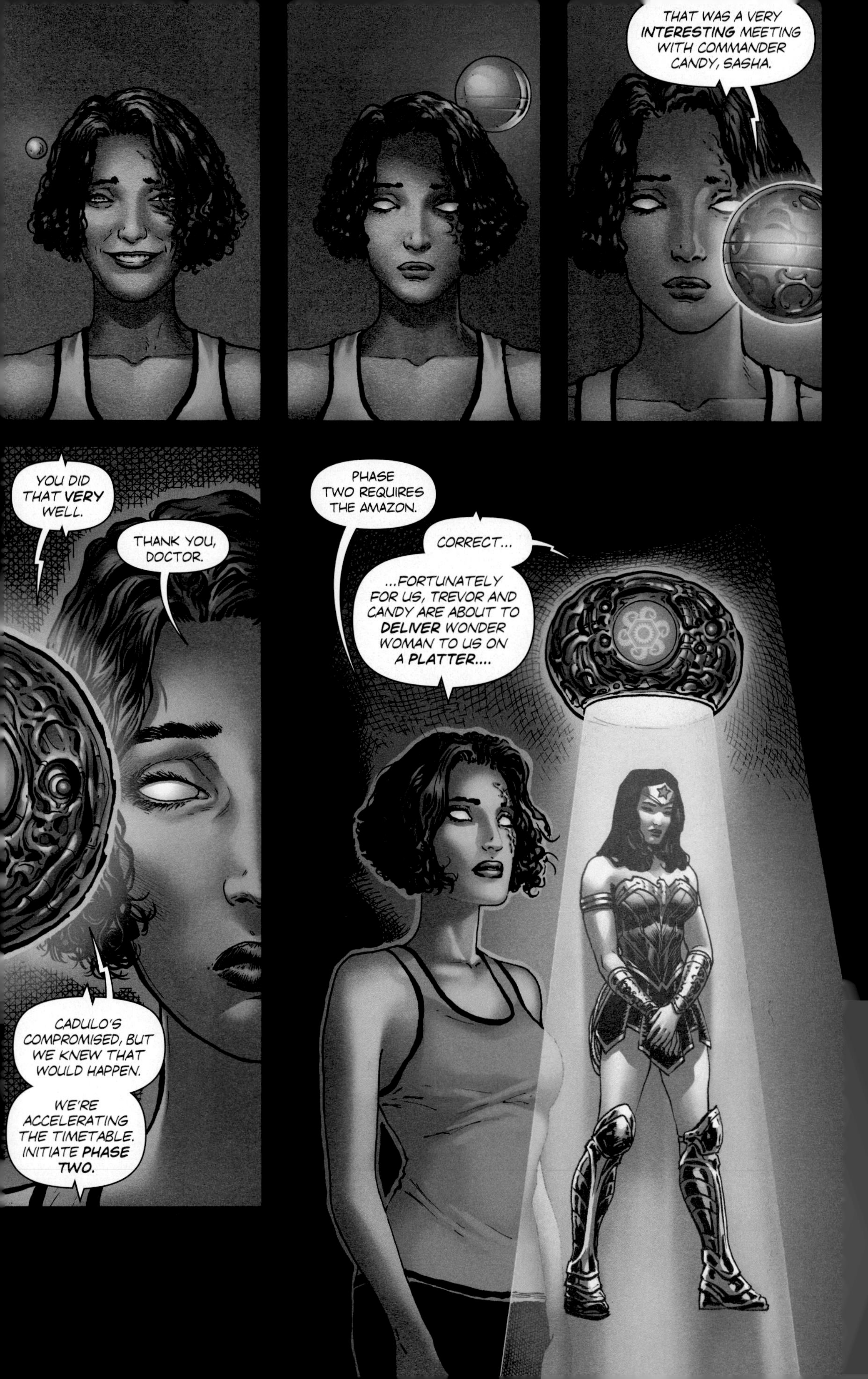
THAT WAS A VERY INTERESTING MEETING WITH COMMANDER CANDY, SASHA.
YOU DID THAT VERY WELL.
THANK YOU, DOCTOR.
CADULO'S COMPROMISED, BUT WE KNEW THAT WOULD HAPPEN.
WE'RE ACCELERATING THE TIMETABLE. INITIATE PHASE TWO.
PHASE TWO REQUIRES THE AMAZON.
CORRECT...
...FORTUNATELY FOR US, TREVOR AND CANDY ARE ABOUT TO DELIVER WONDER WOMAN TO US ON A PLATTER....

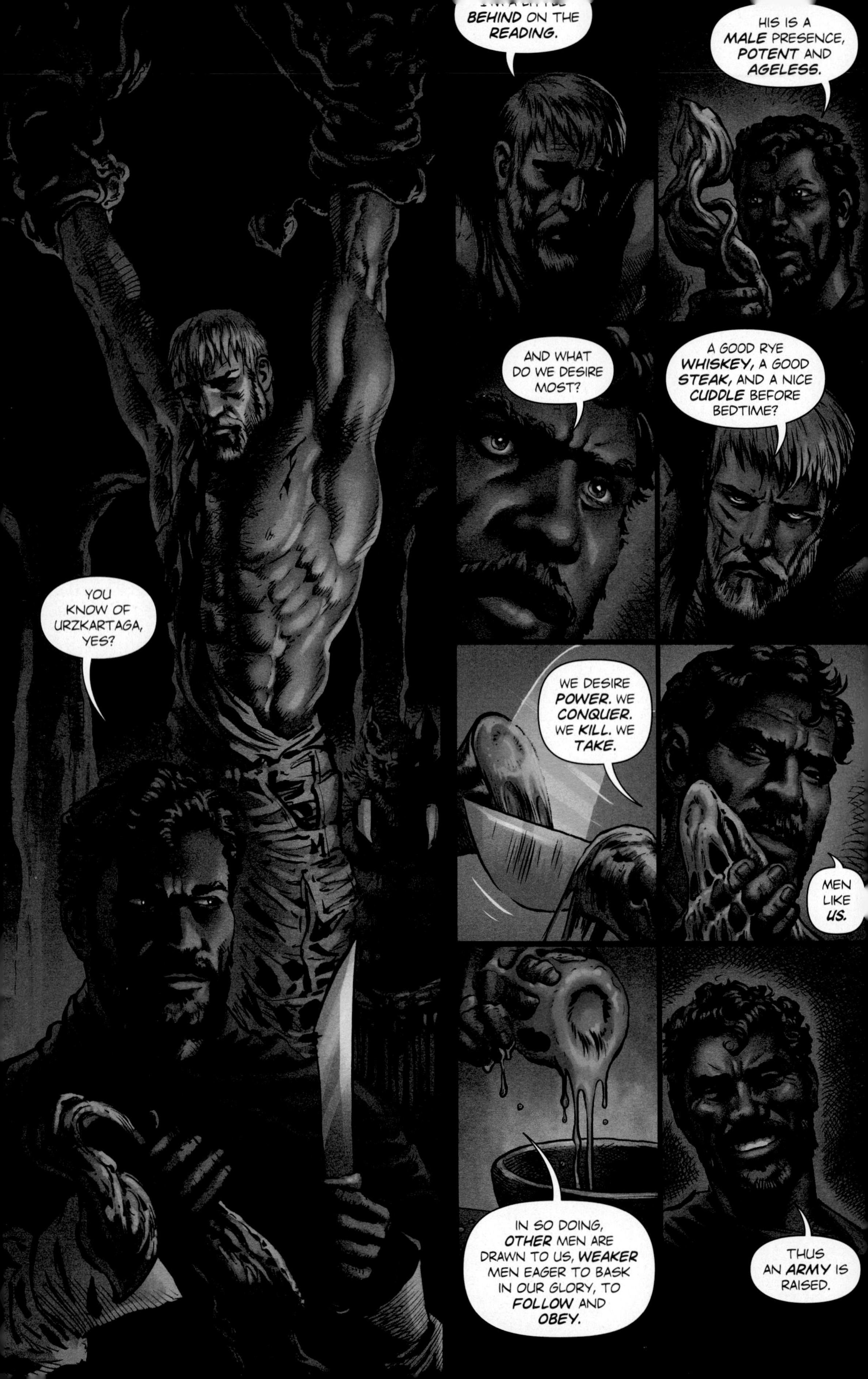
YOU KNOW OF URZKARTAGA, YES?
BEHIND ON THE READING.
HIS IS A MALE PRESENCE, POTENT AND AGELESS.
AND WHAT DO WE DESIRE MOST?
A GOOD RYE WHISKEY, A GOOD STEAK, AND A NICE CUDDLE BEFORE BEDTIME?
WE DESIRE POWER. WE CONQUER. WE KILL. WE TAKE.
MEN LIKE US.
IN SO DOING, OTHER MEN ARE DRAWN TO US, WEAKER MEN EAGER TO BASK IN OUR GLORY, TO FOLLOW AND OBEY.
THUS AN ARMY IS RAISED.

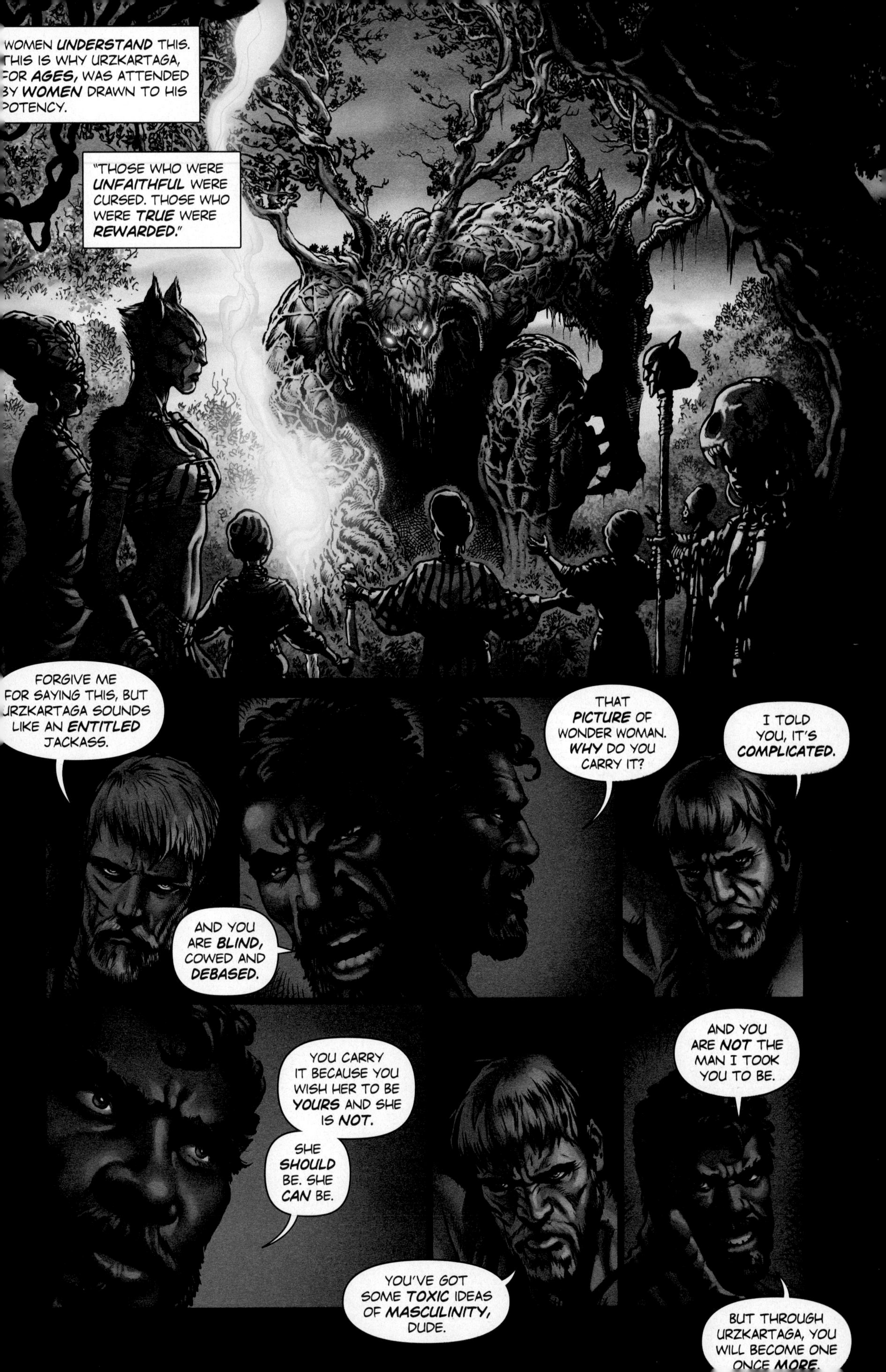
WOMEN UNDERSTAND THIS. THIS IS WHY URZKARTAGA, FOR AGES, WAS ATTENDED BY WOMEN DRAWN TO HIS POTENCY.
"THOSE WHO WERE UNFAITHFUL WERE CURSED. THOSE WHO WERE TRUE WERE REWARDED."
FORGIVE ME FOR SAYING THIS, BUT URZKARTAGA SOUNDS LIKE AN ENTITLED JACKASS.
AND YOU ARE BLIND, COWED AND DEBASED.
THAT PICTURE OF WONDER WOMAN. WHY DO YOU CARRY IT?
I TOLD YOU, IT'S COMPLICATED.
YOU CARRY IT BECAUSE YOU WISH HER TO BE YOURS AND SHE IS NOT.
SHE SHOULD BE. SHE CAN BE.
YOU'VE GOT SOME TOXIC IDEAS OF MASCULINITY, DUDE.
AND YOU ARE NOT THE MAN I TOOK YOU TO BE.
BUT THROUGH URZKARTAGA, YOU WILL BECOME ONE ONCE MORE.

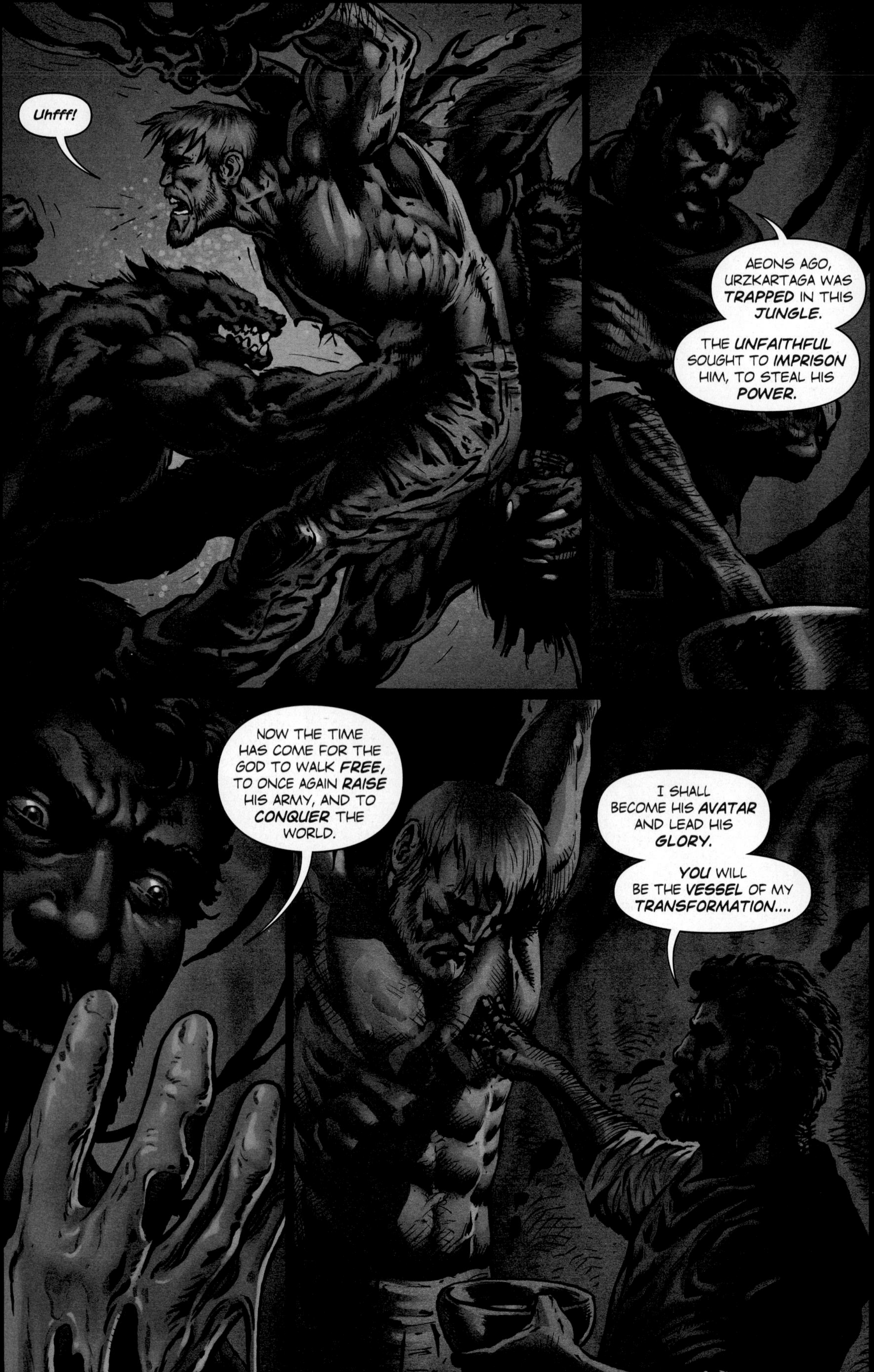
Uhfff!
AEONS AGO, URZKARTAGA WAS TRAPPED IN THIS JUNGLE.
THE UNFAITHFUL SOUGHT TO IMPRISON HIM, TO STEAL HIS POWER.
NOW THE TIME HAS COME FOR THE GOD TO WALK FREE, TO ONCE AGAIN RAISE HIS ARMY, AND TO CONQUER THE WORLD.
I SHALL BECOME HIS AVATAR AND LEAD HIS GLORY.
YOU WILL BE THE VESSEL OF MY TRANSFORMATION....

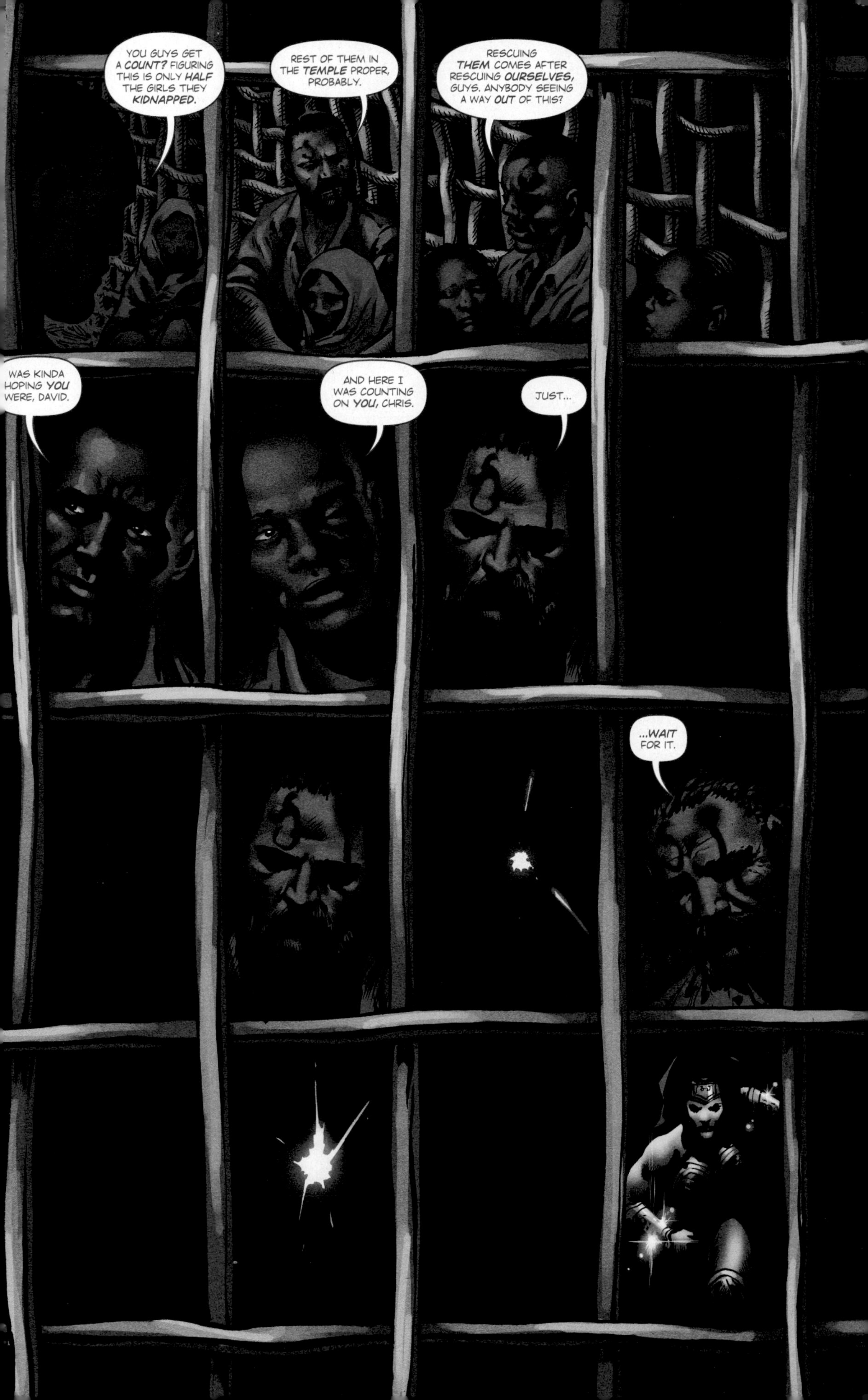
YOU GUYS GET A COUNT? FIGURING THIS IS ONLY HALF THE GIRLS THEY KIDNAPPED.
REST OF THEM IN THE TEMPLE PROPER, PROBABLY.
RESCUING THEM COMES AFTER RESCUING OURSELVES, GUYS. ANYBODY SEEING A WAY OUT OF THIS?
WAS KINDA HOPING YOU WERE, DAVID.
AND HERE I WAS COUNTING ON YOU, CHRIS.
JUST...
...WAIT FOR IT.

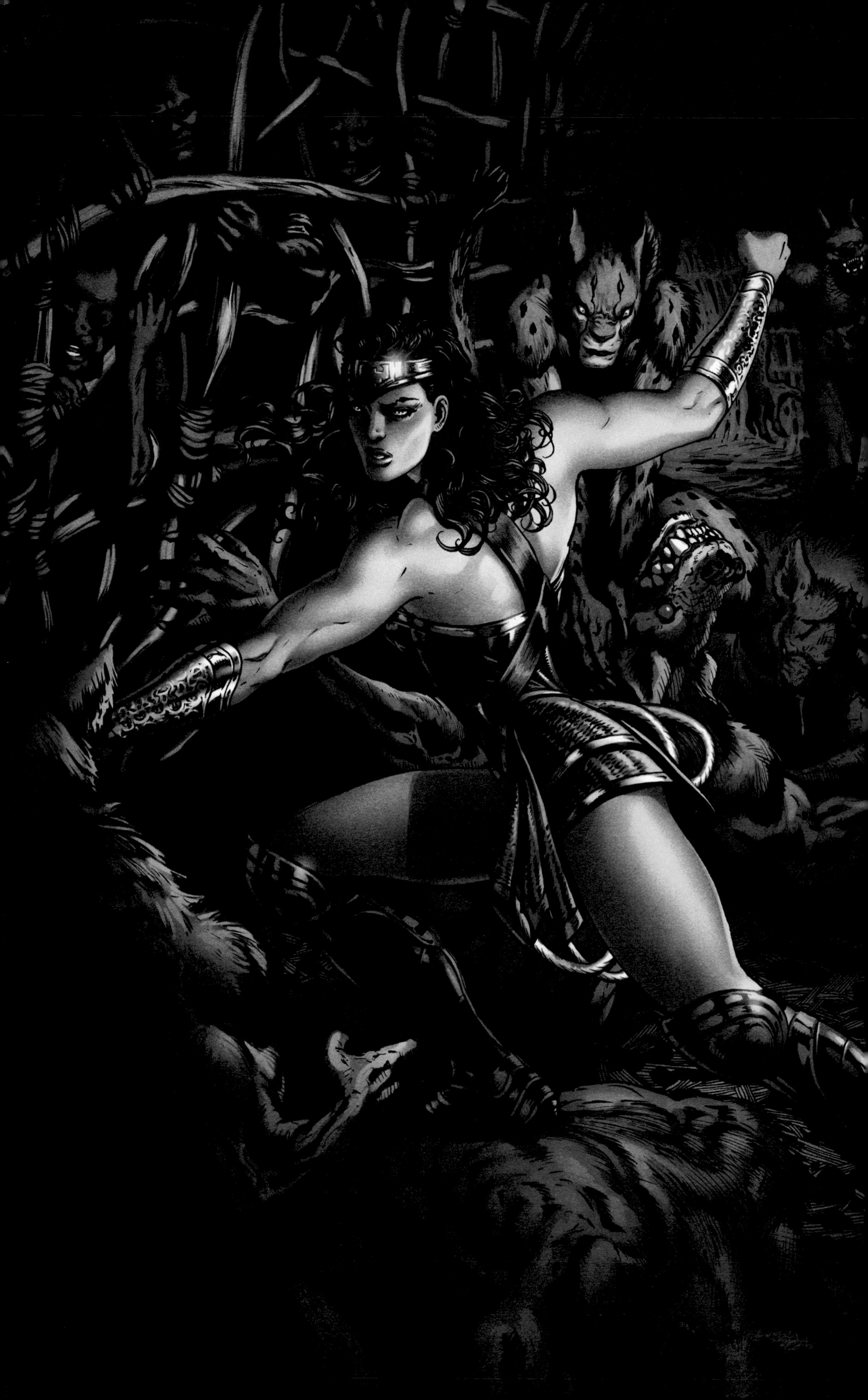

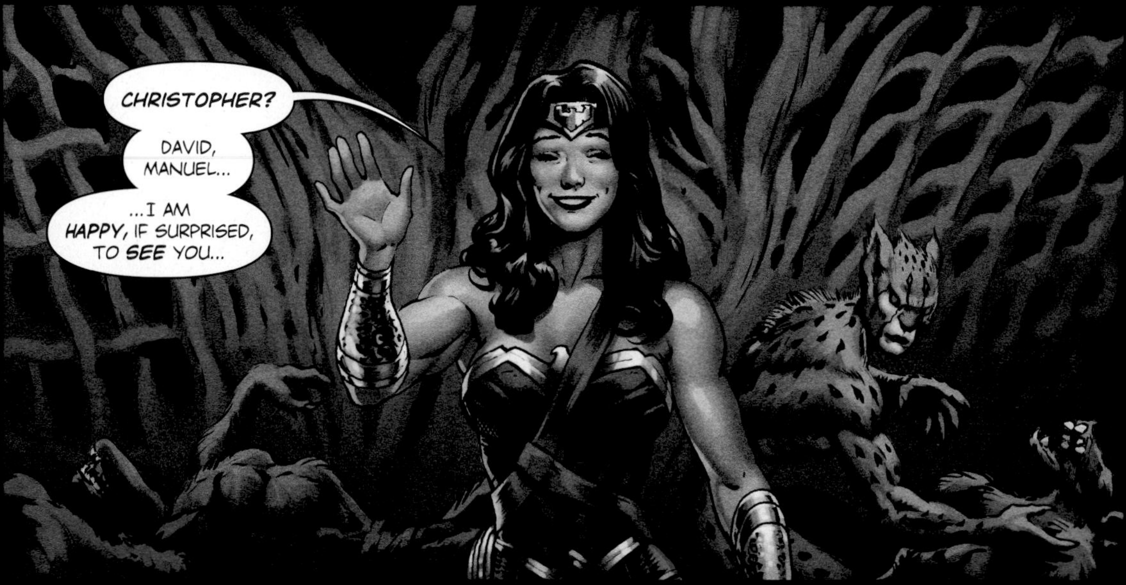
CHRISTOPHER?
DAVID, MANUEL...
...I AM HAPPY, IF SURPRISED, TO SEE YOU...

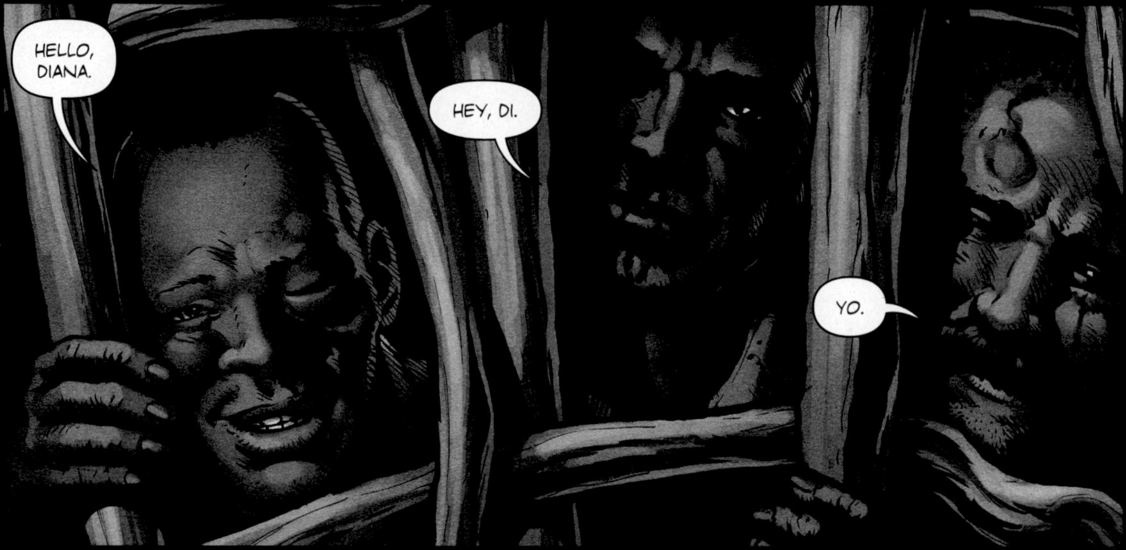
HELLO, DIANA.
HEY, DI.
YO.

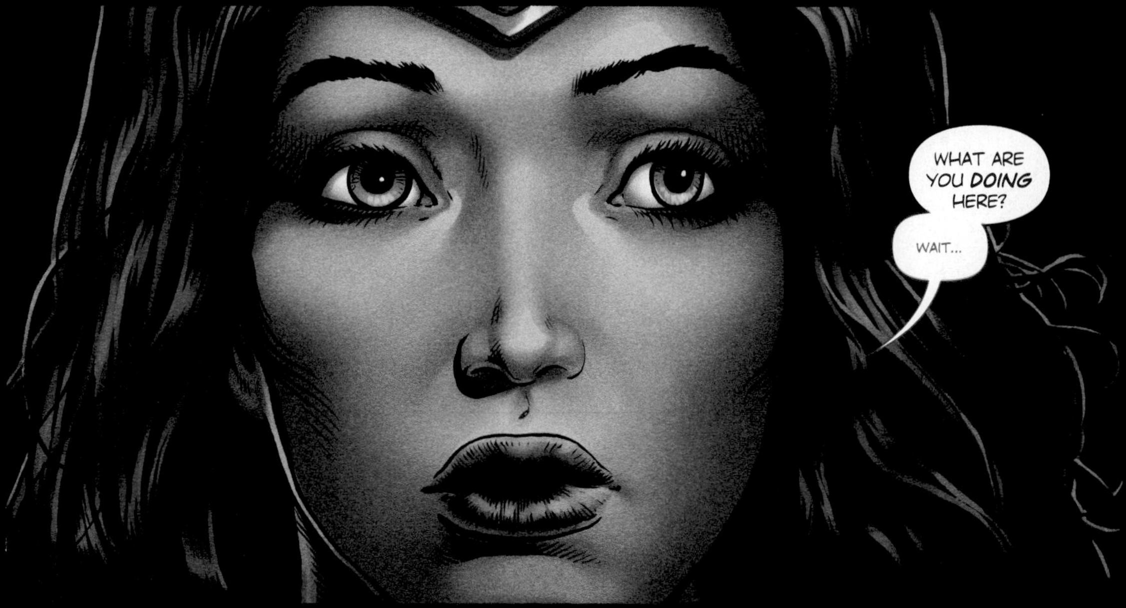
WHAT ARE YOU DOING HERE?
WAIT...

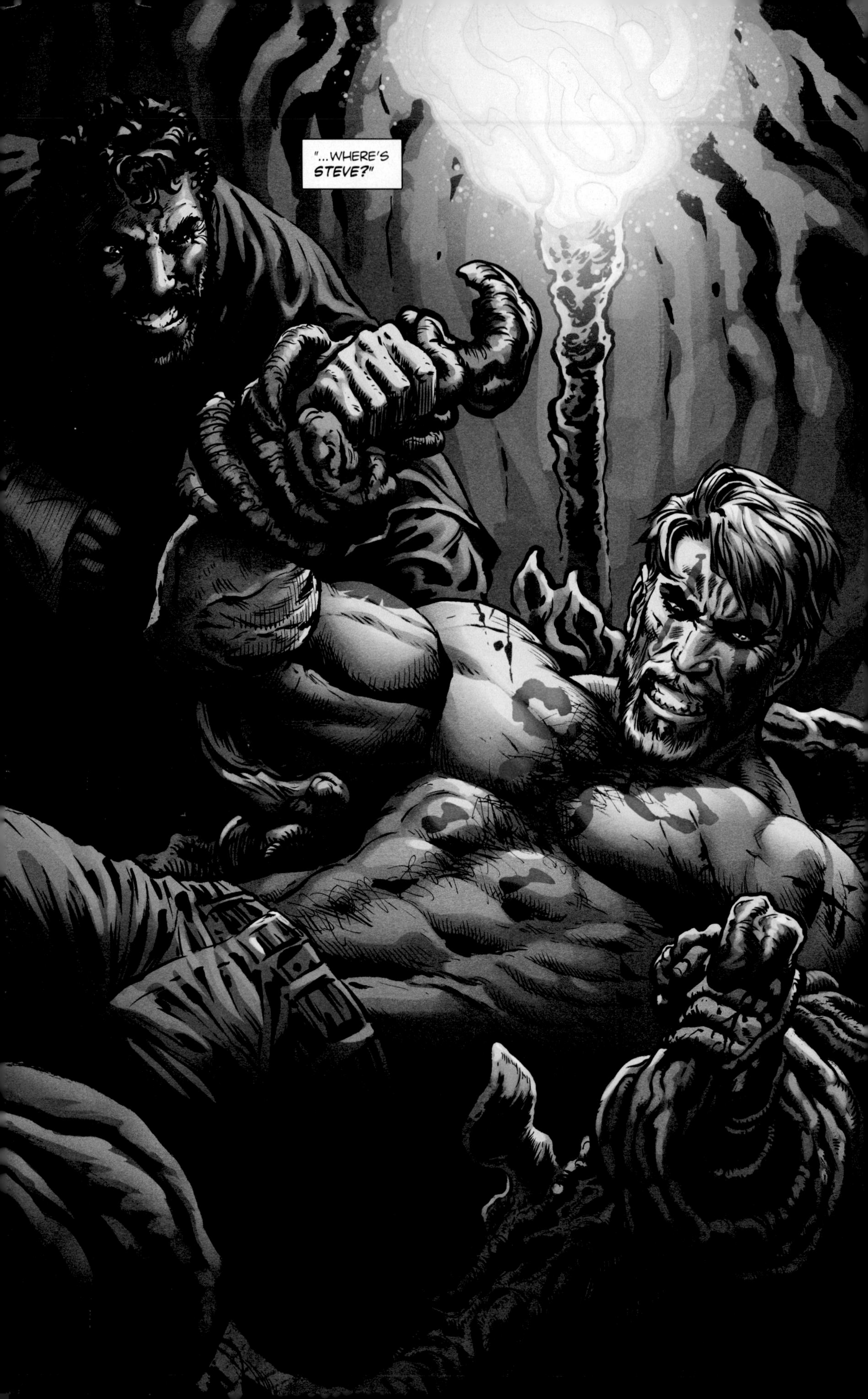
"...WHERE'S STEVE?"

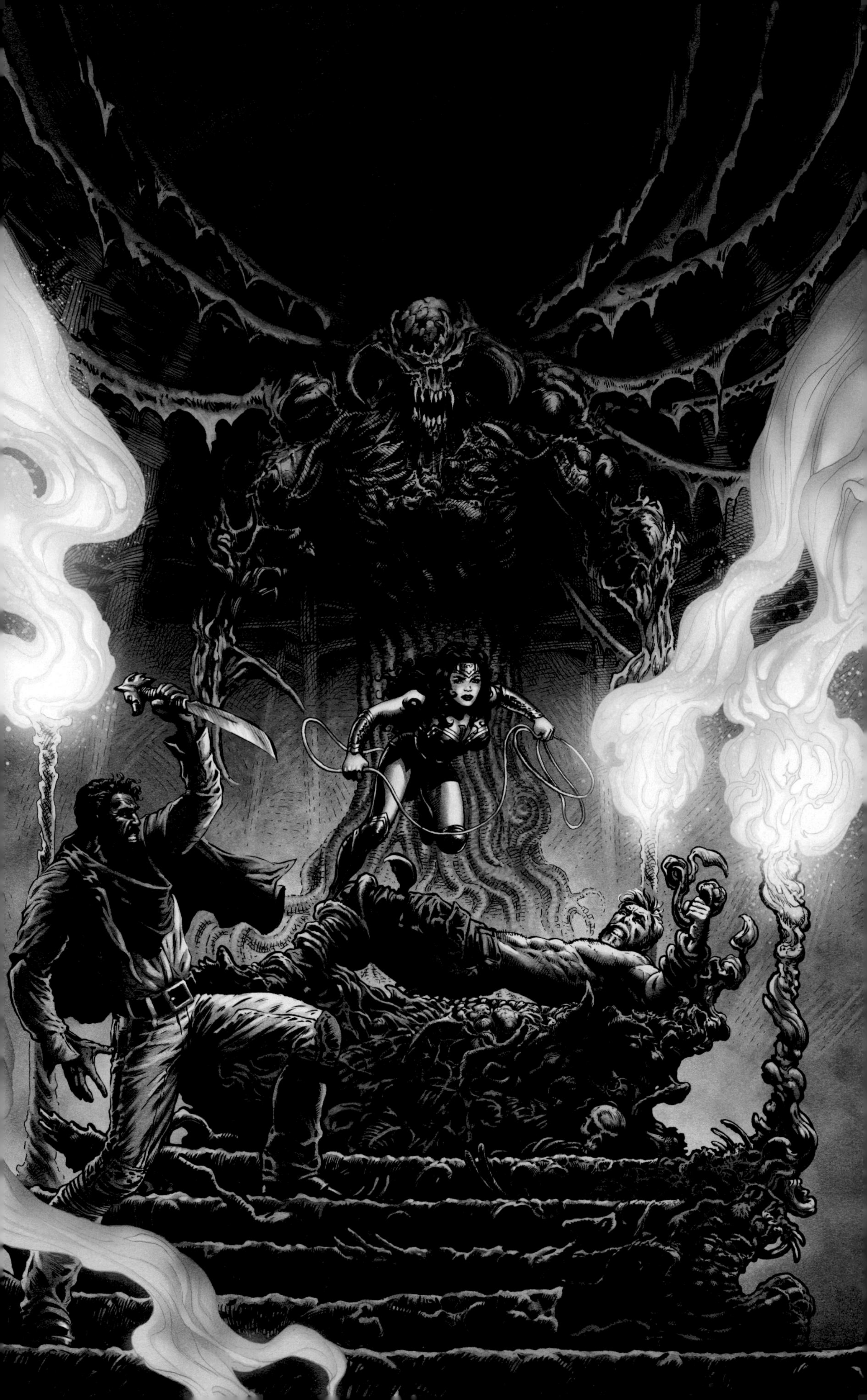

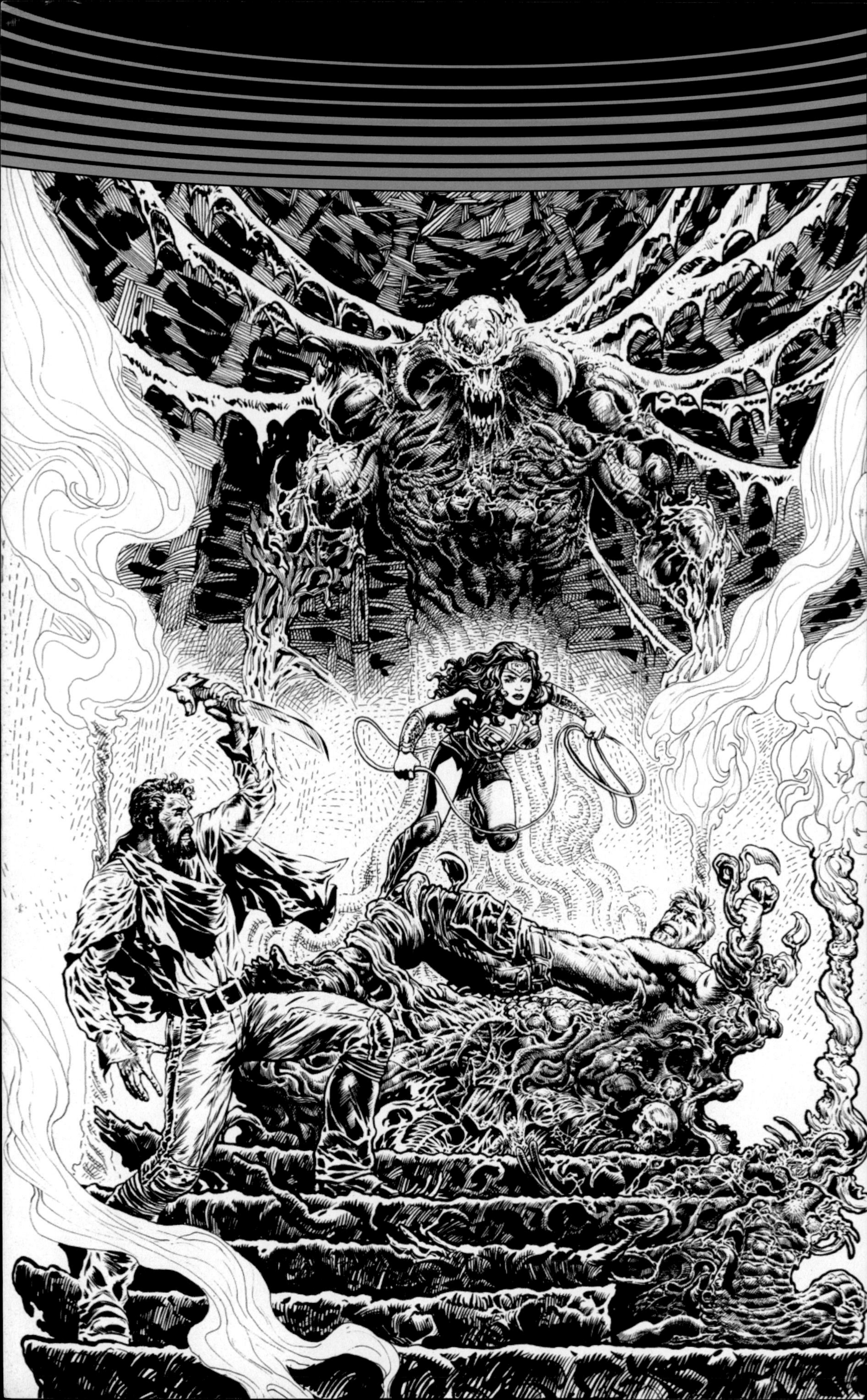

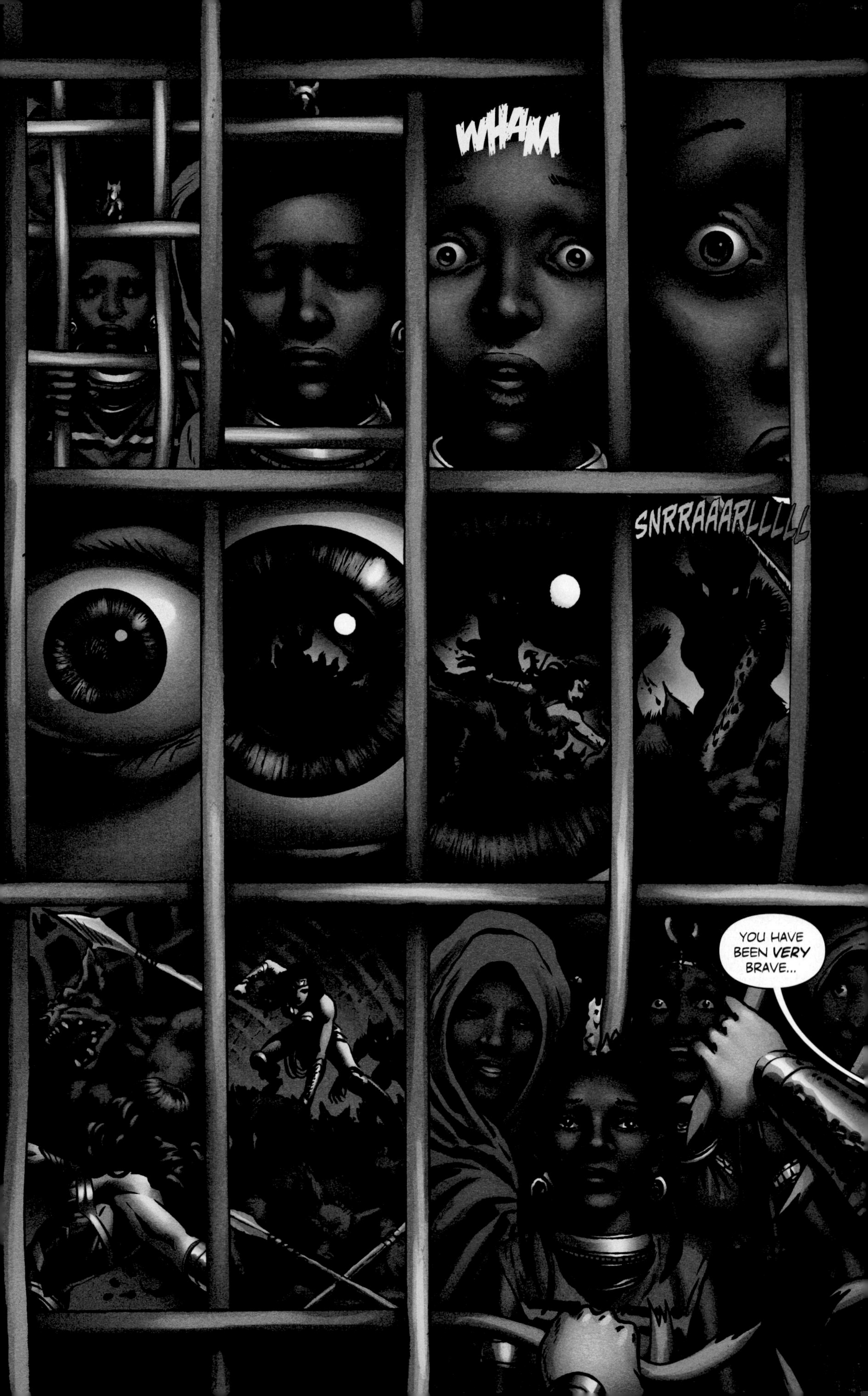
WHAM
SNRRAAARLLLLL
YOU HAVE BEEN VERY BRAVE...

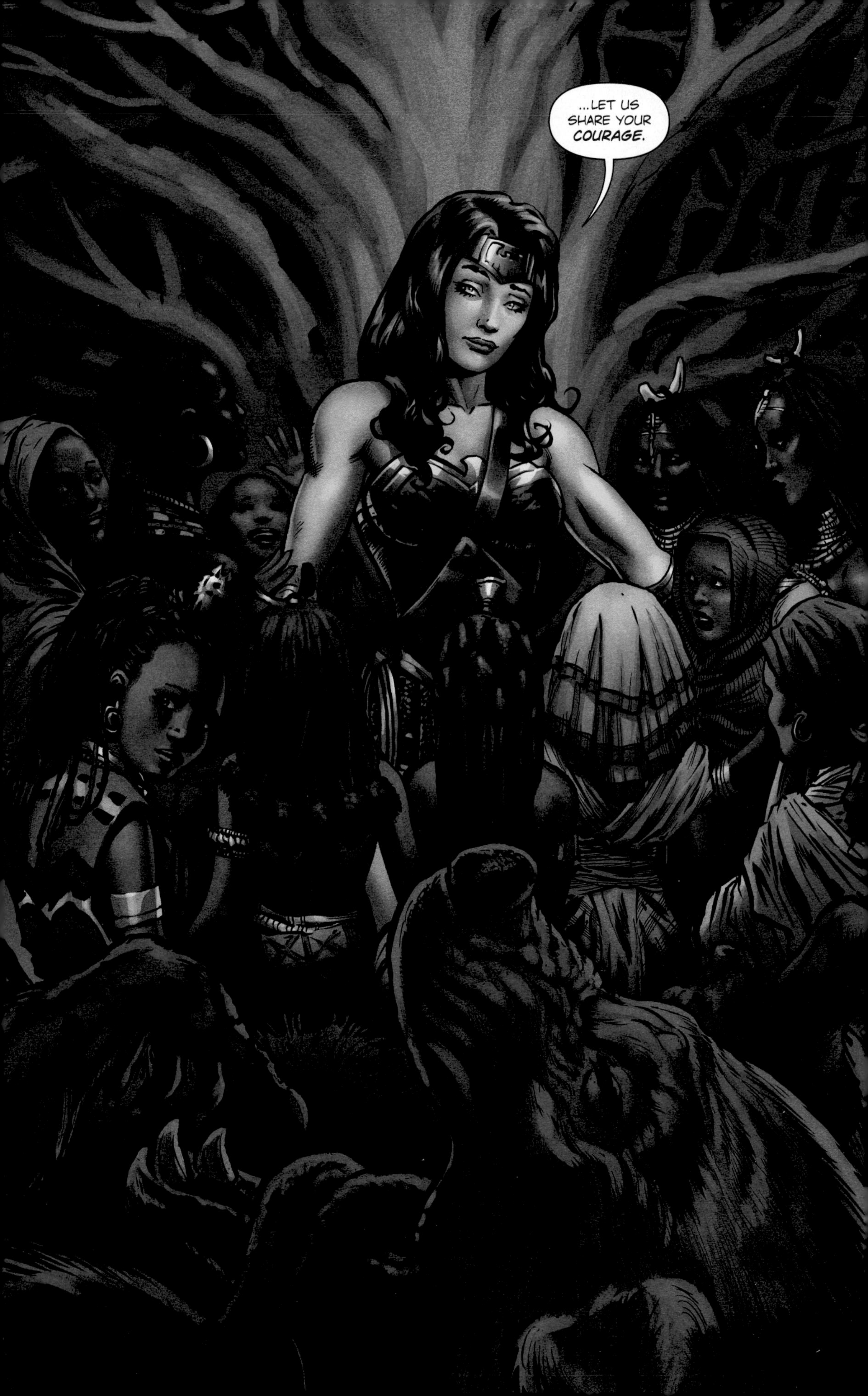
...LET US SHARE YOUR COURAGE.

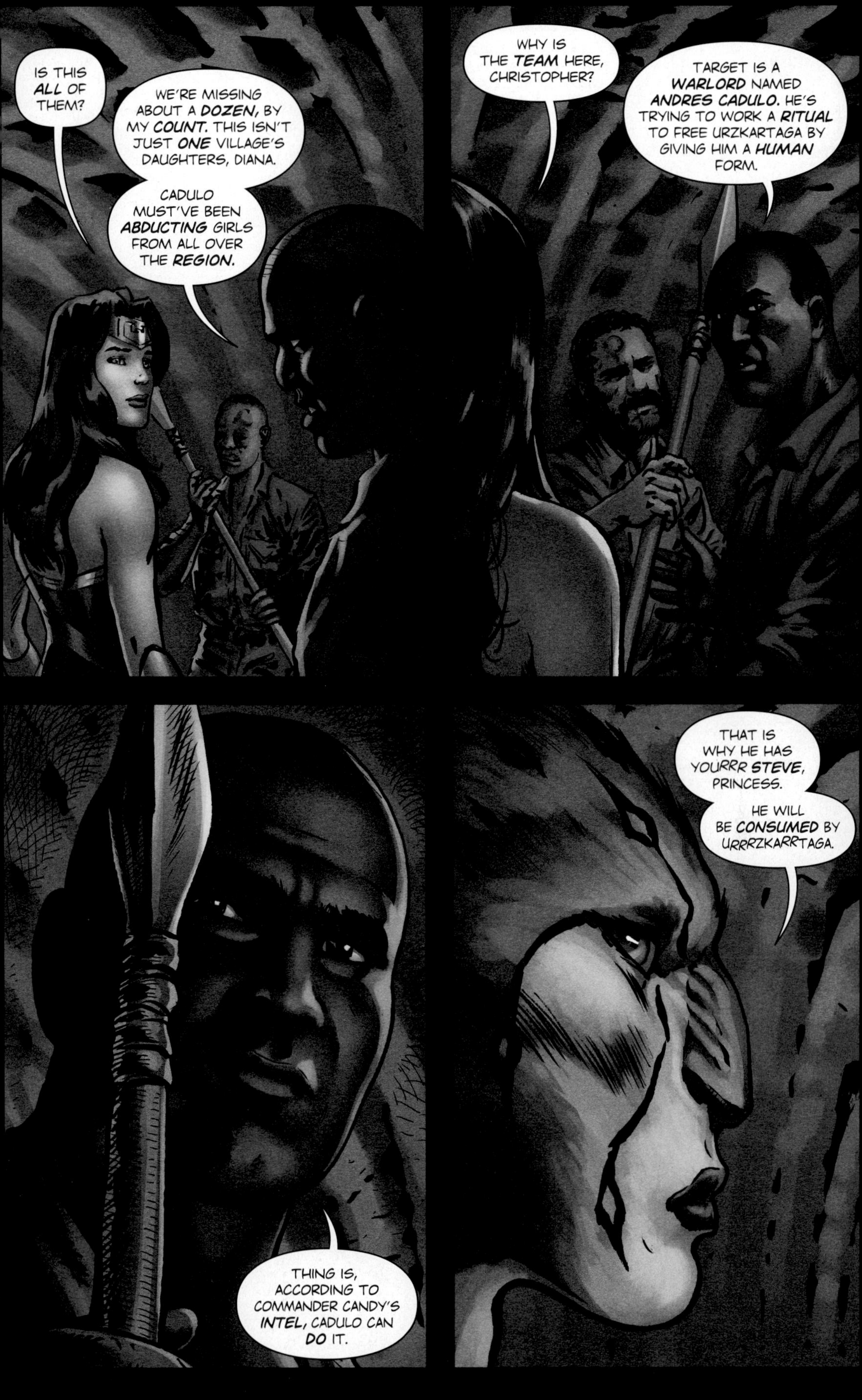
IS THIS ALL OF THEM?
WE'RE MISSING ABOUT A DOZEN, BY MY COUNT. THIS ISN'T JUST ONE VILLAGE'S DAUGHTERS, DIANA.
CADULO MUST'VE BEEN ABDUCTING GIRLS FROM ALL OVER THE REGION.
WHY IS THE TEAM HERE, CHRISTOPHER?
TARGET IS A WARLORD NAMED ANDRES CADULO. HE'S TRYING TO WORK A RITUAL TO FREE URZKARTAGA BY GIVING HIM A HUMAN FORM.
THING IS, ACCORDING TO COMMANDER CANDY'S INTEL, CADULO CAN DO IT.
THAT IS WHY HE HAS YOURRR STEVE, PRINCESS.
HE WILL BE CONSUMED BY URRRZKARRTAGA.

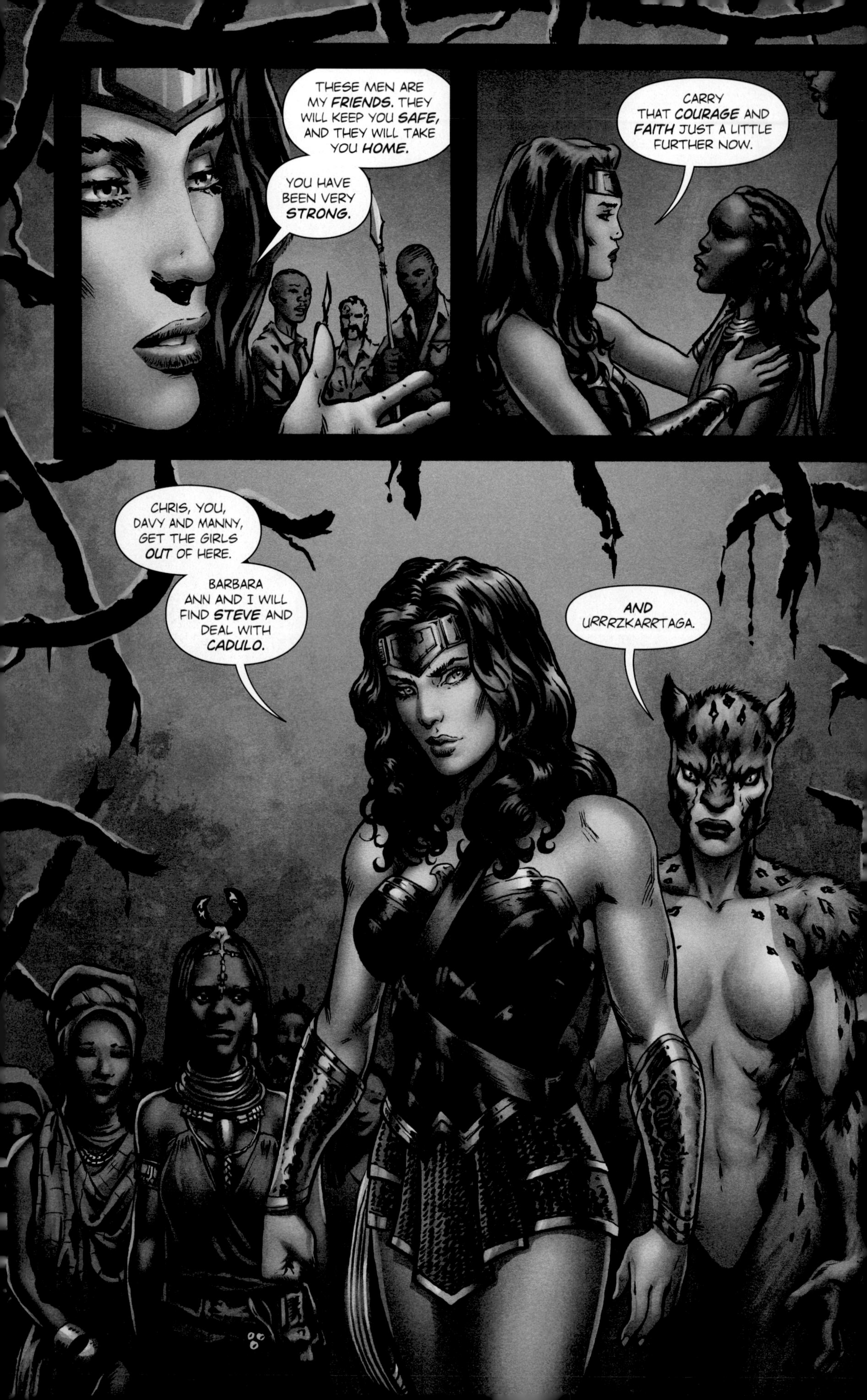
THESE MEN ARE MY FRIENDS. THEY WILL KEEP YOU SAFE, AND THEY WILL TAKE YOU HOME.
YOU HAVE BEEN VERY STRONG.
CARRY THAT COURAGE AND FAITH JUST A LITTLE FURTHER NOW.
CHRIS, YOU, DAVY AND MANNY, GET THE GIRLS OUT OF HERE.
BARBARA ANN AND I WILL FIND STEVE AND DEAL WITH CADULO.
AND URRRZKARRTAGA.

...YOU SURE YOU WANT THE *CHEETAH* WATCHING YOUR *BACK?*

I GOTTA *ASK,* DIANA...

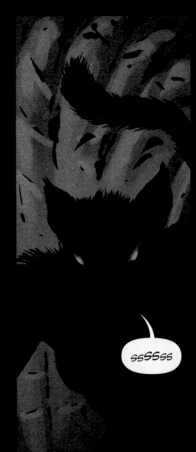

sssSsss

YOURRR *PRRRINCESS* HAS PROMISED TO FREE ME FROM MY *CURRRSE.*

BUT *UNTIL* THEN MY *HUNGERRR* FOR FLESH *BURRNS* ME...

...SO *WATCH* YOURRR *TONGUE.*

GET THE GIRLS TO *SAFETY.*

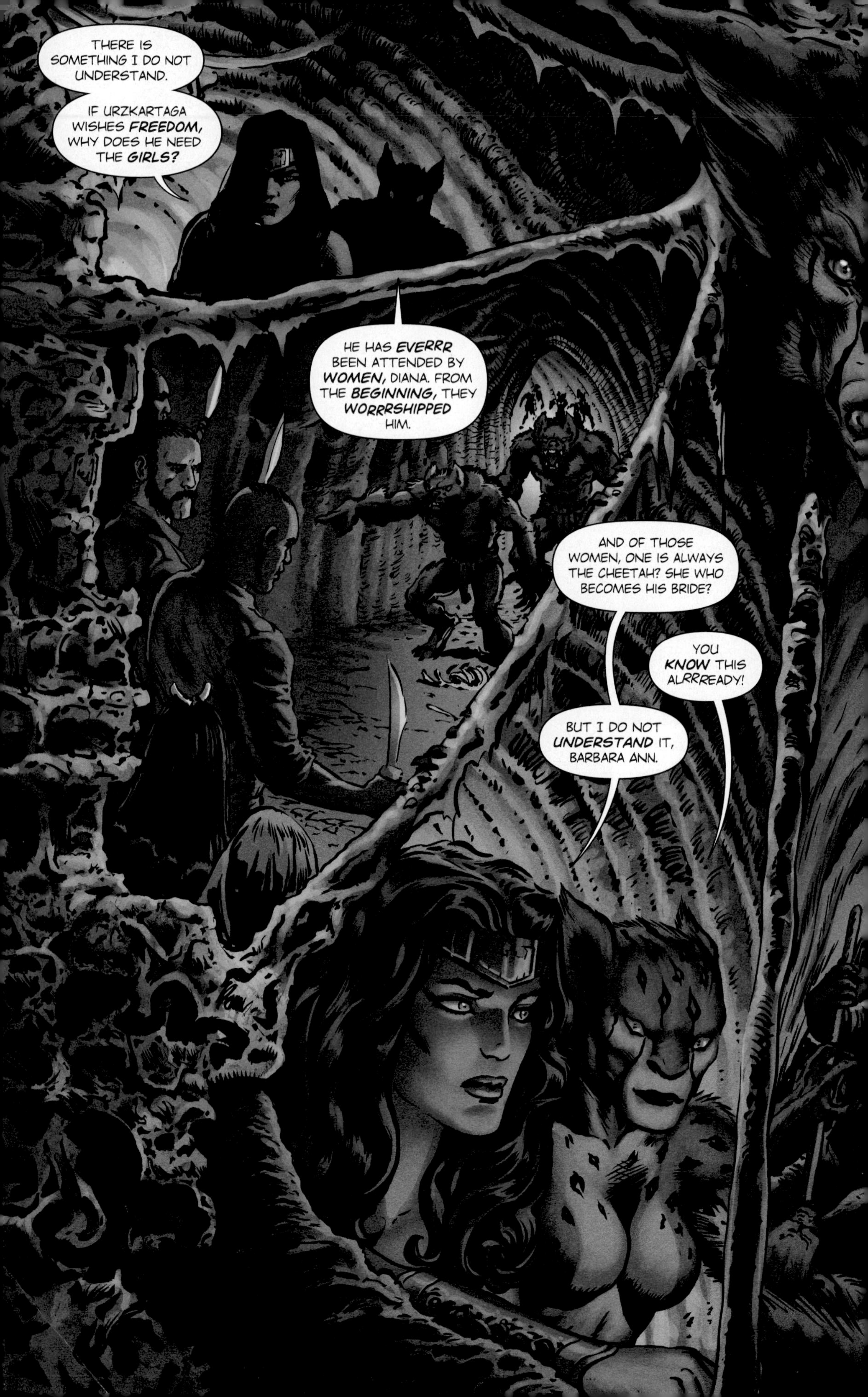
THERE IS SOMETHING I DO NOT UNDERSTAND.
IF URZKARTAGA WISHES **FREEDOM,** WHY DOES HE NEED THE **GIRLS?**
HE HAS **EVERRR** BEEN ATTENDED BY **WOMEN,** DIANA. FROM THE **BEGINNING,** THEY **WORRRSHIPPED** HIM.
AND OF THOSE WOMEN, ONE IS ALWAYS THE CHEETAH? SHE WHO BECOMES HIS BRIDE?
YOU **KNOW** THIS ALRRREADY!
BUT I DO NOT **UNDERSTAND** IT, BARBARA ANN.

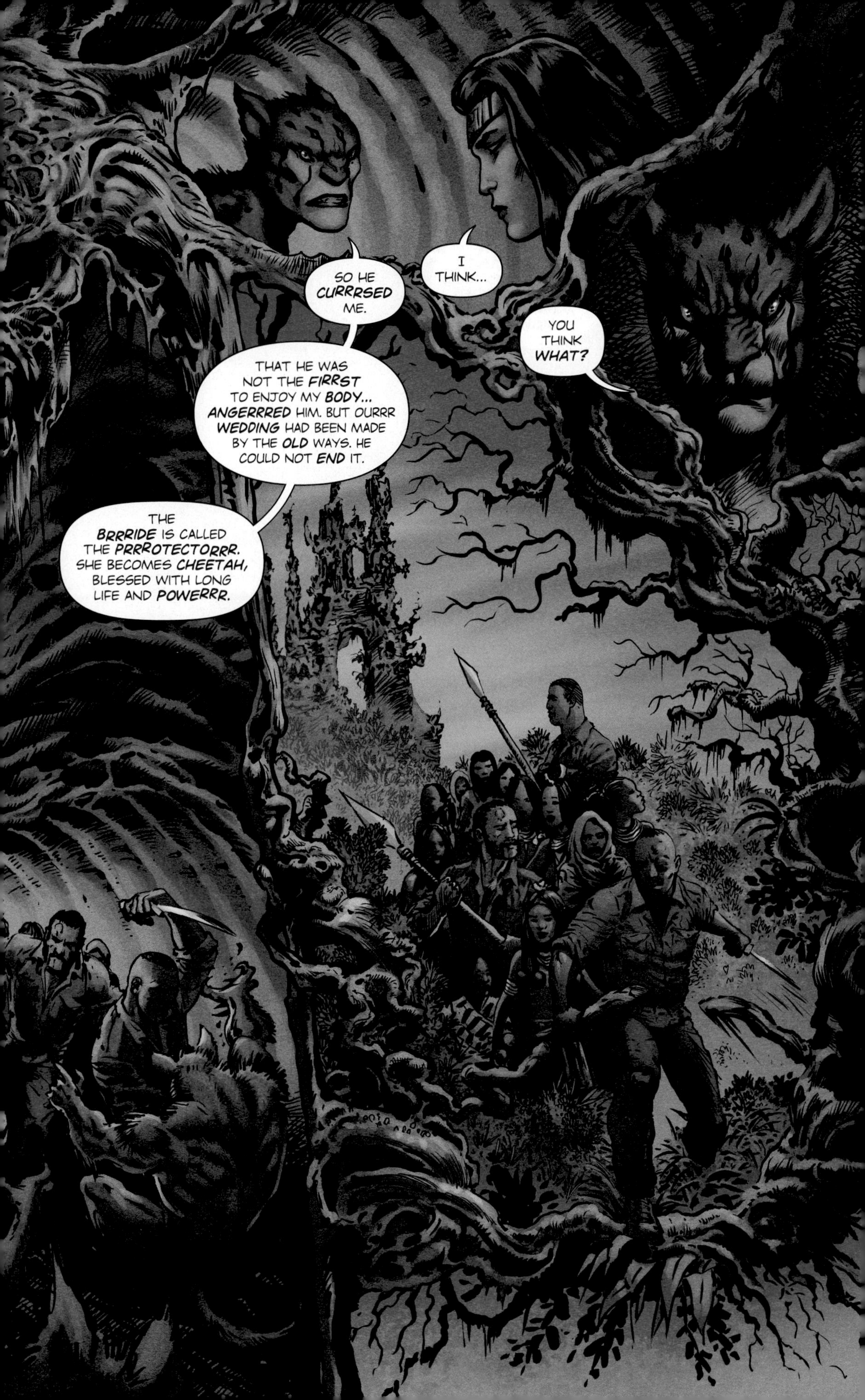
SO HE CURRRSED ME.
I THINK...
YOU THINK WHAT?
THAT HE WAS NOT THE FIRRST TO ENJOY MY BODY... ANGERRRED HIM. BUT OURRR WEDDING HAD BEEN MADE BY THE OLD WAYS. HE COULD NOT END IT.
THE BRRRIDE IS CALLED THE PRRROTECTORRR. SHE BECOMES CHEETAH, BLESSED WITH LONG LIFE AND POWERRR.

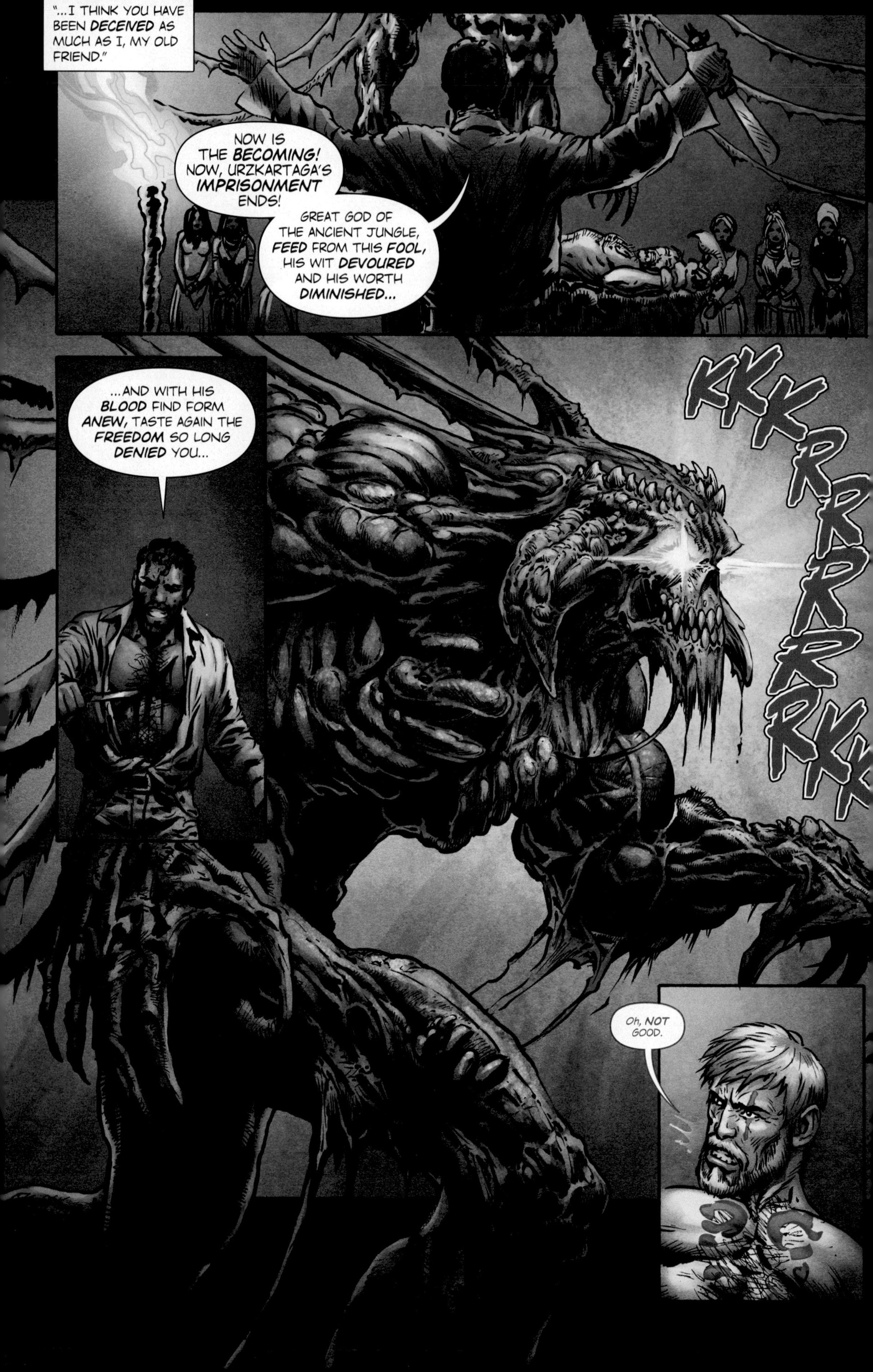

"...I THINK YOU HAVE BEEN DECEIVED AS MUCH AS I, MY OLD FRIEND."
NOW IS THE BECOMING! NOW, URZKARTAGA'S IMPRISONMENT ENDS!
GREAT GOD OF THE ANCIENT JUNGLE, FEED FROM THIS FOOL, HIS WIT DEVOURED AND HIS WORTH DIMINISHED...
...AND WITH HIS BLOOD FIND FORM ANEW, TASTE AGAIN THE FREEDOM SO LONG DENIED YOU...
KKKRRRRRRKK
Oh, NOT GOOD.

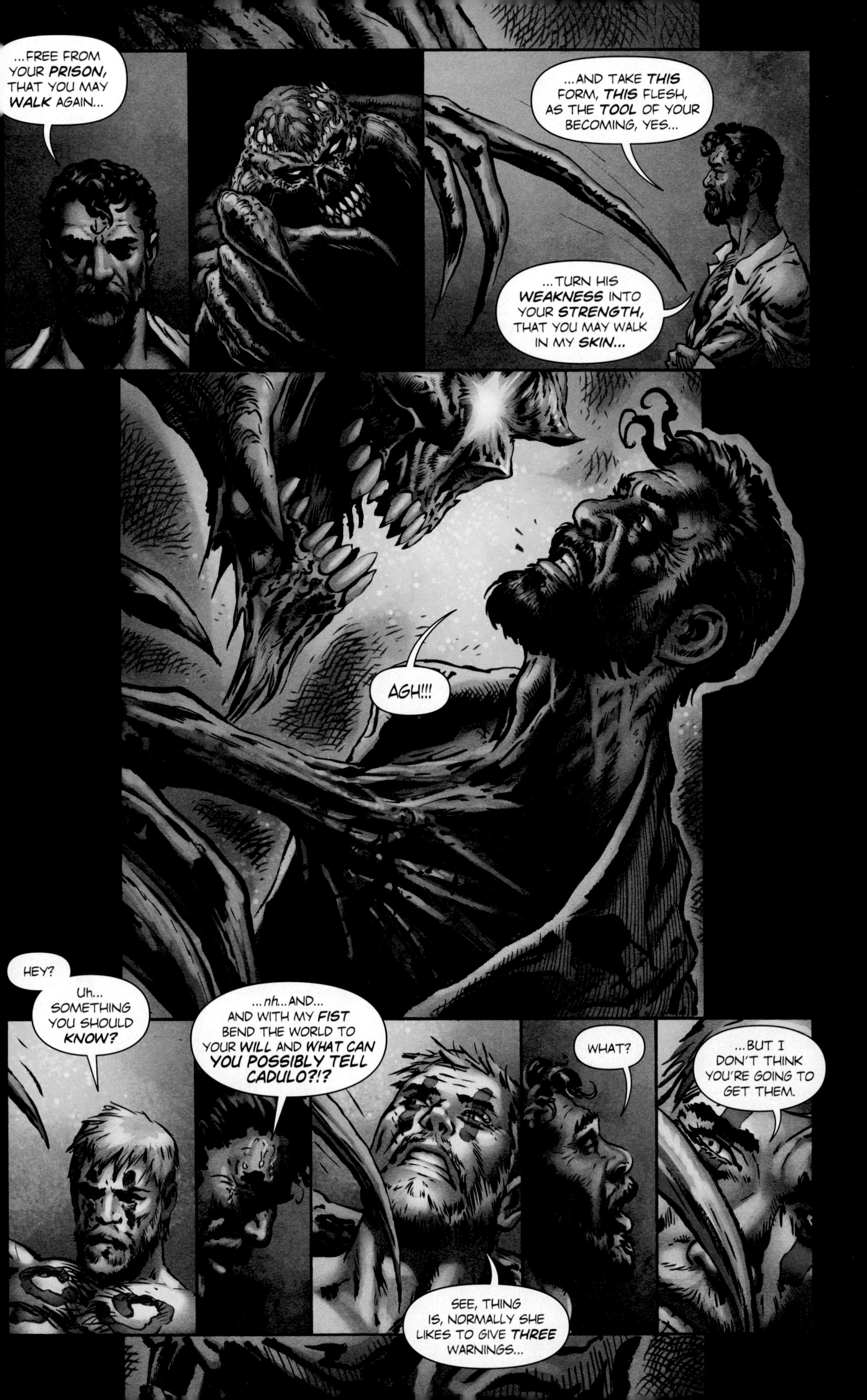
...FREE FROM YOUR PRISON, THAT YOU MAY WALK AGAIN...
...AND TAKE THIS FORM, THIS FLESH, AS THE TOOL OF YOUR BECOMING, YES...
...TURN HIS WEAKNESS INTO YOUR STRENGTH, THAT YOU MAY WALK IN MY SKIN...
AGH!!!
HEY?
Uh... SOMETHING YOU SHOULD KNOW?
...nh...AND... AND WITH MY FIST BEND THE WORLD TO YOUR WILL AND WHAT CAN YOU POSSIBLY TELL CADULO?!?
SEE, THING IS, NORMALLY SHE LIKES TO GIVE THREE WARNINGS...
WHAT?
...BUT I DON'T THINK YOU'RE GOING TO GET THEM.

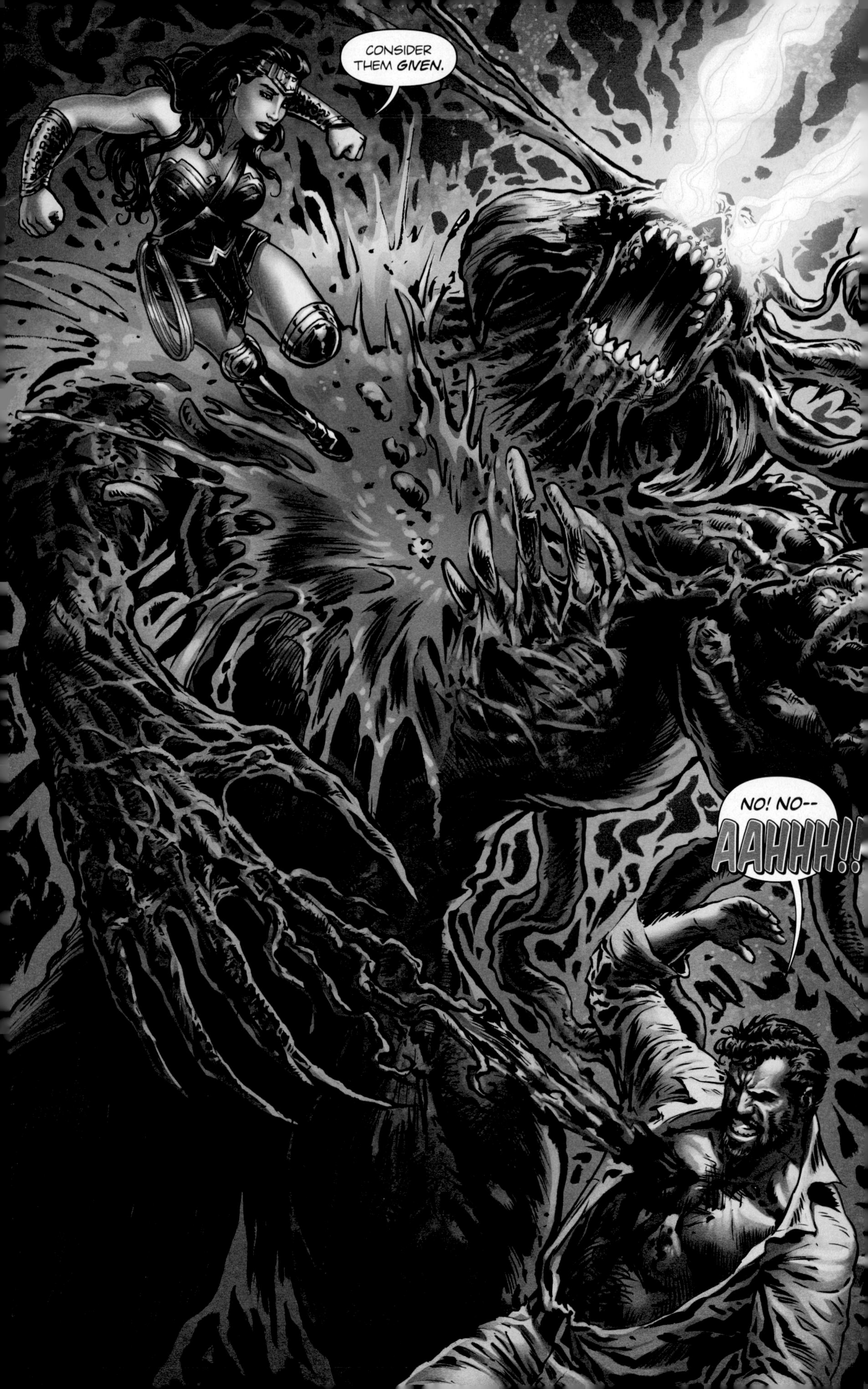
CONSIDER THEM GIVEN.
NO! NO--
AAHHH!!

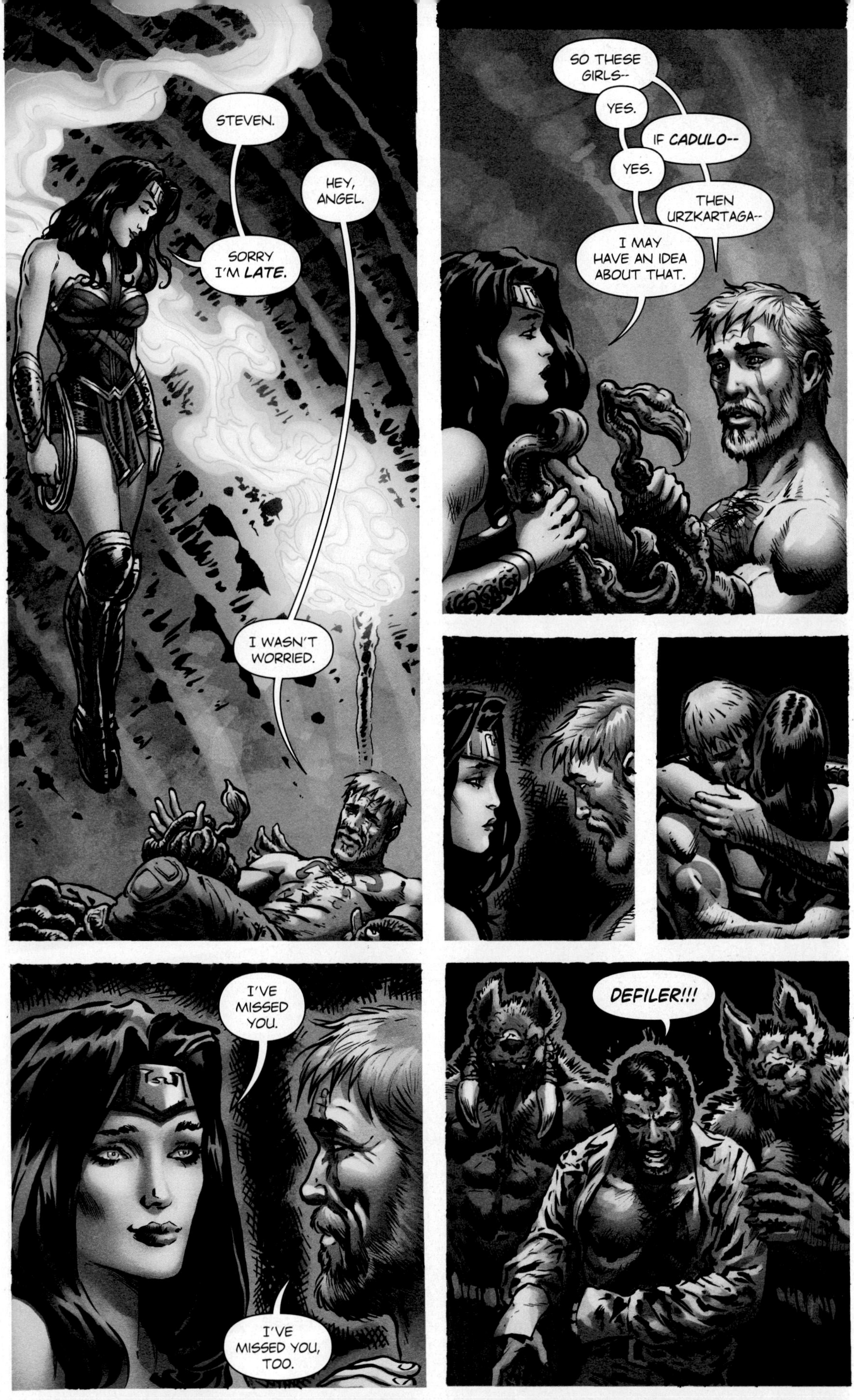
STEVEN.
SORRY I'M LATE.
HEY, ANGEL.
I WASN'T WORRIED.
SO THESE GIRLS--
YES.
IF CADULO--
YES.
THEN URZKARTAGA--
I MAY HAVE AN IDEA ABOUT THAT.
I'VE MISSED YOU.
I'VE MISSED YOU, TOO.
DEFILER!!!

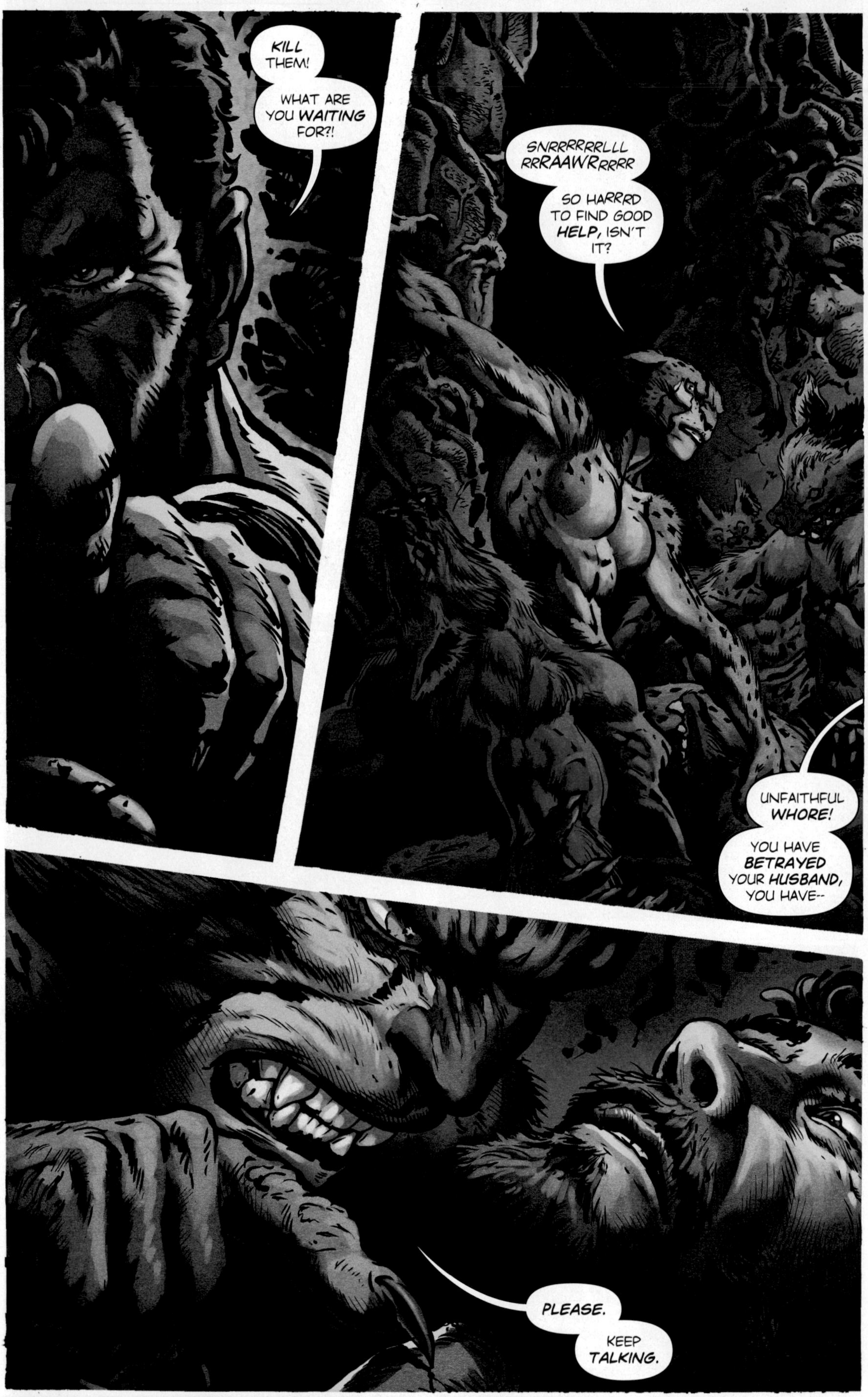
KILL THEM!
WHAT ARE YOU WAITING FOR?!
SNRRRRRRLLL RRRAAWRRRRR
SO HARRRD TO FIND GOOD HELP, ISN'T IT?
UNFAITHFUL WHORE!
YOU HAVE BETRAYED YOUR HUSBAND, YOU HAVE--
PLEASE.
KEEP TALKING.

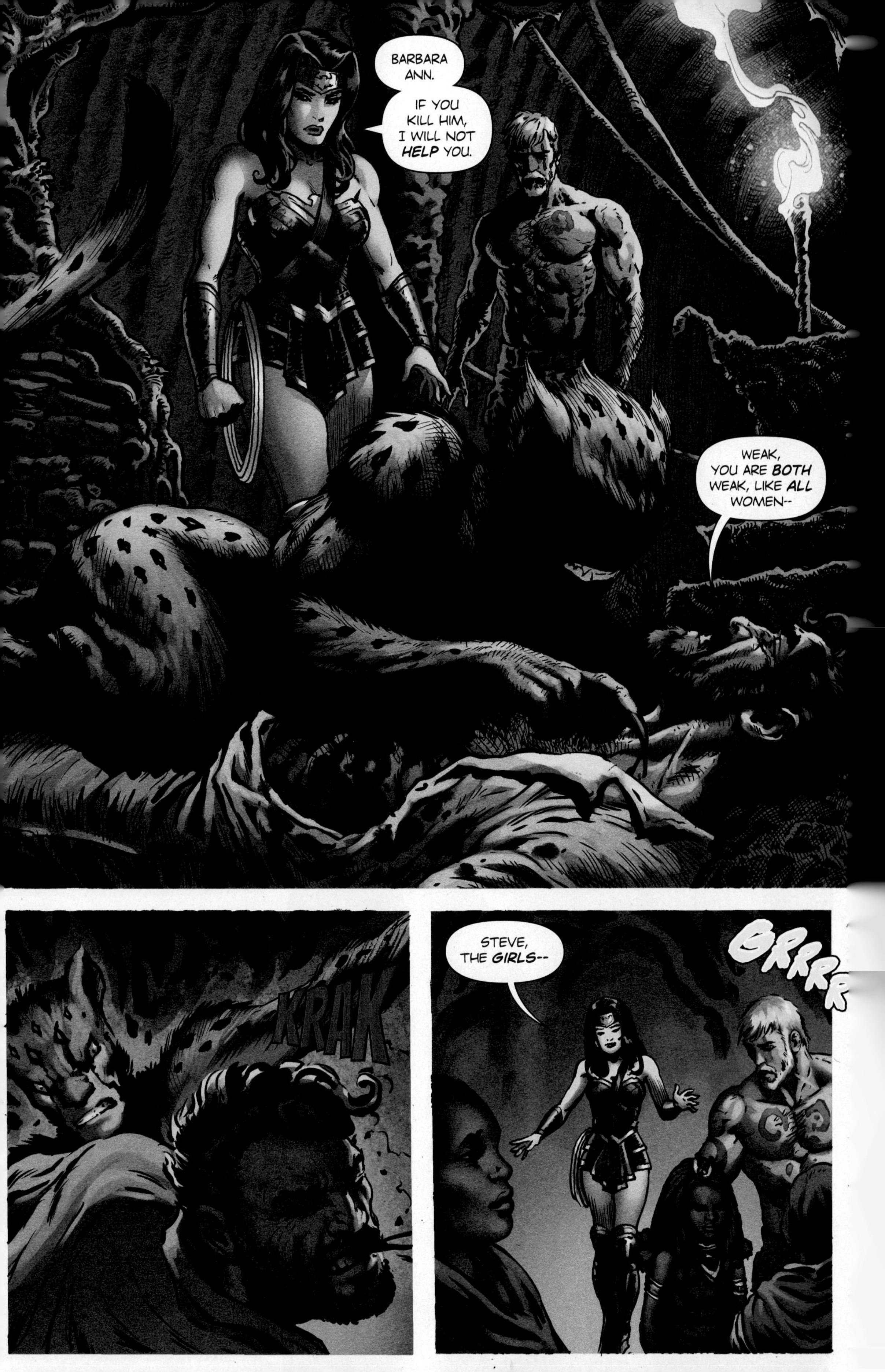
BARBARA ANN.
IF YOU KILL HIM, I WILL NOT HELP YOU.
WEAK, YOU ARE BOTH WEAK, LIKE ALL WOMEN--
KRAK
STEVE, THE GIRLS--
GRRRR

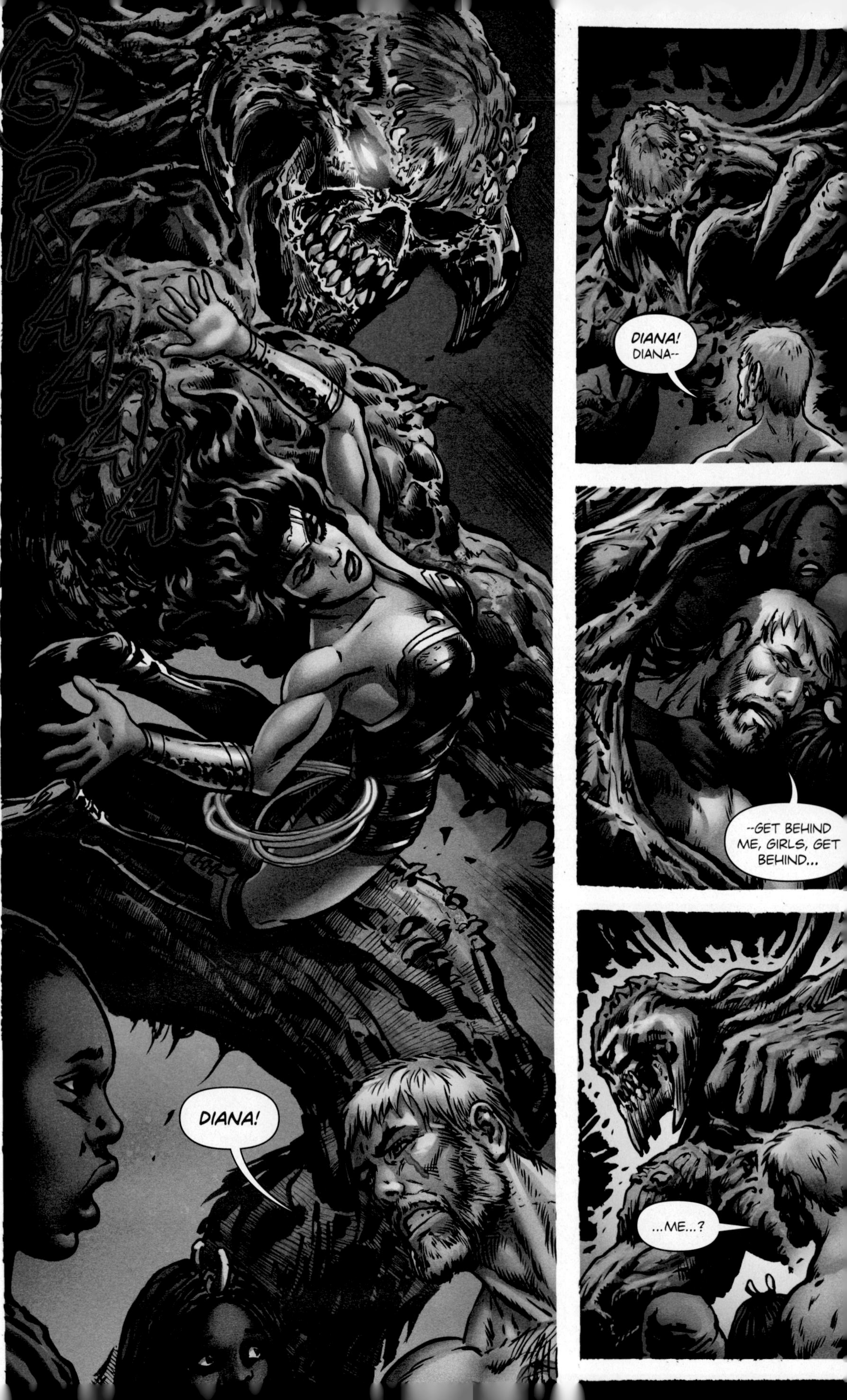
GRAAAAA
DIANA!
DIANA! DIANA--
--GET BEHIND ME, GIRLS, GET BEHIND...
...ME...?

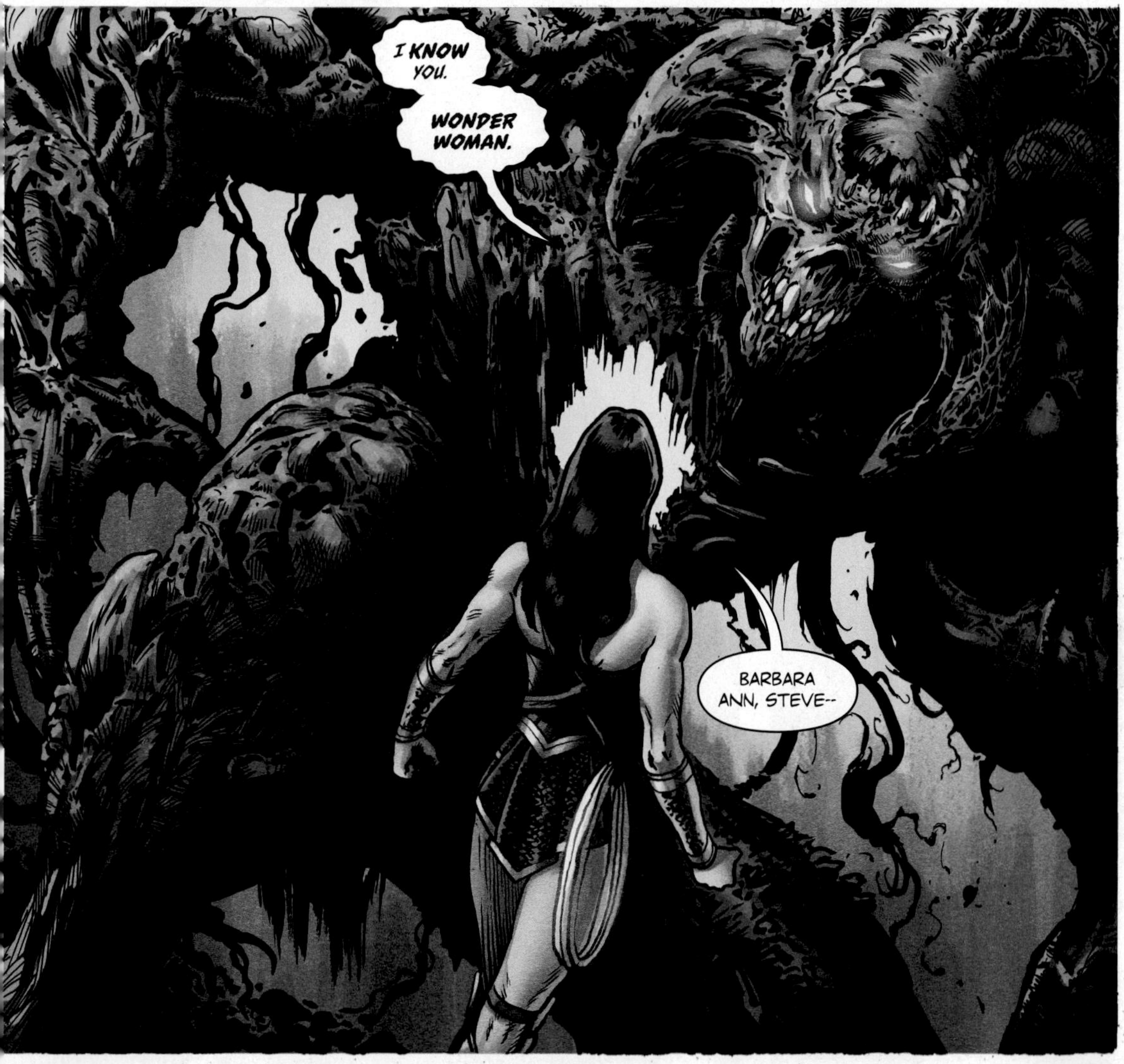
I KNOW YOU.
WONDER WOMAN.
BARBARA ANN, STEVE--

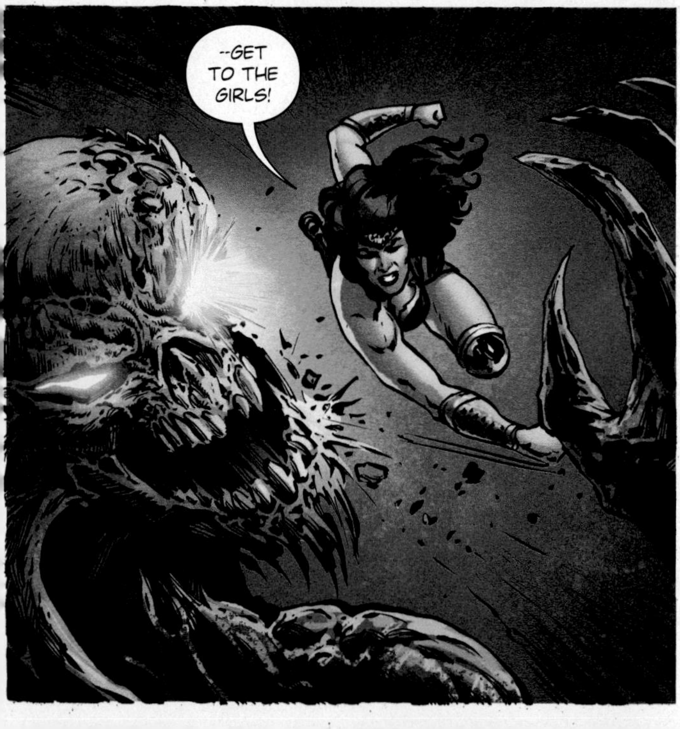
--GET TO THE GIRLS!

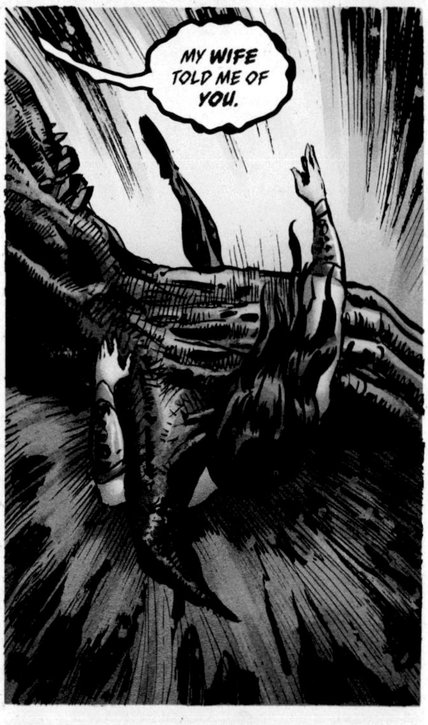
MY WIFE TOLD ME OF YOU.

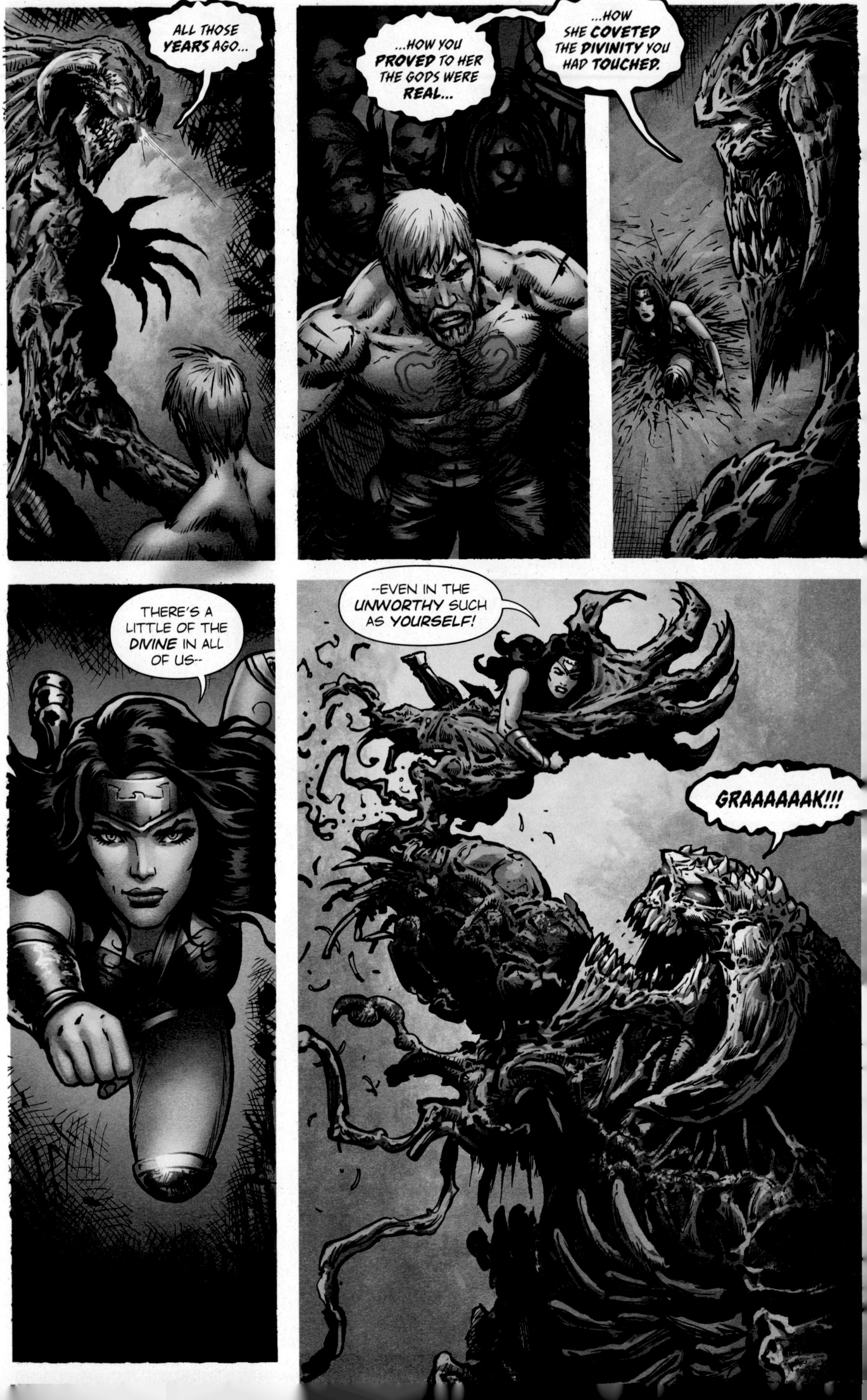
ALL THOSE YEARS AGO...
...HOW YOU PROVED TO HER THE GODS WERE REAL...
...HOW SHE COVETED THE DIVINITY YOU HAD TOUCHED.
THERE'S A LITTLE OF THE DIVINE IN ALL OF US--
--EVEN IN THE UNWORTHY SUCH AS YOURSELF!
GRAAAAAAK!!!

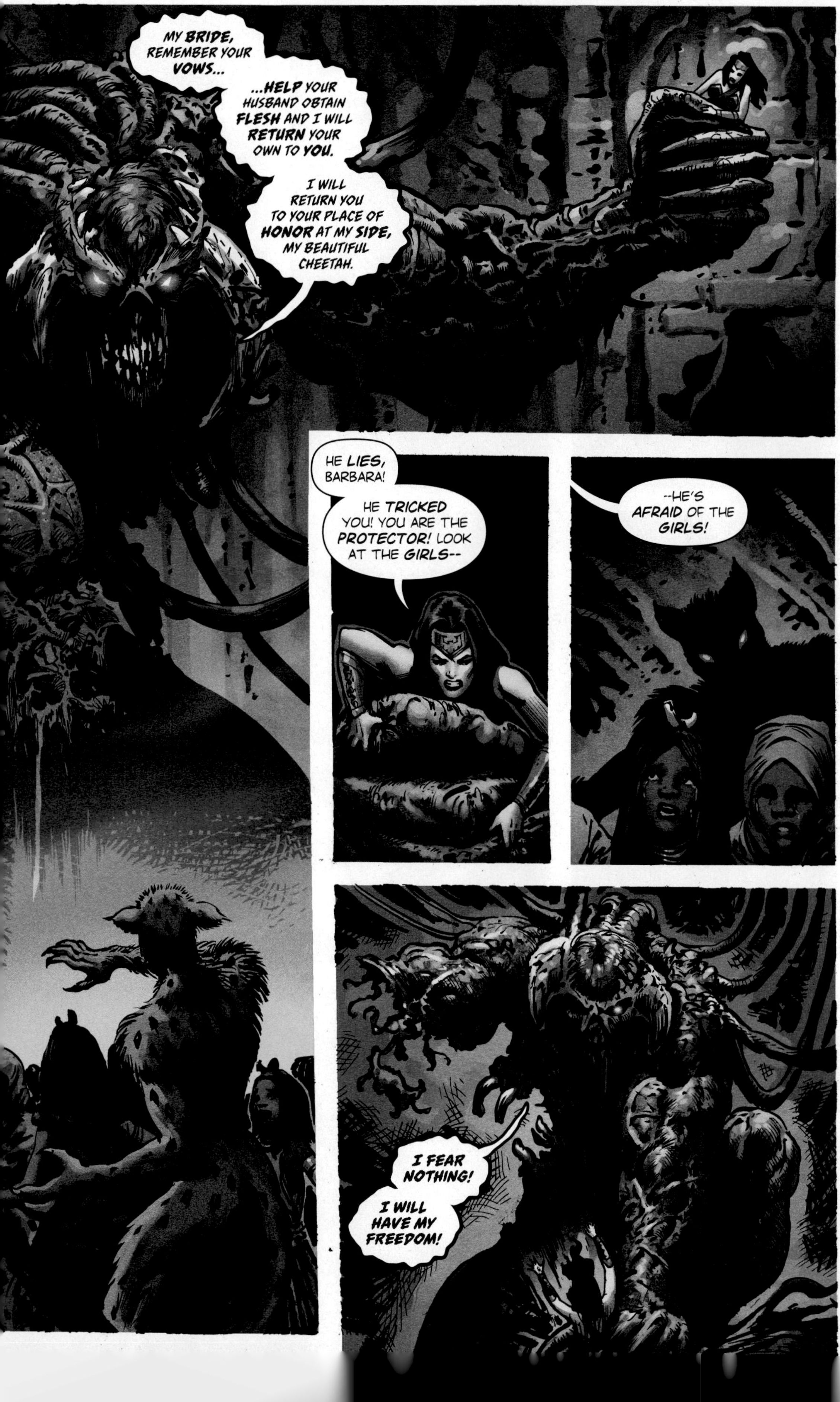

MY BRIDE, REMEMBER YOUR VOWS...
...HELP YOUR HUSBAND OBTAIN FLESH AND I WILL RETURN YOUR OWN TO YOU.
I WILL RETURN YOU TO YOUR PLACE OF HONOR AT MY SIDE, MY BEAUTIFUL CHEETAH.
HE LIES, BARBARA!
HE TRICKED YOU! YOU ARE THE PROTECTOR! LOOK AT THE GIRLS--
--HE'S AFRAID OF THE GIRLS!
I FEAR NOTHING!
I WILL HAVE MY FREEDOM!

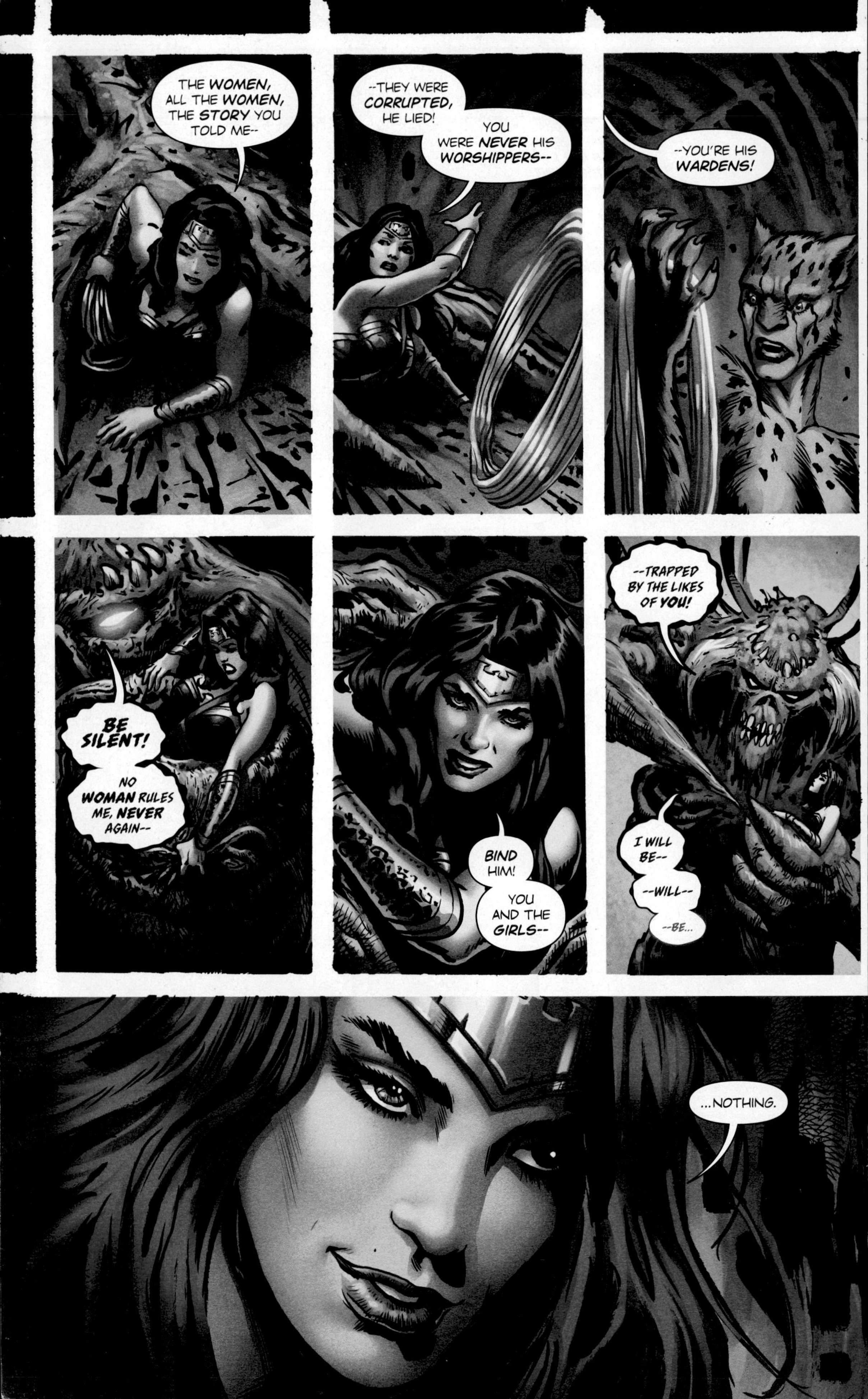
THE WOMEN, ALL THE WOMEN, THE STORY YOU TOLD ME--
--THEY WERE CORRUPTED, HE LIED!
YOU WERE NEVER HIS WORSHIPPERS--
--YOU'RE HIS WARDENS!
BE SILENT!
NO WOMAN RULES ME, NEVER AGAIN--
BIND HIM!
YOU AND THE GIRLS--
--TRAPPED BY THE LIKES OF YOU!
I WILL BE--
--WILL--
--BE...
...NOTHING.

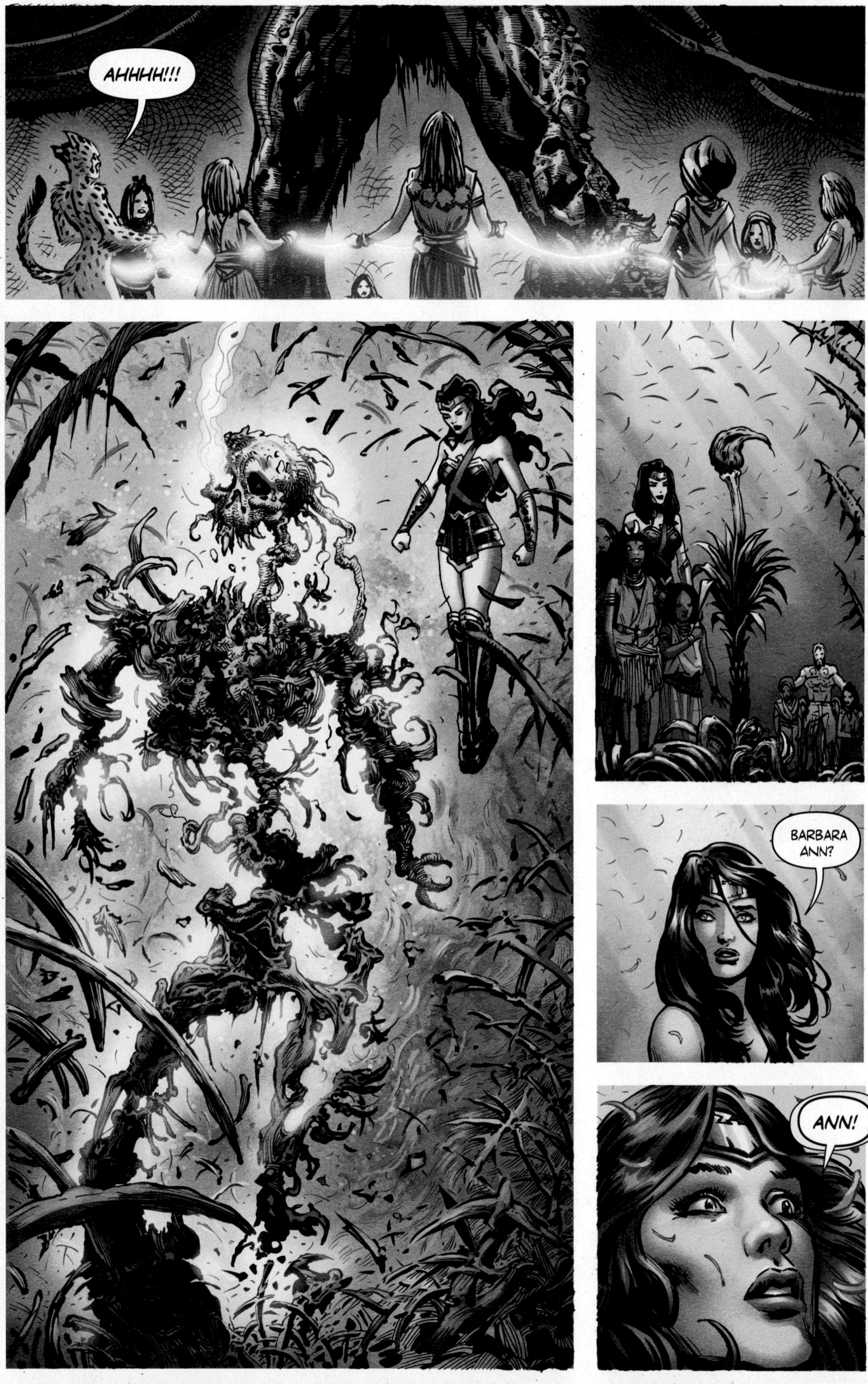
AHHHH!!!
BARBARA ANN?
ANN!

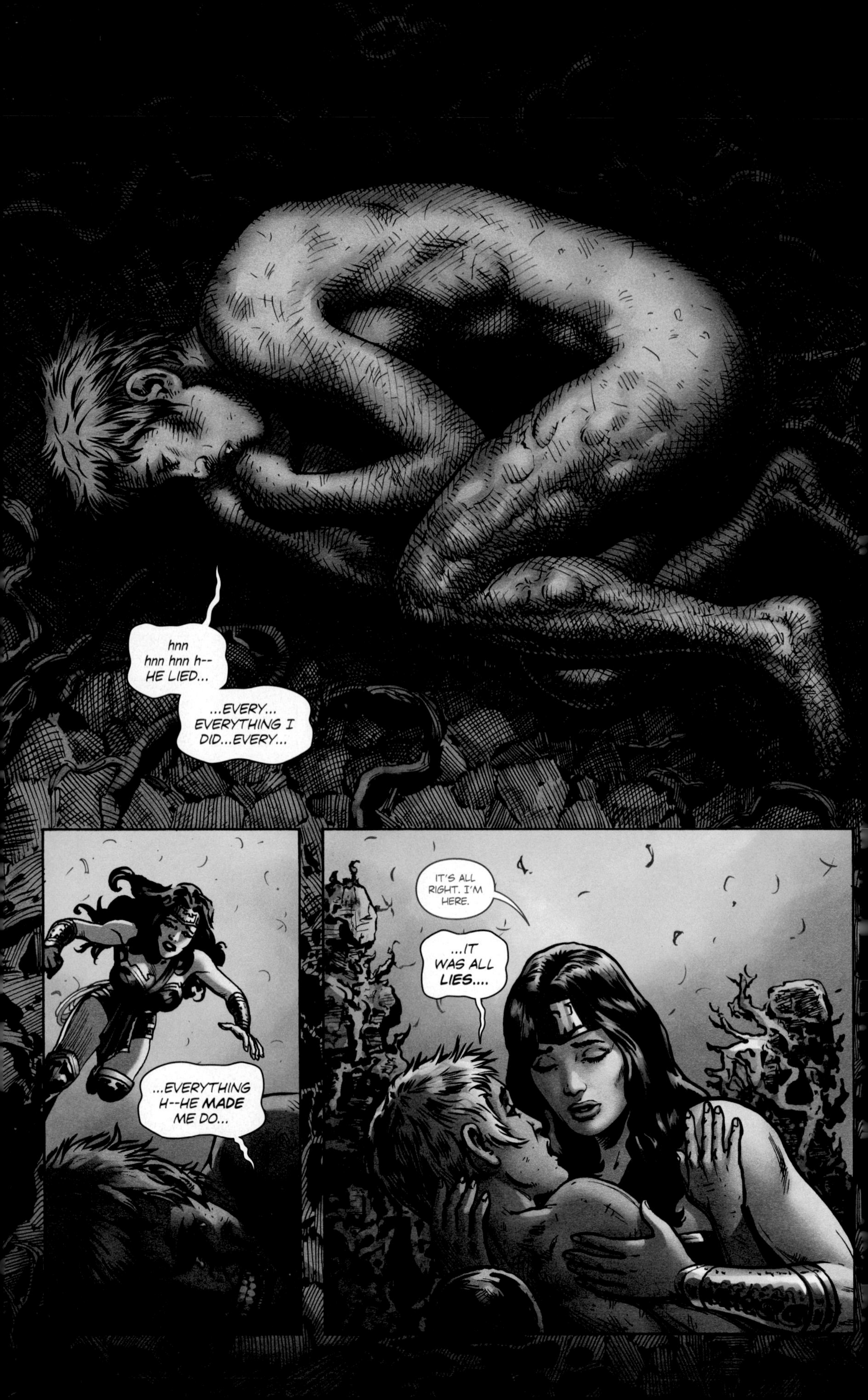
hnn
hnn hnn h--
HE LIED...
...EVERY...
EVERYTHING I
DID...EVERY...
...EVERYTHING
H--HE MADE
ME DO...
IT'S ALL
RIGHT. I'M
HERE.
...IT
WAS ALL
LIES....

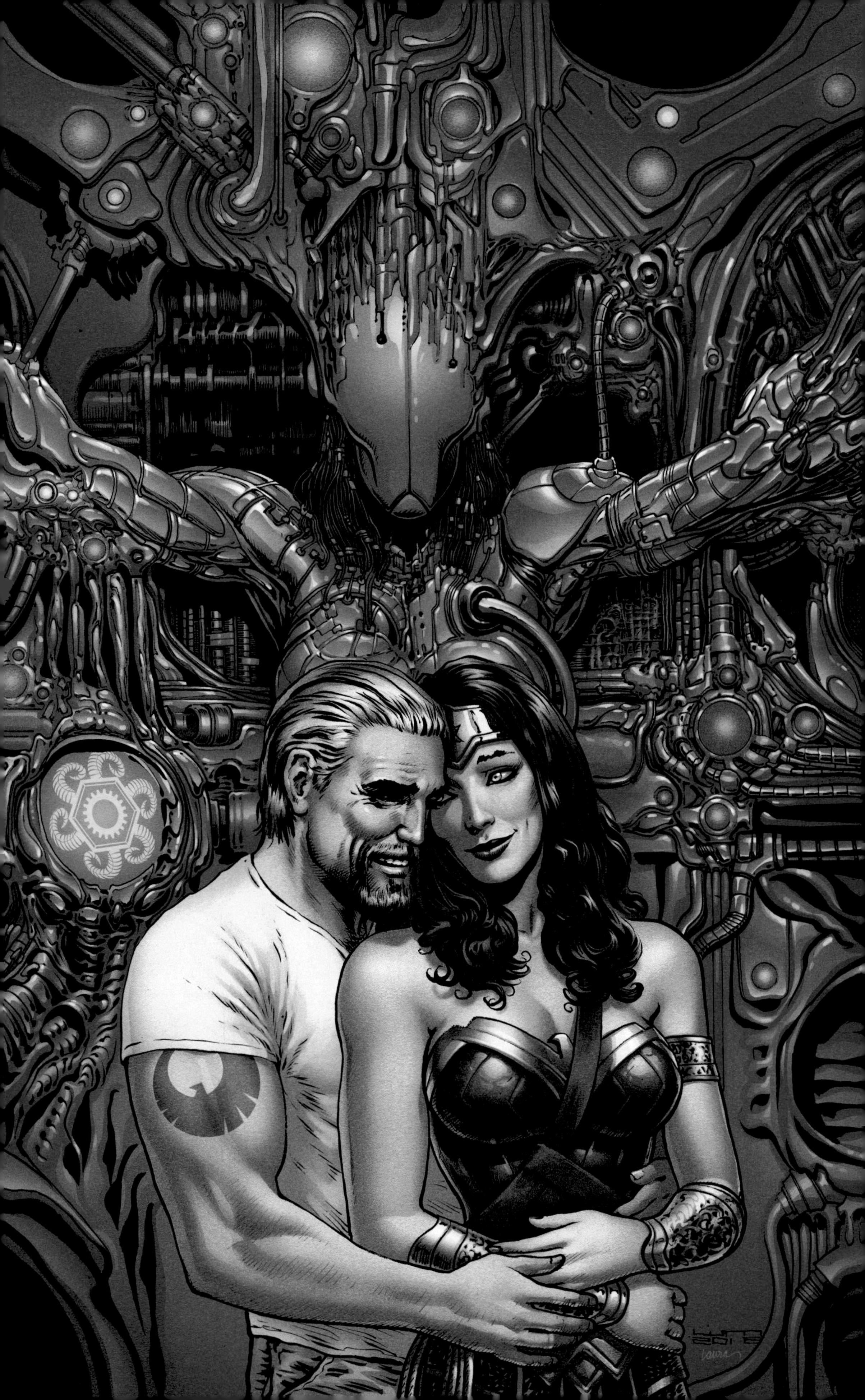

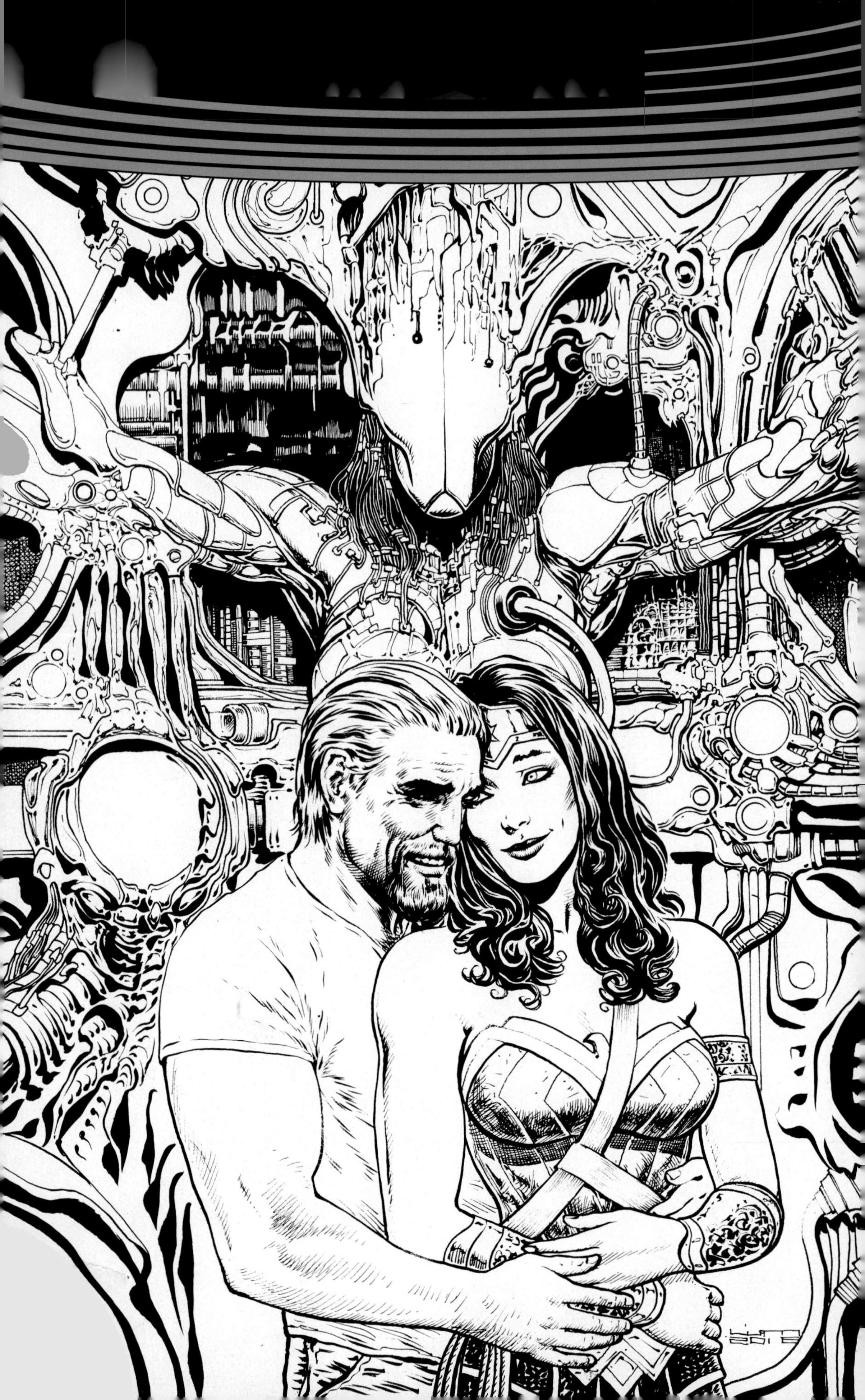

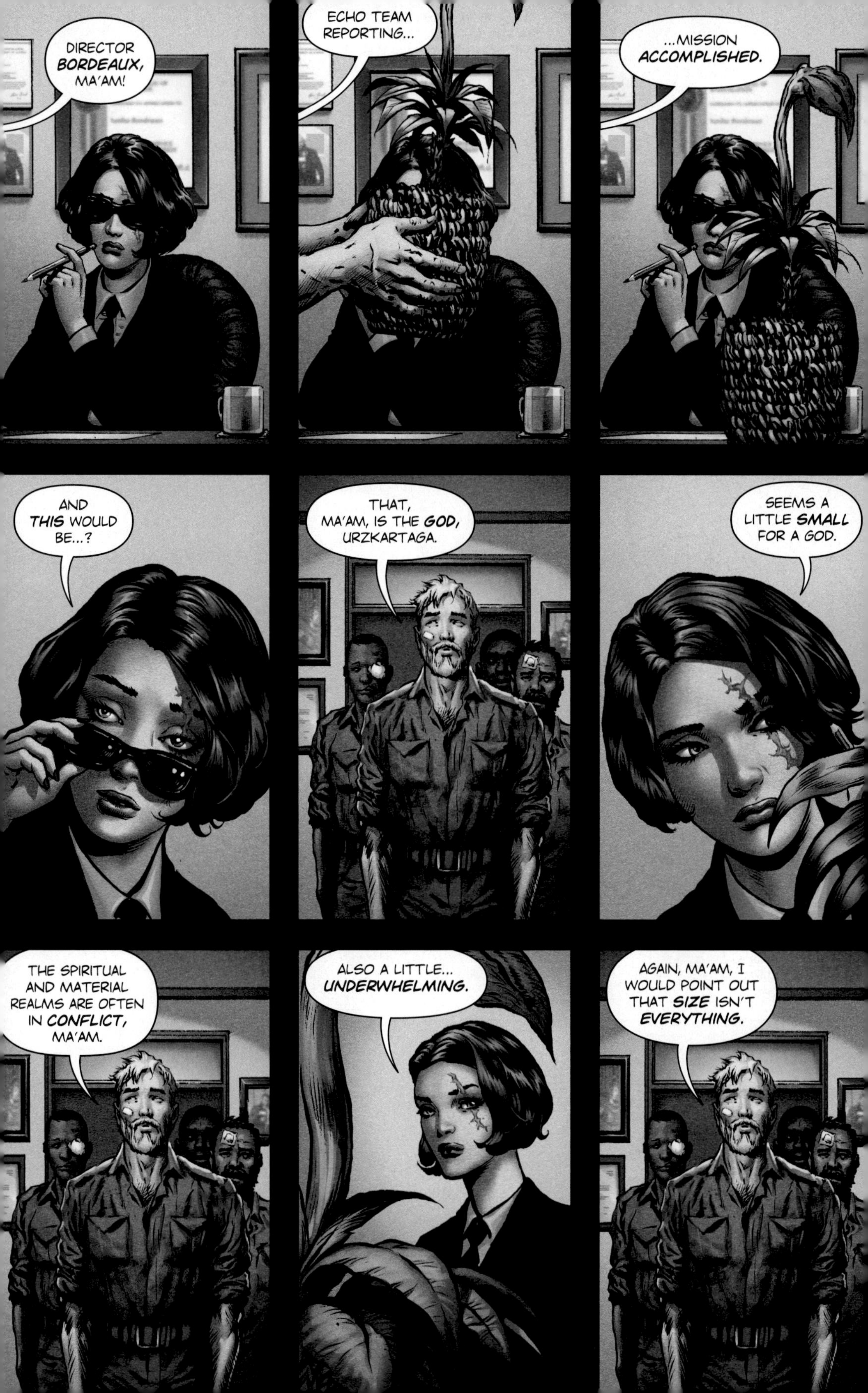
DIRECTOR BORDEAUX, MA'AM!
ECHO TEAM REPORTING...
...MISSION ACCOMPLISHED.
AND THIS WOULD BE...?
THAT, MA'AM, IS THE GOD, URZKARTAGA.
SEEMS A LITTLE SMALL FOR A GOD.
THE SPIRITUAL AND MATERIAL REALMS ARE OFTEN IN CONFLICT, MA'AM.
ALSO A LITTLE... UNDERWHELMING.
AGAIN, MA'AM, I WOULD POINT OUT THAT SIZE ISN'T EVERYTHING.

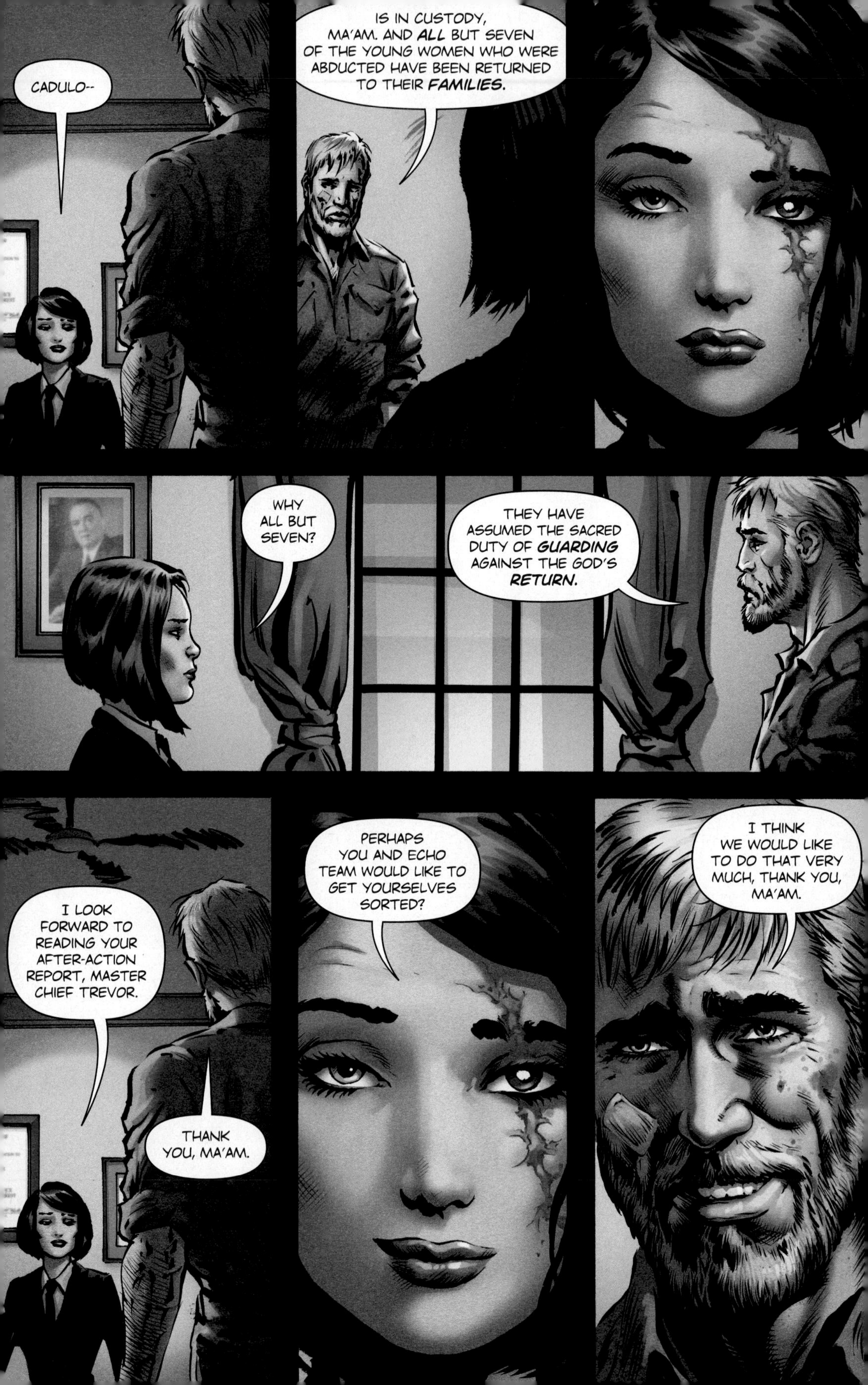
CADULO--
IS IN CUSTODY, MA'AM. AND ALL BUT SEVEN OF THE YOUNG WOMEN WHO WERE ABDUCTED HAVE BEEN RETURNED TO THEIR FAMILIES.
WHY ALL BUT SEVEN?
THEY HAVE ASSUMED THE SACRED DUTY OF GUARDING AGAINST THE GOD'S RETURN.
I LOOK FORWARD TO READING YOUR AFTER-ACTION REPORT, MASTER CHIEF TREVOR.
THANK YOU, MA'AM.
PERHAPS YOU AND ECHO TEAM WOULD LIKE TO GET YOURSELVES SORTED?
I THINK WE WOULD LIKE TO DO THAT VERY MUCH, THANK YOU, MA'AM.

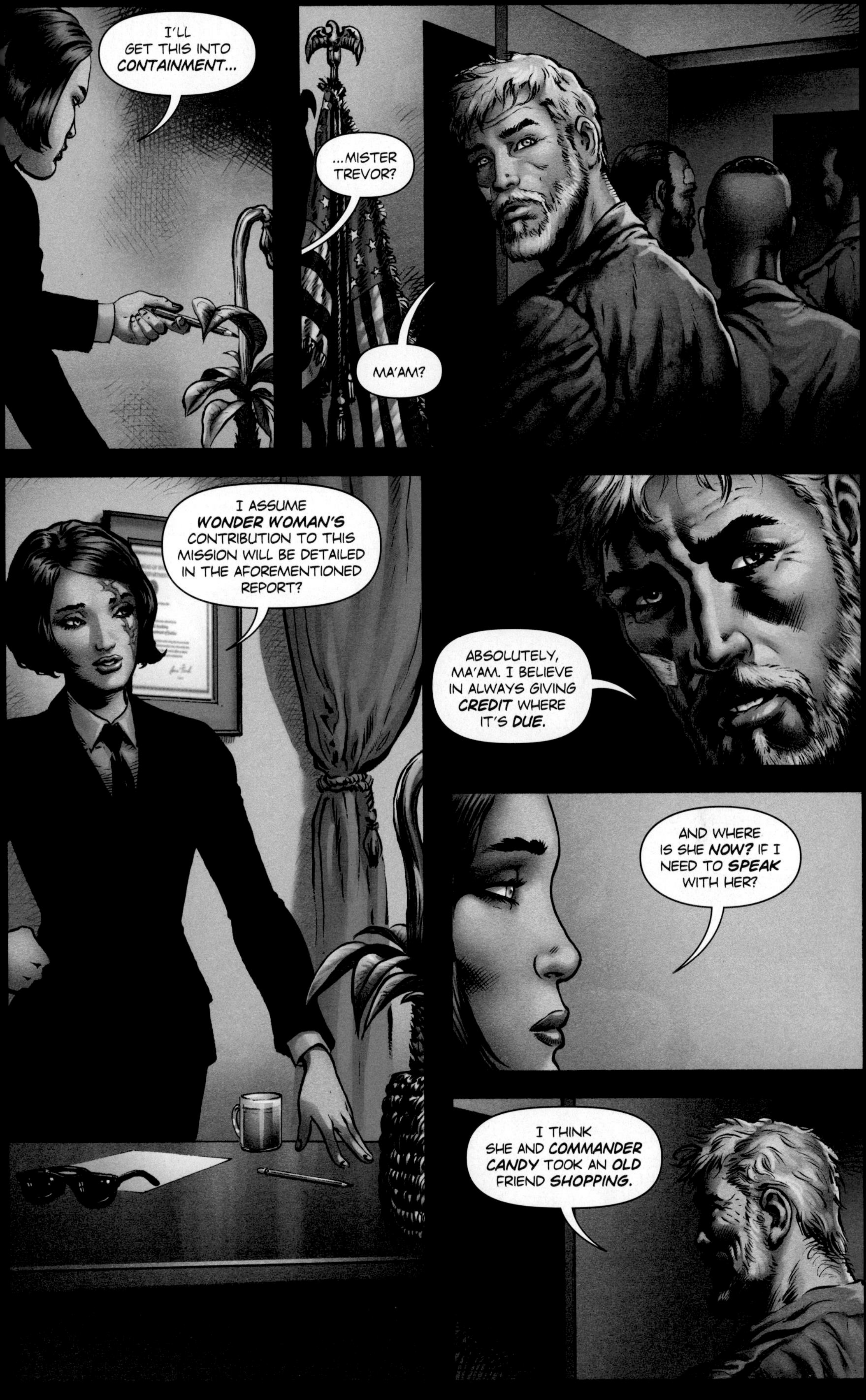
I'LL GET THIS INTO CONTAINMENT...
...MISTER TREVOR?
MA'AM?
I ASSUME WONDER WOMAN'S CONTRIBUTION TO THIS MISSION WILL BE DETAILED IN THE AFOREMENTIONED REPORT?
ABSOLUTELY, MA'AM. I BELIEVE IN ALWAYS GIVING CREDIT WHERE IT'S DUE.
AND WHERE IS SHE NOW? IF I NEED TO SPEAK WITH HER?
I THINK SHE AND COMMANDER CANDY TOOK AN OLD FRIEND SHOPPING.

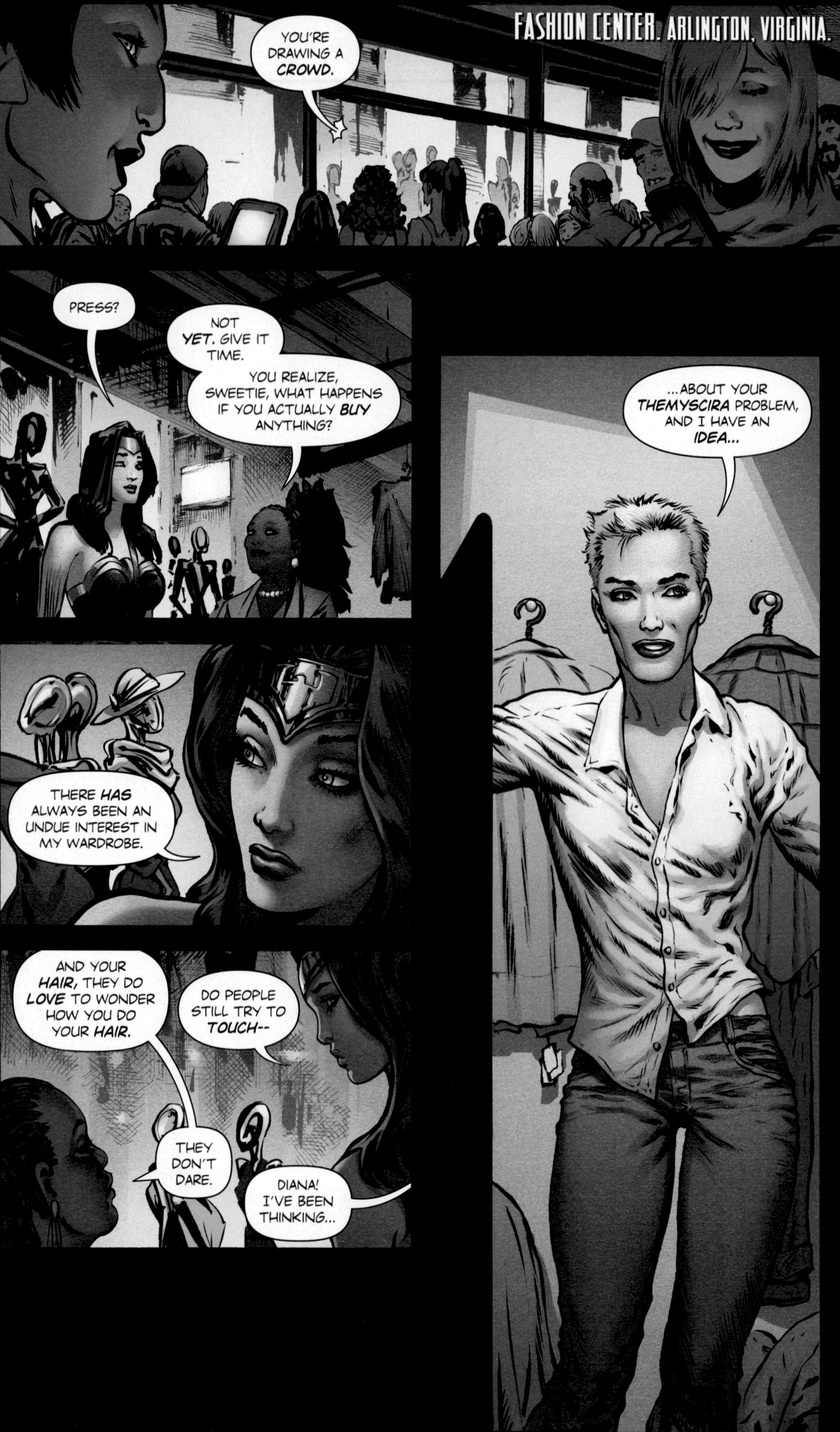
FASHION CENTER. ARLINGTON, VIRGINIA.
YOU'RE DRAWING A CROWD.
PRESS?
NOT YET. GIVE IT TIME.
YOU REALIZE, SWEETIE, WHAT HAPPENS IF YOU ACTUALLY BUY ANYTHING?
THERE HAS ALWAYS BEEN AN UNDUE INTEREST IN MY WARDROBE.
AND YOUR HAIR, THEY DO LOVE TO WONDER HOW YOU DO YOUR HAIR.
DO PEOPLE STILL TRY TO TOUCH--
THEY DON'T DARE.
DIANA! I'VE BEEN THINKING...
...ABOUT YOUR THEMYSCIRA PROBLEM, AND I HAVE AN IDEA...

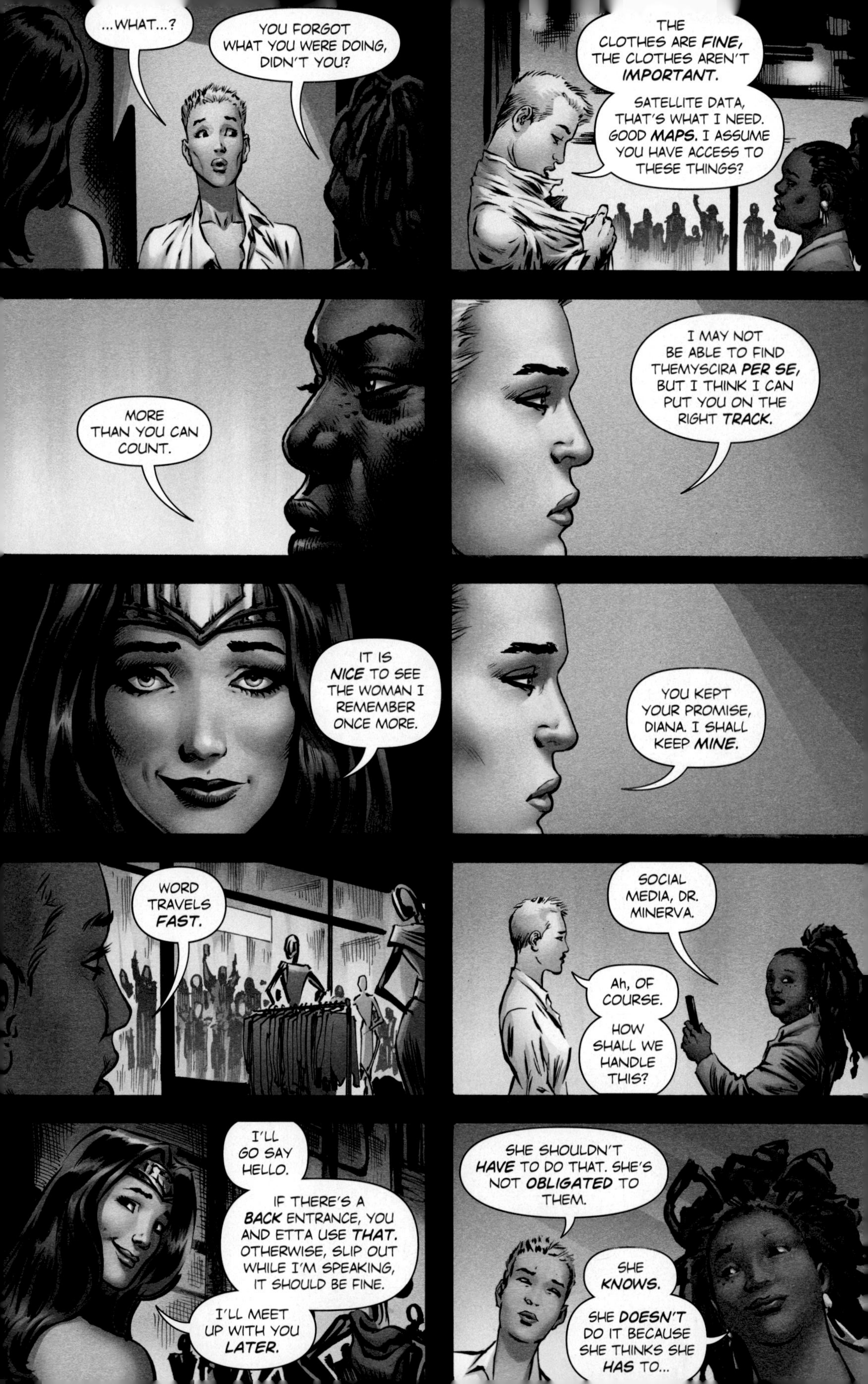
...WHAT...?
YOU FORGOT WHAT YOU WERE DOING, DIDN'T YOU?
THE CLOTHES ARE FINE, THE CLOTHES AREN'T IMPORTANT.
SATELLITE DATA, THAT'S WHAT I NEED. GOOD MAPS. I ASSUME YOU HAVE ACCESS TO THESE THINGS?
MORE THAN YOU CAN COUNT.
I MAY NOT BE ABLE TO FIND THEMYSCIRA PER SE, BUT I THINK I CAN PUT YOU ON THE RIGHT TRACK.
IT IS NICE TO SEE THE WOMAN I REMEMBER ONCE MORE.
YOU KEPT YOUR PROMISE, DIANA. I SHALL KEEP MINE.
WORD TRAVELS FAST.
SOCIAL MEDIA, DR. MINERVA.
Ah, OF COURSE.
HOW SHALL WE HANDLE THIS?
I'LL GO SAY HELLO.
IF THERE'S A BACK ENTRANCE, YOU AND ETTA USE THAT. OTHERWISE, SLIP OUT WHILE I'M SPEAKING, IT SHOULD BE FINE.
I'LL MEET UP WITH YOU LATER.
SHE SHOULDN'T HAVE TO DO THAT. SHE'S NOT OBLIGATED TO THEM.
SHE KNOWS.
SHE DOESN'T DO IT BECAUSE SHE THINKS SHE HAS TO...

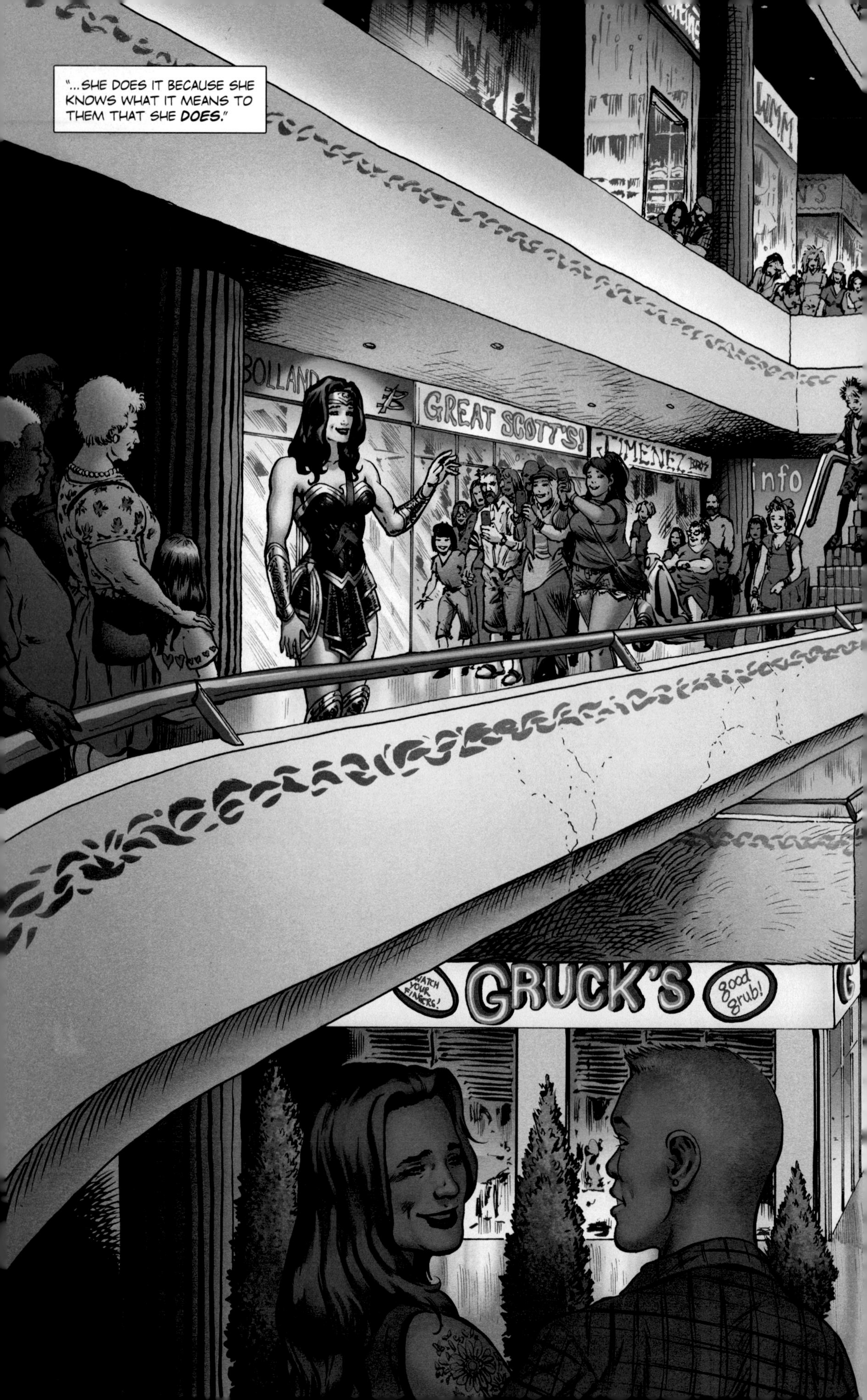
"...SHE DOES IT BECAUSE SHE KNOWS WHAT IT MEANS TO THEM THAT SHE **DOES**."
BOLLAND
GREAT SCOTT'S!
JIMENEZ BROS
info
WATCH YOUR FINGERS!
GRUCK'S
good grub!

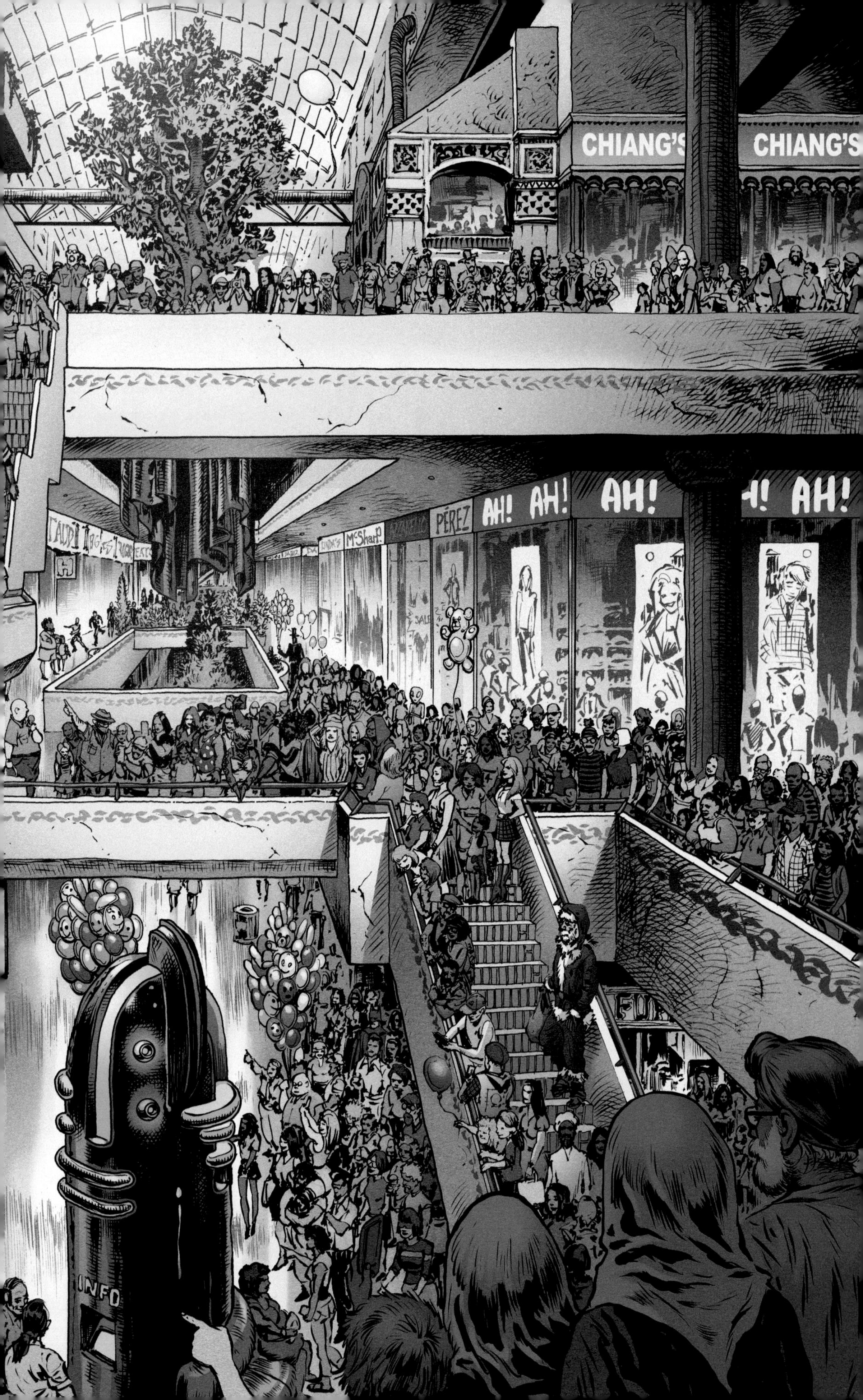
CHIANG'S
CHIANG'S
PÉREZ
AH! AH!
AH!
AH!
INFO

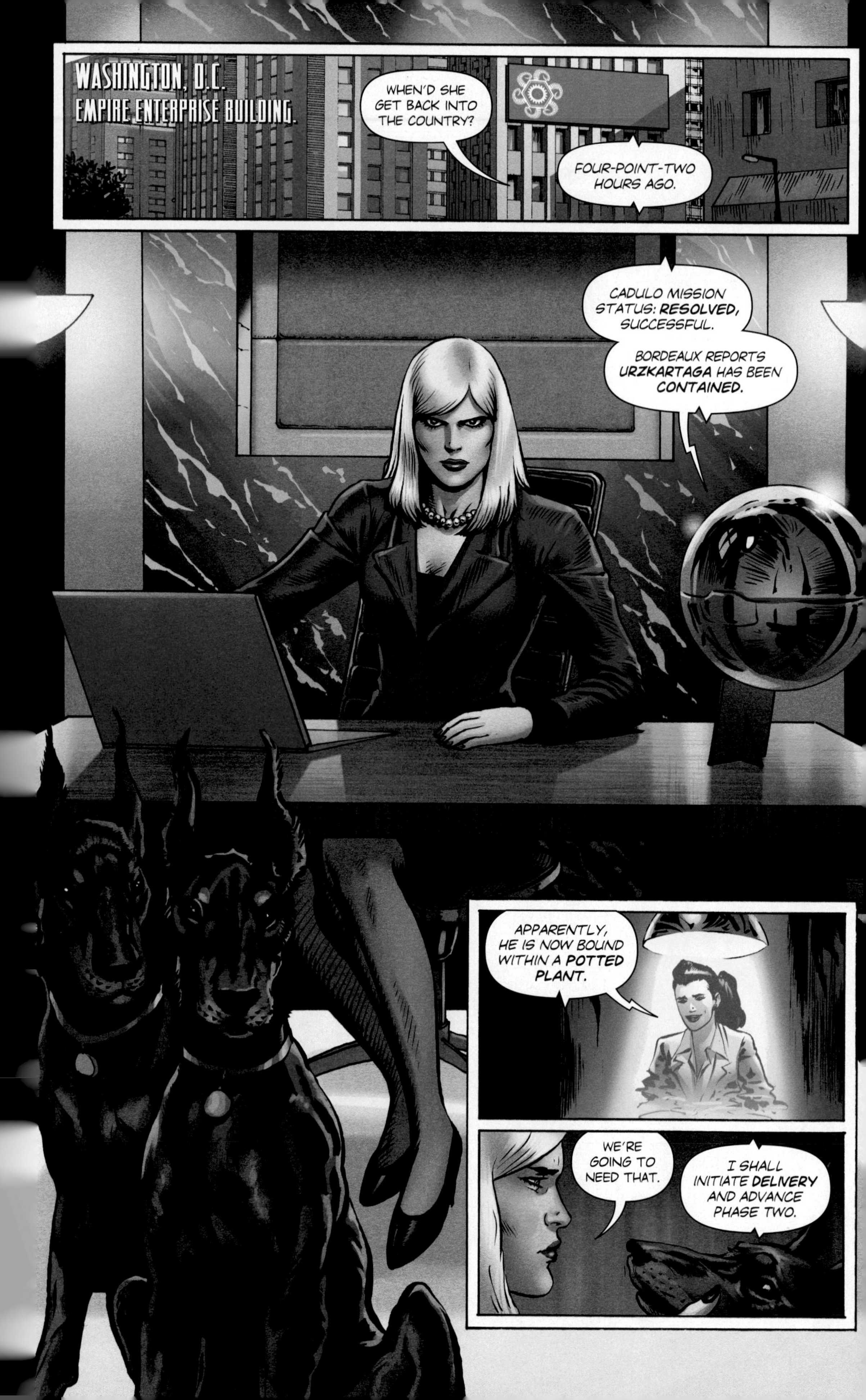
WASHINGTON, D.C.
EMPIRE ENTERPRISE BUILDING.
WHEN'D SHE GET BACK INTO THE COUNTRY?
FOUR-POINT-TWO HOURS AGO.
CADULO MISSION STATUS: **RESOLVED,** SUCCESSFUL.
BORDEAUX REPORTS **URZKARTAGA** HAS BEEN **CONTAINED.**
APPARENTLY, HE IS NOW BOUND WITHIN A **POTTED PLANT.**
WE'RE GOING TO NEED THAT.
I SHALL INITIATE **DELIVERY** AND ADVANCE PHASE TWO.

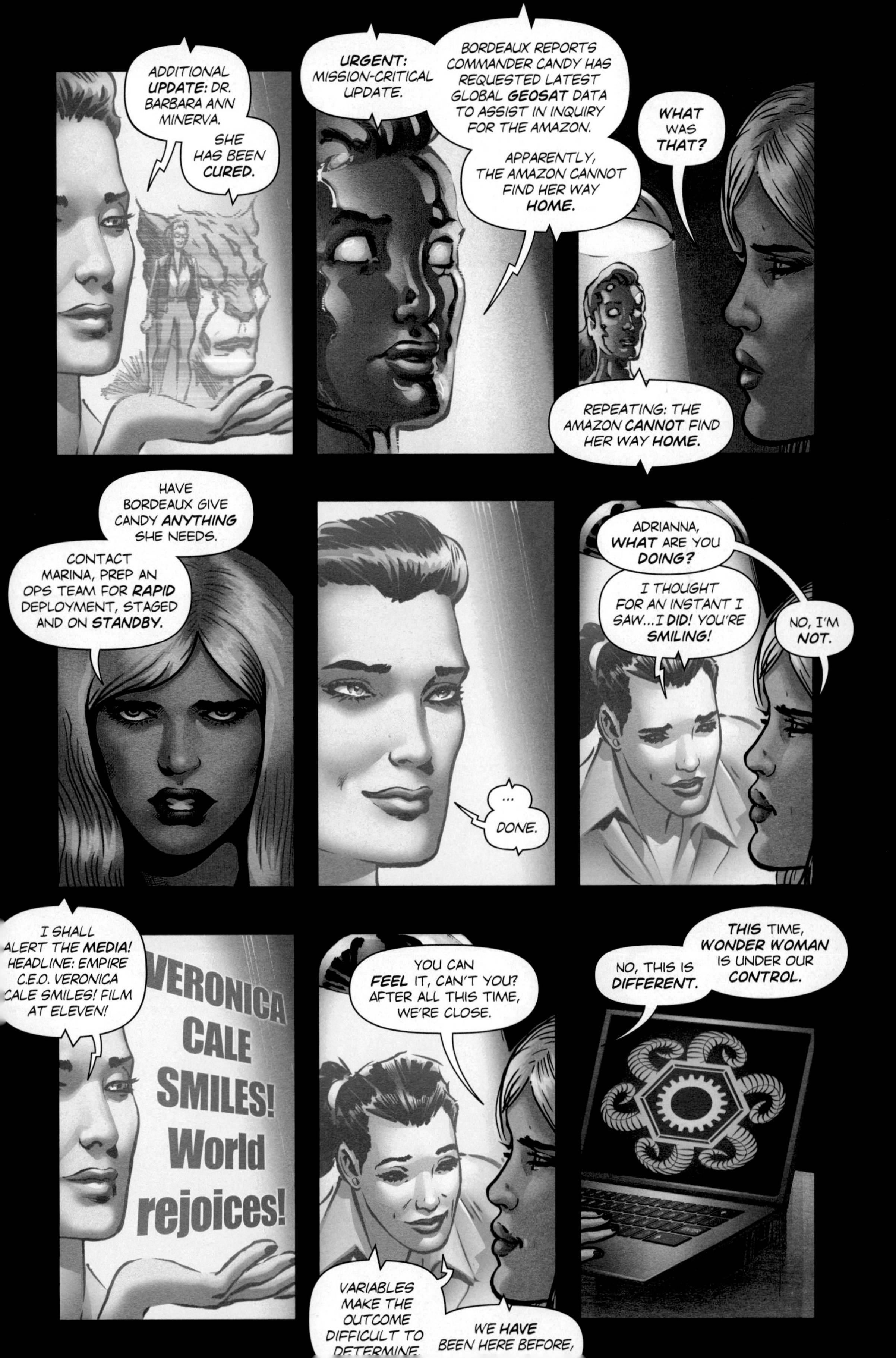
ADDITIONAL UPDATE: DR. BARBARA ANN MINERVA.
SHE HAS BEEN CURED.
URGENT: MISSION-CRITICAL UPDATE.
BORDEAUX REPORTS COMMANDER CANDY HAS REQUESTED LATEST GLOBAL GEOSAT DATA TO ASSIST IN INQUIRY FOR THE AMAZON.
APPARENTLY, THE AMAZON CANNOT FIND HER WAY HOME.
WHAT WAS THAT?
REPEATING: THE AMAZON CANNOT FIND HER WAY HOME.
HAVE BORDEAUX GIVE CANDY ANYTHING SHE NEEDS.
CONTACT MARINA, PREP AN OPS TEAM FOR RAPID DEPLOYMENT, STAGED AND ON STANDBY.
...
DONE.
ADRIANNA, WHAT ARE YOU DOING?
I THOUGHT FOR AN INSTANT I SAW...I DID! YOU'RE SMILING!
NO, I'M NOT.
I SHALL ALERT THE MEDIA! HEADLINE: EMPIRE C.E.O. VERONICA CALE SMILES! FILM AT ELEVEN!
VERONICA CALE SMILES! World rejoices!
YOU CAN FEEL IT, CAN'T YOU? AFTER ALL THIS TIME, WE'RE CLOSE.
VARIABLES MAKE THE OUTCOME DIFFICULT TO DETERMINE.
WE HAVE BEEN HERE BEFORE,
NO, THIS IS DIFFERENT.
THIS TIME, WONDER WOMAN IS UNDER OUR CONTROL.

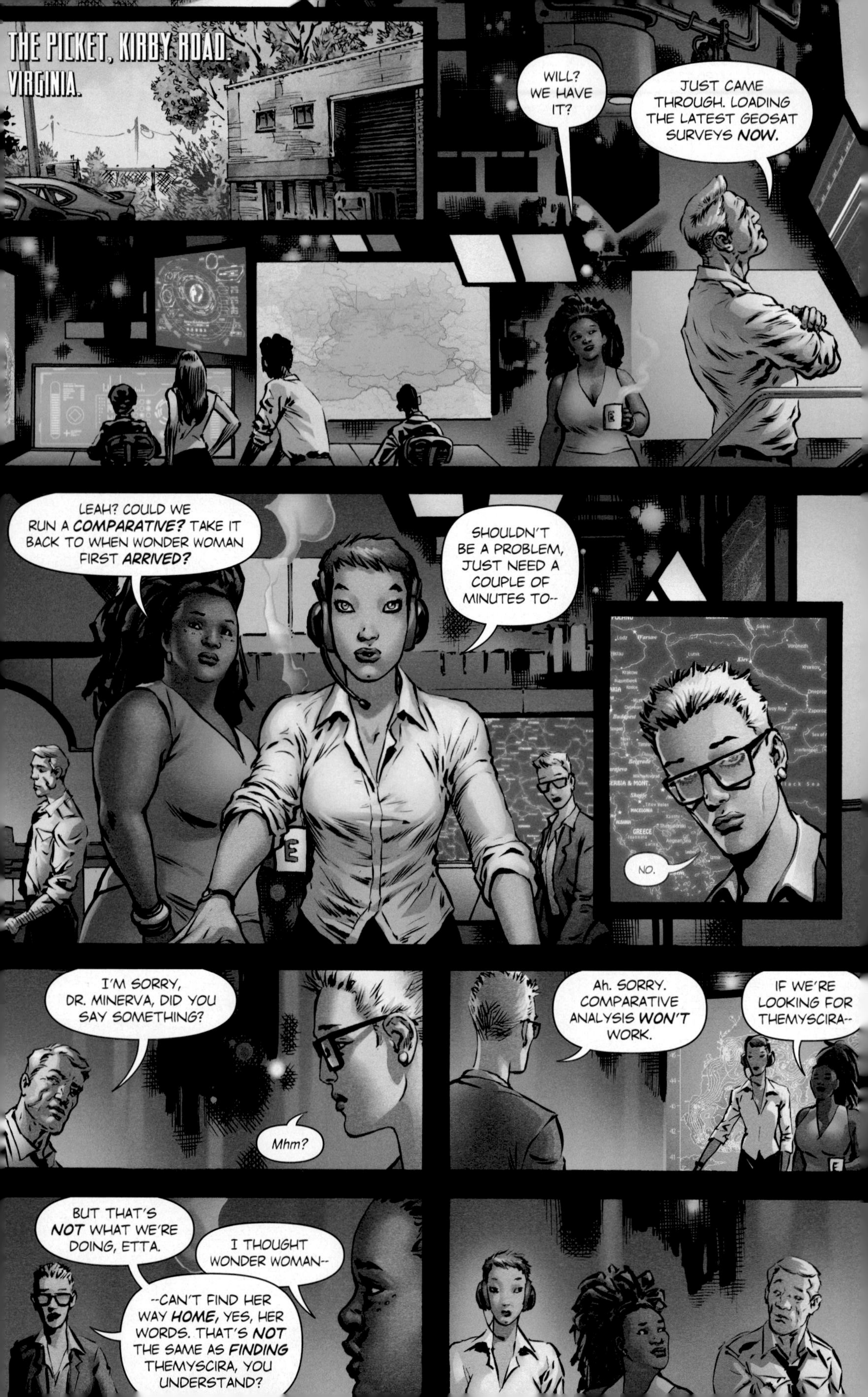
THE PICKET, KIRBY ROAD. VIRGINIA.
WILL? WE HAVE IT?
JUST CAME THROUGH. LOADING THE LATEST GEOSAT SURVEYS NOW.
LEAH? COULD WE RUN A COMPARATIVE? TAKE IT BACK TO WHEN WONDER WOMAN FIRST ARRIVED?
SHOULDN'T BE A PROBLEM, JUST NEED A COUPLE OF MINUTES TO--
NO.
I'M SORRY, DR. MINERVA, DID YOU SAY SOMETHING?
Mhm?
Ah. SORRY. COMPARATIVE ANALYSIS WON'T WORK.
IF WE'RE LOOKING FOR THEMYSCIRA--
BUT THAT'S NOT WHAT WE'RE DOING, ETTA.
I THOUGHT WONDER WOMAN--
--CAN'T FIND HER WAY HOME, YES, HER WORDS. THAT'S NOT THE SAME AS FINDING THEMYSCIRA, YOU UNDERSTAND?

IT'S **PROTECTED** BY THE PATRON GODS OF THE AMAZONS. IT DOESN'T HAVE A **LITERAL** LOCATION, BUT RATHER A **SPIRITUAL** ONE.

YOU HAVE TO BE **ALLOWED** TO ENTER.

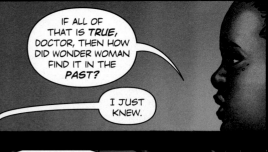

IF ALL OF THAT IS **TRUE**, DOCTOR, THEN HOW DID WONDER WOMAN FIND IT IN THE **PAST**?

I JUST KNEW.

I ALWAYS JUST...**KNEW**.

I DON'T THINK IT'S **LOST**. I THINK IT'S **HIDDEN**, THE WAY IT'S **ALWAYS** BEEN HIDDEN.

AND NOW HIDDEN FROM **ME**, AS WELL.

I'M NOT SURE MUCH STAYS HIDDEN FROM YOU FOR **LONG**, DIANA.

YOU'LL LET ME KNOW IF THERE'S ANYTHING I CAN DO TO **HELP**?

WE KNOW HOW TO CONTACT YOU, DI. YOU GO DO WHAT YOU'RE GONNA DO.

ALL RIGHT.

IF THERE'S **ANYTHING** YOU NEED--

GIRL. GO. GET **OUT** OF HERE.

COMMANDER? WHERE'S SHE GOING?

SHE'S GOT A **DATE**.

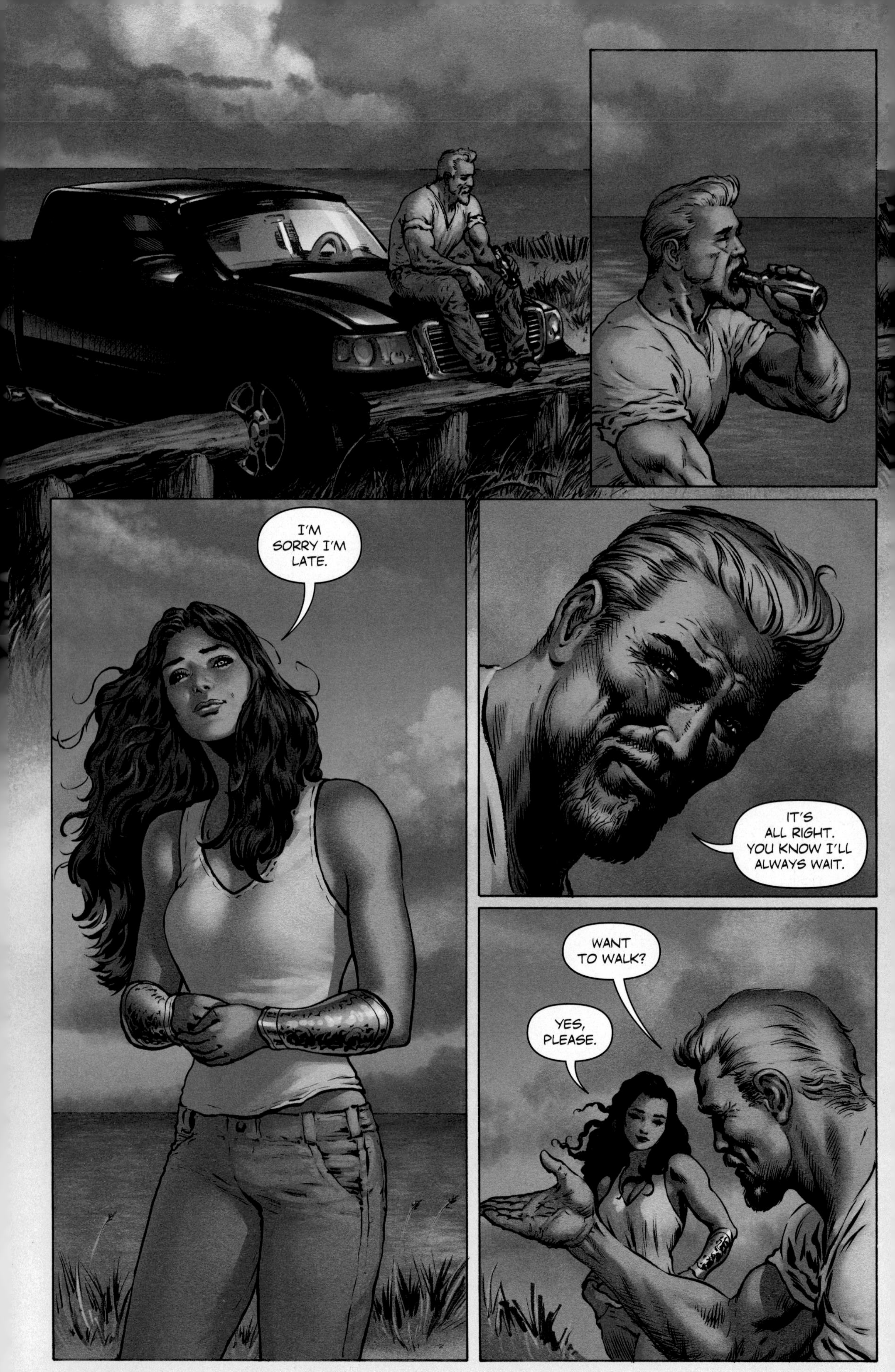
I'M SORRY I'M LATE.
IT'S ALL RIGHT. YOU KNOW I'LL ALWAYS WAIT.
WANT TO WALK?
YES, PLEASE.

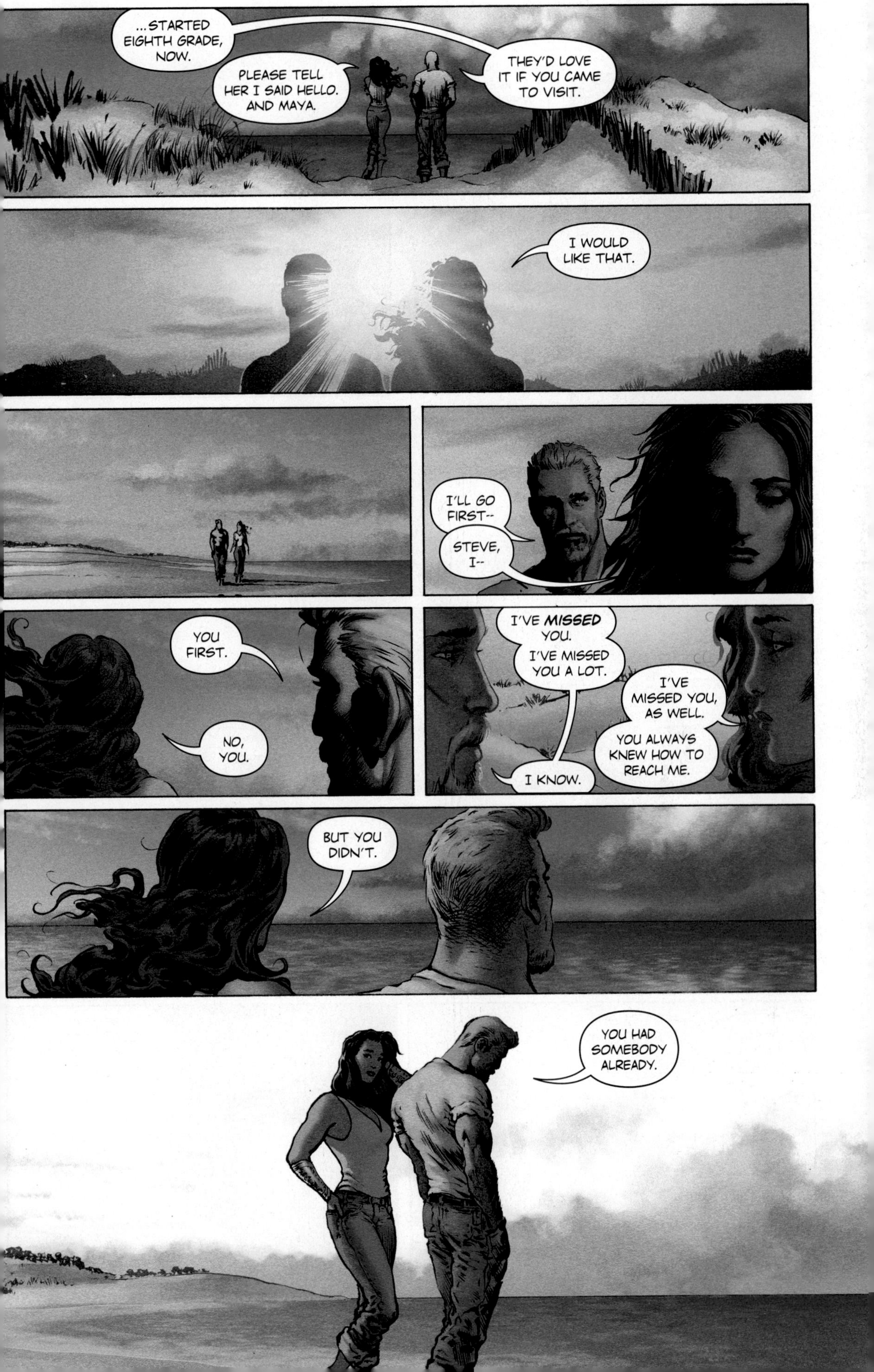
...STARTED EIGHTH GRADE, NOW.
PLEASE TELL HER I SAID HELLO. AND MAYA.
THEY'D LOVE IT IF YOU CAME TO VISIT.
I WOULD LIKE THAT.
I'LL GO FIRST--
STEVE, I--
YOU FIRST.
NO, YOU.
I'VE **MISSED** YOU.
I'VE MISSED YOU A LOT.
I'VE MISSED YOU, AS WELL.
YOU ALWAYS KNEW HOW TO REACH ME.
I KNOW.
BUT YOU DIDN'T.
YOU HAD SOMEBODY ALREADY.

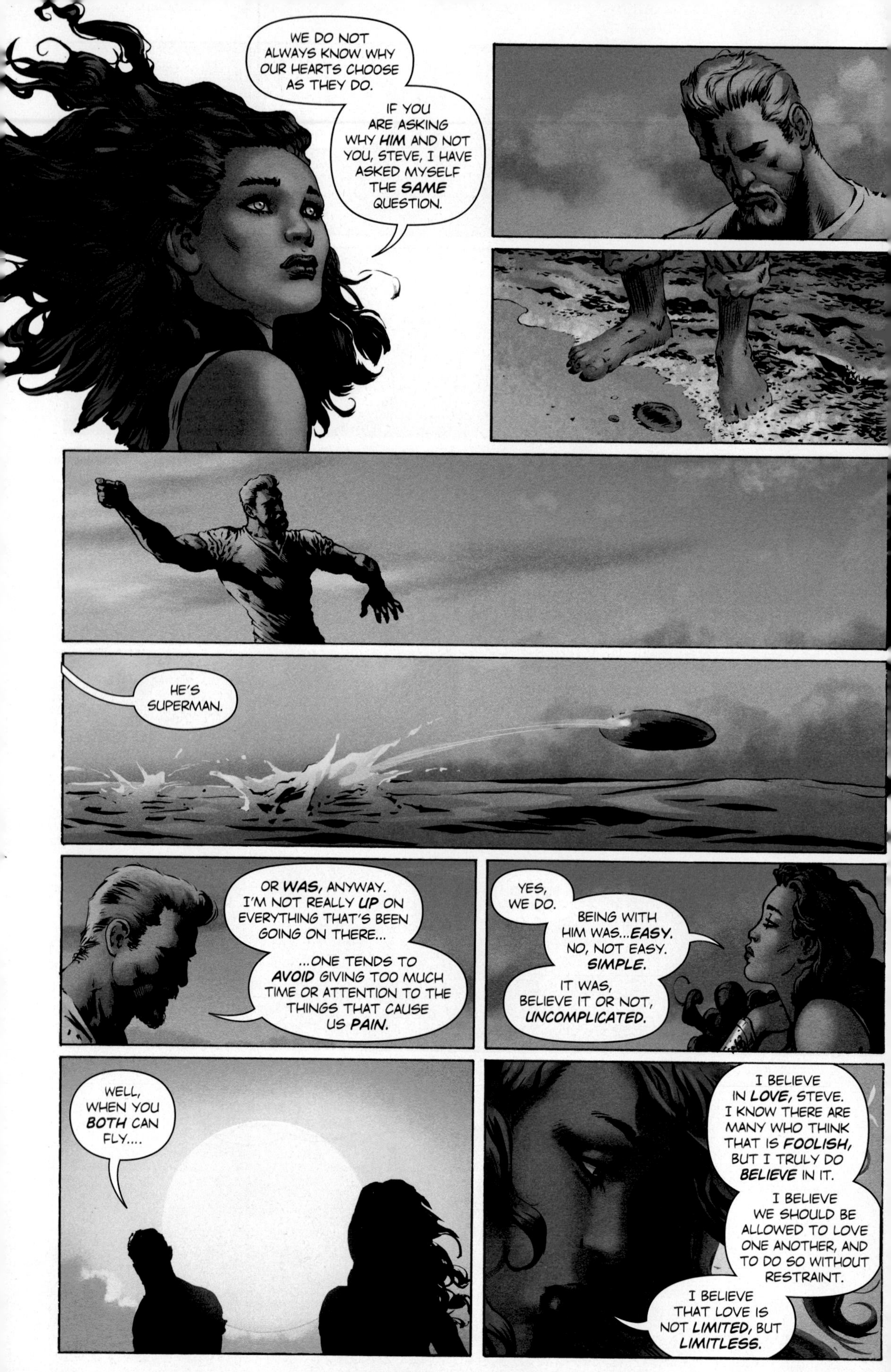
WE DO NOT ALWAYS KNOW WHY OUR HEARTS CHOOSE AS THEY DO.
IF YOU ARE ASKING WHY *HIM* AND NOT YOU, STEVE, I HAVE ASKED MYSELF THE *SAME* QUESTION.
HE'S SUPERMAN.
OR *WAS,* ANYWAY. I'M NOT REALLY *UP* ON EVERYTHING THAT'S BEEN GOING ON THERE...
...ONE TENDS TO *AVOID* GIVING TOO MUCH TIME OR ATTENTION TO THE THINGS THAT CAUSE US *PAIN.*
YES, WE DO.
BEING WITH HIM WAS...*EASY.* NO, NOT EASY. *SIMPLE.*
IT WAS, BELIEVE IT OR NOT, *UNCOMPLICATED.*
WELL, WHEN YOU *BOTH* CAN FLY....
I BELIEVE IN *LOVE,* STEVE. I KNOW THERE ARE MANY WHO THINK THAT IS *FOOLISH,* BUT I TRULY DO *BELIEVE* IN IT.
I BELIEVE WE SHOULD BE ALLOWED TO LOVE ONE ANOTHER, AND TO DO SO WITHOUT RESTRAINT.
I BELIEVE THAT LOVE IS NOT *LIMITED,* BUT *LIMITLESS.*

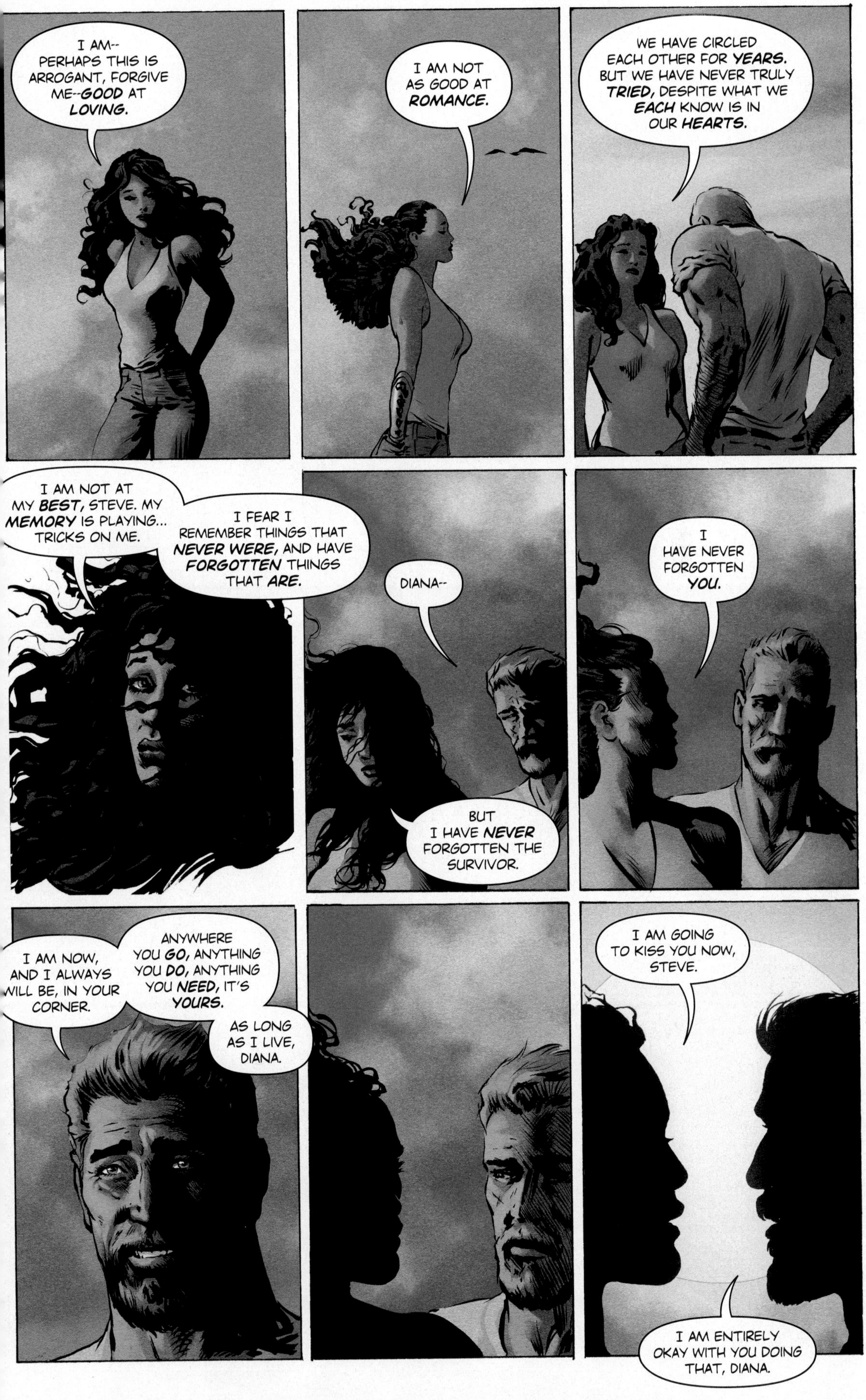
I AM-- PERHAPS THIS IS ARROGANT, FORGIVE ME--GOOD AT LOVING.
I AM NOT AS GOOD AT ROMANCE.
WE HAVE CIRCLED EACH OTHER FOR YEARS. BUT WE HAVE NEVER TRULY TRIED, DESPITE WHAT WE EACH KNOW IS IN OUR HEARTS.
I AM NOT AT MY BEST, STEVE. MY MEMORY IS PLAYING... TRICKS ON ME.
I FEAR I REMEMBER THINGS THAT NEVER WERE, AND HAVE FORGOTTEN THINGS THAT ARE.
DIANA--
BUT I HAVE NEVER FORGOTTEN THE SURVIVOR.
I HAVE NEVER FORGOTTEN YOU.
I AM NOW, AND I ALWAYS WILL BE, IN YOUR CORNER.
ANYWHERE YOU GO, ANYTHING YOU DO, ANYTHING YOU NEED, IT'S YOURS.
AS LONG AS I LIVE, DIANA.
I AM GOING TO KISS YOU NOW, STEVE.
I AM ENTIRELY OKAY WITH YOU DOING THAT, DIANA.

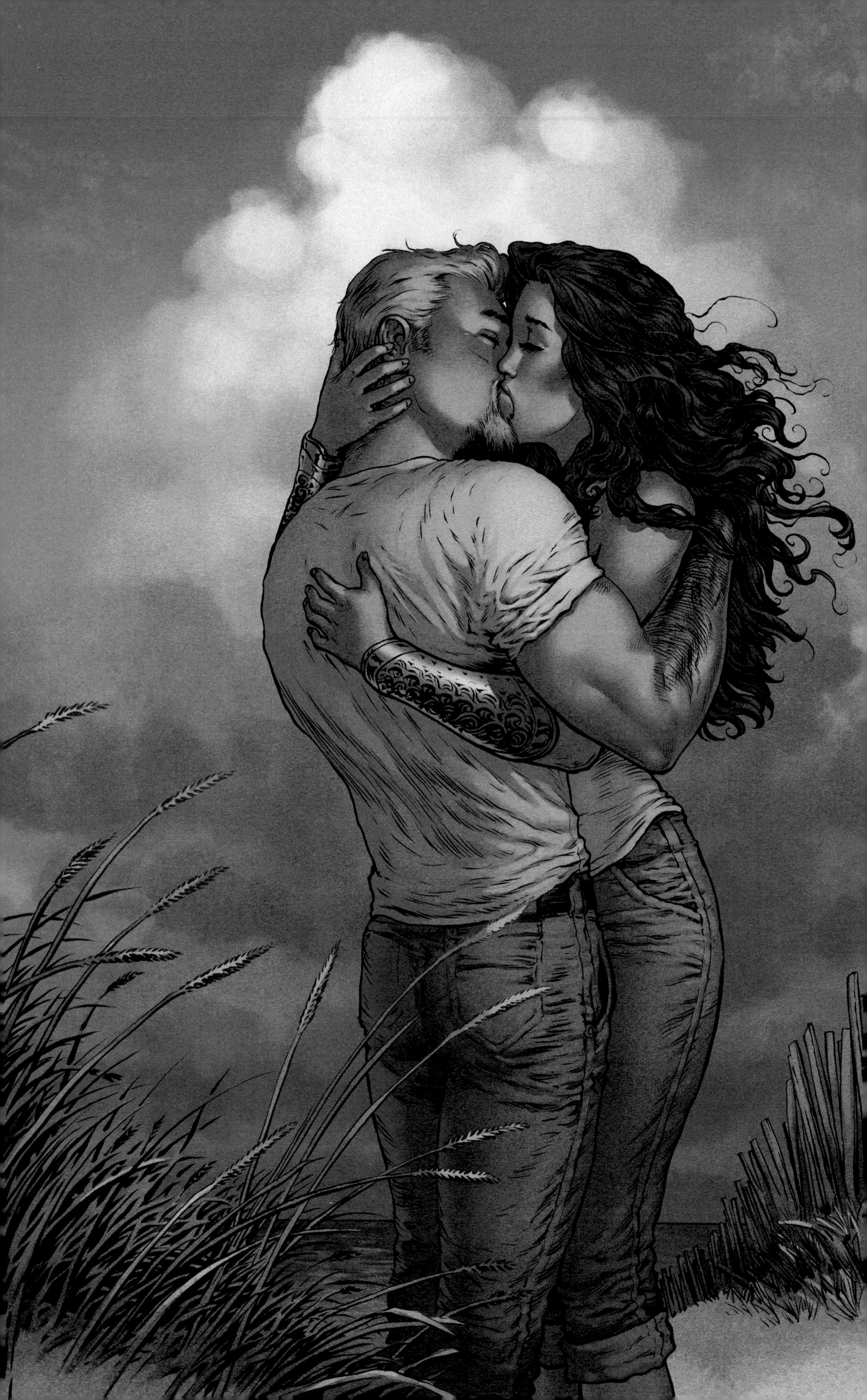

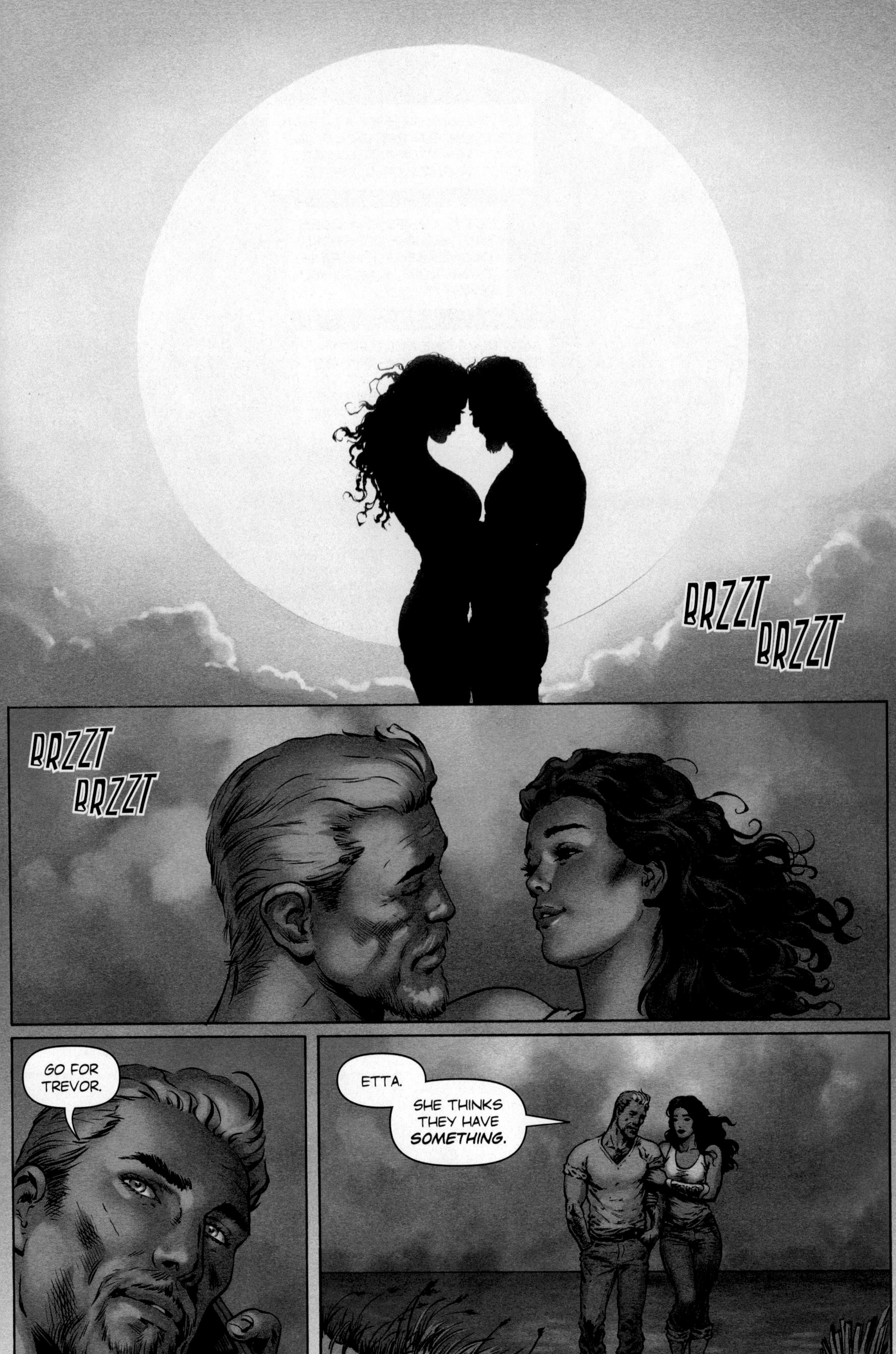
BRZZT BRZZT
BRZZT BRZZT
GO FOR TREVOR.
ETTA.
SHE THINKS THEY HAVE SOMETHING.

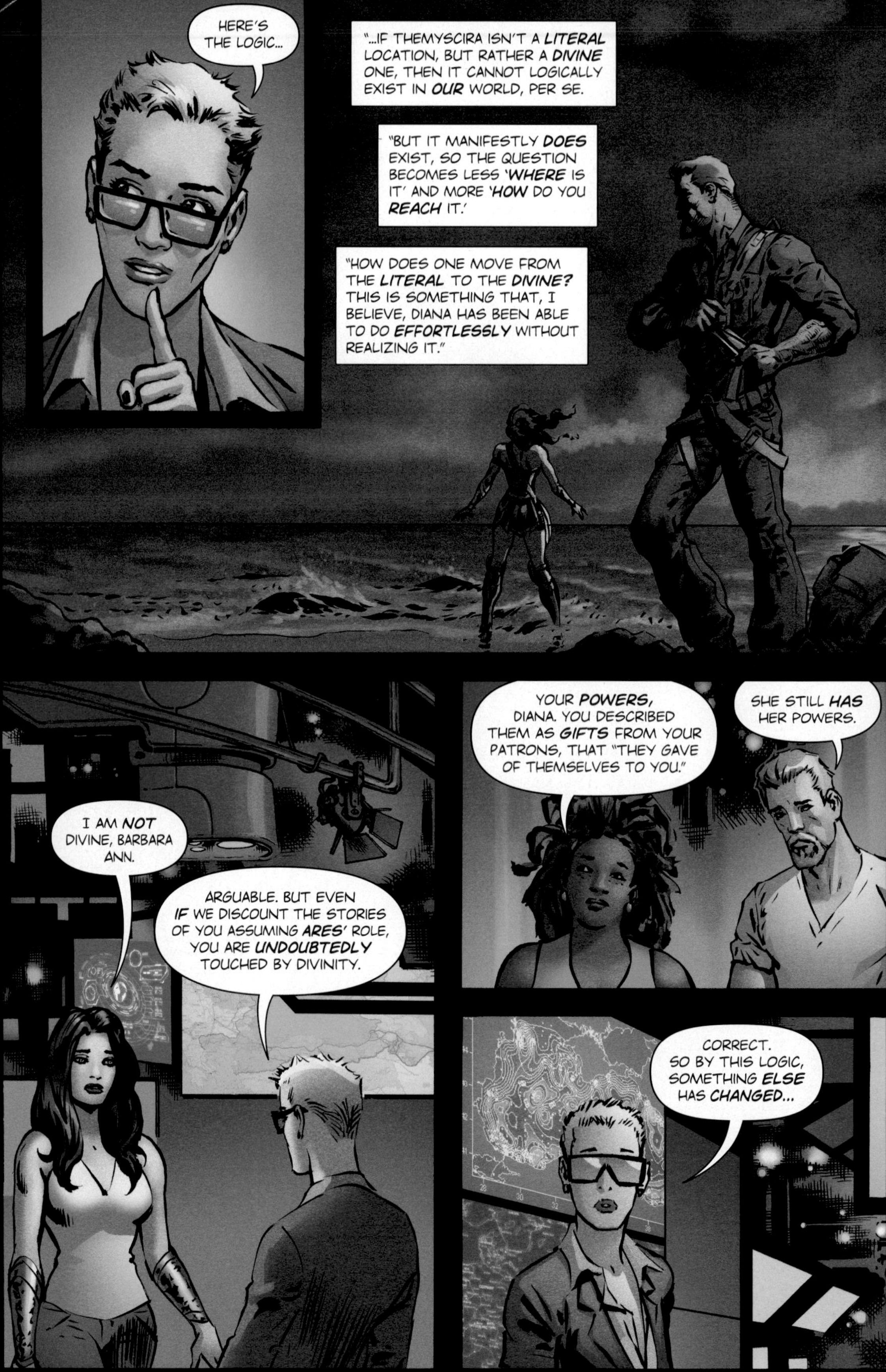
HERE'S THE LOGIC...
"...IF THEMYSCIRA ISN'T A LITERAL LOCATION, BUT RATHER A DIVINE ONE, THEN IT CANNOT LOGICALLY EXIST IN OUR WORLD, PER SE.
"BUT IT MANIFESTLY DOES EXIST, SO THE QUESTION BECOMES LESS 'WHERE IS IT' AND MORE 'HOW DO YOU REACH IT.'
"HOW DOES ONE MOVE FROM THE LITERAL TO THE DIVINE? THIS IS SOMETHING THAT, I BELIEVE, DIANA HAS BEEN ABLE TO DO EFFORTLESSLY WITHOUT REALIZING IT."
I AM NOT DIVINE, BARBARA ANN.
ARGUABLE. BUT EVEN IF WE DISCOUNT THE STORIES OF YOU ASSUMING ARES' ROLE, YOU ARE UNDOUBTEDLY TOUCHED BY DIVINITY.
YOUR POWERS, DIANA. YOU DESCRIBED THEM AS GIFTS FROM YOUR PATRONS, THAT "THEY GAVE OF THEMSELVES TO YOU."
SHE STILL HAS HER POWERS.
CORRECT. SO BY THIS LOGIC, SOMETHING ELSE HAS CHANGED...

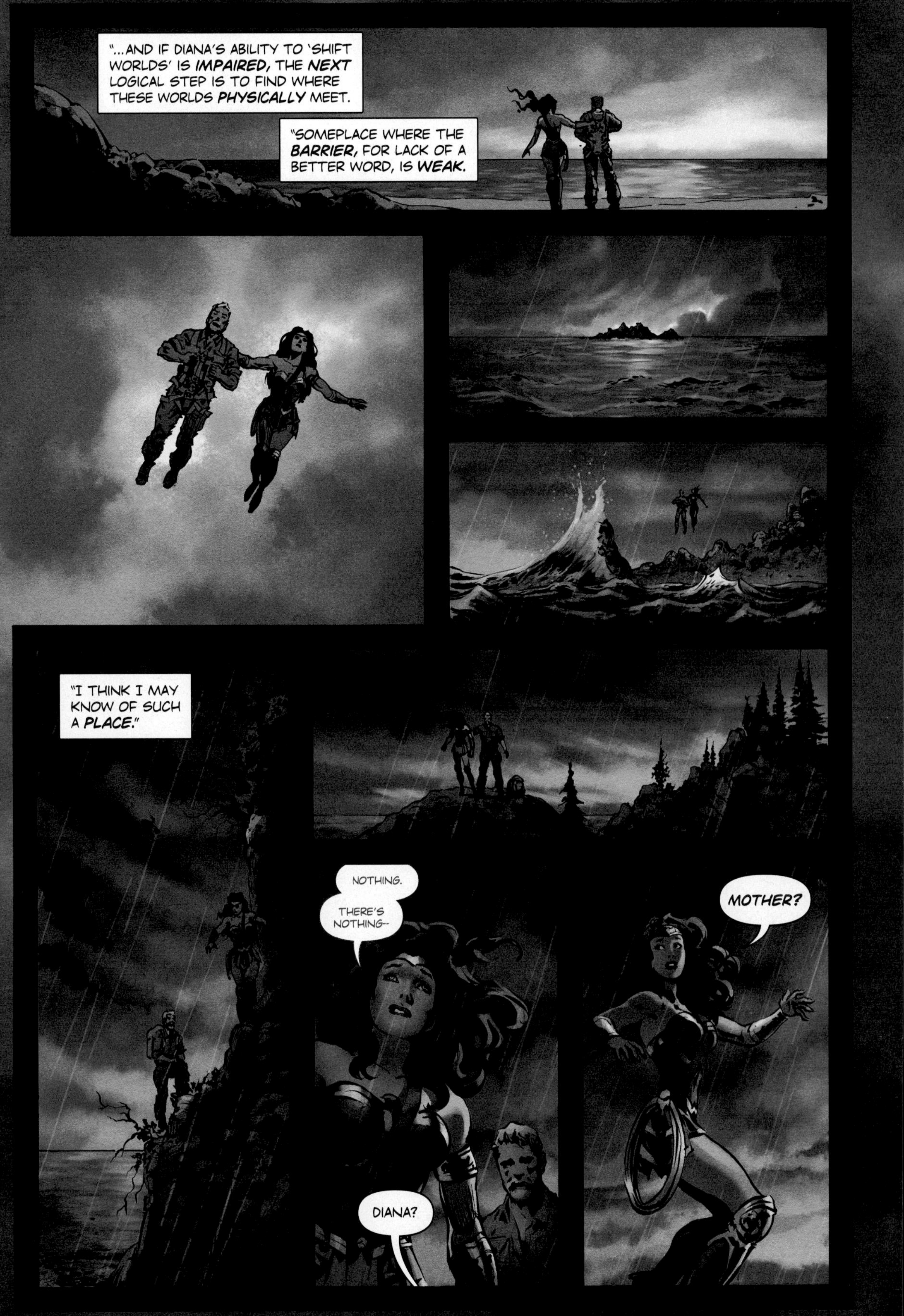
"...AND IF DIANA'S ABILITY TO 'SHIFT WORLDS' IS IMPAIRED, THE NEXT LOGICAL STEP IS TO FIND WHERE THESE WORLDS PHYSICALLY MEET.
"SOMEPLACE WHERE THE BARRIER, FOR LACK OF A BETTER WORD, IS WEAK.
"I THINK I MAY KNOW OF SUCH A PLACE."
NOTHING.
THERE'S NOTHING--
DIANA?
MOTHER?

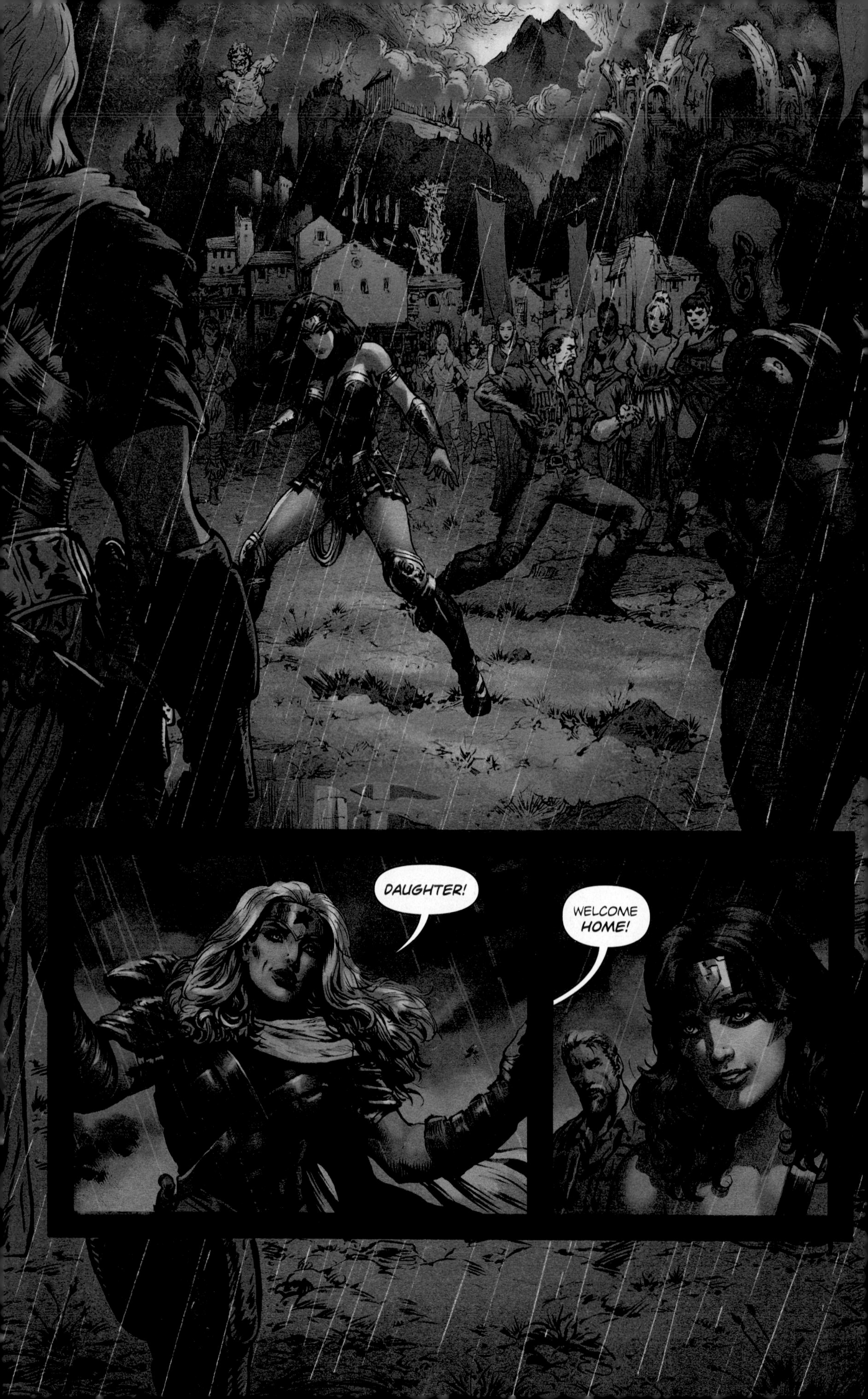
DAUGHTER!
WELCOME HOME!

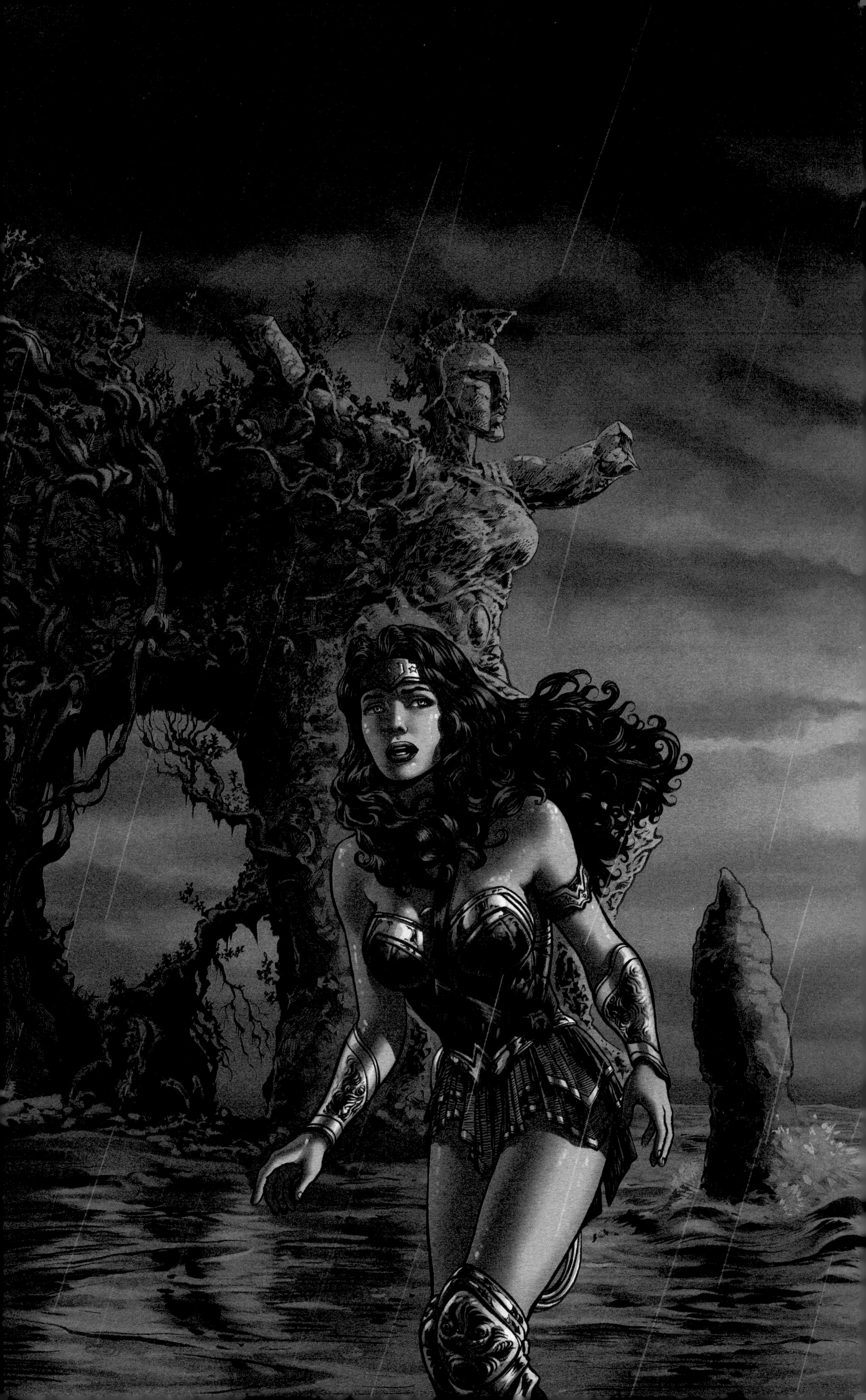

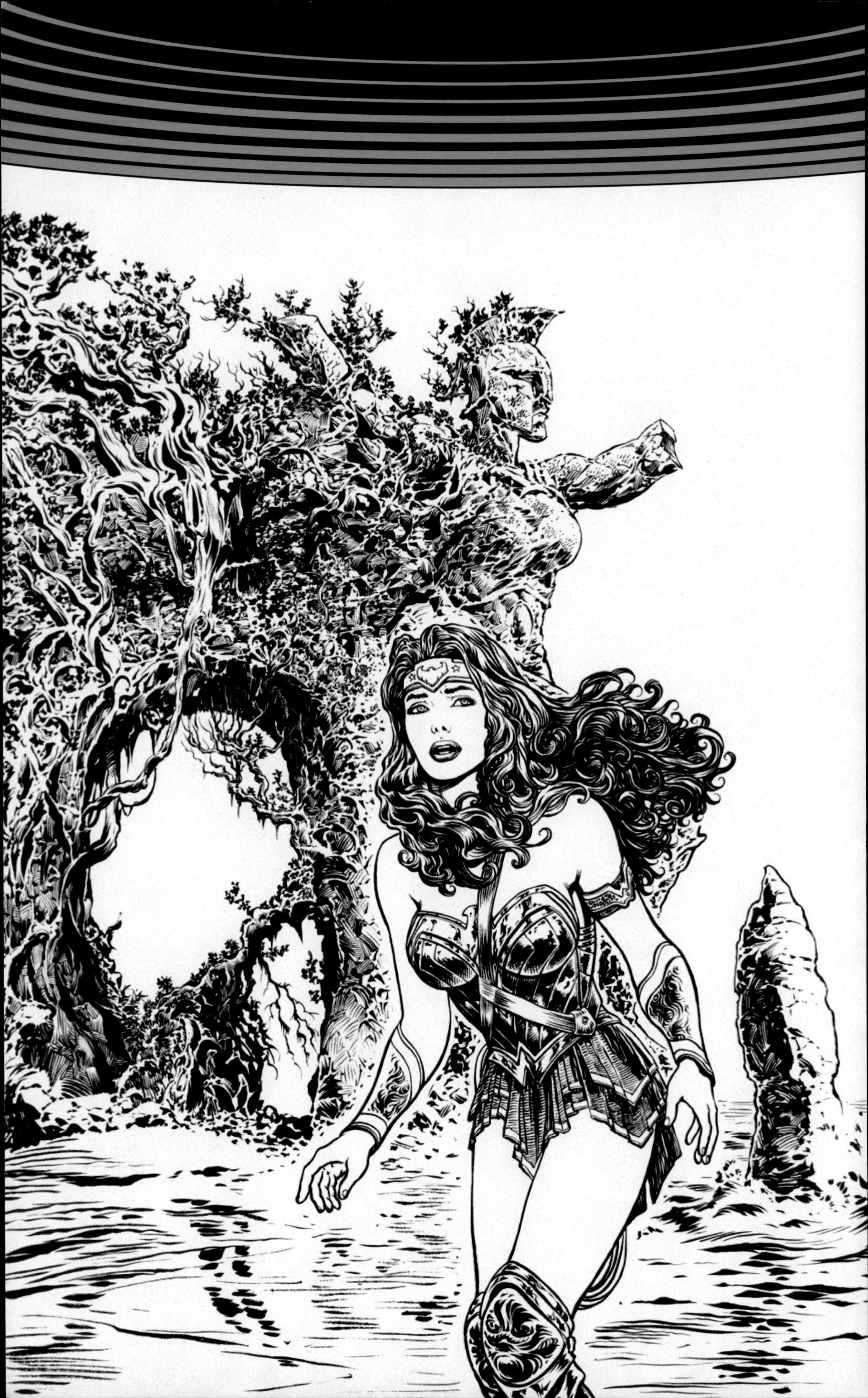

HE PICKET.

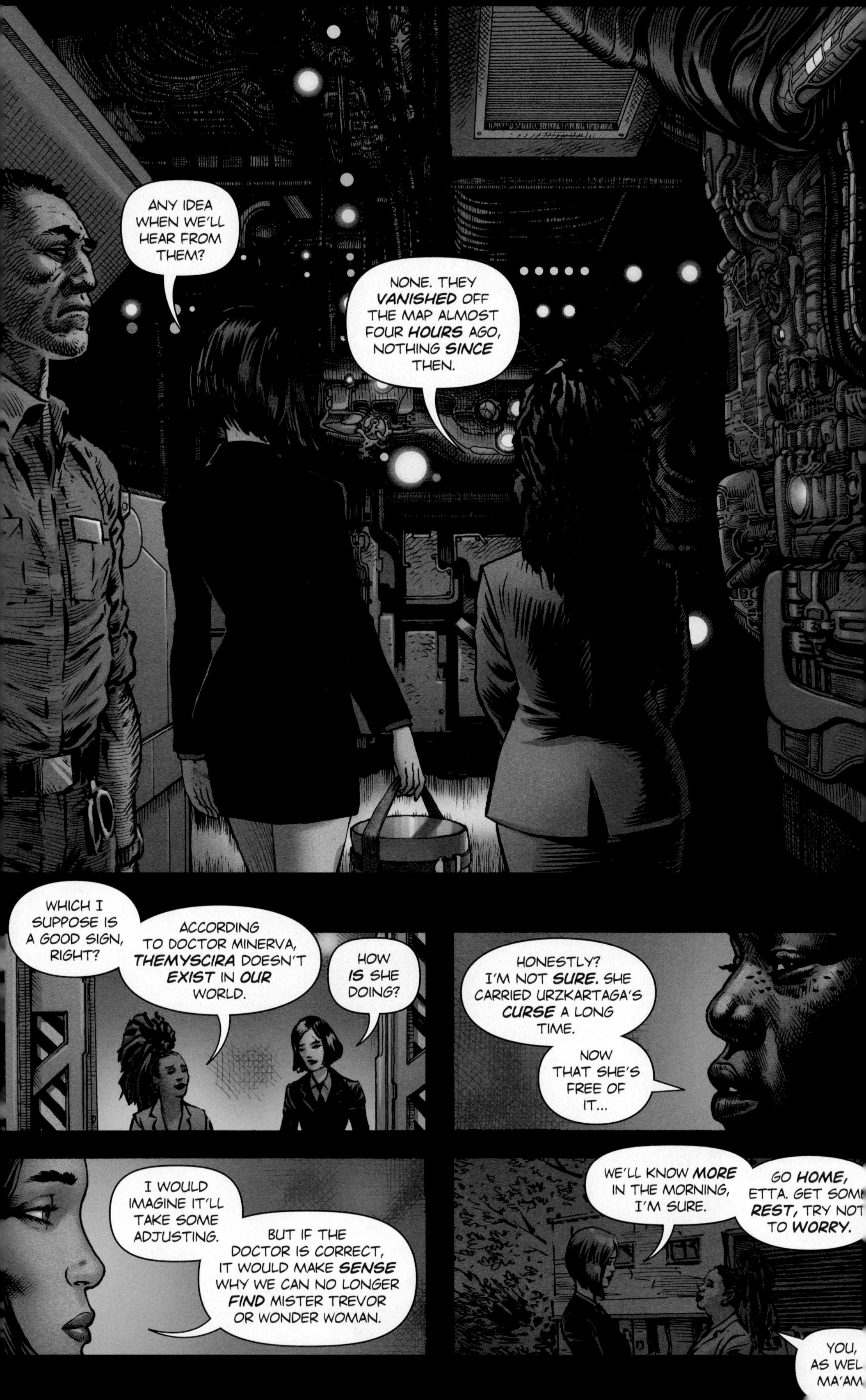
ANY IDEA WHEN WE'LL HEAR FROM THEM?
NONE. THEY VANISHED OFF THE MAP ALMOST FOUR HOURS AGO, NOTHING SINCE THEN.
WHICH I SUPPOSE IS A GOOD SIGN, RIGHT?
ACCORDING TO DOCTOR MINERVA, THEMYSCIRA DOESN'T EXIST IN OUR WORLD.
HOW IS SHE DOING?
HONESTLY? I'M NOT SURE. SHE CARRIED URZKARTAGA'S CURSE A LONG TIME.
NOW THAT SHE'S FREE OF IT...
I WOULD IMAGINE IT'LL TAKE SOME ADJUSTING.
BUT IF THE DOCTOR IS CORRECT, IT WOULD MAKE SENSE WHY WE CAN NO LONGER FIND MISTER TREVOR OR WONDER WOMAN.
WE'LL KNOW MORE IN THE MORNING, I'M SURE.
GO HOME, ETTA. GET SOM
REST, TRY NOT TO WORRY.
YOU, AS WEL MA'AM

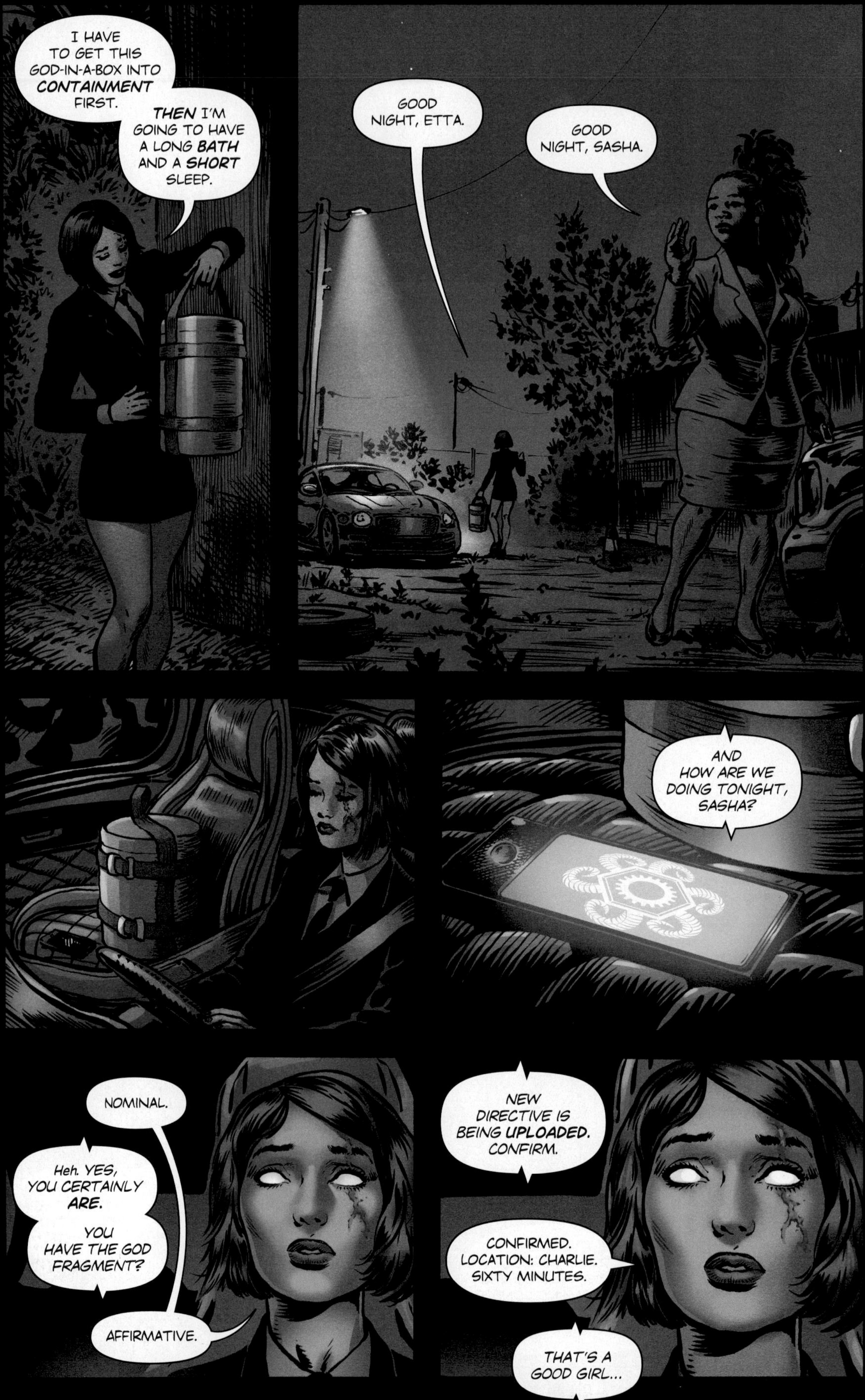
I HAVE TO GET THIS GOD-IN-A-BOX INTO CONTAINMENT FIRST.
THEN I'M GOING TO HAVE A LONG BATH AND A SHORT SLEEP.
GOOD NIGHT, ETTA.
GOOD NIGHT, SASHA.
AND HOW ARE WE DOING TONIGHT, SASHA?
NOMINAL.
Heh. YES, YOU CERTAINLY ARE.
YOU HAVE THE GOD FRAGMENT?
AFFIRMATIVE.
NEW DIRECTIVE IS BEING UPLOADED. CONFIRM.
CONFIRMED. LOCATION: CHARLIE. SIXTY MINUTES.
THAT'S A GOOD GIRL...

...SEE YOU SOON....

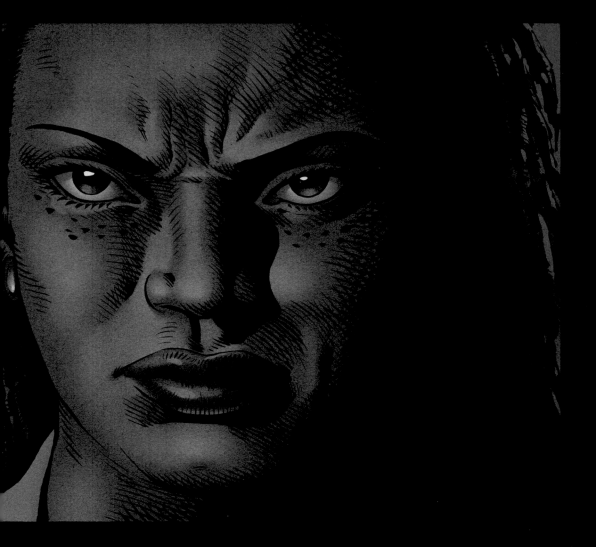

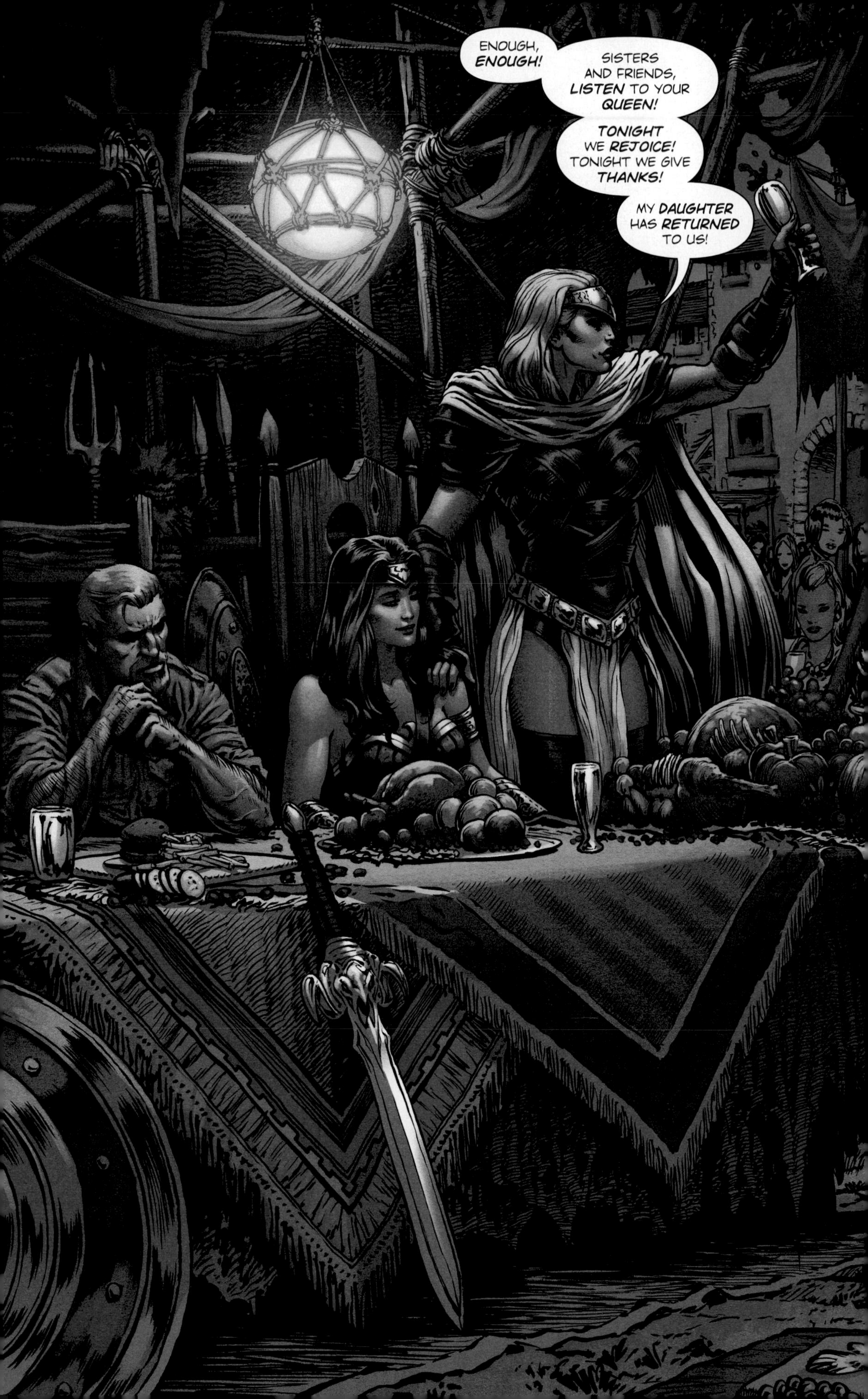
ENOUGH, ENOUGH!
SISTERS AND FRIENDS, LISTEN TO YOUR QUEEN!
TONIGHT WE REJOICE! TONIGHT WE GIVE THANKS!
MY DAUGHTER HAS RETURNED TO US!

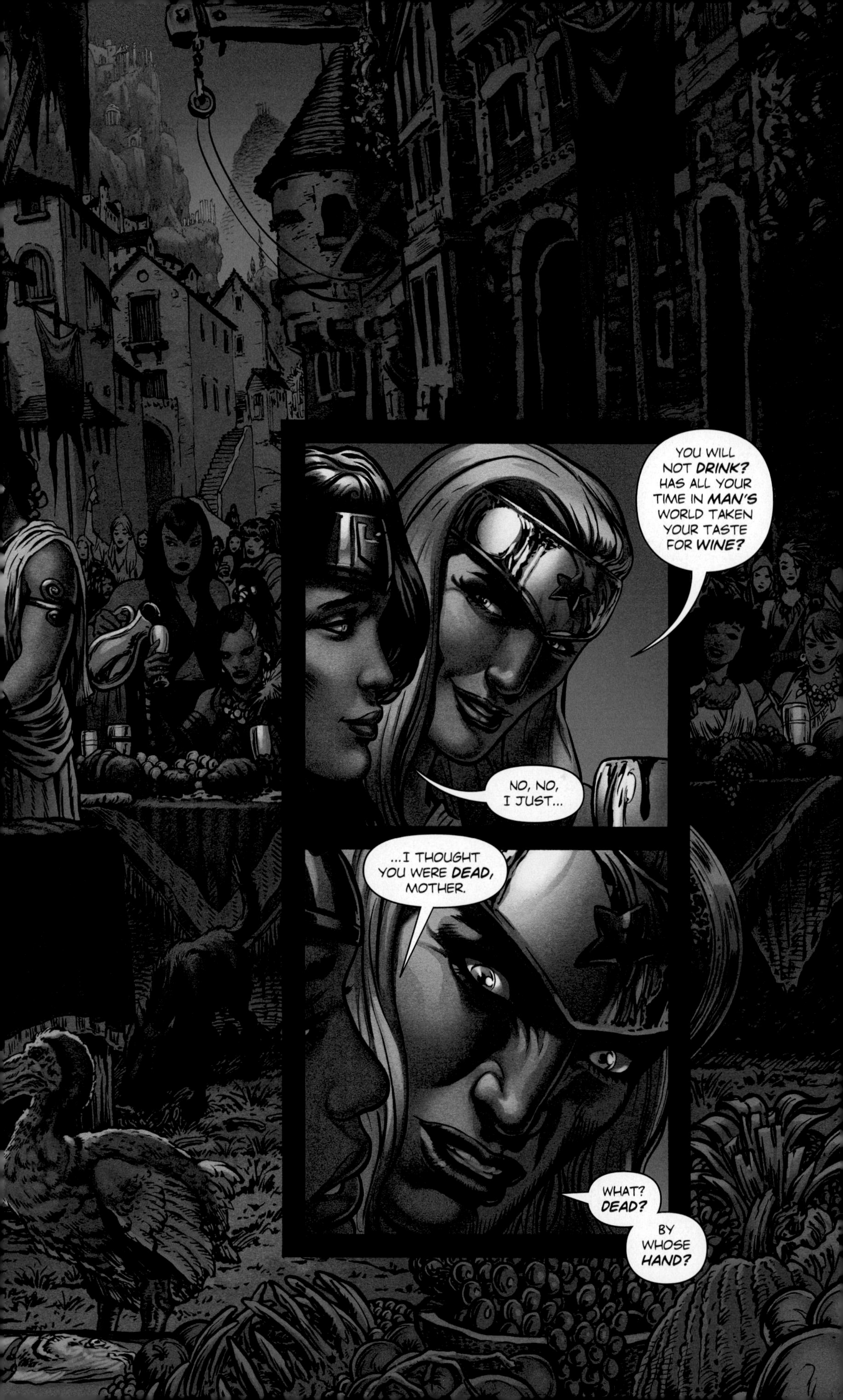
YOU WILL NOT DRINK? HAS ALL YOUR TIME IN MAN'S WORLD TAKEN YOUR TASTE FOR WINE?
NO, NO, I JUST...
...I THOUGHT YOU WERE DEAD, MOTHER.
WHAT? DEAD?
BY WHOSE HAND?

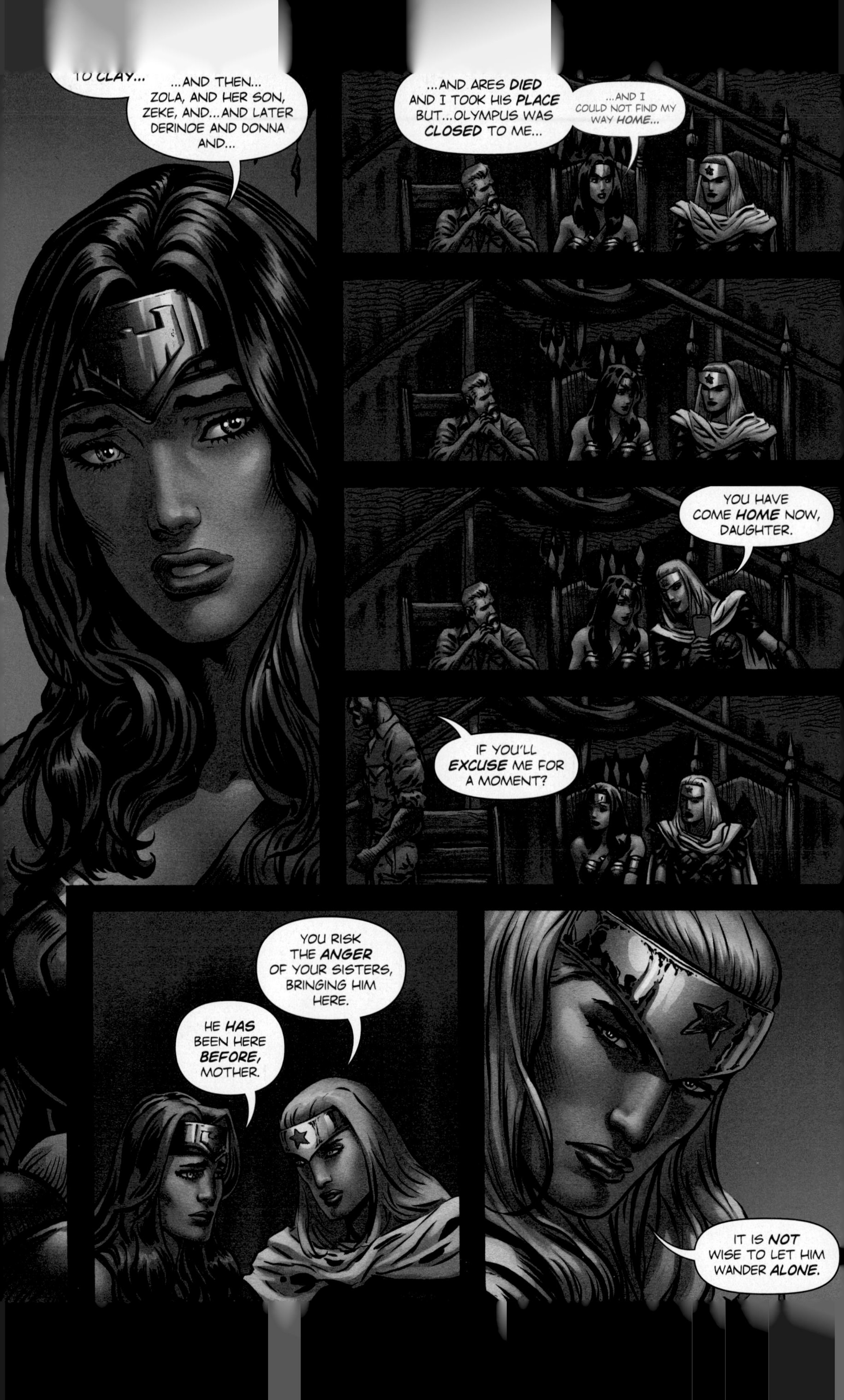
TO CLAY...
...AND THEN... ZOLA, AND HER SON, ZEKE, AND...AND LATER DERINOE AND DONNA AND...
...AND ARES DIED AND I TOOK HIS PLACE BUT...OLYMPUS WAS CLOSED TO ME...
...AND I COULD NOT FIND MY WAY HOME...
YOU HAVE COME HOME NOW, DAUGHTER.
IF YOU'LL EXCUSE ME FOR A MOMENT?
YOU RISK THE ANGER OF YOUR SISTERS, BRINGING HIM HERE.
HE HAS BEEN HERE BEFORE, MOTHER.
IT IS NOT WISE TO LET HIM WANDER ALONE.

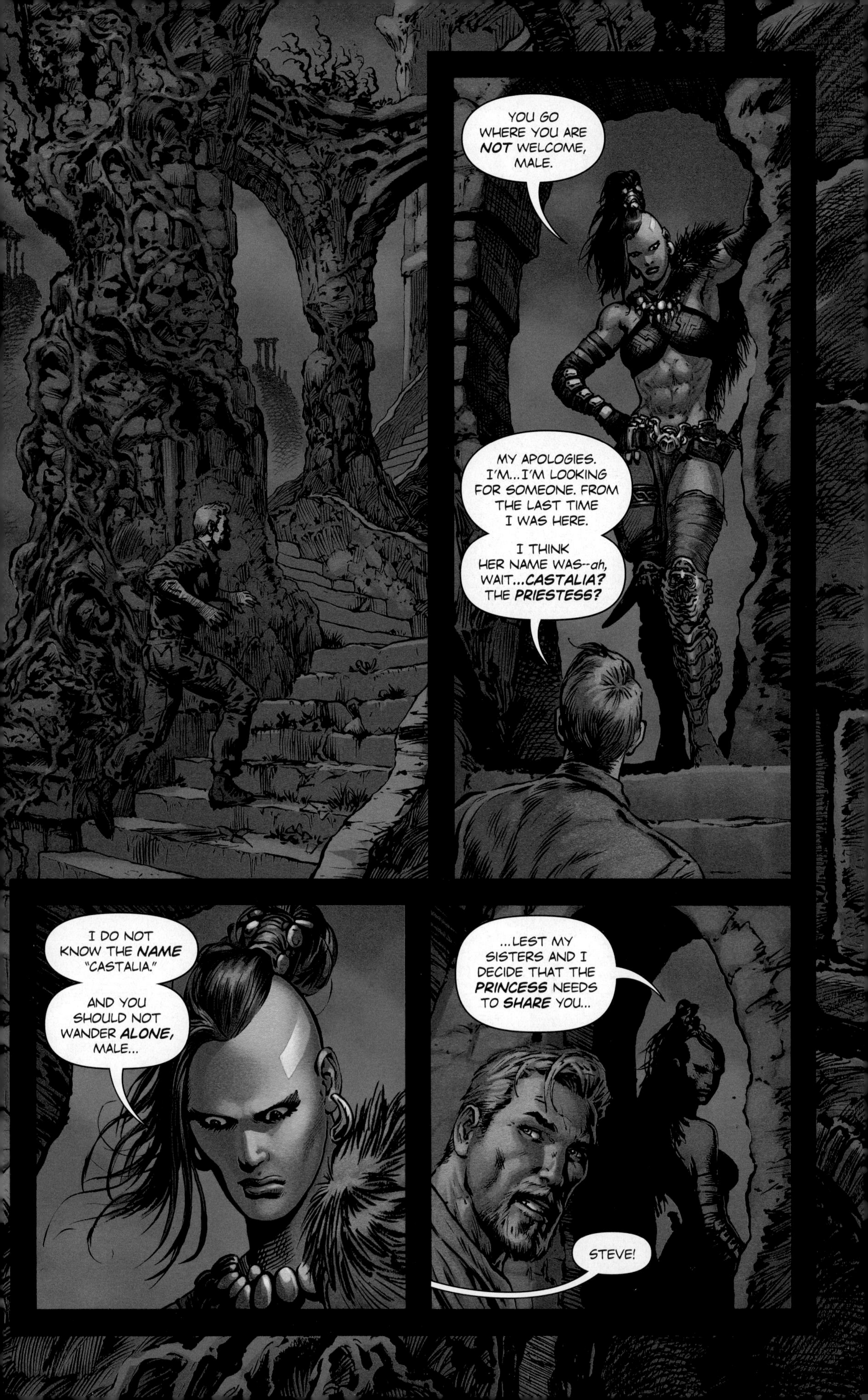

YOU GO WHERE YOU ARE ***NOT*** WELCOME, MALE.
MY APOLOGIES. I'M...I'M LOOKING FOR SOMEONE. FROM THE LAST TIME I WAS HERE.
I THINK HER NAME WAS--*ah,* WAIT...***CASTALIA?*** THE ***PRIESTESS?***
I DO NOT KNOW THE ***NAME*** "CASTALIA."
AND YOU SHOULD NOT WANDER ***ALONE,*** MALE...
...LEST MY SISTERS AND I DECIDE THAT THE ***PRINCESS*** NEEDS TO ***SHARE*** YOU...
STEVE!

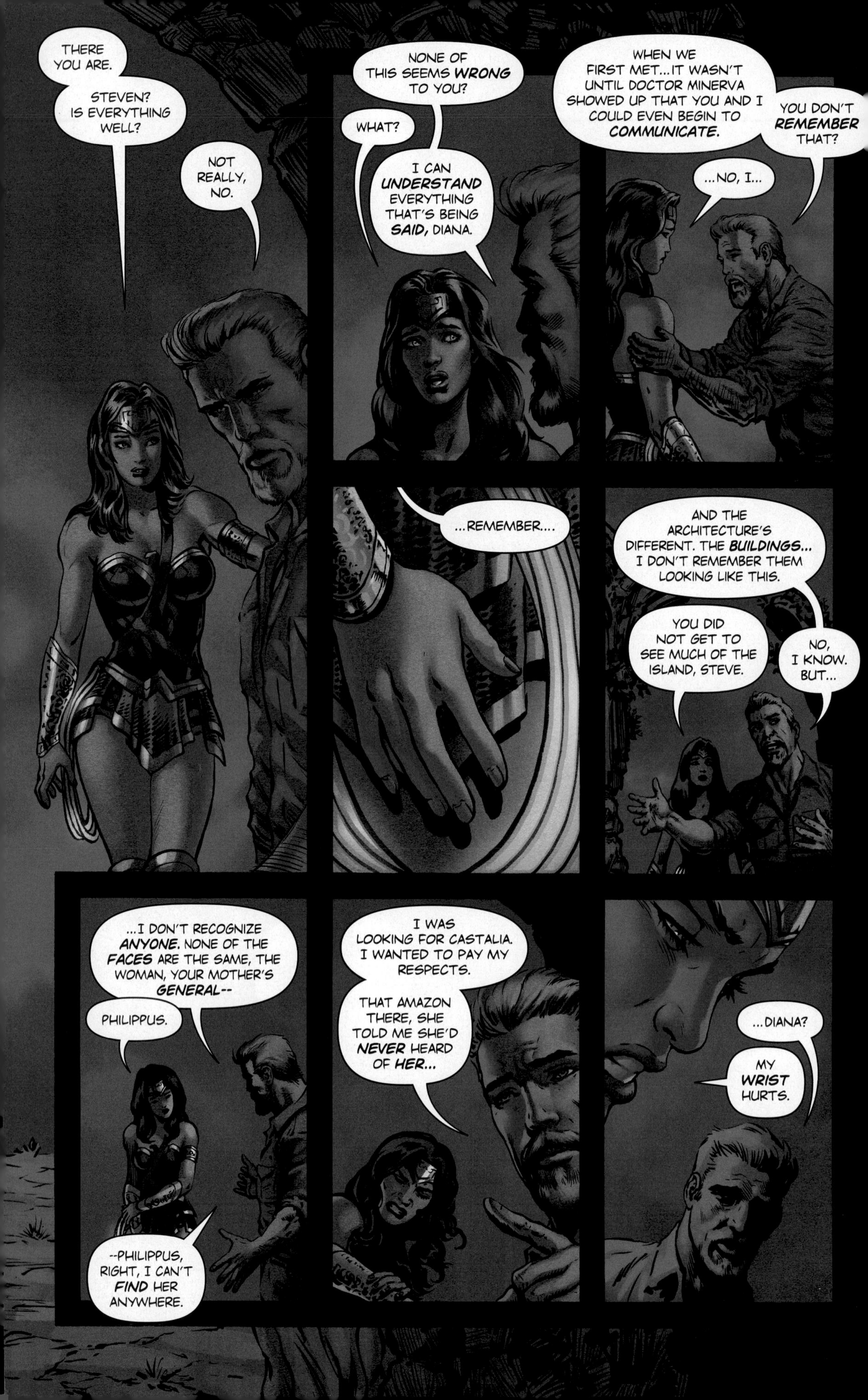
THERE YOU ARE.
STEVEN? IS EVERYTHING WELL?
NOT REALLY, NO.
NONE OF THIS SEEMS **WRONG** TO YOU?
WHAT?
I CAN **UNDERSTAND** EVERYTHING THAT'S BEING **SAID,** DIANA.
WHEN WE FIRST MET...IT WASN'T UNTIL DOCTOR MINERVA SHOWED UP THAT YOU AND I COULD EVEN BEGIN TO **COMMUNICATE.**
YOU DON'T **REMEMBER** THAT?
...NO, I...
...REMEMBER....
AND THE ARCHITECTURE'S DIFFERENT. THE **BUILDINGS...** I DON'T REMEMBER THEM LOOKING LIKE THIS.
YOU DID NOT GET TO SEE MUCH OF THE ISLAND, STEVE.
NO, I KNOW. BUT...
...I DON'T RECOGNIZE **ANYONE.** NONE OF THE **FACES** ARE THE SAME, THE WOMAN, YOUR MOTHER'S **GENERAL--**
PHILIPPUS.
--PHILIPPUS, RIGHT, I CAN'T **FIND** HER ANYWHERE.
I WAS LOOKING FOR CASTALIA. I WANTED TO PAY MY RESPECTS.
THAT AMAZON THERE, SHE TOLD ME SHE'D **NEVER** HEARD OF **HER...**
...DIANA?
MY **WRIST** HURTS.

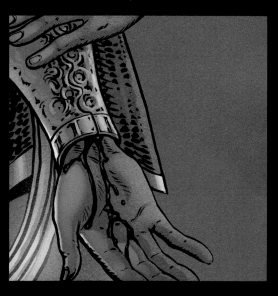

COME
WITH ME.
QUICKLY.

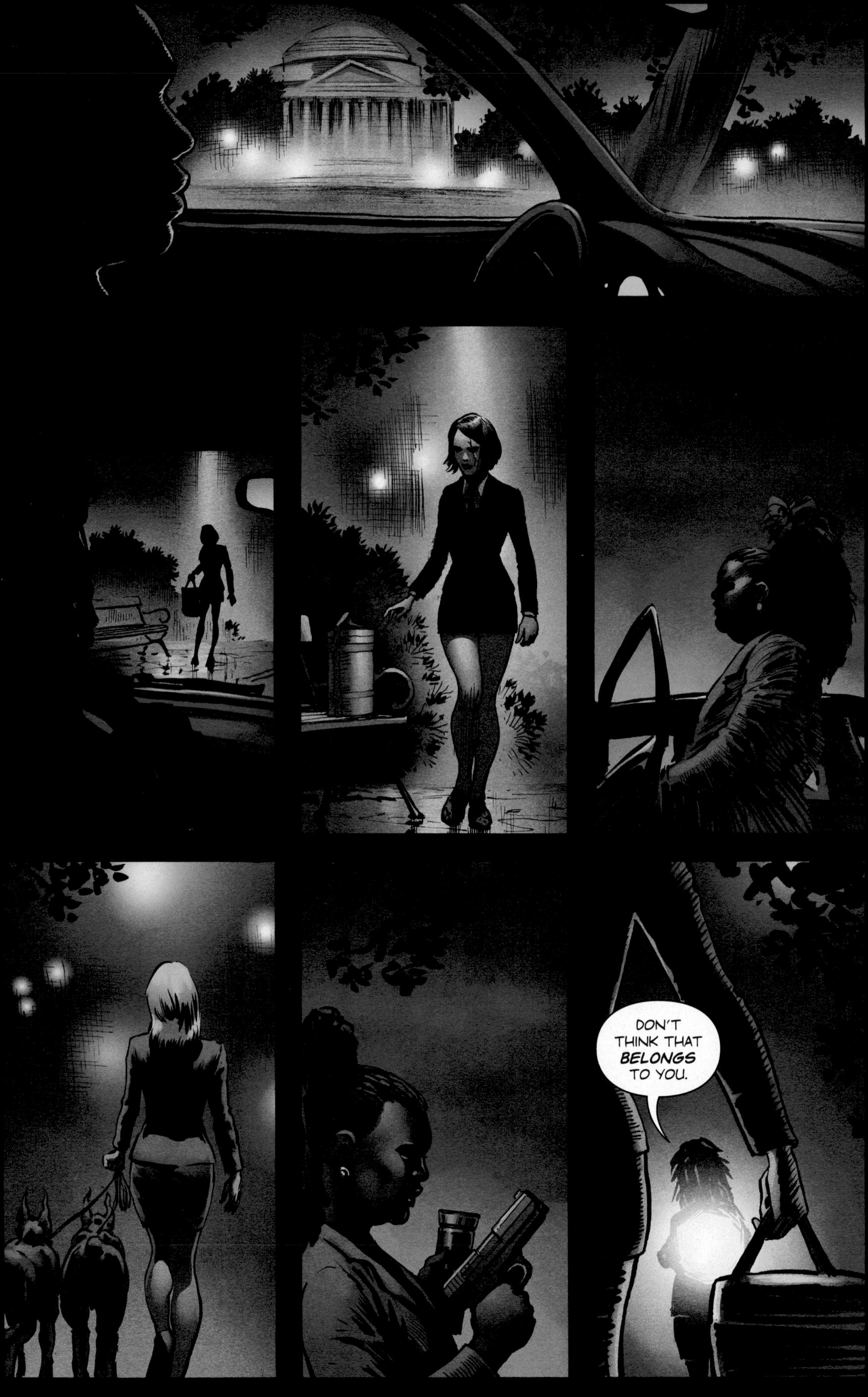
DON'T THINK THAT BELONGS TO YOU.

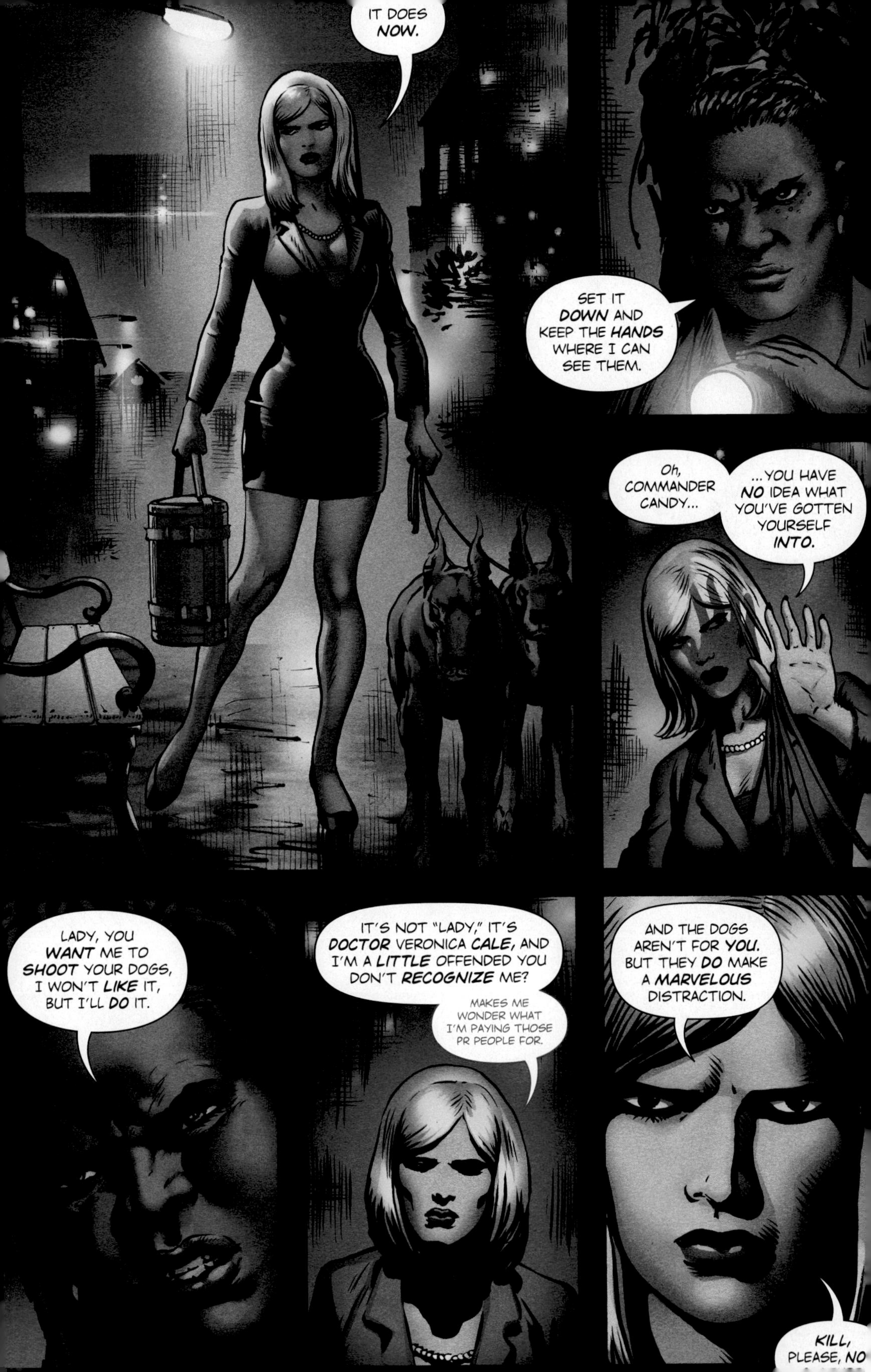

IT DOES NOW.
SET IT DOWN AND KEEP THE HANDS WHERE I CAN SEE THEM.
Oh, COMMANDER CANDY...
...YOU HAVE NO IDEA WHAT YOU'VE GOTTEN YOURSELF INTO.
LADY, YOU WANT ME TO SHOOT YOUR DOGS, I WON'T LIKE IT, BUT I'LL DO IT.
IT'S NOT "LADY," IT'S DOCTOR VERONICA CALE, AND I'M A LITTLE OFFENDED YOU DON'T RECOGNIZE ME?
MAKES ME WONDER WHAT I'M PAYING THOSE PR PEOPLE FOR.
AND THE DOGS AREN'T FOR YOU. BUT THEY DO MAKE A MARVELOUS DISTRACTION.
KILL, PLEASE, NO

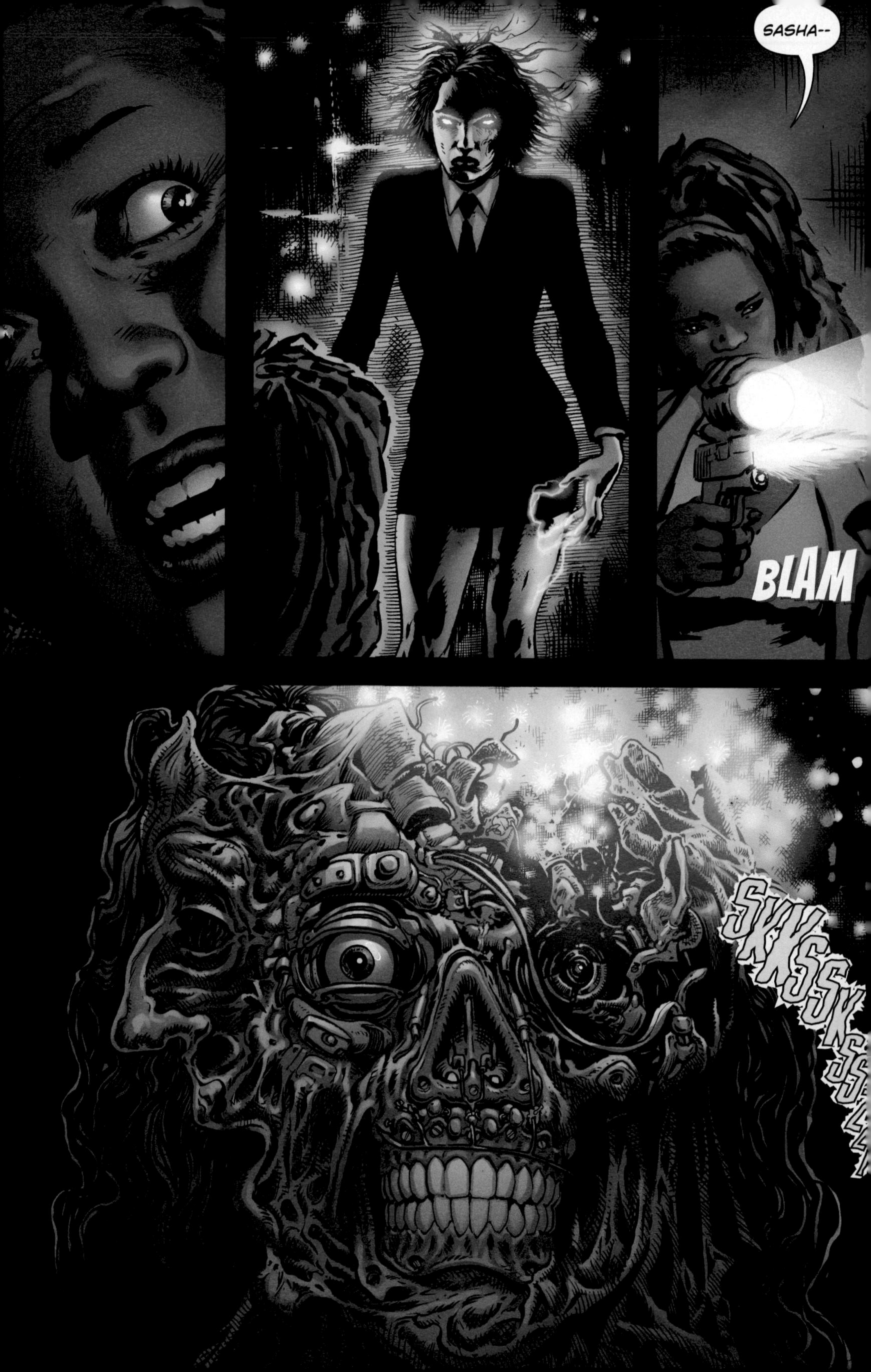
SASHA--
BLAM
SKKSSKSSSZZ

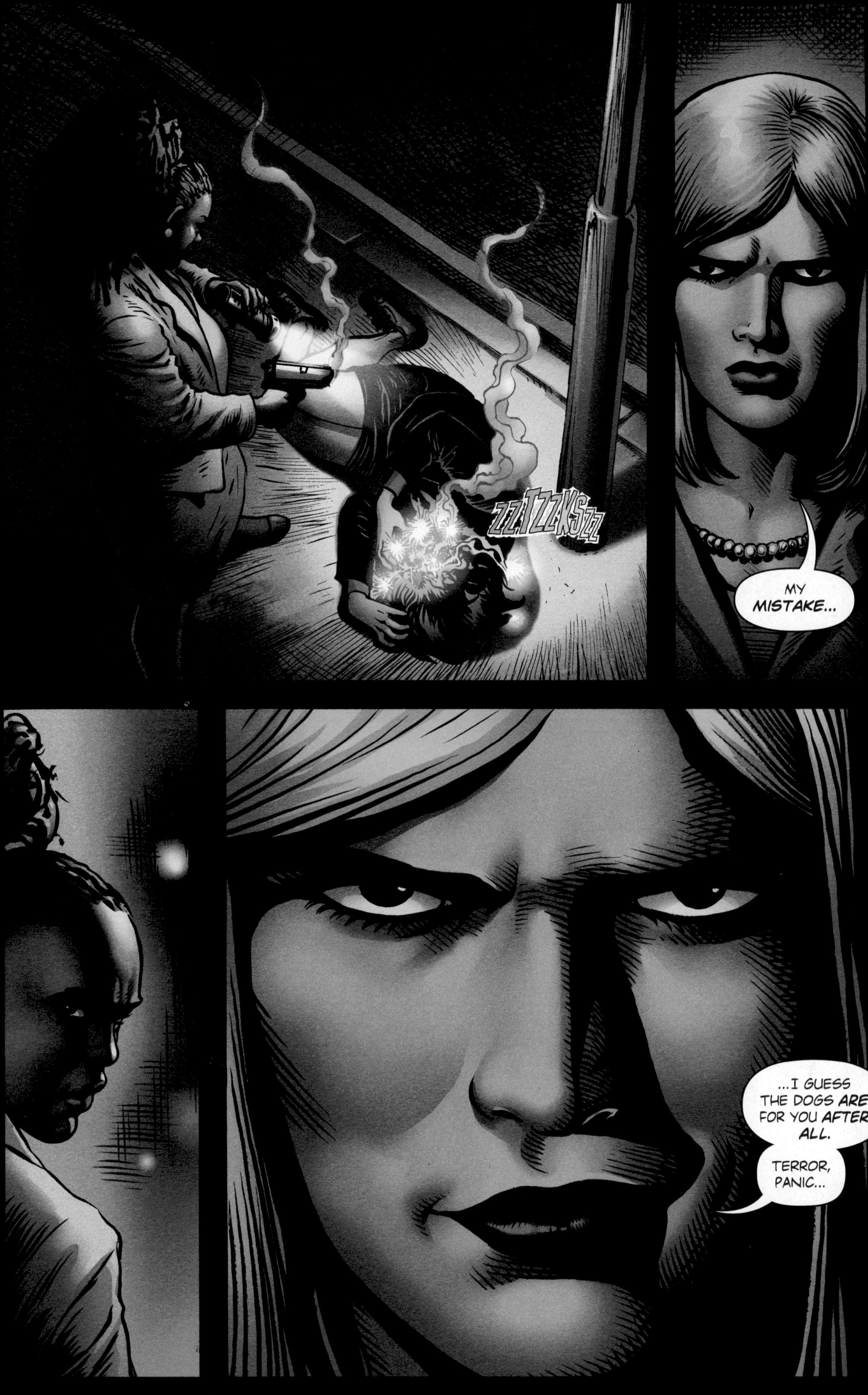
ZZ TZZKSZZ
MY MISTAKE...
...I GUESS THE DOGS ARE FOR YOU AFTER ALL.
TERROR, PANIC...

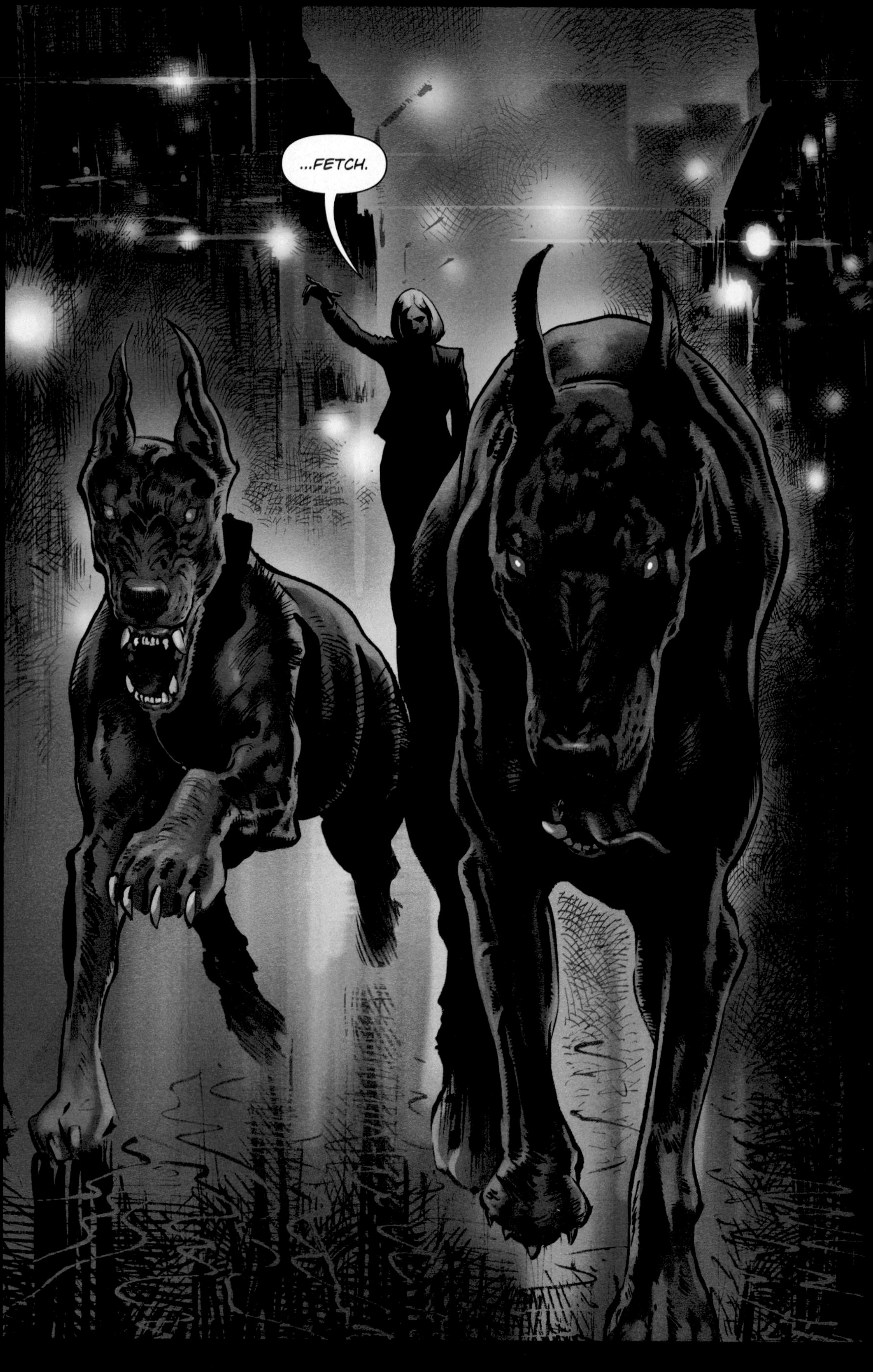
...FETCH.

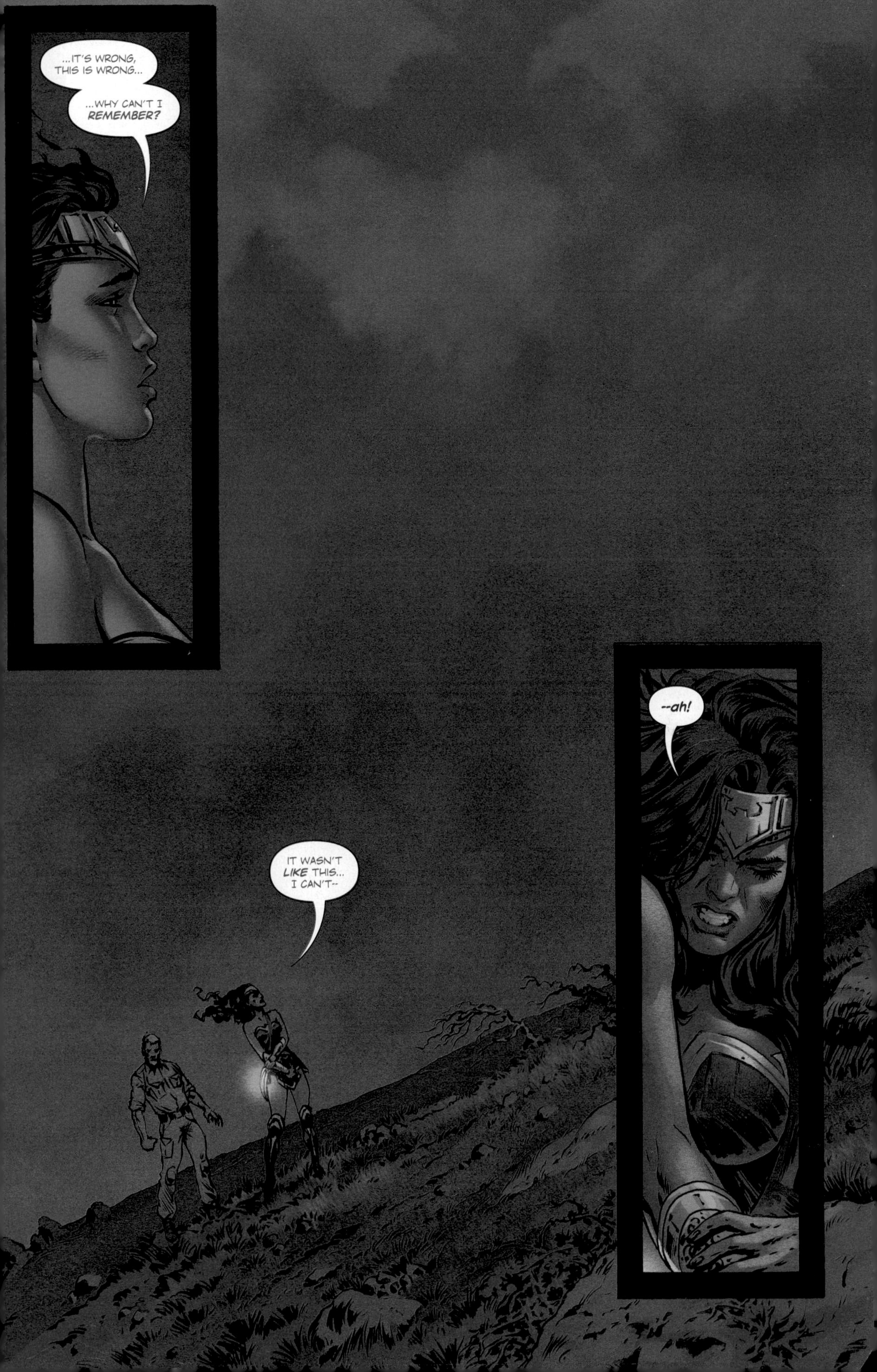
...IT'S WRONG, THIS IS WRONG...
...WHY CAN'T I *REMEMBER?*
IT WASN'T *LIKE* THIS... I CAN'T--
--ah!

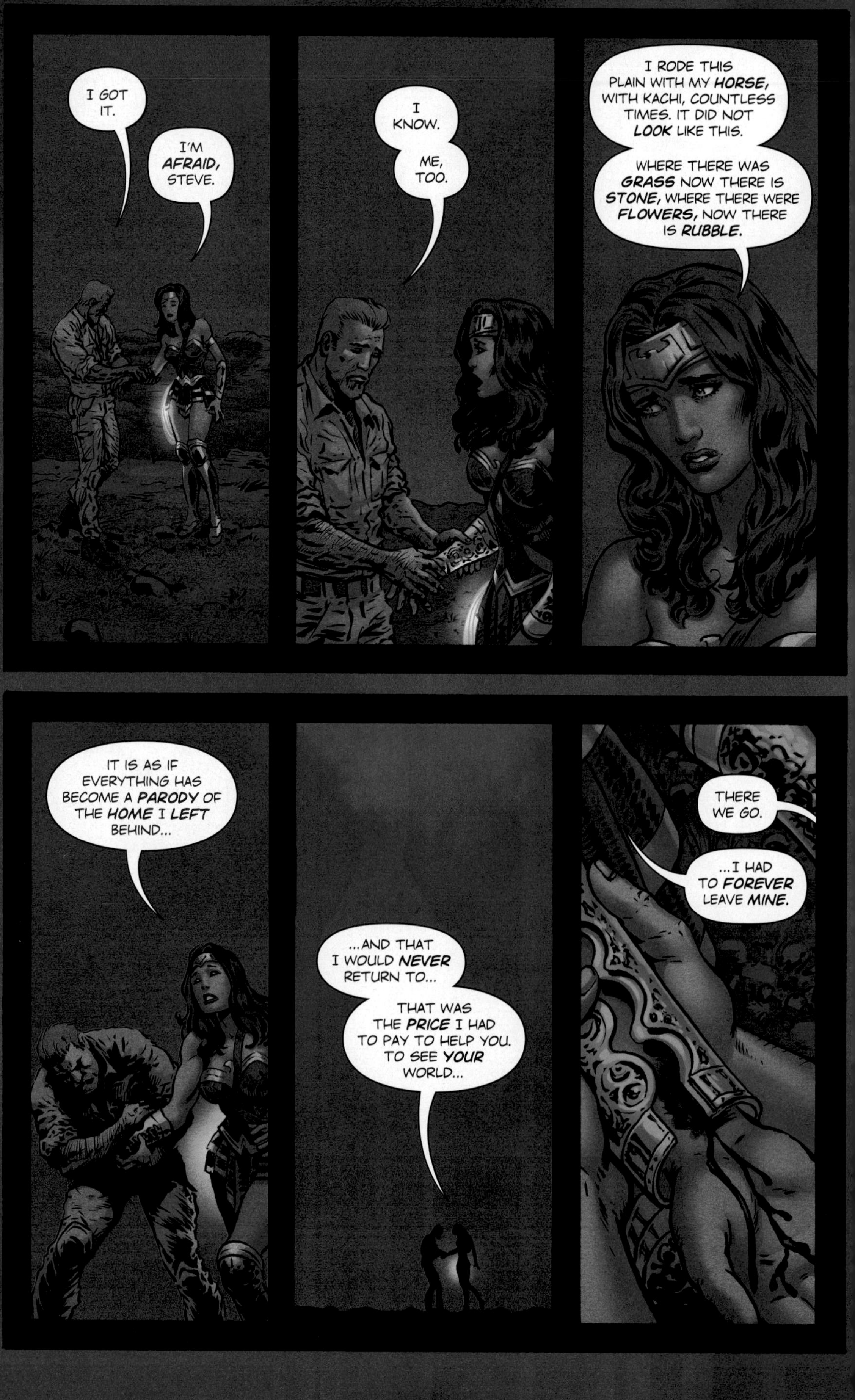
I GOT IT.
I'M AFRAID, STEVE.
I KNOW.
ME, TOO.
I RODE THIS PLAIN WITH MY HORSE, WITH KACHI, COUNTLESS TIMES. IT DID NOT LOOK LIKE THIS.
WHERE THERE WAS GRASS NOW THERE IS STONE, WHERE THERE WERE FLOWERS, NOW THERE IS RUBBLE.
IT IS AS IF EVERYTHING HAS BECOME A PARODY OF THE HOME I LEFT BEHIND...
...AND THAT I WOULD NEVER RETURN TO...
THAT WAS THE PRICE I HAD TO PAY TO HELP YOU. TO SEE YOUR WORLD...
THERE WE GO.
...I HAD TO FOREVER LEAVE MINE.

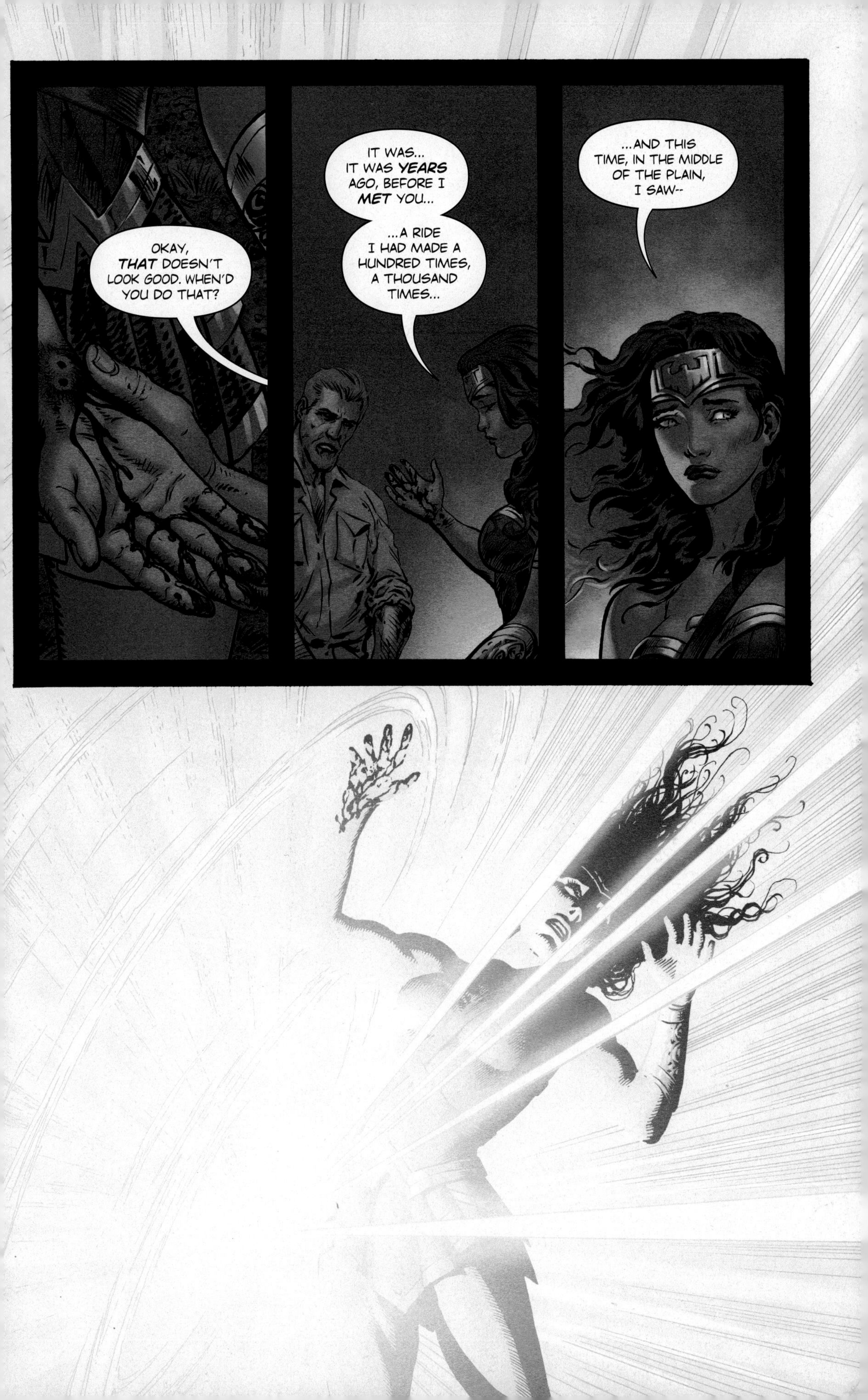
OKAY, THAT DOESN'T LOOK GOOD. WHEN'D YOU DO THAT?
IT WAS... IT WAS YEARS AGO, BEFORE I MET YOU...
...A RIDE I HAD MADE A HUNDRED TIMES, A THOUSAND TIMES...
...AND THIS TIME, IN THE MIDDLE OF THE PLAIN, I SAW--

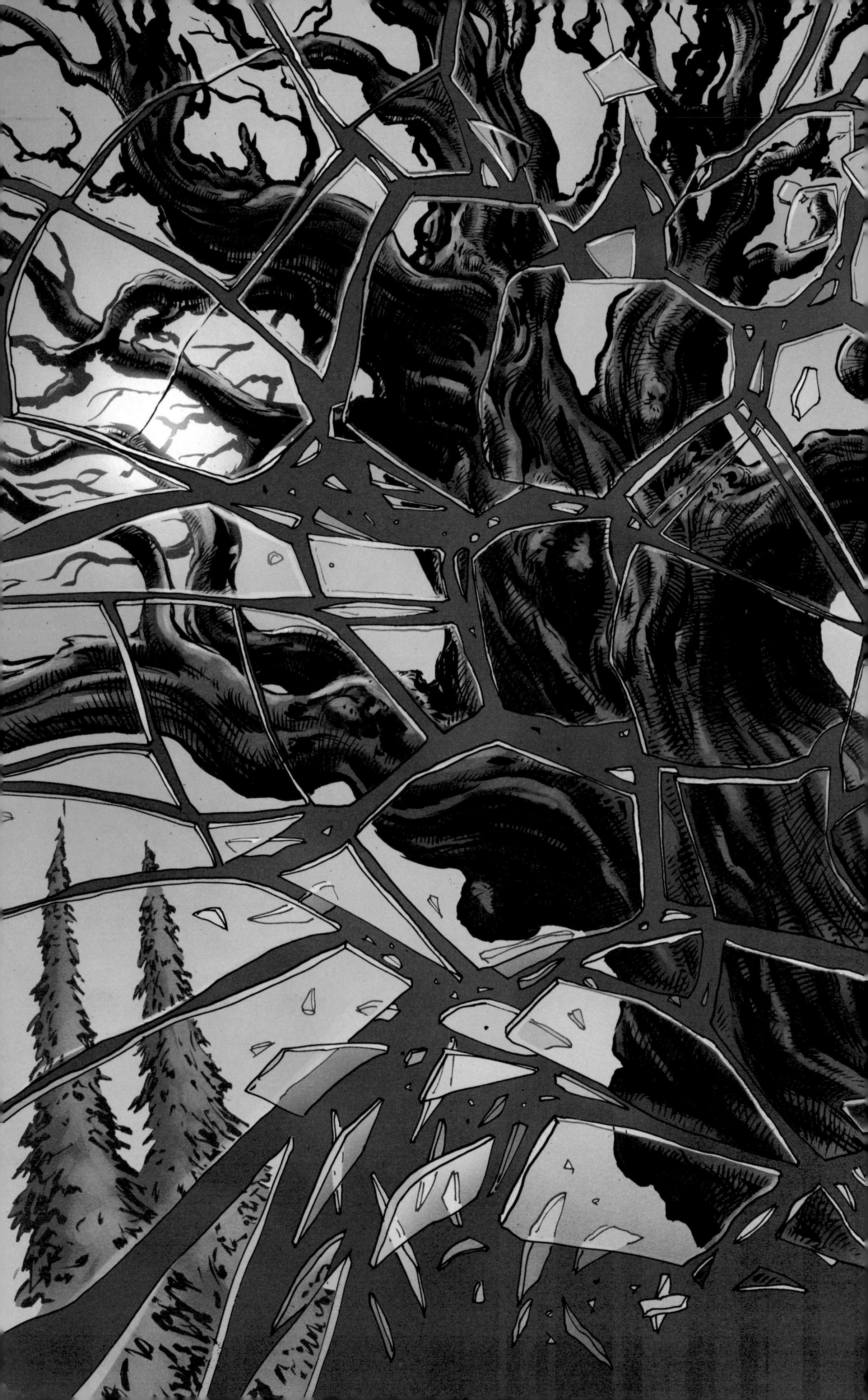

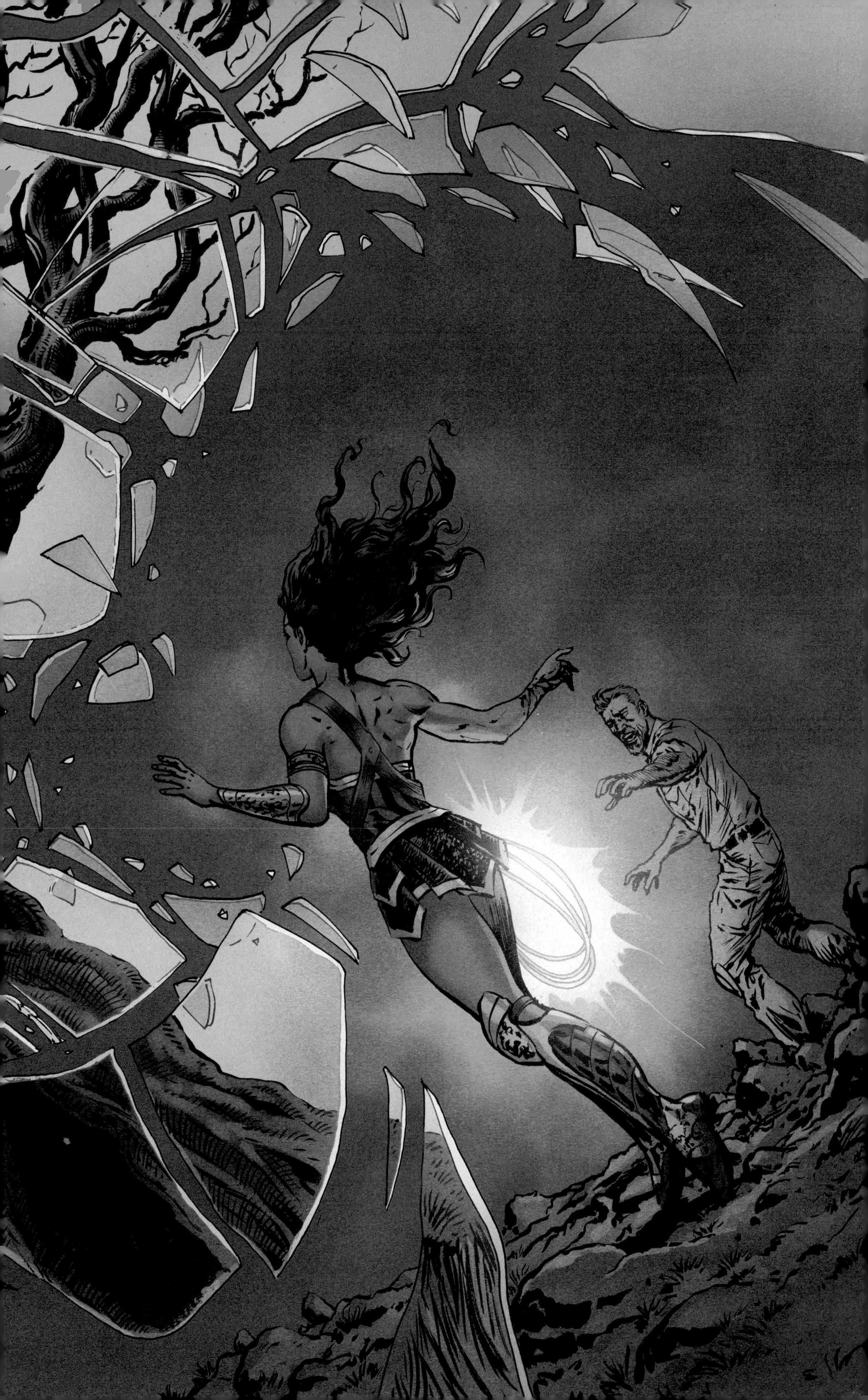

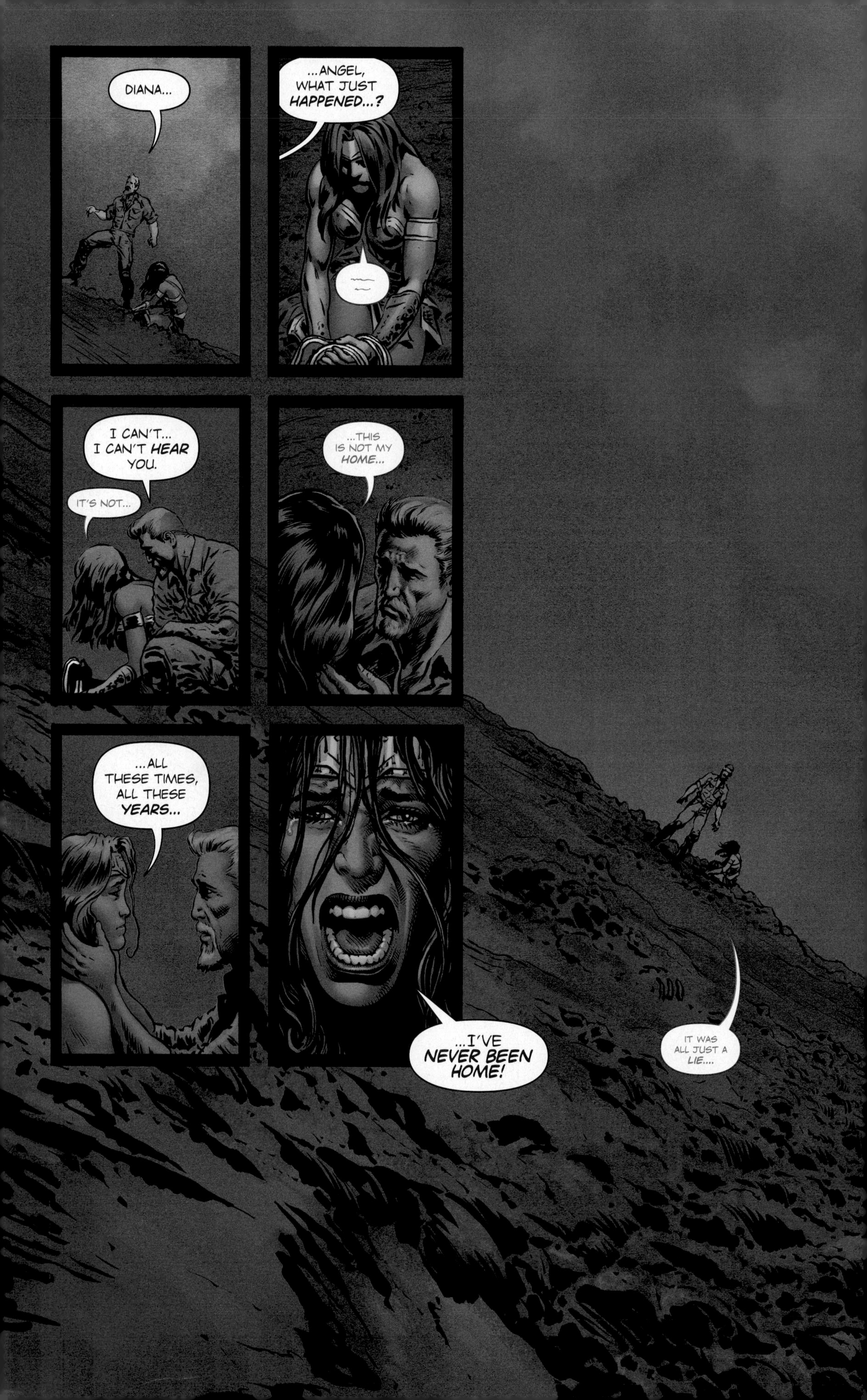
DIANA...
...ANGEL, WHAT JUST HAPPENED...?
I CAN'T... I CAN'T HEAR YOU.
IT'S NOT...
...THIS IS NOT MY HOME...
...ALL THESE TIMES, ALL THESE YEARS...
...I'VE NEVER BEEN HOME!
IT WAS ALL JUST A LIE....

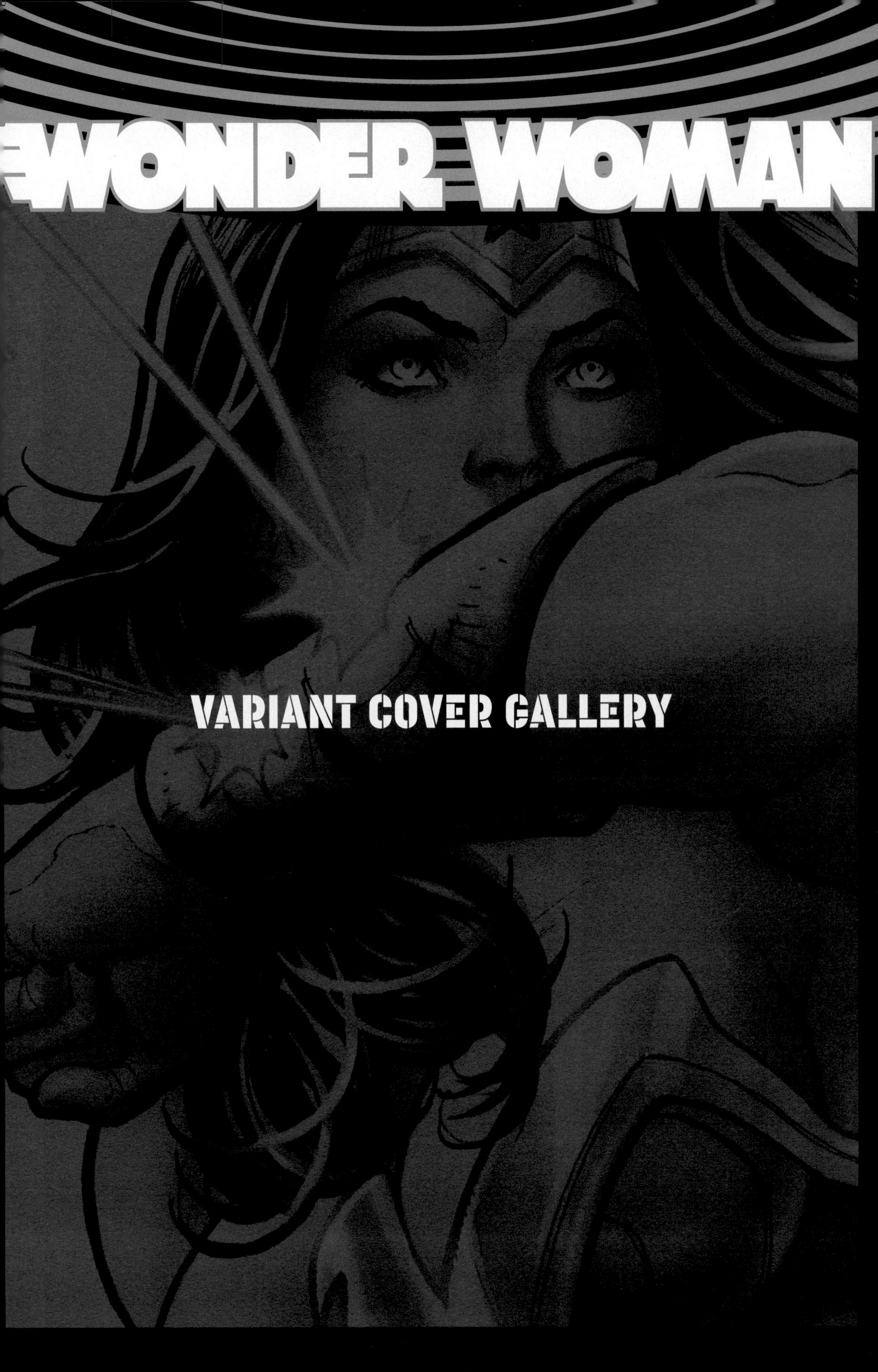
WONDER WOMAN

VARIANT COVER GALLERY

WONDER WOMAN: REBIRTH #1 variant cover by STANLEY "ARTGERM" LAU

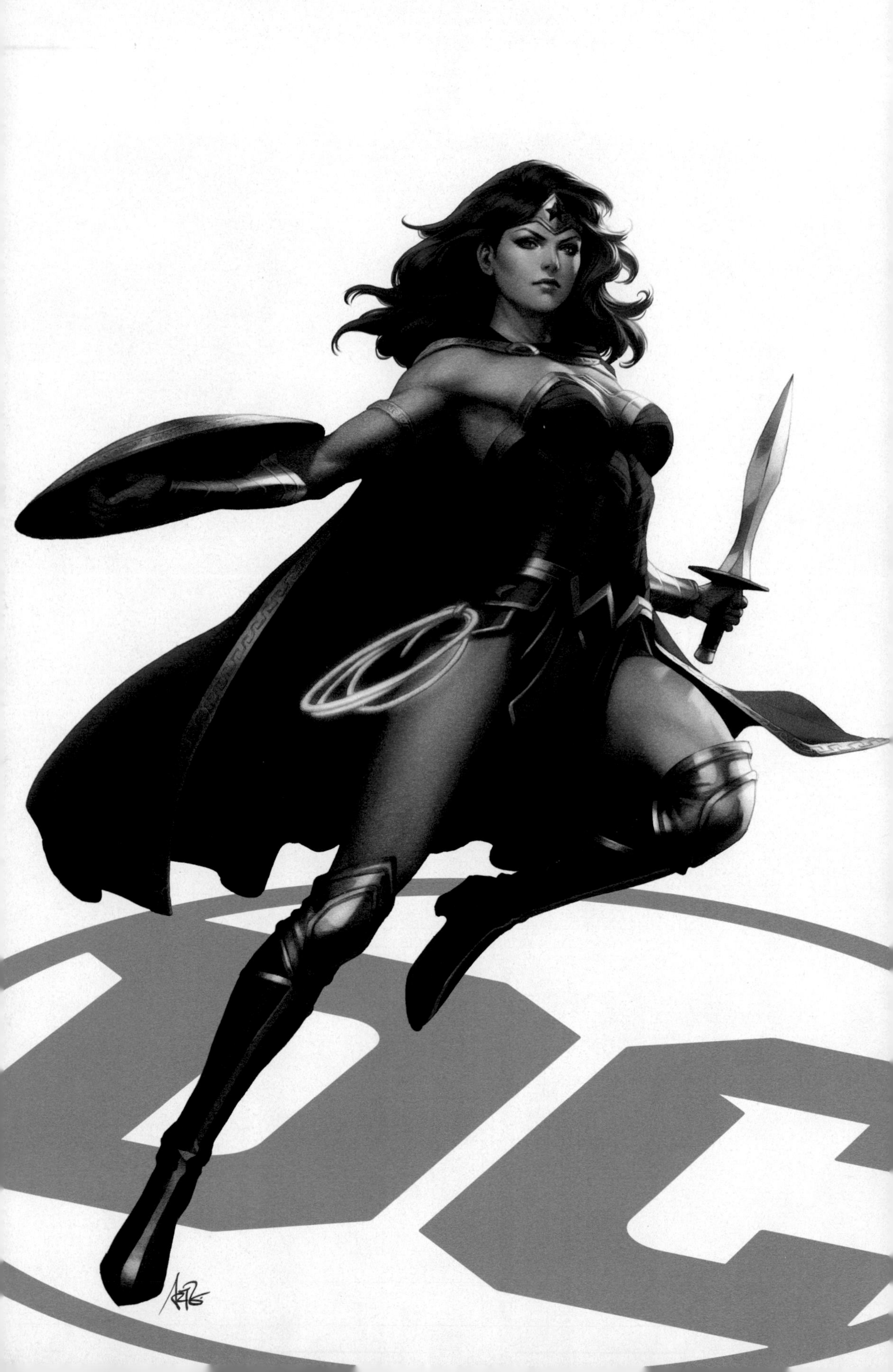

WONDER WOMAN: REBIRTH #1 Warner Brothers Studio Tour variant cover by MATTHEW CLARK with WENDY BROOME

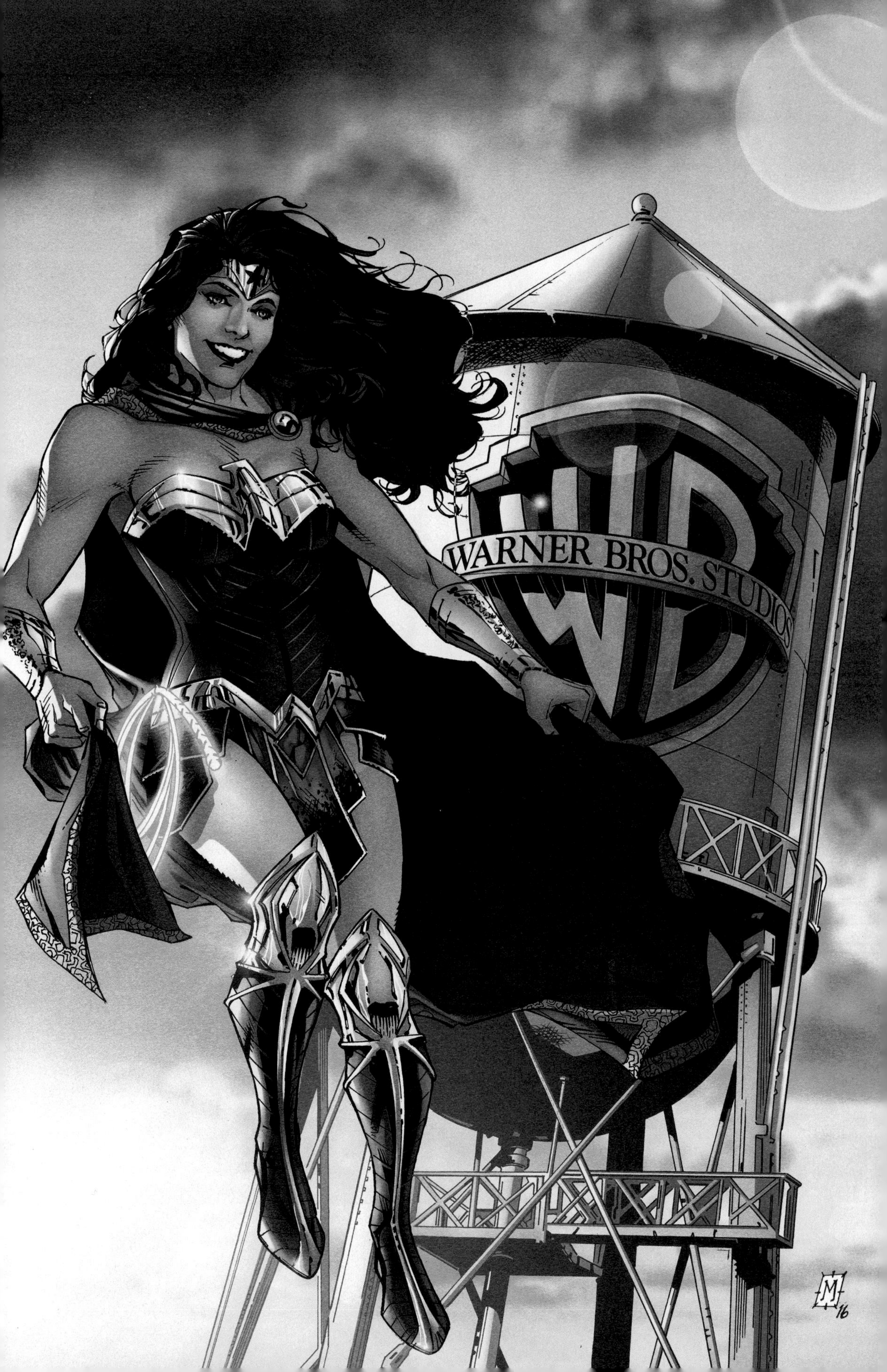
WB
WARNER BROS. STUDIOS
M '16

WONDER WOMAN #1 variant cover by FRANK CHO and NEI RUFFINO

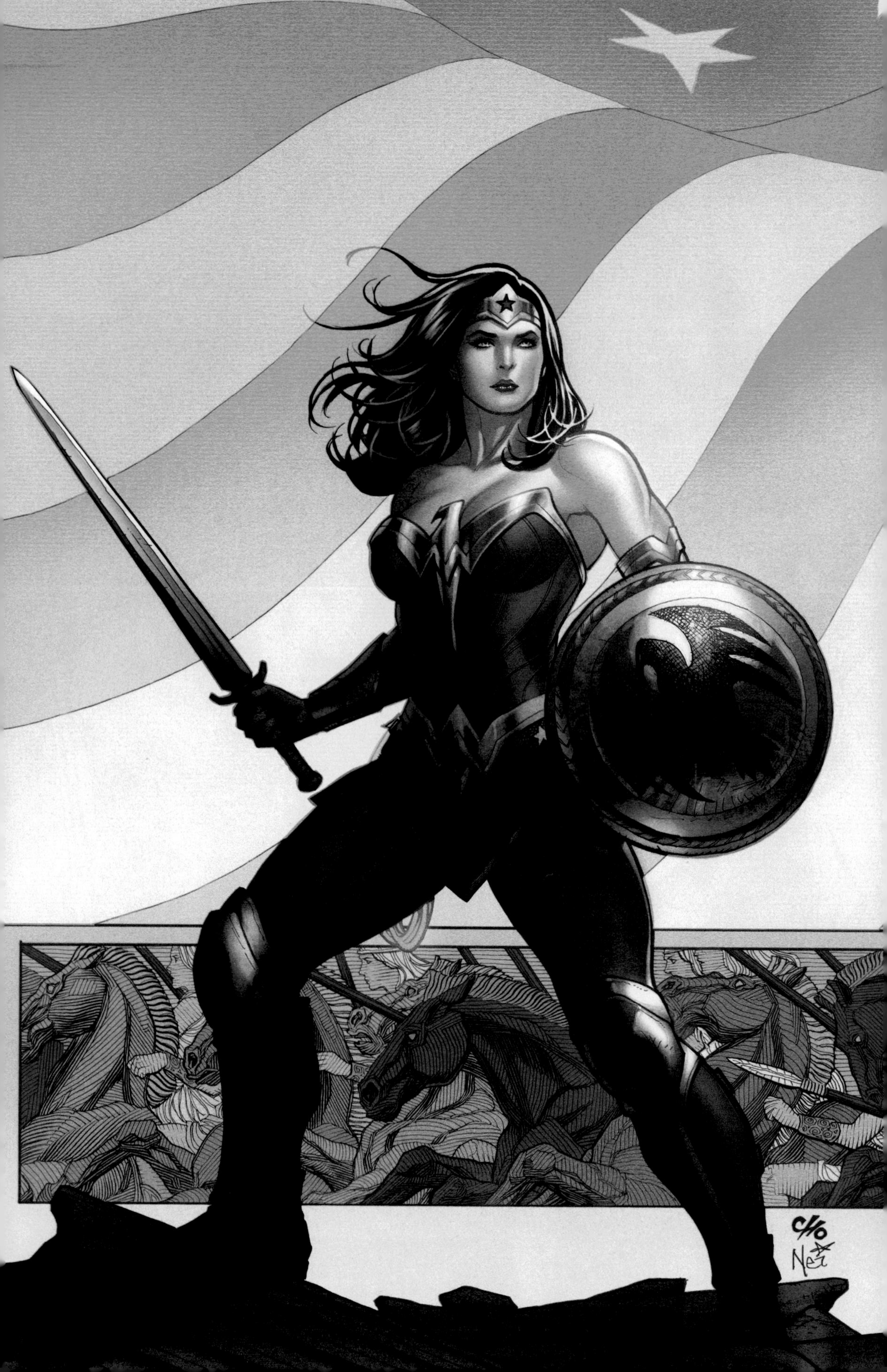

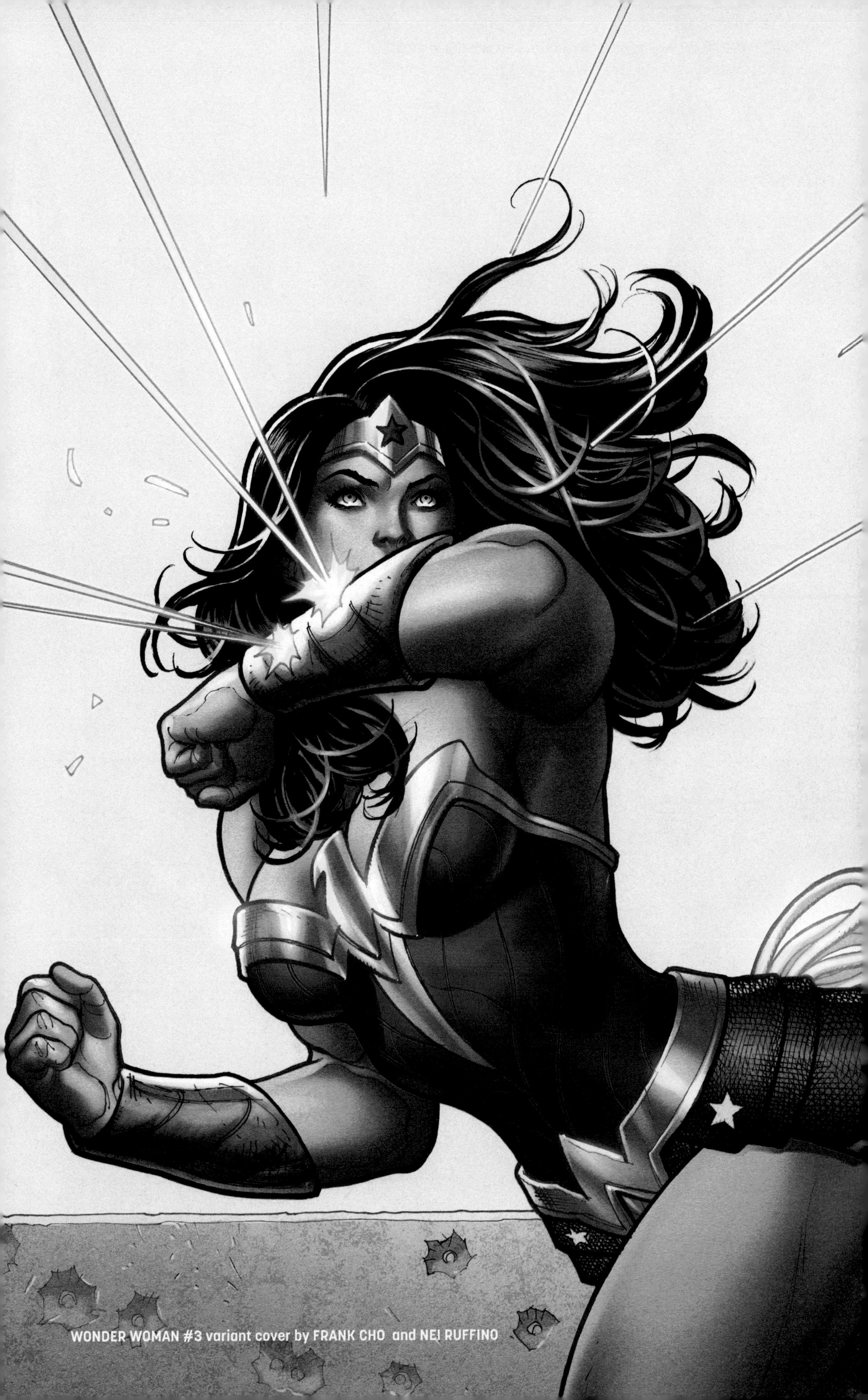

WONDER WOMAN #3 variant cover by FRANK CHO and NEI RUFFINO

WONDER WOMAN #5 variant cover by FRANK CHO and NEI RUFFINO

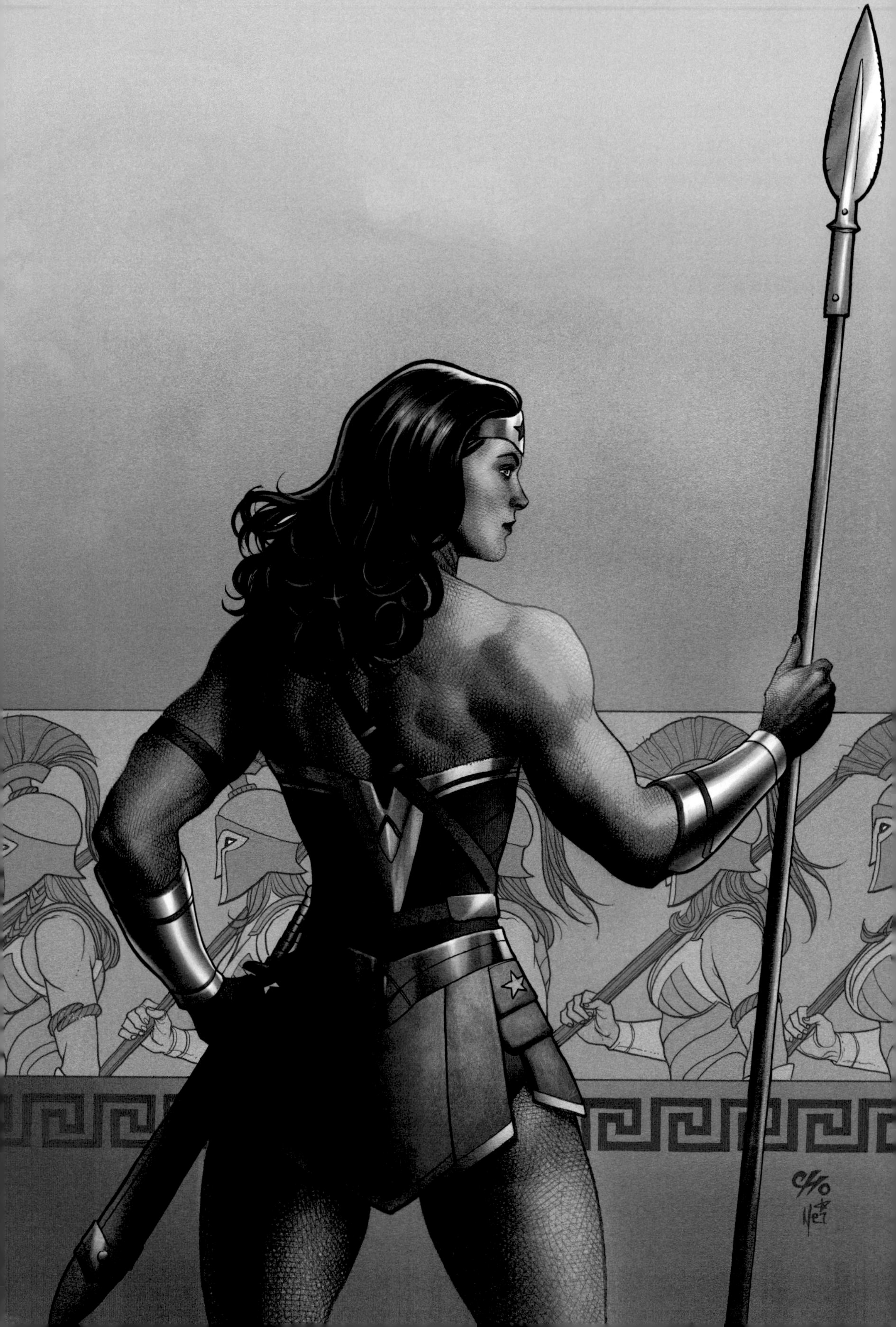

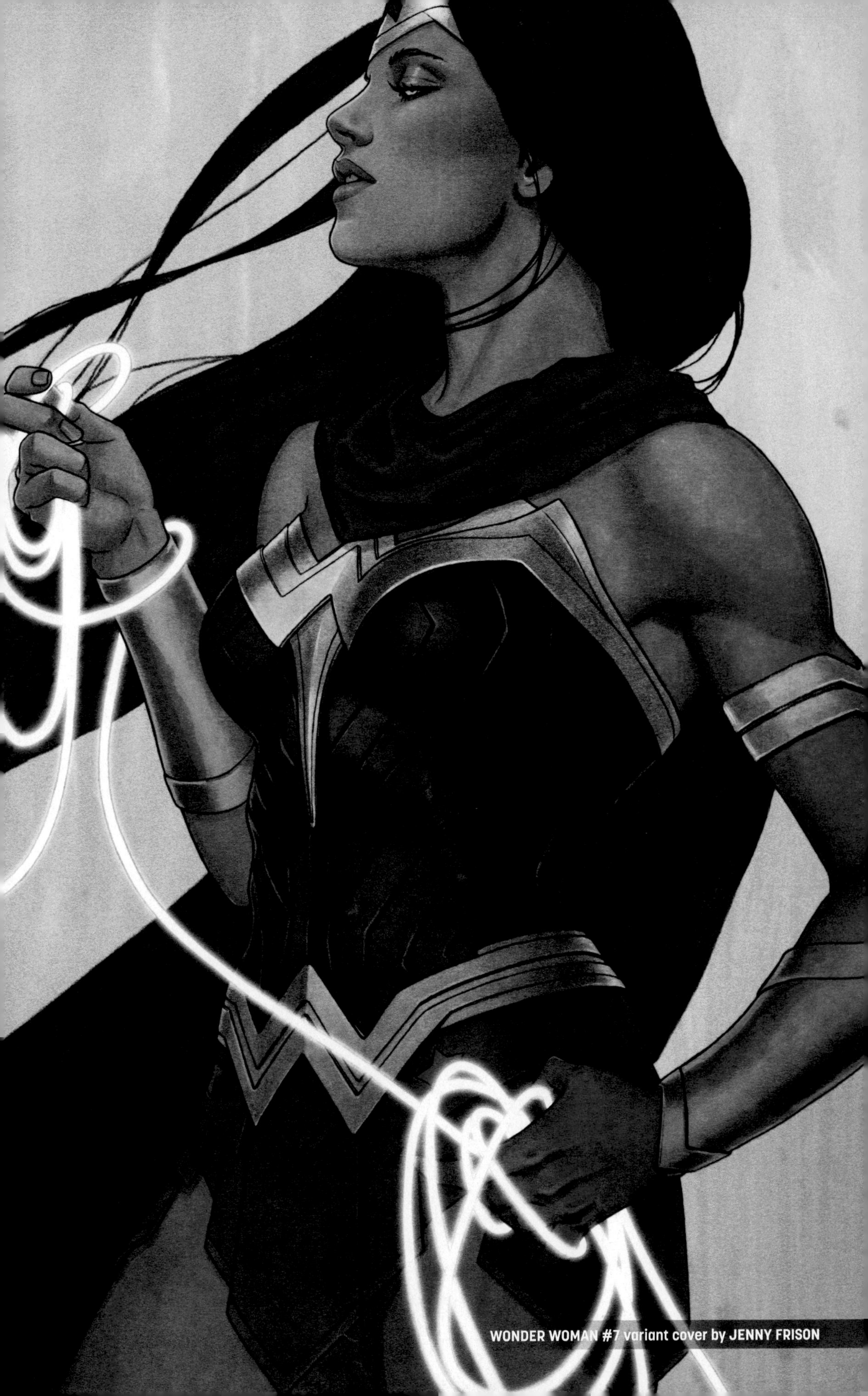

WONDER WOMAN #7 variant cover by JENNY FRISON

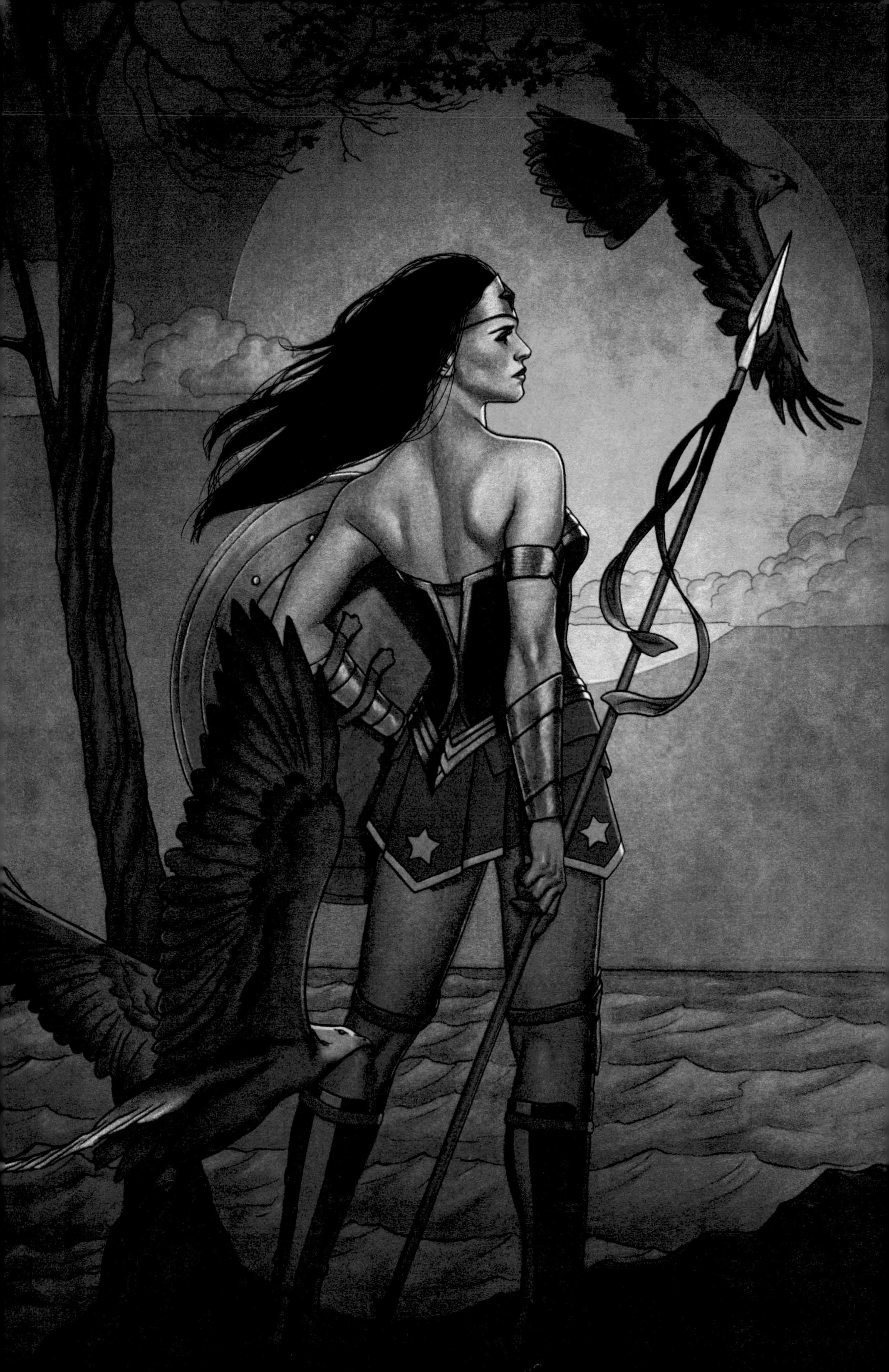

WONDER WOMAN #9 variant cover by JENNY FRISON

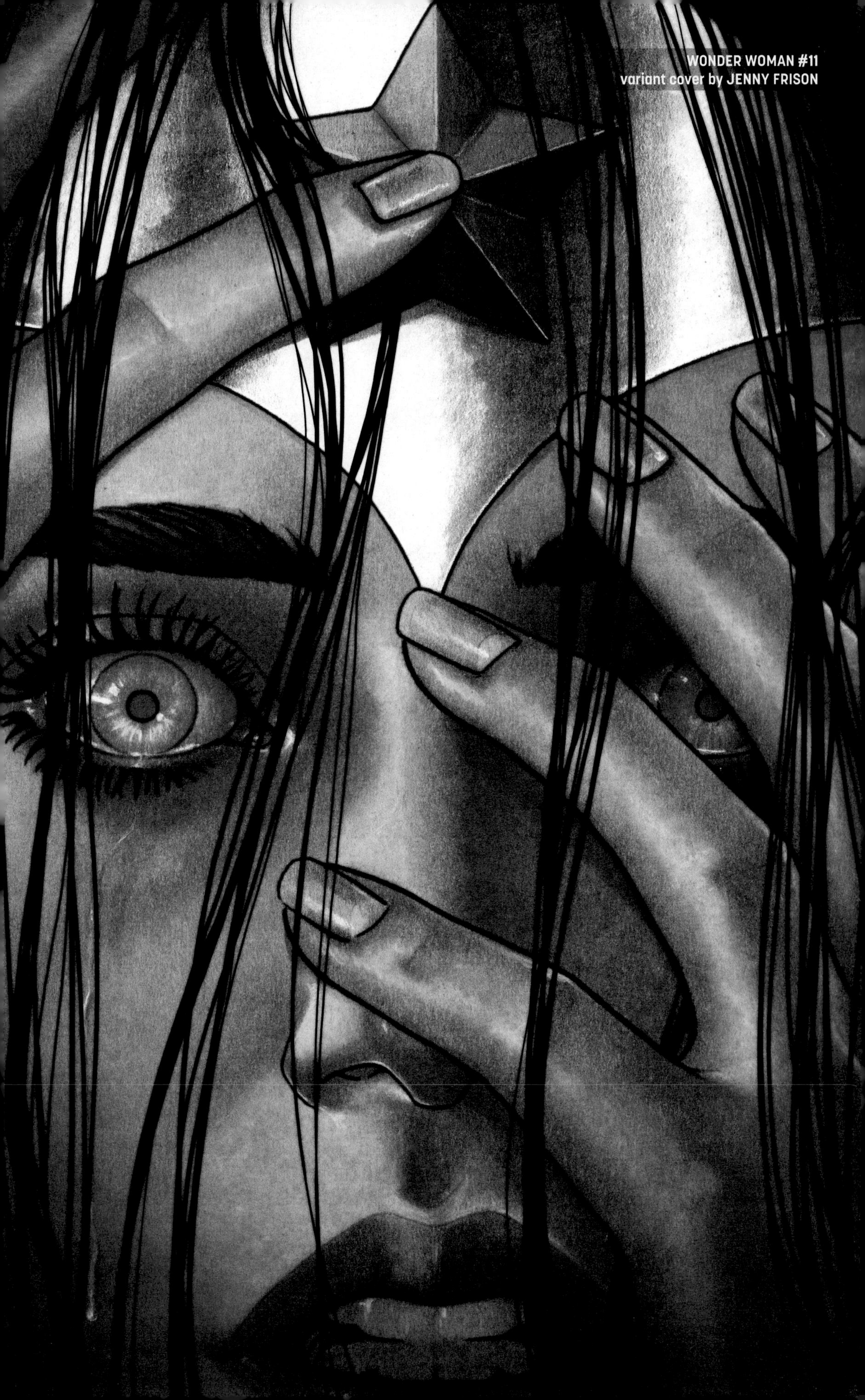

WONDER WOMAN #11
variant cover by JENNY FRISON

WONDER WOMAN COSTUME REDESIGN

COSTUME REDESIGN BY TONY S. DANIEL

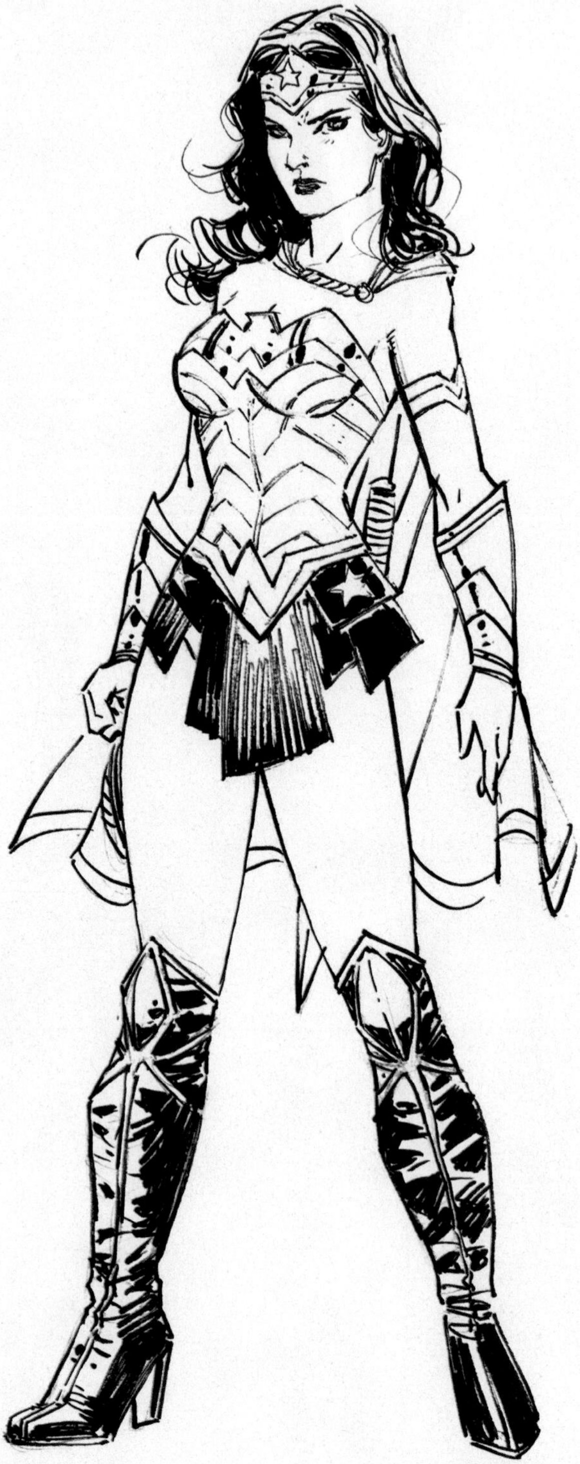

ILLUSTRATION BY JIM LEE, SCOTT WILLIAMS & ALEX SINCLAIR

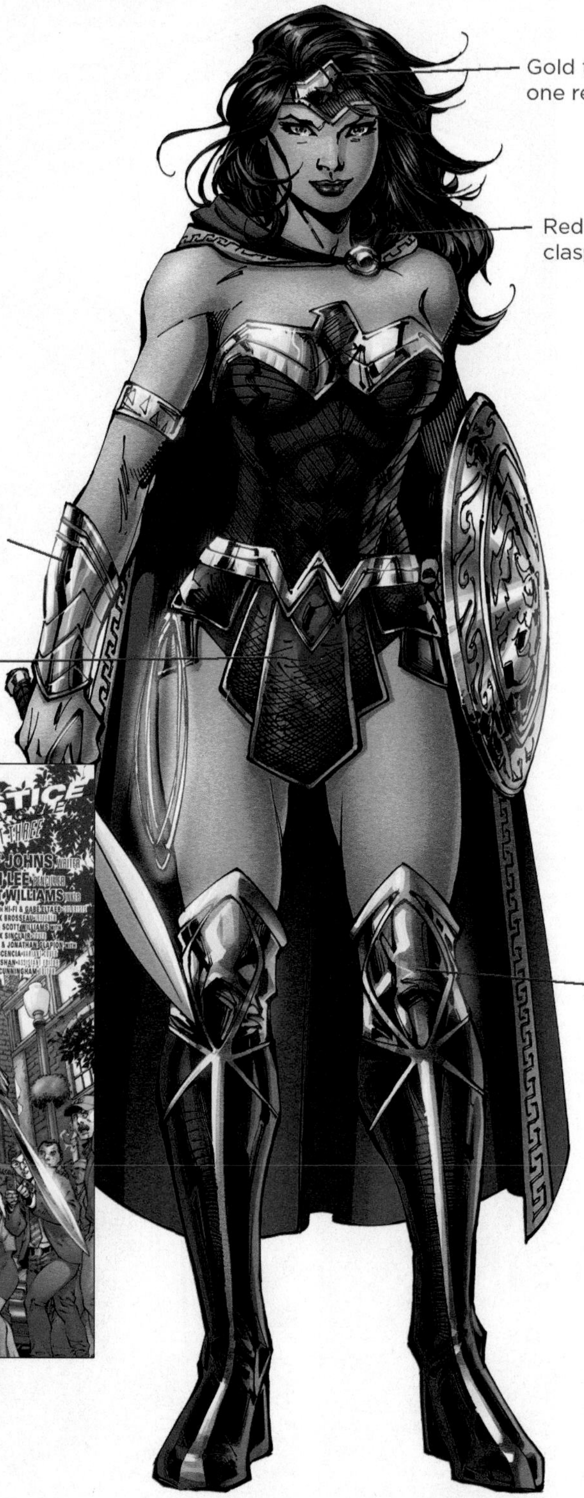
Gold tiara with one red star
Red cape with gold clasp and edge
Silver forearm guards with recessed detailing
Blue leather skirt with gold edges and two stars
Red knee-high boots with gold knee guards and accents

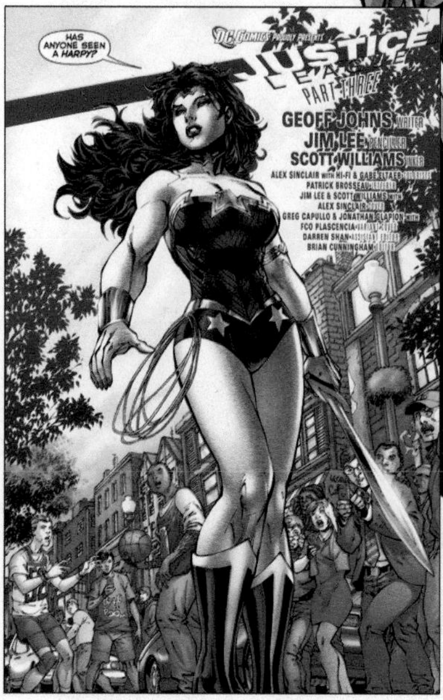
HAS ANYONE SEEN A HARPY?
JUSTICE LEAGUE
PART THREE
GEOFF JOHNS
JIM LEE
SCOTT WILLIAMS

Previous New 52 design

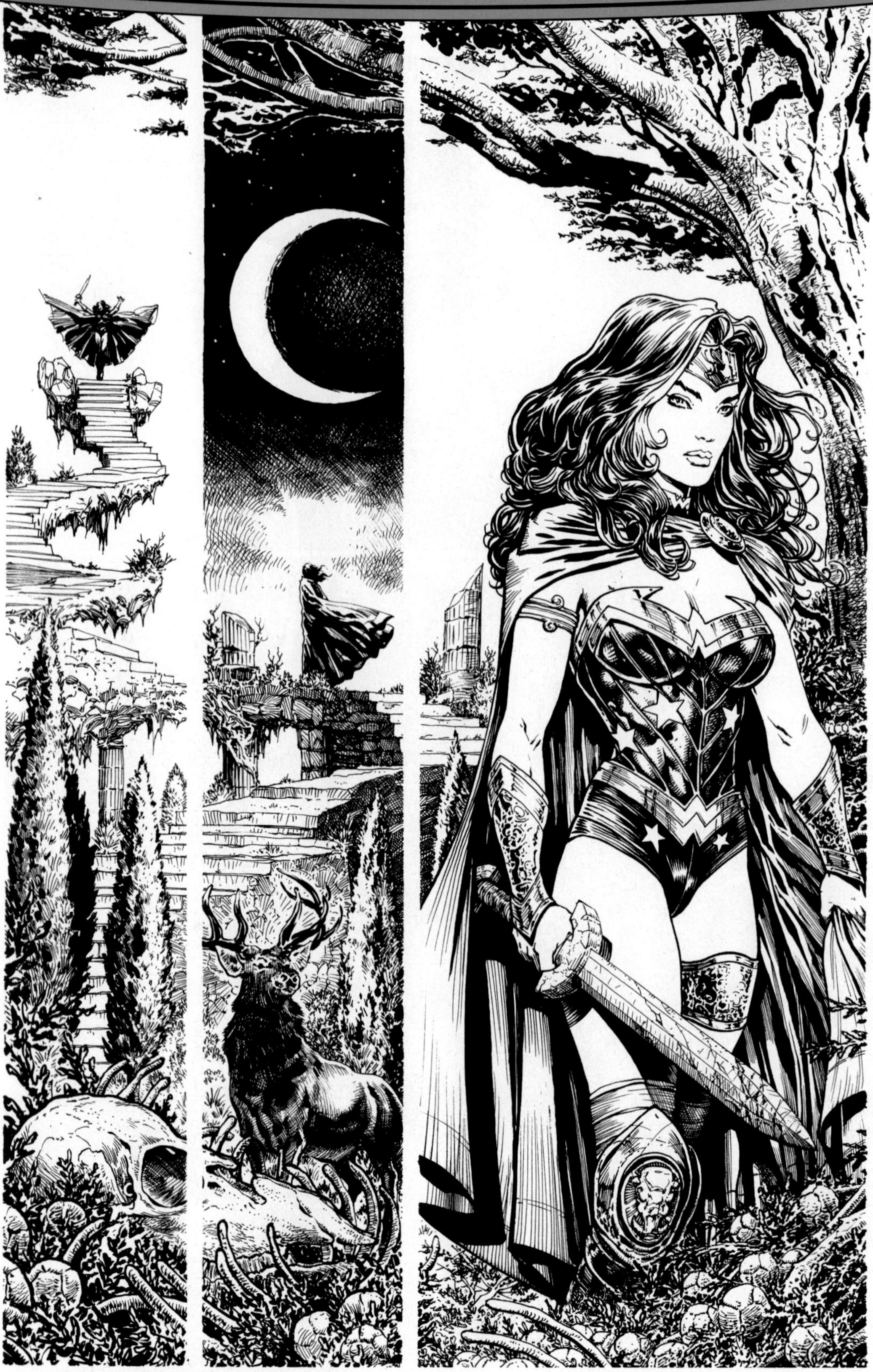

PRE-SERIES TEST PAGE BY LIAM SHARP

ROUGH PENCILS TO FINAL INKS FOR WONDER WOMAN #1, PAGE 1

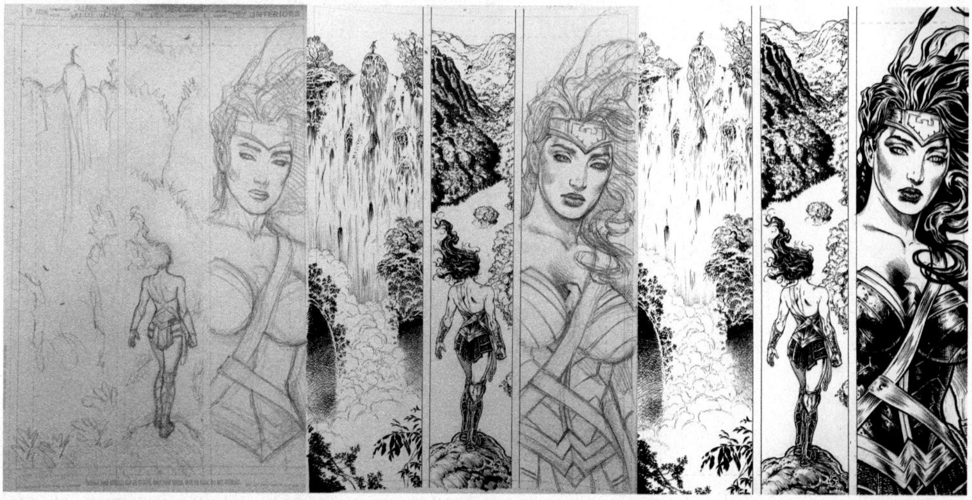

ROUGH PENCILS TO FINAL INKS FOR WONDER WOMAN: REBIRTH #1, PAGE 15

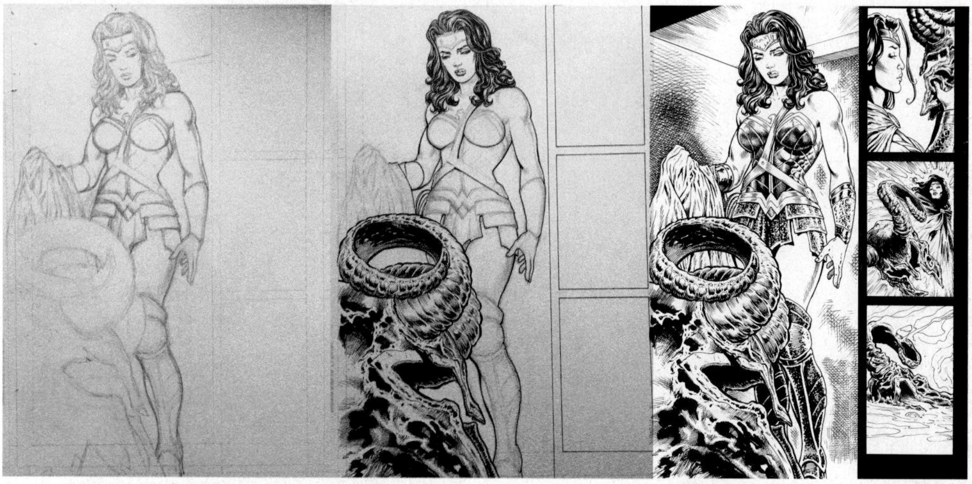

ROUGH PENCILS TO FINAL INKS FOR WONDER WOMAN #7 COVER

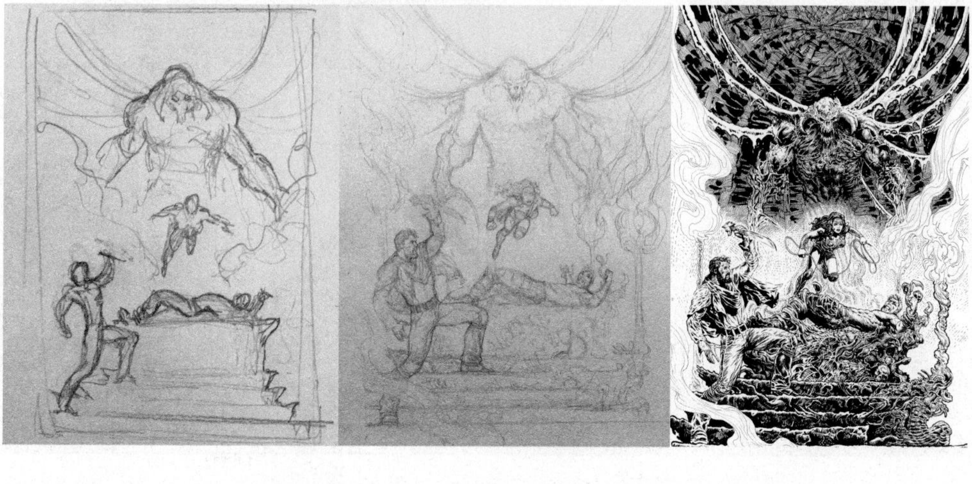

Page progression for WONDER WOMAN #1, page 20

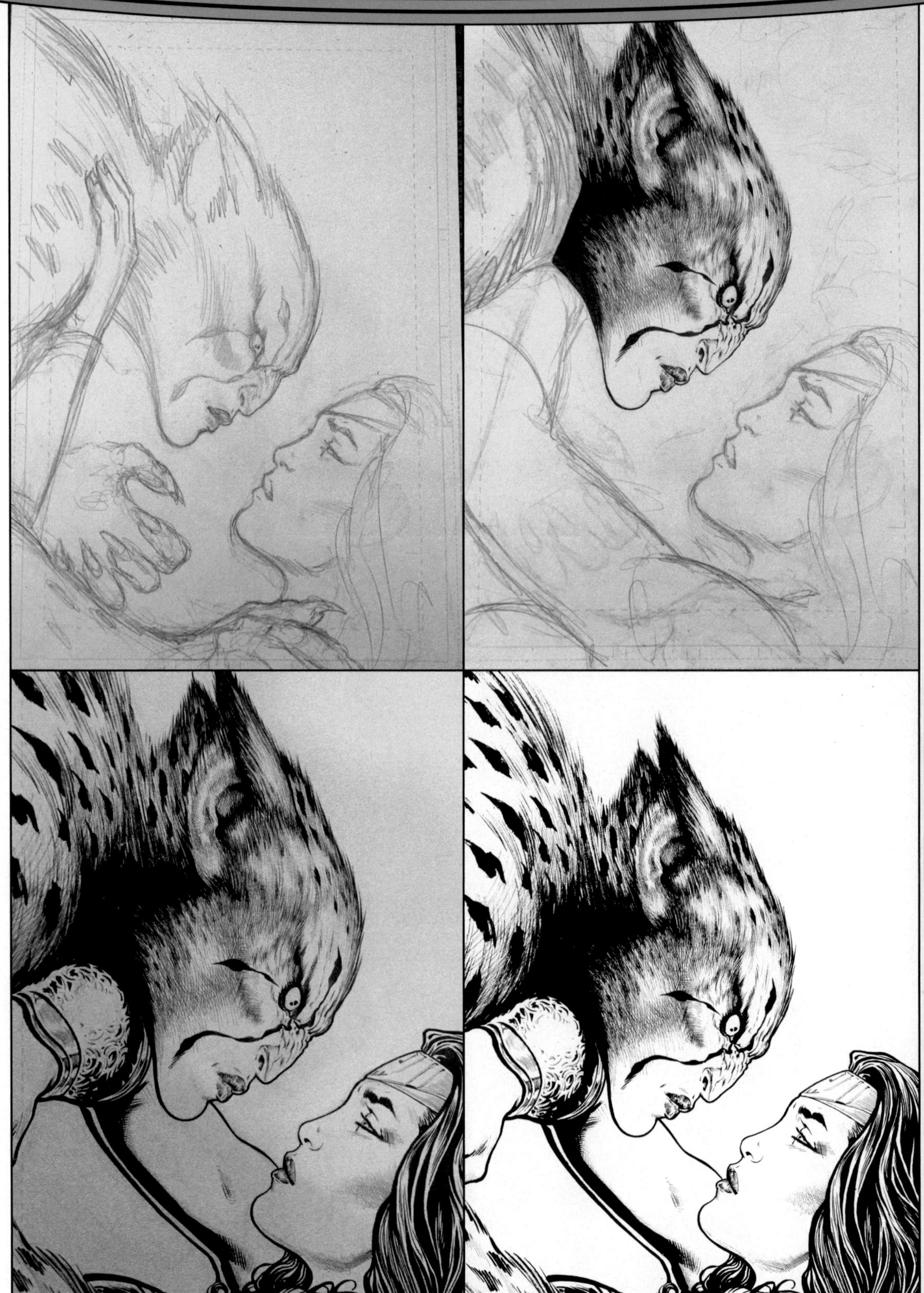

Page progression for WONDER WOMAN #3, page 17

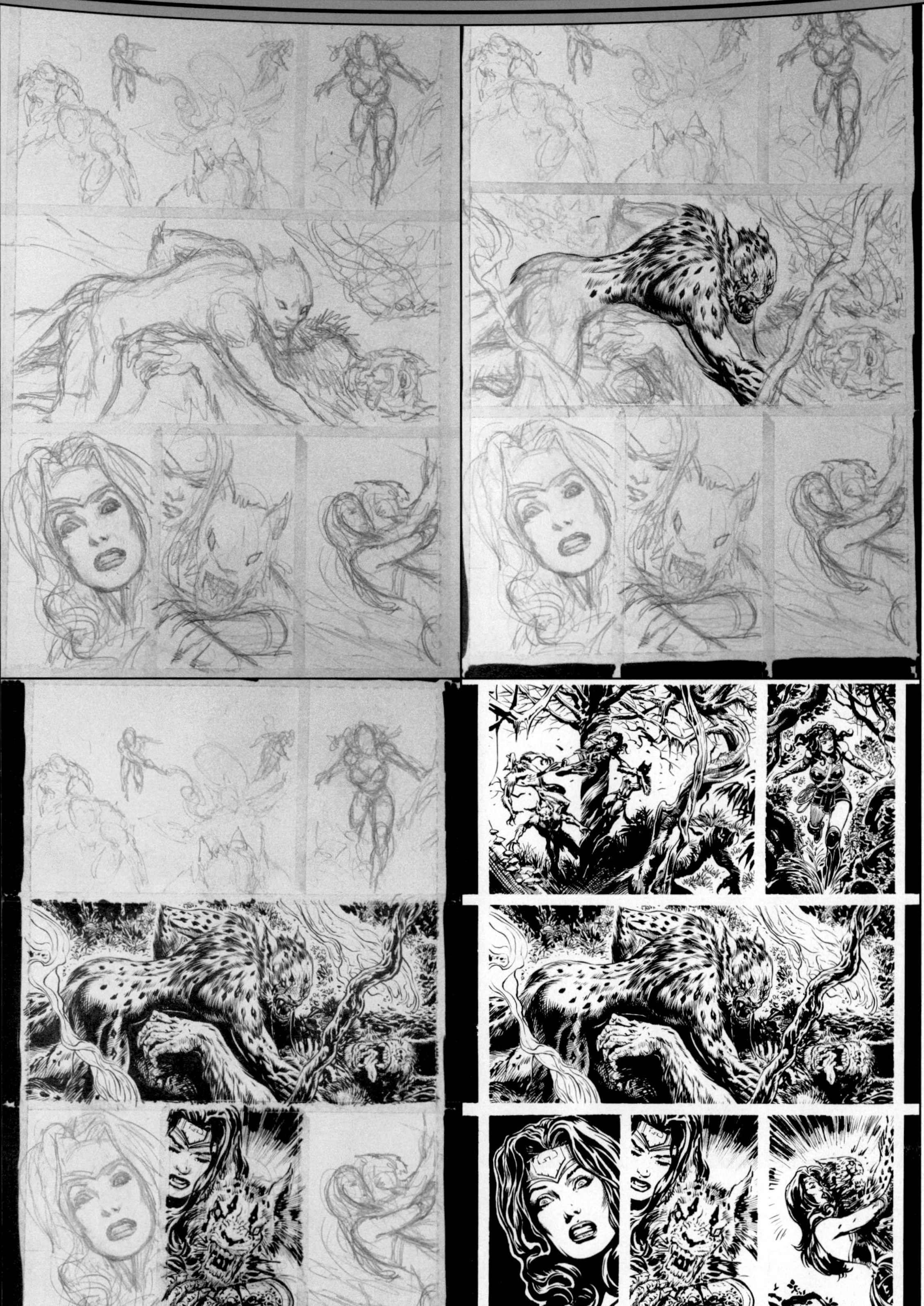

Page progression for WONDER WOMAN: REBIRTH #1, pages 18-19

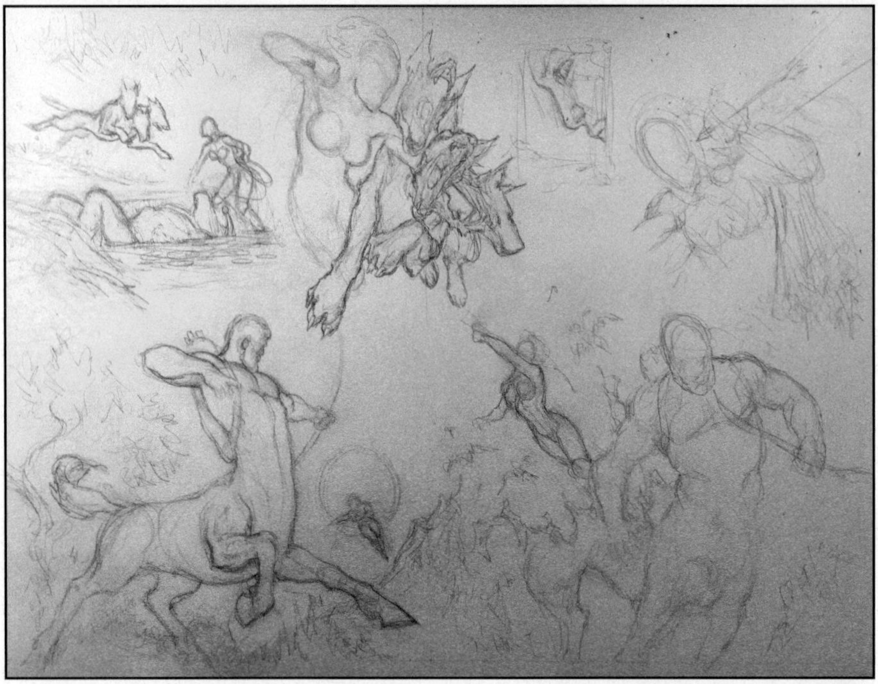

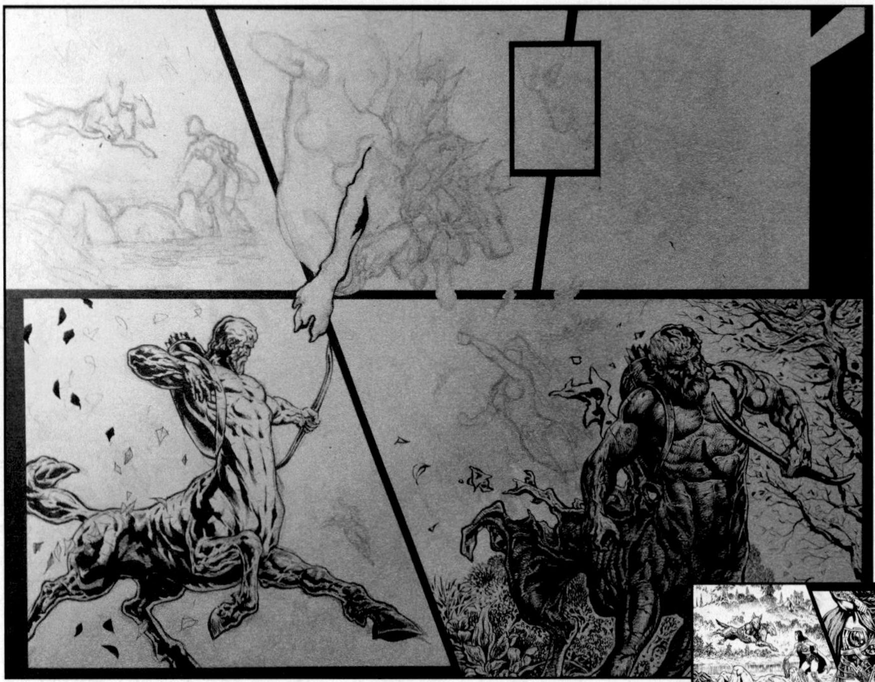

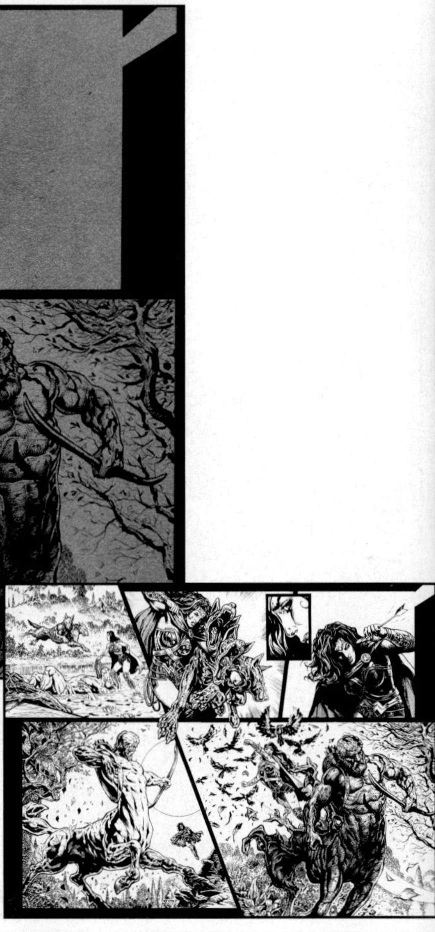

In-process art for WONDER WOMAN: REBIRTH #1, page 16

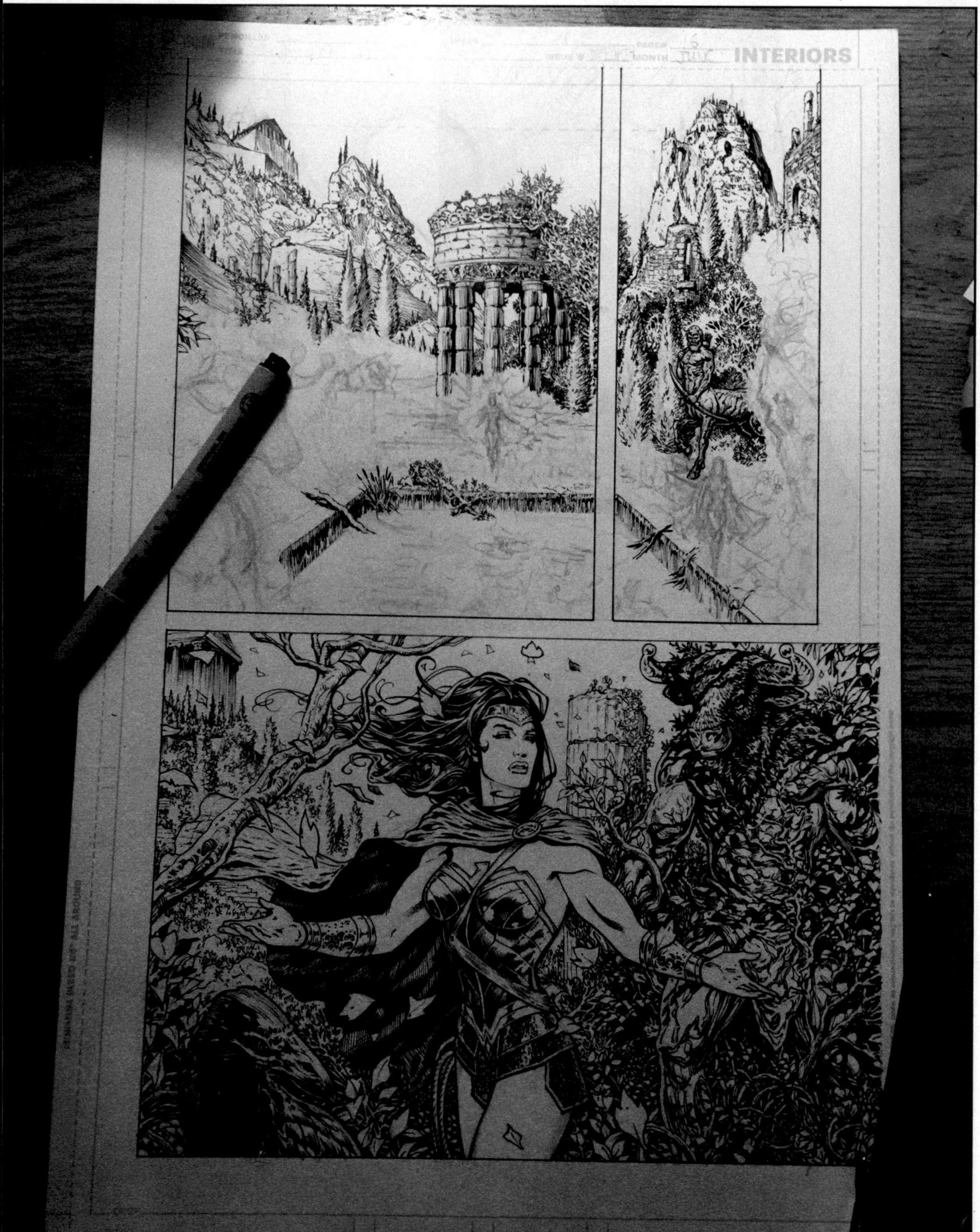
INTERIORS
DOUBLE PAGE SPREAD: CUT AS SHOWN, BUTT PAGE EDGES, TAPE ON BACK. DO NOT OVERLAP

Unused alternate and final cover inks for WONDER WOMAN: REBIRTH #1 and WONDER WOMAN #1

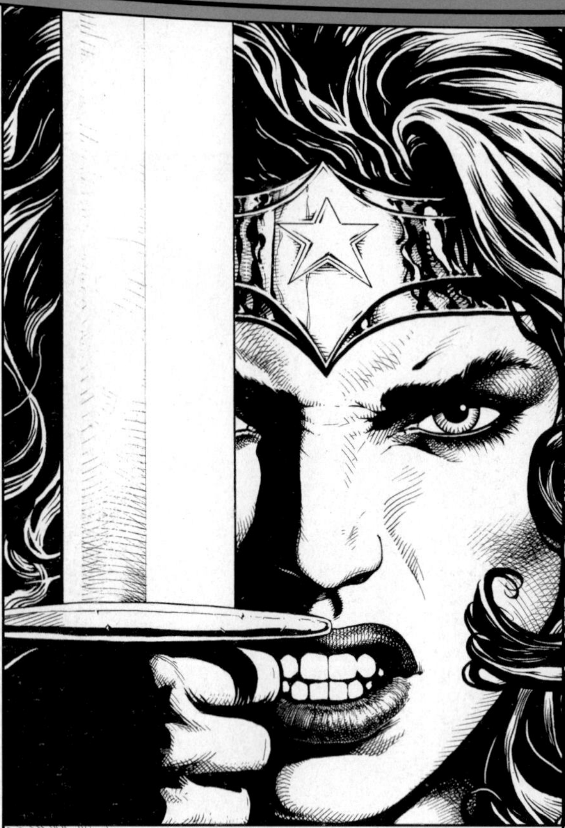

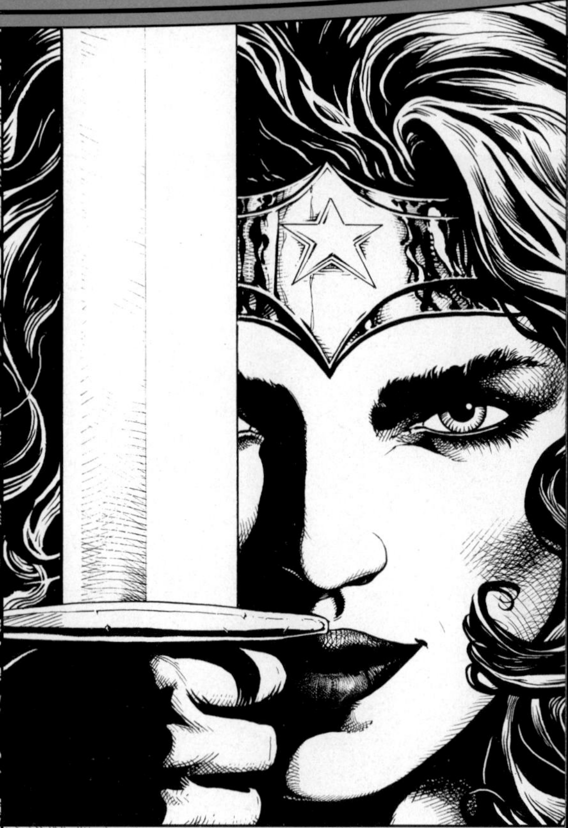

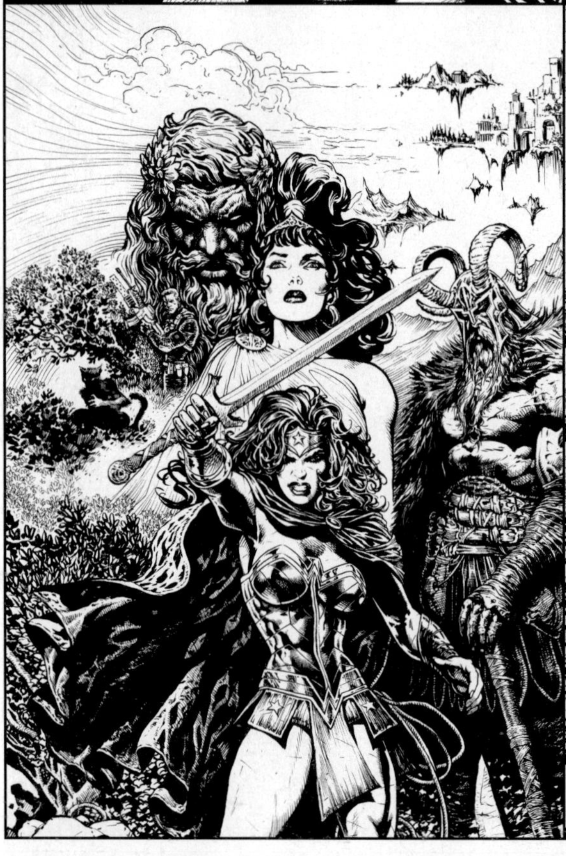

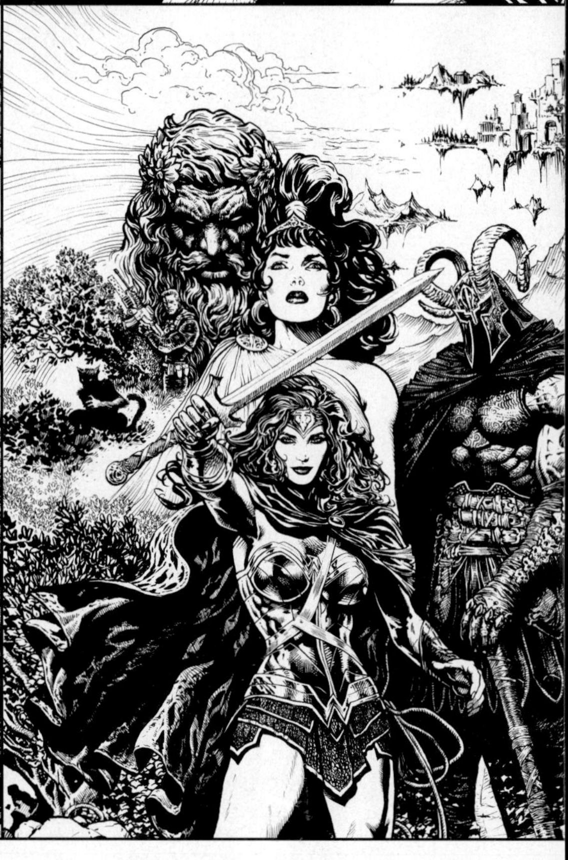